JUSTICE LEAGUE BEYOND

KONSTRICTION

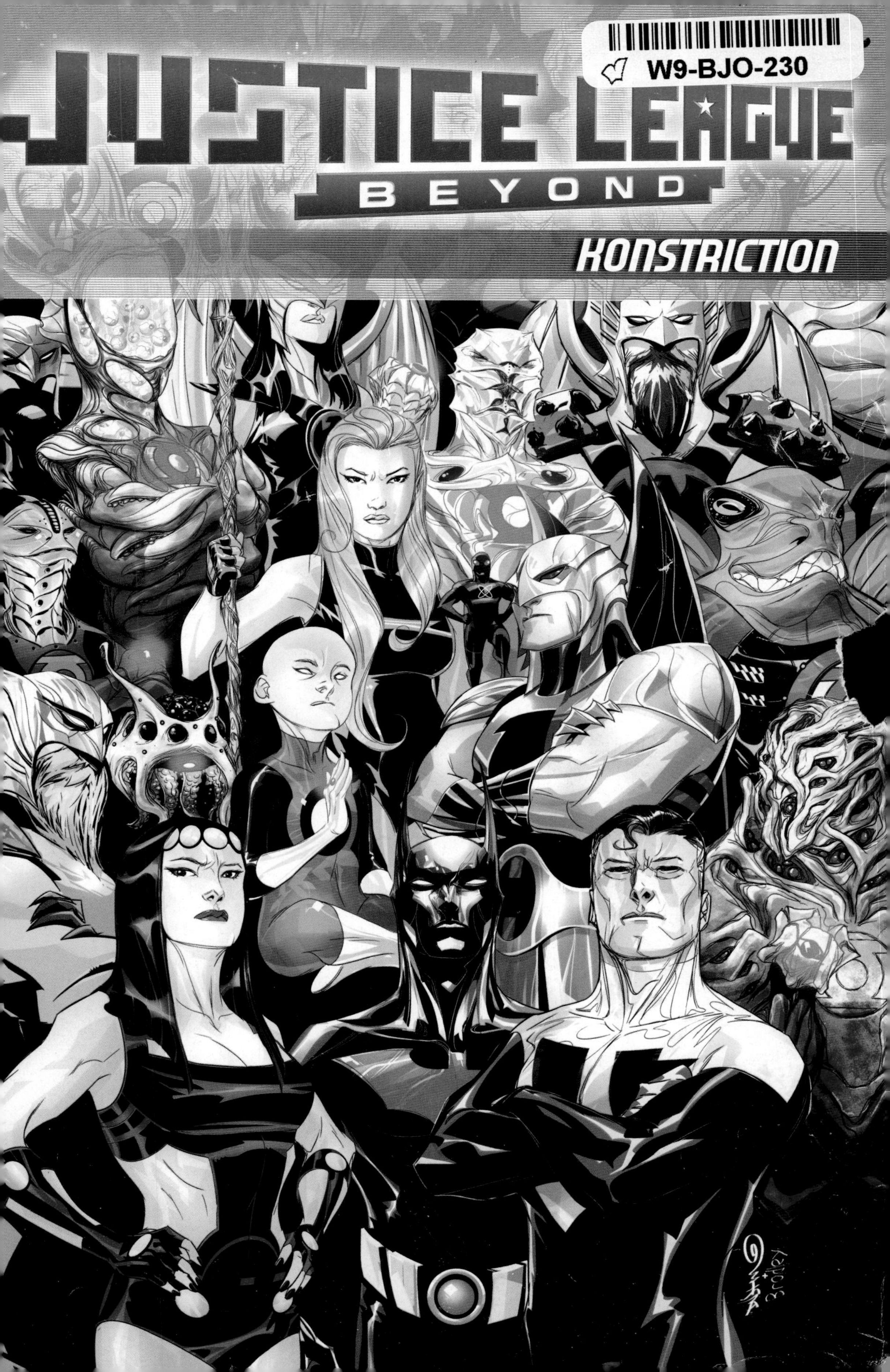

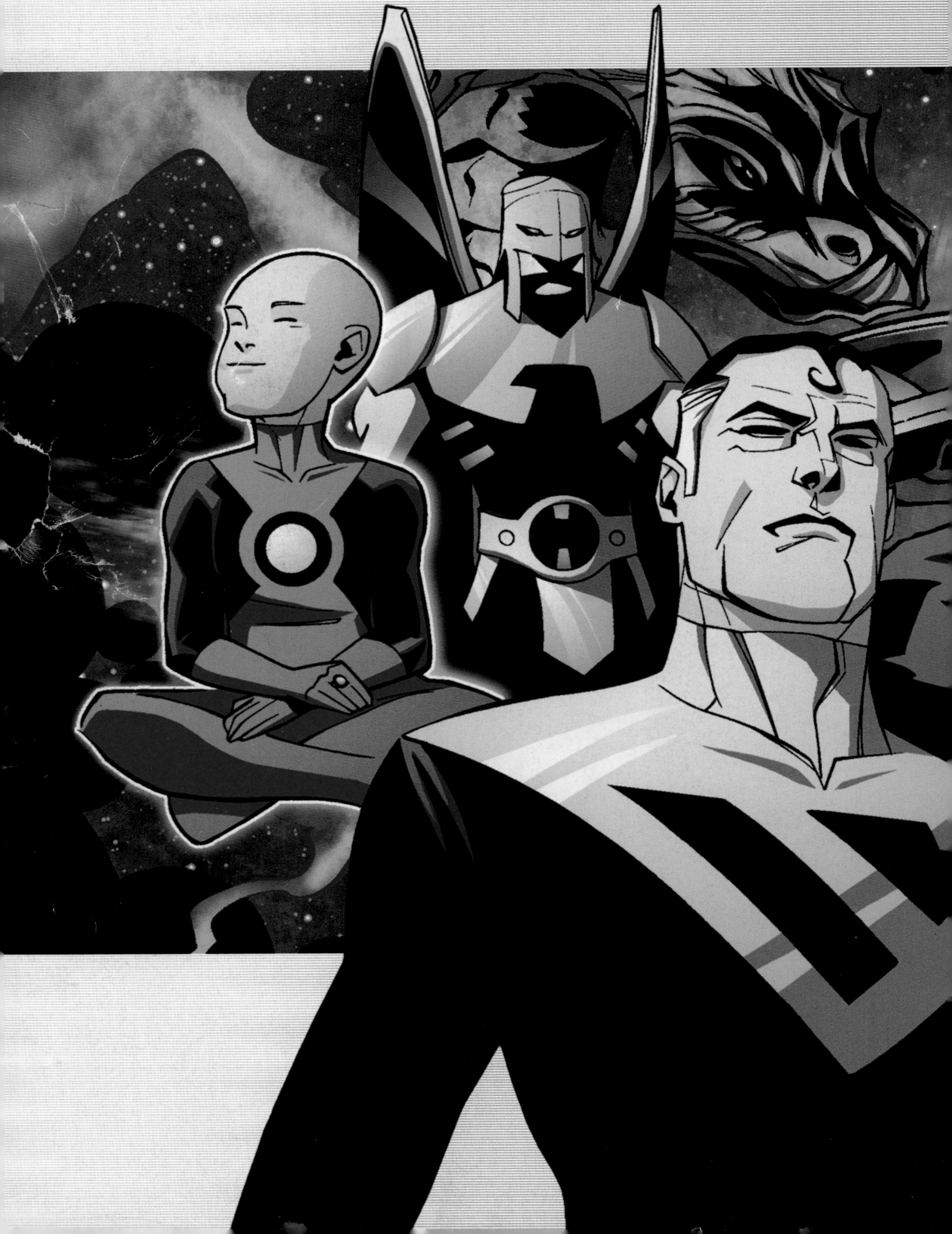

JUSTICE LEAGUE BEYOND

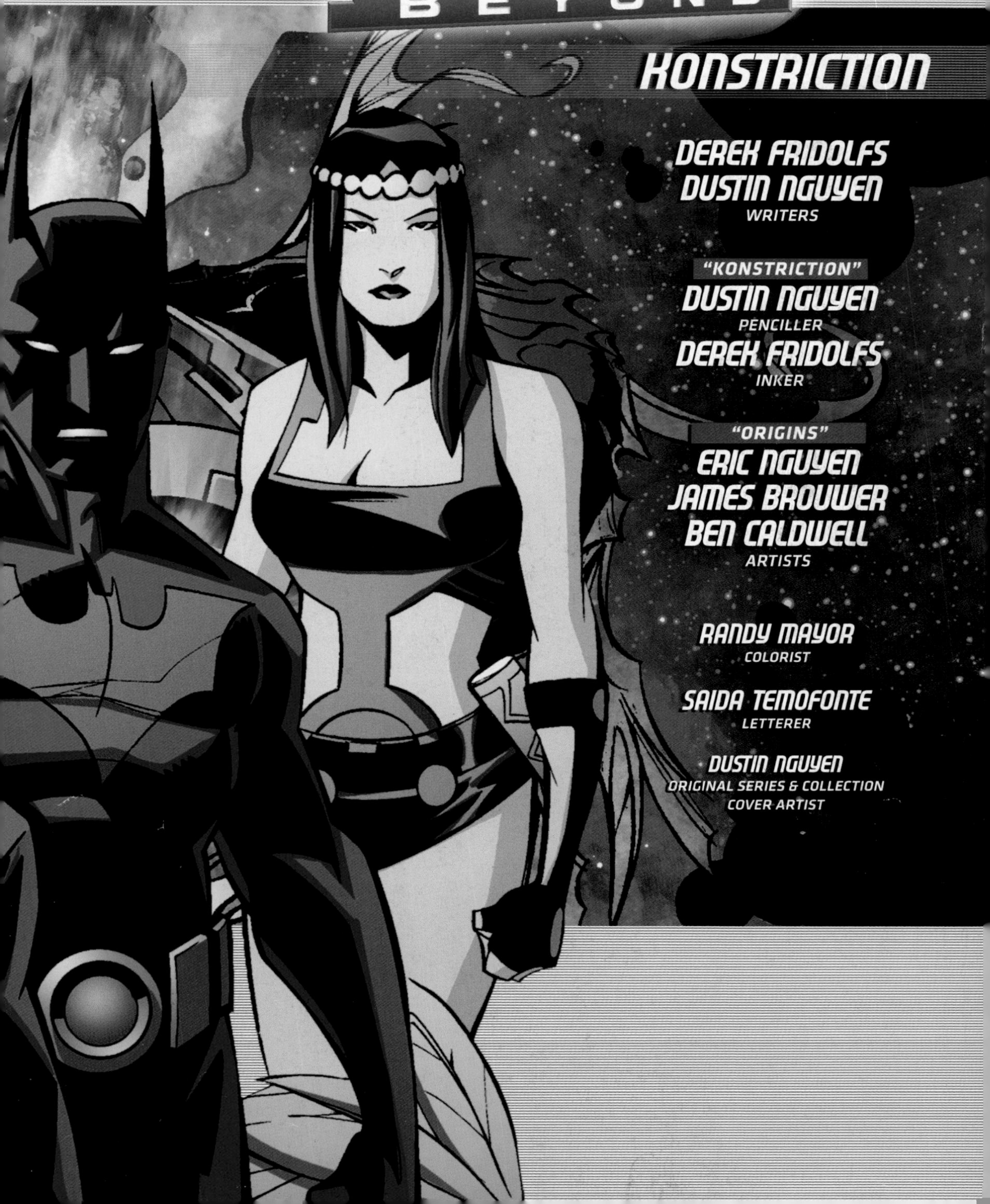

KONSTRICTION

DEREK FRIDOLFS
DUSTIN NGUYEN
WRITERS

"KONSTRICTION"
DUSTIN NGUYEN
PENCILLER
DEREK FRIDOLFS
INKER

"ORIGINS"
ERIC NGUYEN
JAMES BROUWER
BEN CALDWELL
ARTISTS

RANDY MAYOR
COLORIST

SAIDA TEMOFONTE
LETTERER

DUSTIN NGUYEN
ORIGINAL SERIES & COLLECTION
COVER ARTIST

Ben Abernathy

Alex Antone Editors – Original Series

Kristy Quinn Associate Editor – Original Series

Jeb Woodard Group Editor – Collected Editions

Robin Wildman Editor – Collected Edition

Curtis King Jr. Publication Design

Bob Harras Senior VP – Editor-in-Chief, DC Comics

Diane Nelson President

Dan DiDio and **Jim Lee** Co-Publishers

Geoff Johns Chief Creative Officer

Amit Desai Senior VP – Marketing & Global Franchise Management

Nairi Gardiner Senior VP – Finance

Sam Ades VP – Digital Marketing

Bobbie Chase VP – Talent Development

Mark Chiarello Senior VP – Art, Design & Collected Editions

John Cunningham VP – Content Strategy

Anne DePies VP – Strategy Planning & Reporting

Don Falletti VP – Manufacturing Operations

Lawrence Ganem VP – Editorial Administration & Talent Relations

Alison Gill Senior VP – Manufacturing & Operations

Hank Kanalz Senior VP – Editorial Strategy & Administration

Jay Kogan VP – Legal Affairs

Derek Maddalena Senior VP – Sales & Business Development

Dan Miron VP – Sales Planning & Trade Development

Nick Napolitano VP – Manufacturing Administration

Carol Roeder VP – Marketing

Eddie Scannell VP – Mass Account & Digital Sales

Susan Sheppard VP – Business Affairs

Courtney Simmons Senior VP – Publicity & Communications

Jim (Ski) Sokolowski VP – Comic Book Specialty & Newsstand Sales

JUSTICE LEAGUE BEYOND: KONSTRICTION

Published by DC Comics. Cover and compilation Copyright © 2013 DC Comics. All Rights Reserved.

Originally published in single magazine form in JUSTICE LEAGUE BEYOND DIGITAL CHAPTERS 1-16 Copyright © 2012 DC Comics. All Rights Reserved. All characters, their distinctive likenesses and related elements featured in this publication are trademarks of DC Comics. The stories, characters and incidents featured in this publication are entirely fictional. DC Comics does not read or accept unsolicited ideas, stories or artwork.

DC Comics, 4000 Warner Blvd., Burbank, CA 91522
A Warner Bros. Entertainment Company.
Printed by RR Donnelley, Salem, VA, USA. 8/28/15. Second Printing.
ISBN: 978-1-4012-4023-3

Library of Congress Cataloging-in-Publication Data

Nguyen, Dustin.
    Justice League Beyond : Konstriction / Dustin Nguyen, Derek Fridolfs.
       pages cm
    "Originally published in single magazine form in JUSTICE LEAGUE BEYOND digital chapters 1-16."
    ISBN 978-1-4012-4023-3
    1. Graphic novels. I. Fridolfs, Derek. II. Title. III. Title: Konstriction.
    PN6728.J87N48 2013
    741.5'973—dc23
                                    2012050766

PEFC Certified

Printed on paper from sustainably managed forests, controlled sources

PEFC/29-31-75   www.pefc.org

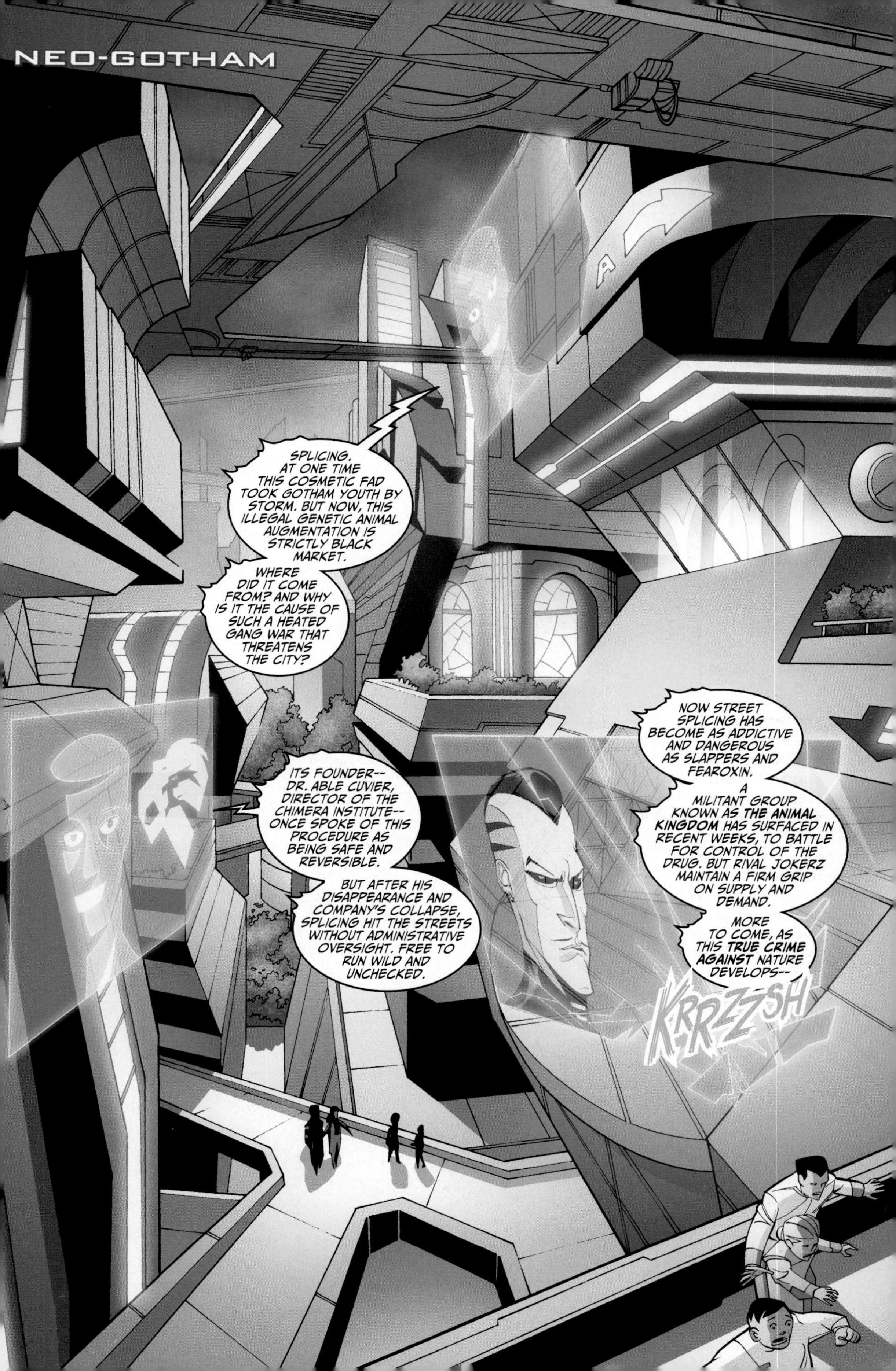
NEO-GOTHAM
SPLICING. AT ONE TIME THIS COSMETIC FAD TOOK GOTHAM YOUTH BY STORM. BUT NOW, THIS ILLEGAL GENETIC ANIMAL AUGMENTATION IS STRICTLY BLACK MARKET.
WHERE DID IT COME FROM? AND WHY IS IT THE CAUSE OF SUCH A HEATED GANG WAR THAT THREATENS THE CITY?
ITS FOUNDER-- DR. ABLE CUVIER, DIRECTOR OF THE CHIMERA INSTITUTE-- ONCE SPOKE OF THIS PROCEDURE AS BEING SAFE AND REVERSIBLE.
BUT AFTER HIS DISAPPEARANCE AND COMPANY'S COLLAPSE, SPLICING HIT THE STREETS WITHOUT ADMINISTRATIVE OVERSIGHT. FREE TO RUN WILD AND UNCHECKED.
NOW STREET SPLICING HAS BECOME AS ADDICTIVE AND DANGEROUS AS SLAPPERS AND FEAROXIN.
A MILITANT GROUP KNOWN AS **THE ANIMAL KINGDOM** HAS SURFACED IN RECENT WEEKS, TO BATTLE FOR CONTROL OF THE DRUG. BUT RIVAL JOKERZ MAINTAIN A FIRM GRIP ON SUPPLY AND DEMAND.
MORE TO COME, AS THIS **TRUE CRIME AGAINST** NATURE DEVELOPS--
KRRZZSH

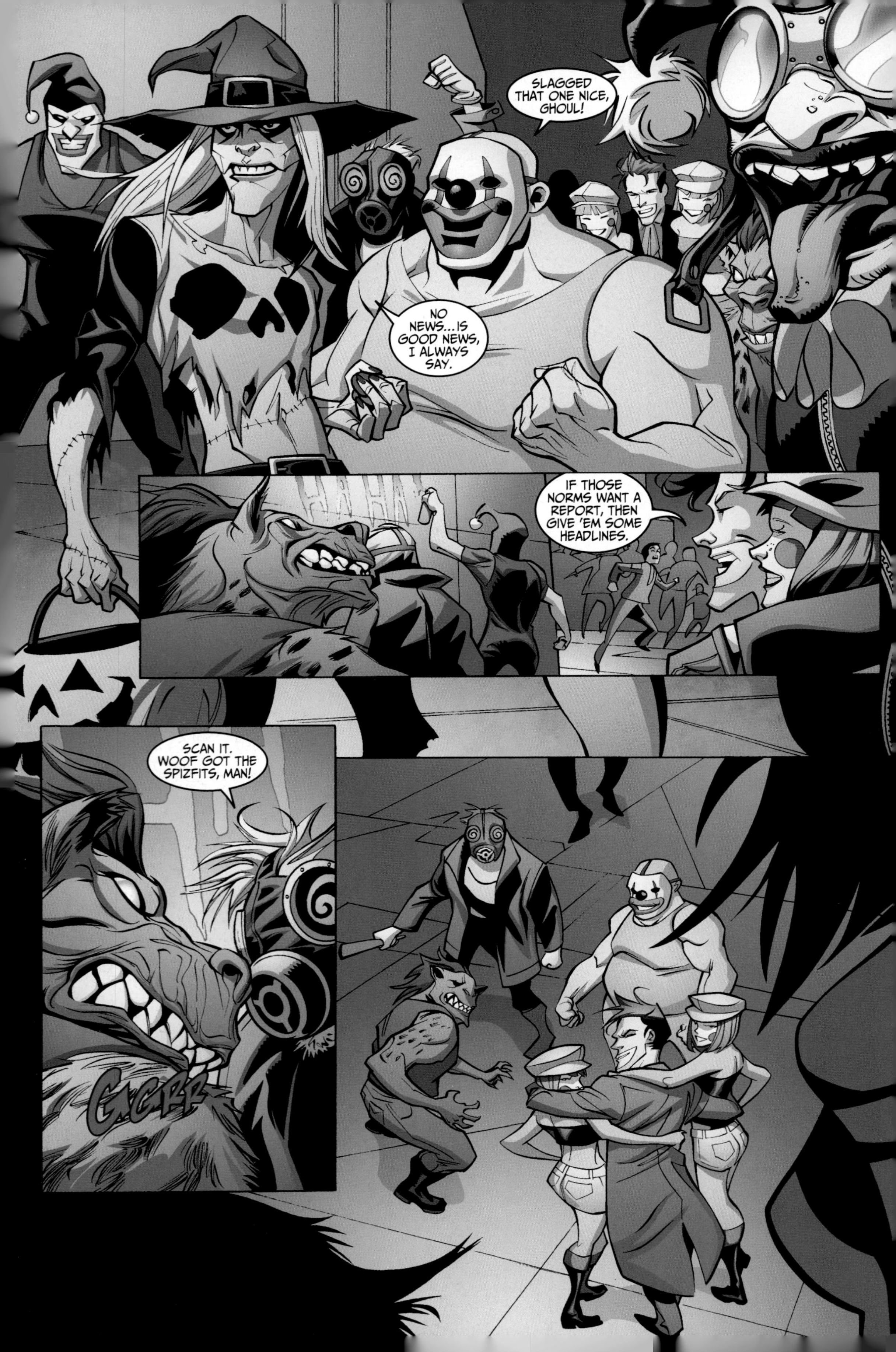
SLAGGED THAT ONE NICE, GHOUL!
NO NEWS...IS GOOD NEWS, I ALWAYS SAY.
IF THOSE NORMS WANT A REPORT, THEN GIVE 'EM SOME HEADLINES.
SCAN IT. WOOF GOT THE SPIZFITS, MAN!
GGRR

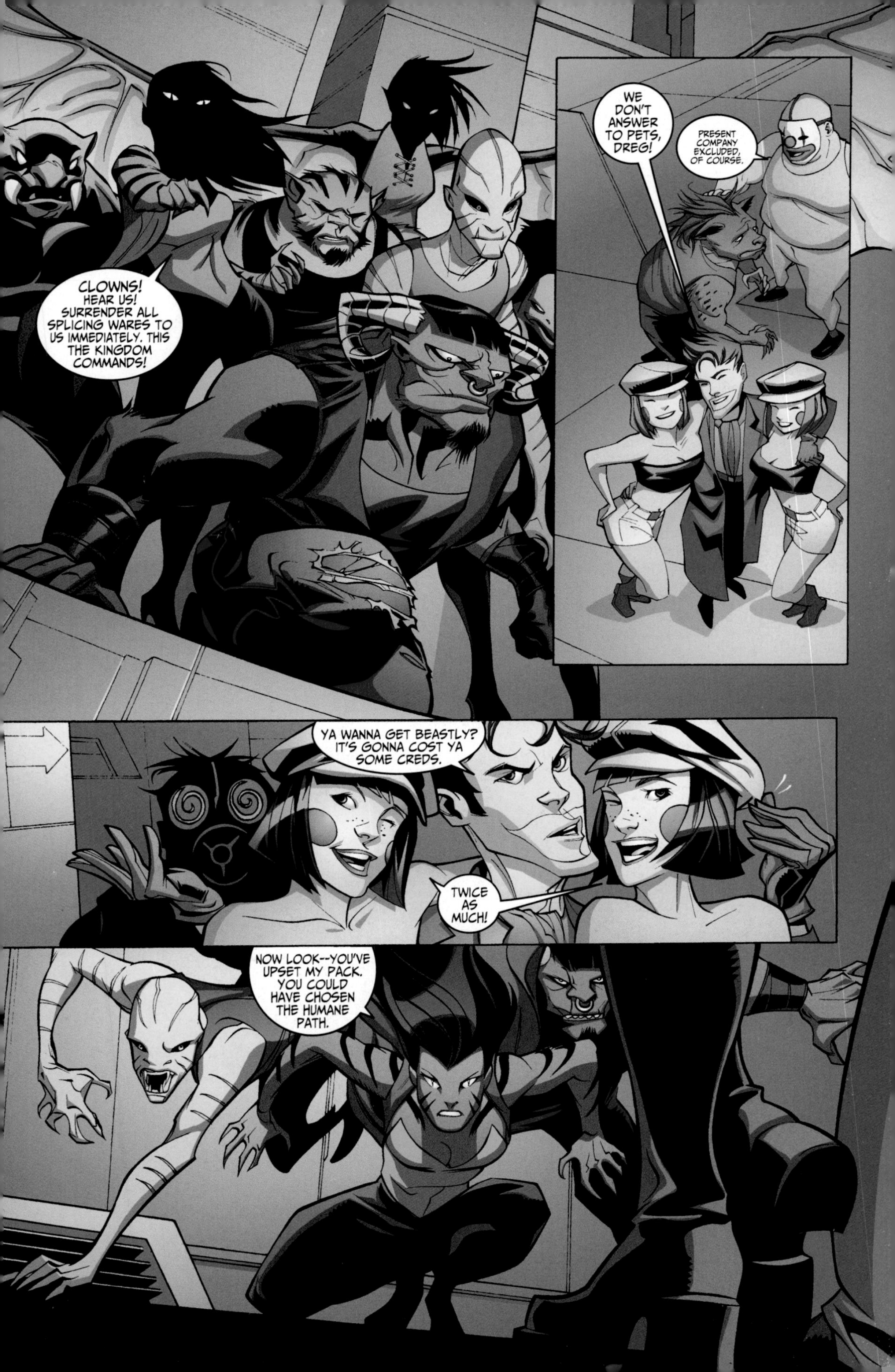

CLOWNS! HEAR US! SURRENDER ALL SPLICING WARES TO US IMMEDIATELY. THIS THE KINGDOM COMMANDS!
WE DON'T ANSWER TO PETS, DREG!
PRESENT COMPANY EXCLUDED, OF COURSE.
YA WANNA GET BEASTLY? IT'S GONNA COST YA SOME CREDS.
TWICE AS MUCH!
NOW LOOK--YOU'VE UPSET MY PACK. YOU COULD HAVE CHOSEN THE HUMANE PATH.

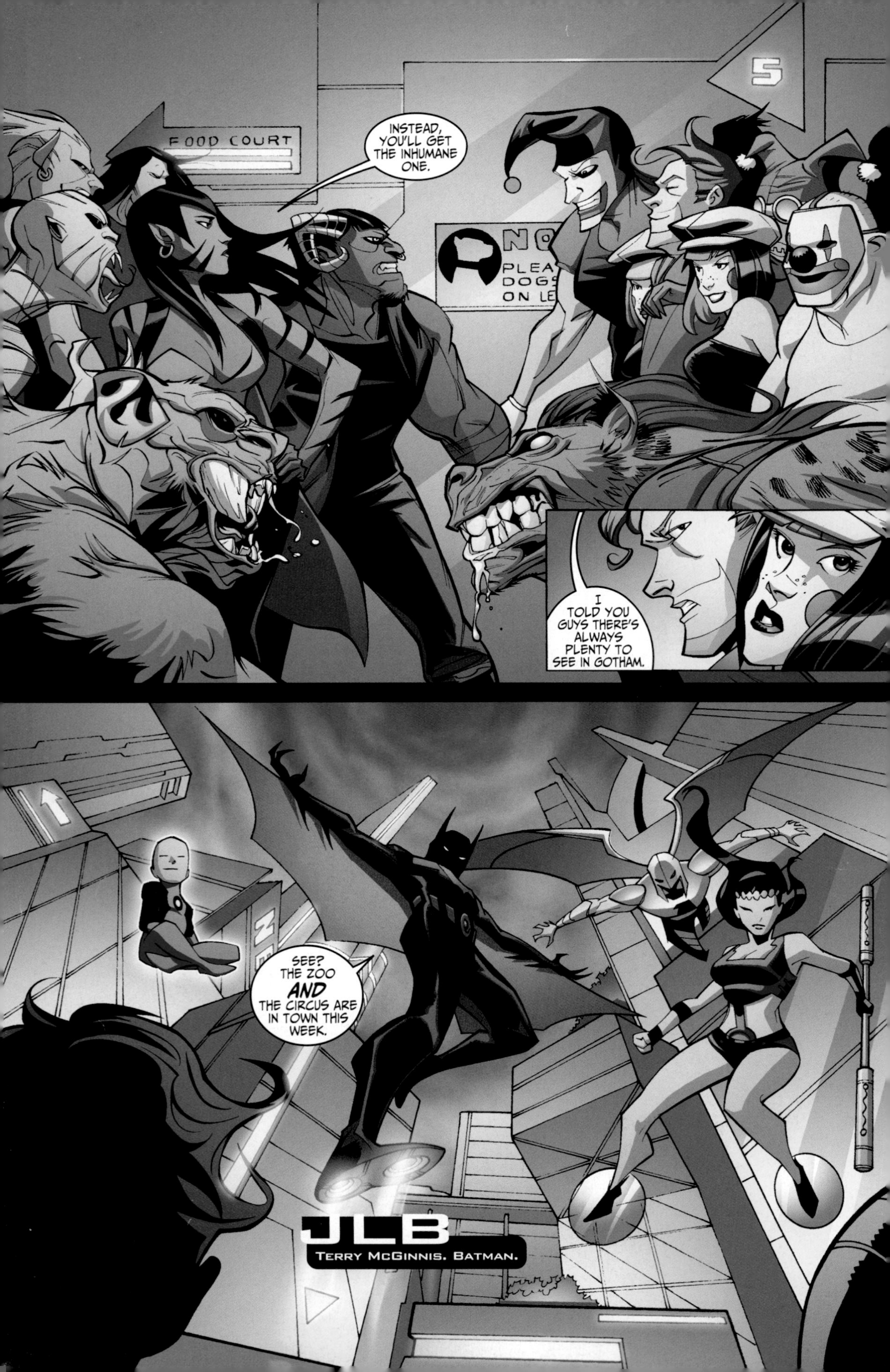

5
FOOD COURT
INSTEAD, YOU'LL GET THE INHUMANE ONE.
I TOLD YOU GUYS THERE'S ALWAYS PLENTY TO SEE IN GOTHAM.
SEE? THE ZOO AND THE CIRCUS ARE IN TOWN THIS WEEK.
JLB
TERRY McGINNIS. BATMAN.

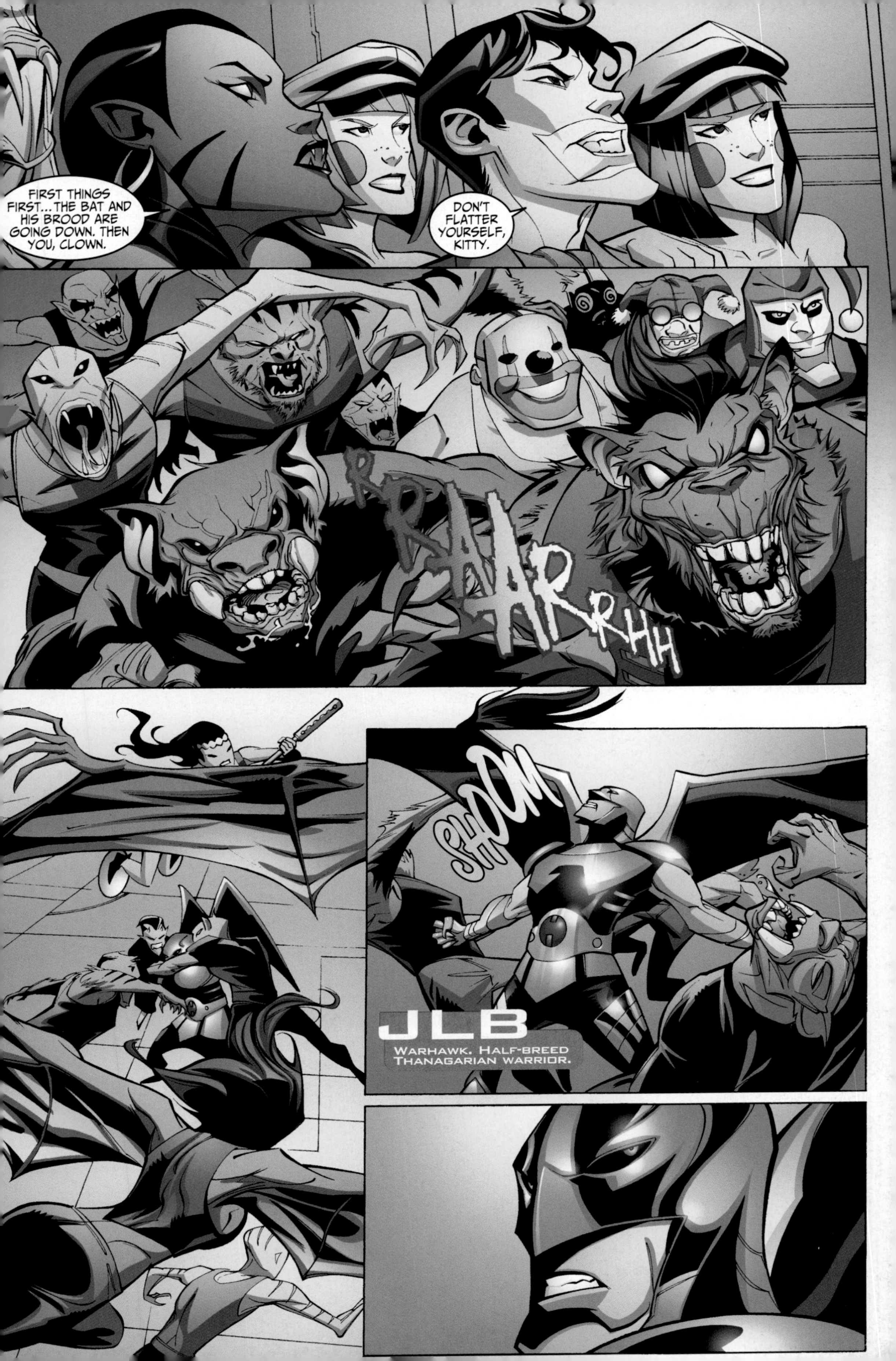
FIRST THINGS FIRST... THE BAT AND HIS BROOD ARE GOING DOWN. THEN YOU, CLOWN.
DON'T FLATTER YOURSELF, KITTY.
RRAARRRHH
SHOOM
JLB
WARHAWK. HALF-BREED THANAGARIAN WARRIOR.

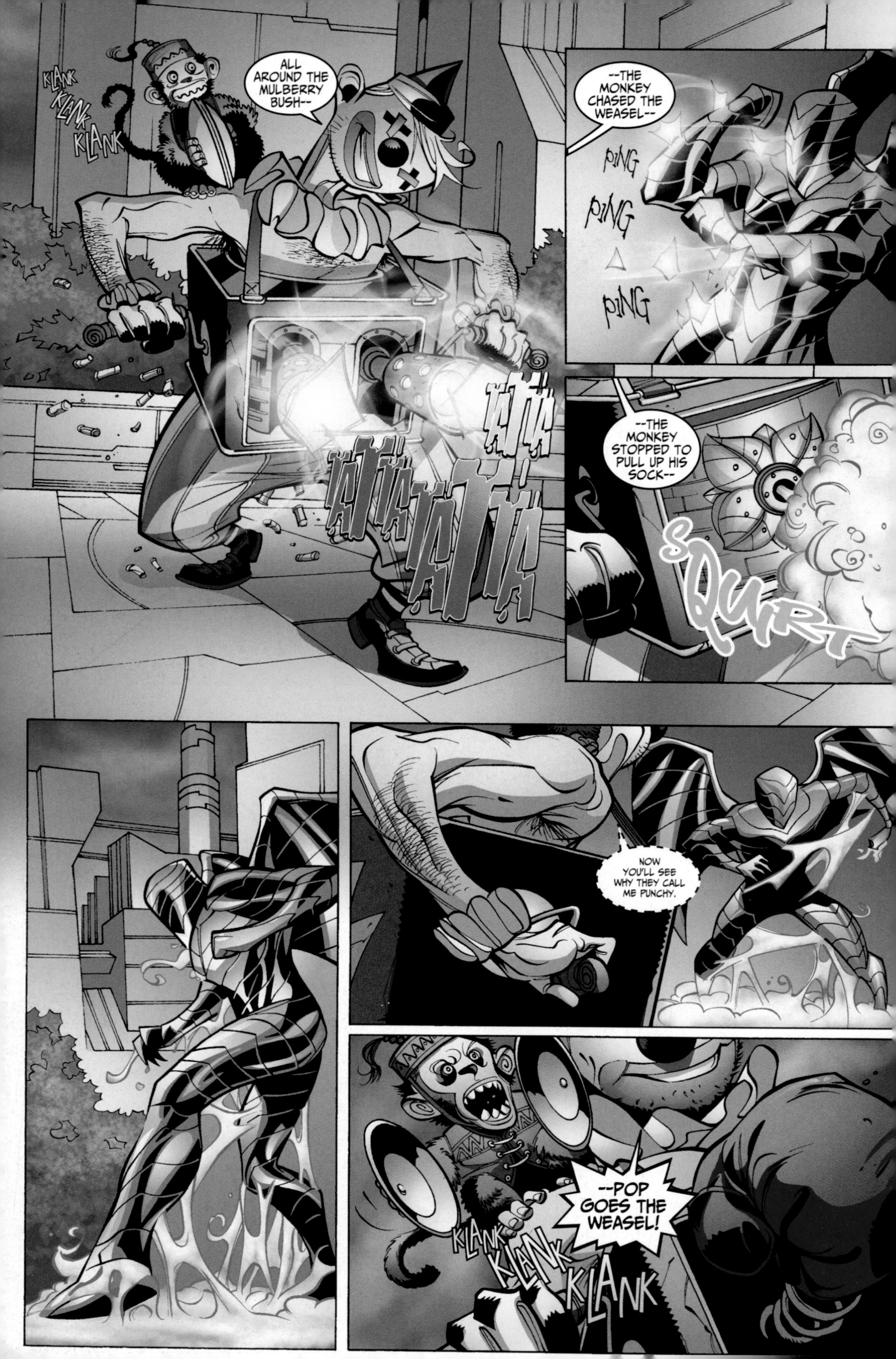
KLANK
KLANK
KLANK
ALL AROUND THE MULBERRY BUSH--
--THE MONKEY CHASED THE WEASEL--
PING
PING
PING
--THE MONKEY STOPPED TO PULL UP HIS SOCK--
SQUIRT
NOW YOU'LL SEE WHY THEY CALL ME PUNCHY.
--POP GOES THE WEASEL!
KLANK
KLANK
KLANK

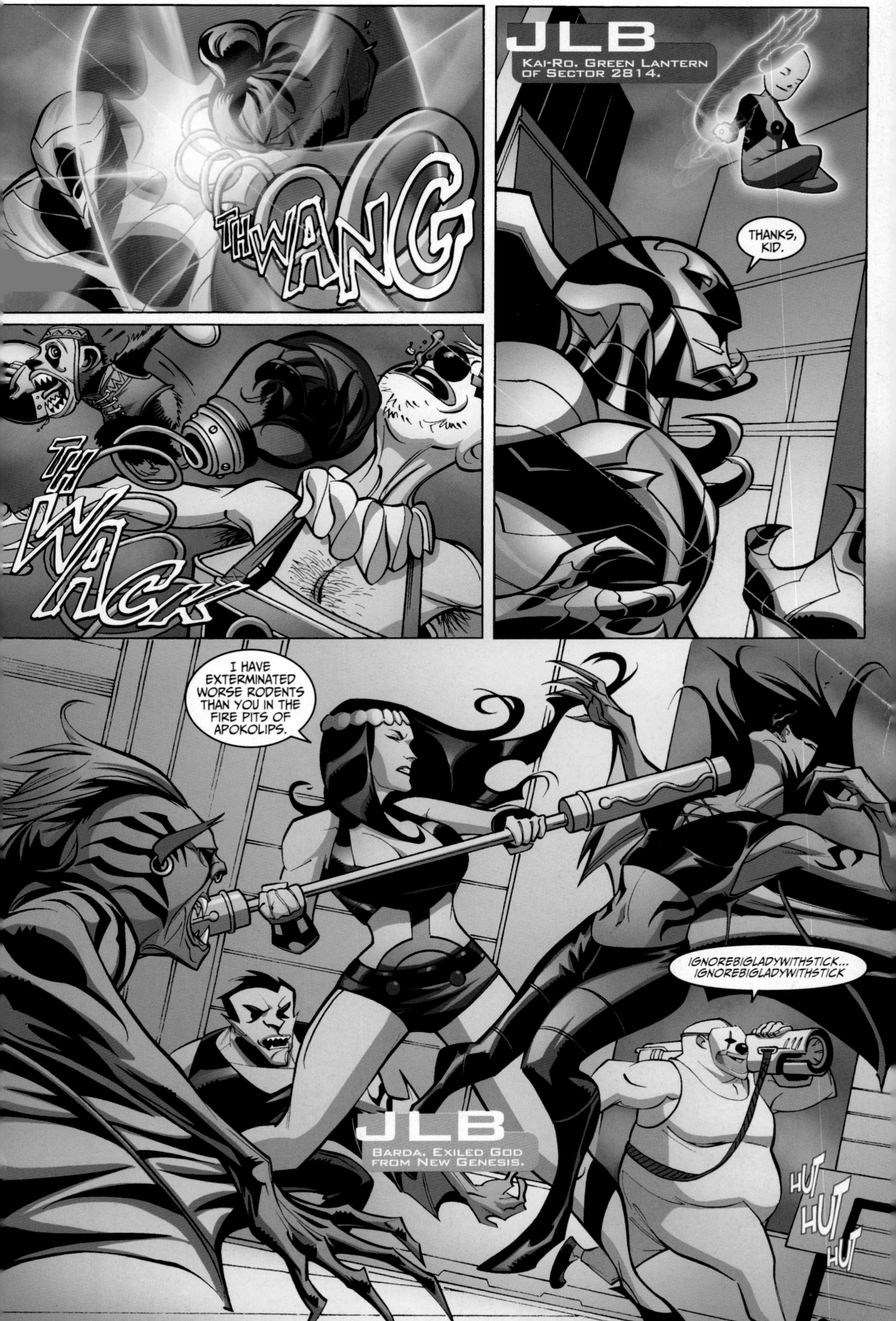
THWANG
JLB
KAI-RO. GREEN LANTERN OF SECTOR 2814.
THANKS, KID.
THWACK
I HAVE EXTERMINATED WORSE RODENTS THAN YOU IN THE FIRE PITS OF APOKOLIPS.
IGNOREBIGLADYWITHSTICK... IGNOREBIGLADYWITHSTICK
JLB
BARDA. EXILED GOD FROM NEW GENESIS.
HUT HUT HUT

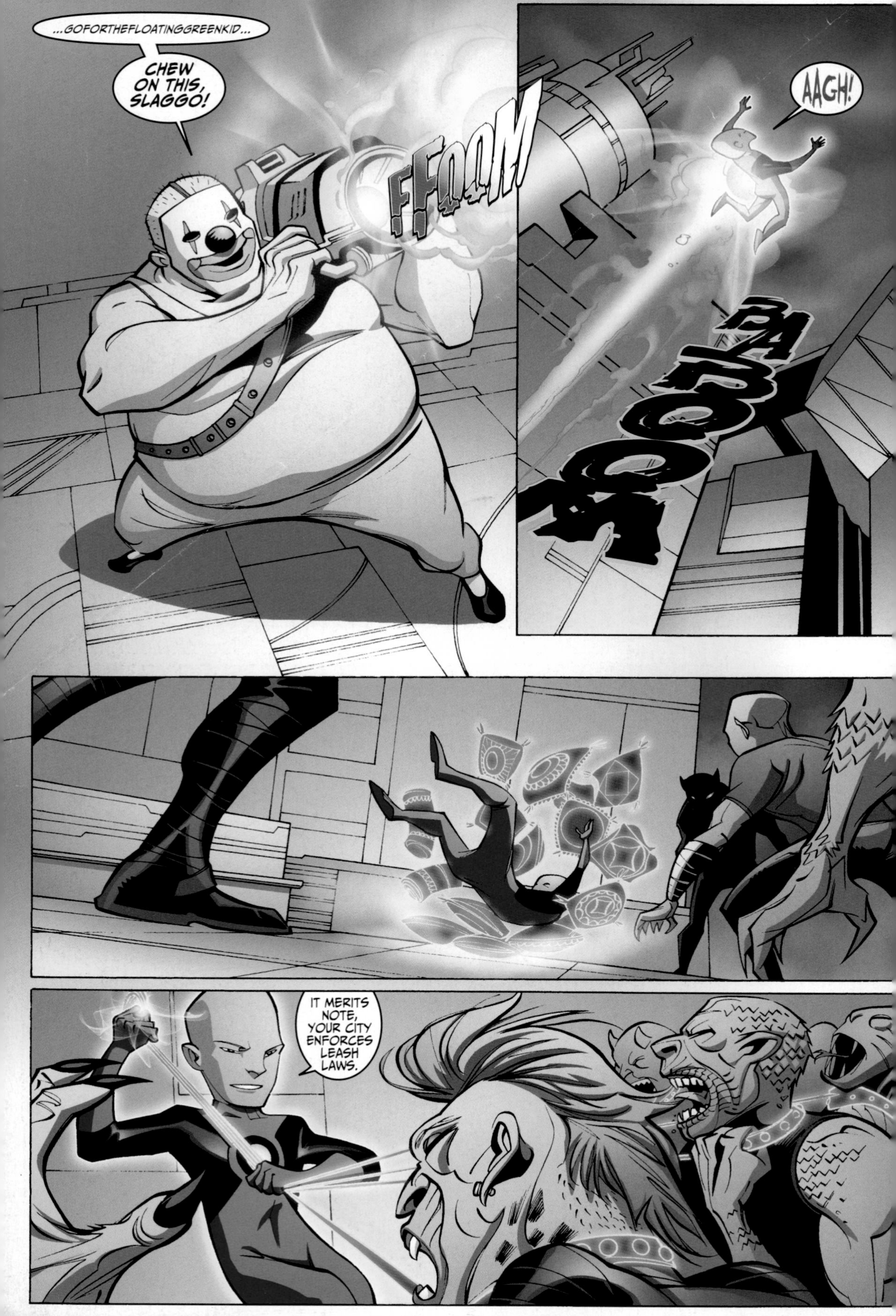
...GOFORTHEFLOATINGGREENKID...
CHEW ON THIS, SLAGGO!
FFOOM
AAGH!
BADOOM
IT MERITS NOTE, YOUR CITY ENFORCES LEASH LAWS.

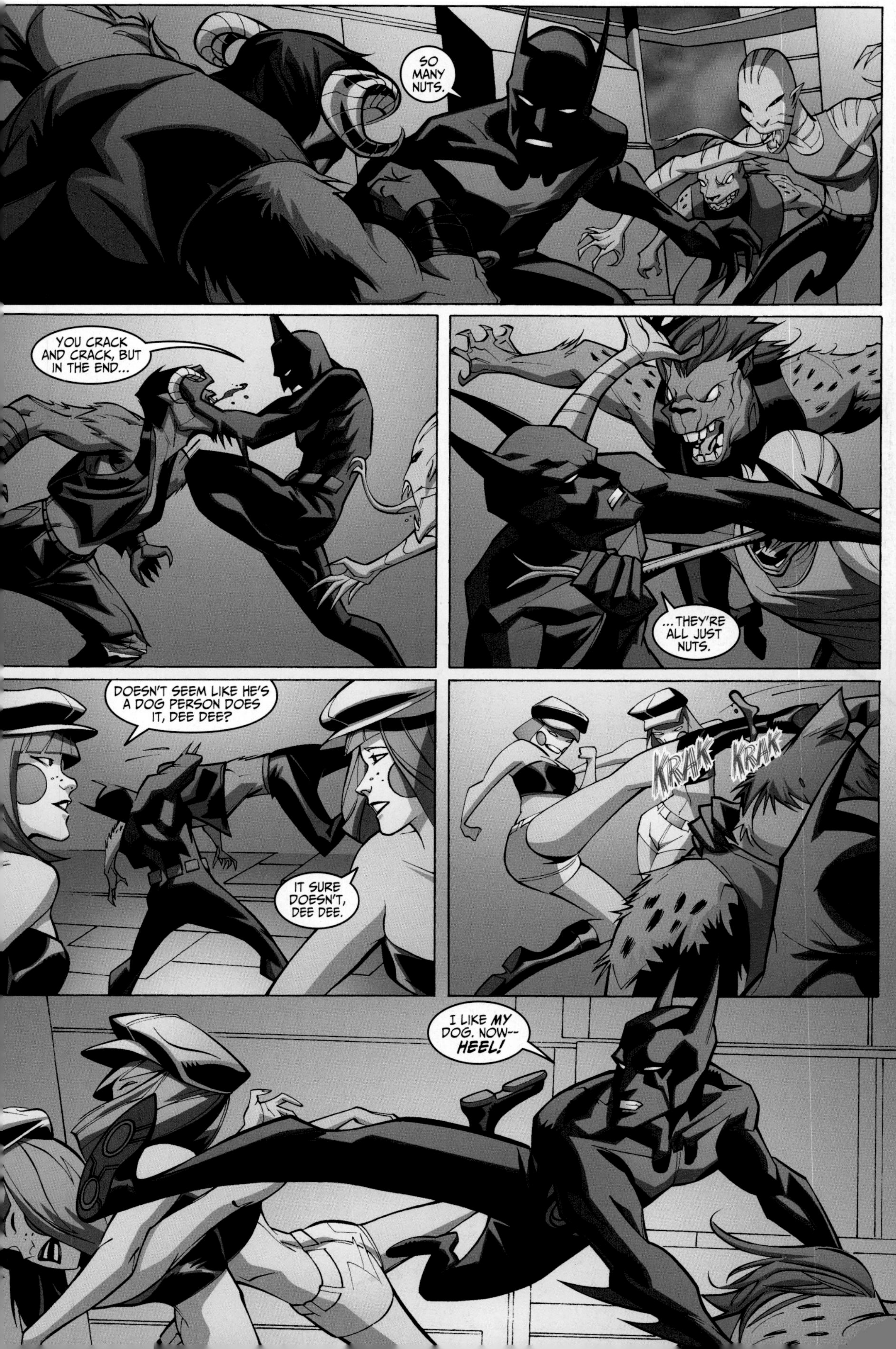
SO MANY NUTS.
YOU CRACK AND CRACK, BUT IN THE END...
...THEY'RE ALL JUST NUTS.
DOESN'T SEEM LIKE HE'S A DOG PERSON DOES IT, DEE DEE?
IT SURE DOESN'T, DEE DEE.
KRAK KRAK
I LIKE MY DOG. NOW-- HEEL!

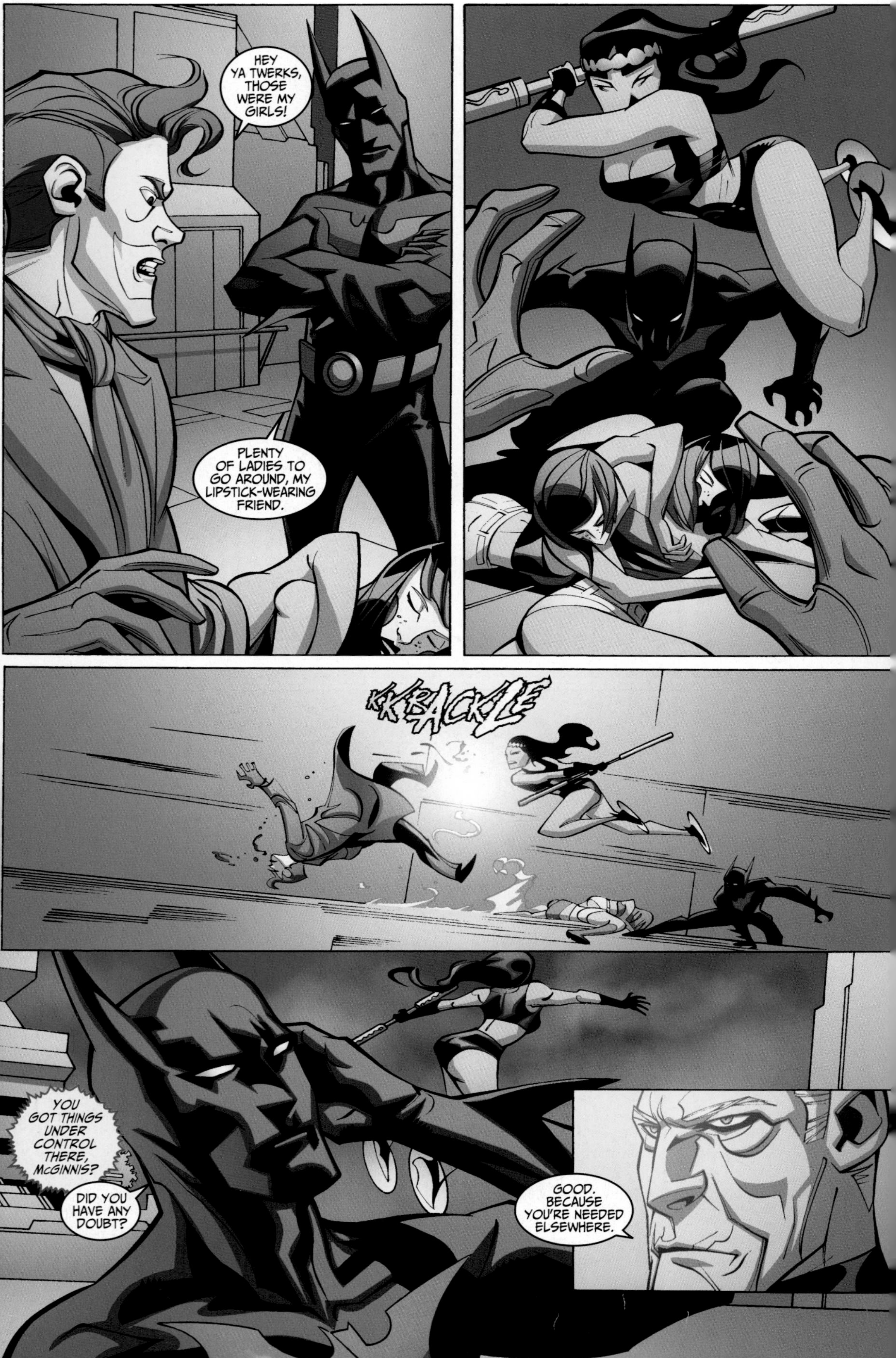
HEY YA TWERKS, THOSE WERE MY GIRLS!
PLENTY OF LADIES TO GO AROUND, MY LIPSTICK-WEARING FRIEND.
KKRACKLE
YOU GOT THINGS UNDER CONTROL THERE, McGINNIS?
DID YOU HAVE ANY DOUBT?
GOOD. BECAUSE YOU'RE NEEDED ELSEWHERE.

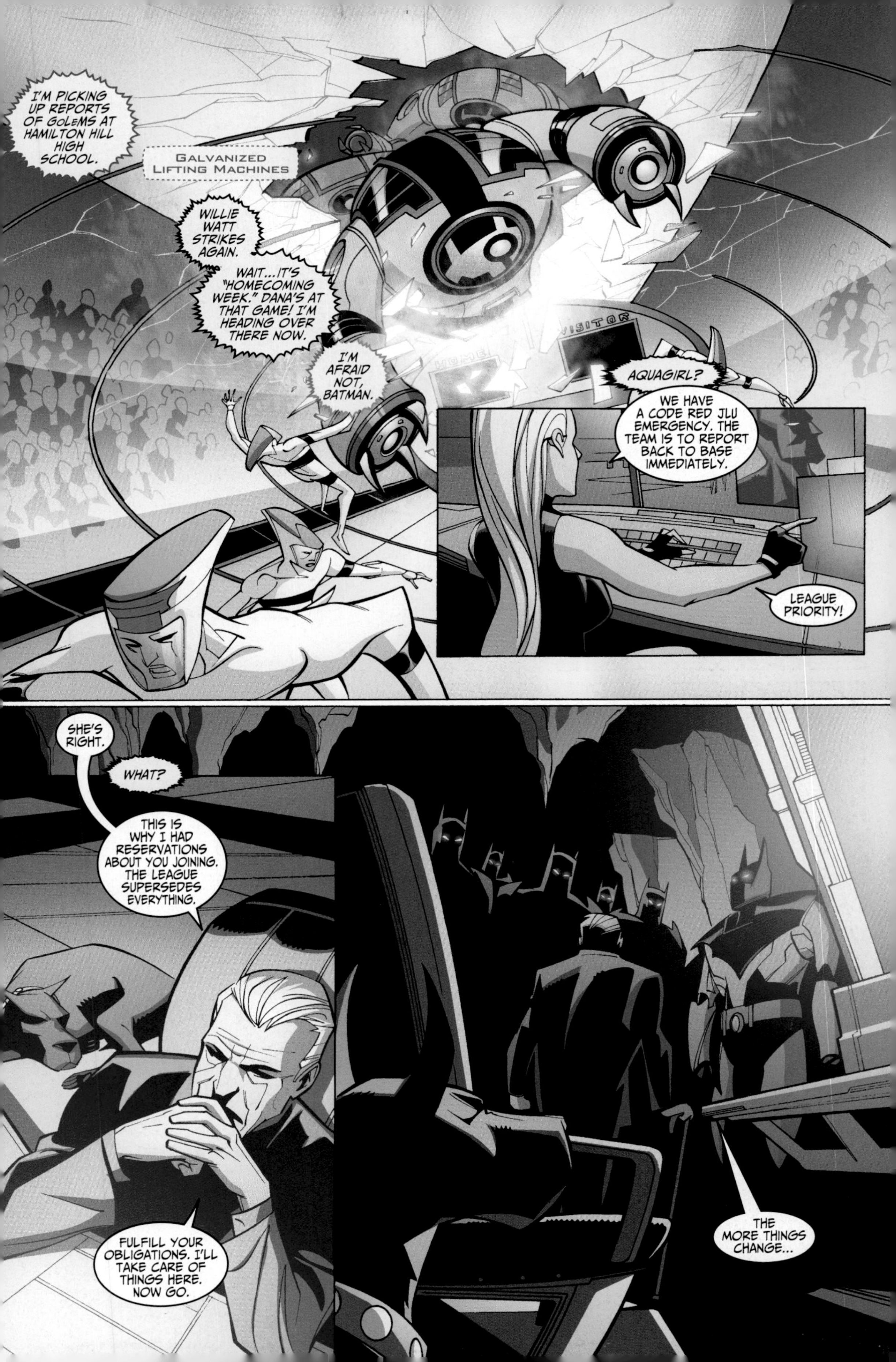
I'M PICKING UP REPORTS OF GoLeMS AT HAMILTON HILL HIGH SCHOOL.
GALVANIZED LIFTING MACHINES
WILLIE WATT STRIKES AGAIN.
WAIT...IT'S "HOMECOMING WEEK." DANA'S AT THAT GAME! I'M HEADING OVER THERE NOW.
I'M AFRAID NOT, BATMAN.
AQUAGIRL?
WE HAVE A CODE RED JLU EMERGENCY. THE TEAM IS TO REPORT BACK TO BASE IMMEDIATELY.
LEAGUE PRIORITY!
SHE'S RIGHT.
WHAT?
THIS IS WHY I HAD RESERVATIONS ABOUT YOU JOINING. THE LEAGUE SUPERSEDES EVERYTHING.
FULFILL YOUR OBLIGATIONS. I'LL TAKE CARE OF THINGS HERE. NOW GO.
THE MORE THINGS CHANGE...

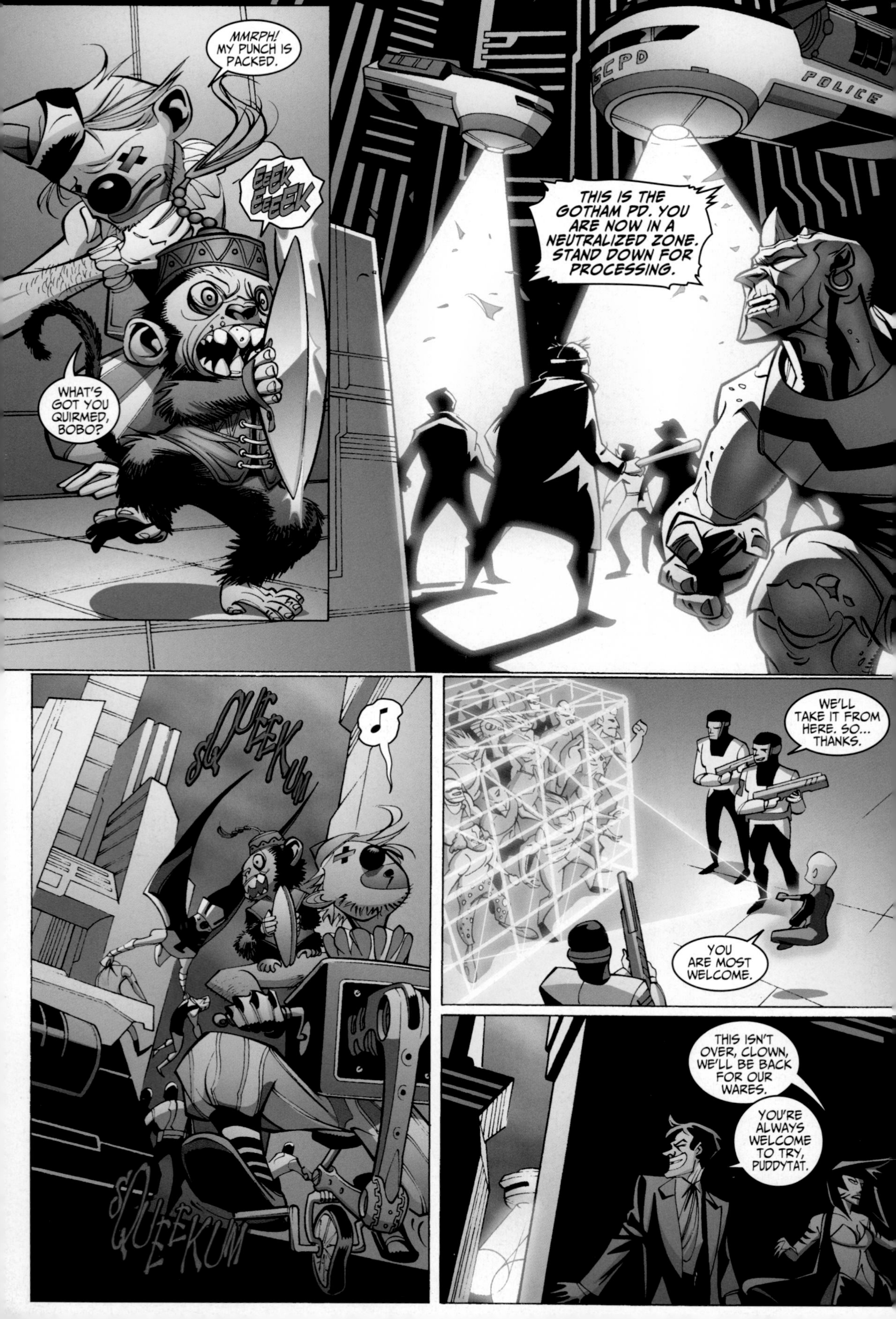
MMRPH! MY PUNCH IS PACKED.
EEEK EEEEK
WHAT'S GOT YOU QUIRMED, BOBO?
THIS IS THE GOTHAM PD. YOU ARE NOW IN A NEUTRALIZED ZONE. STAND DOWN FOR PROCESSING.
GCPD
POLICE
SQUEEKUM
♪
SQUEEKUM
WE'LL TAKE IT FROM HERE. SO... THANKS.
YOU ARE MOST WELCOME.
THIS ISN'T OVER, CLOWN, WE'LL BE BACK FOR OUR WARES.
YOU'RE ALWAYS WELCOME TO TRY, PUDDYTAT.

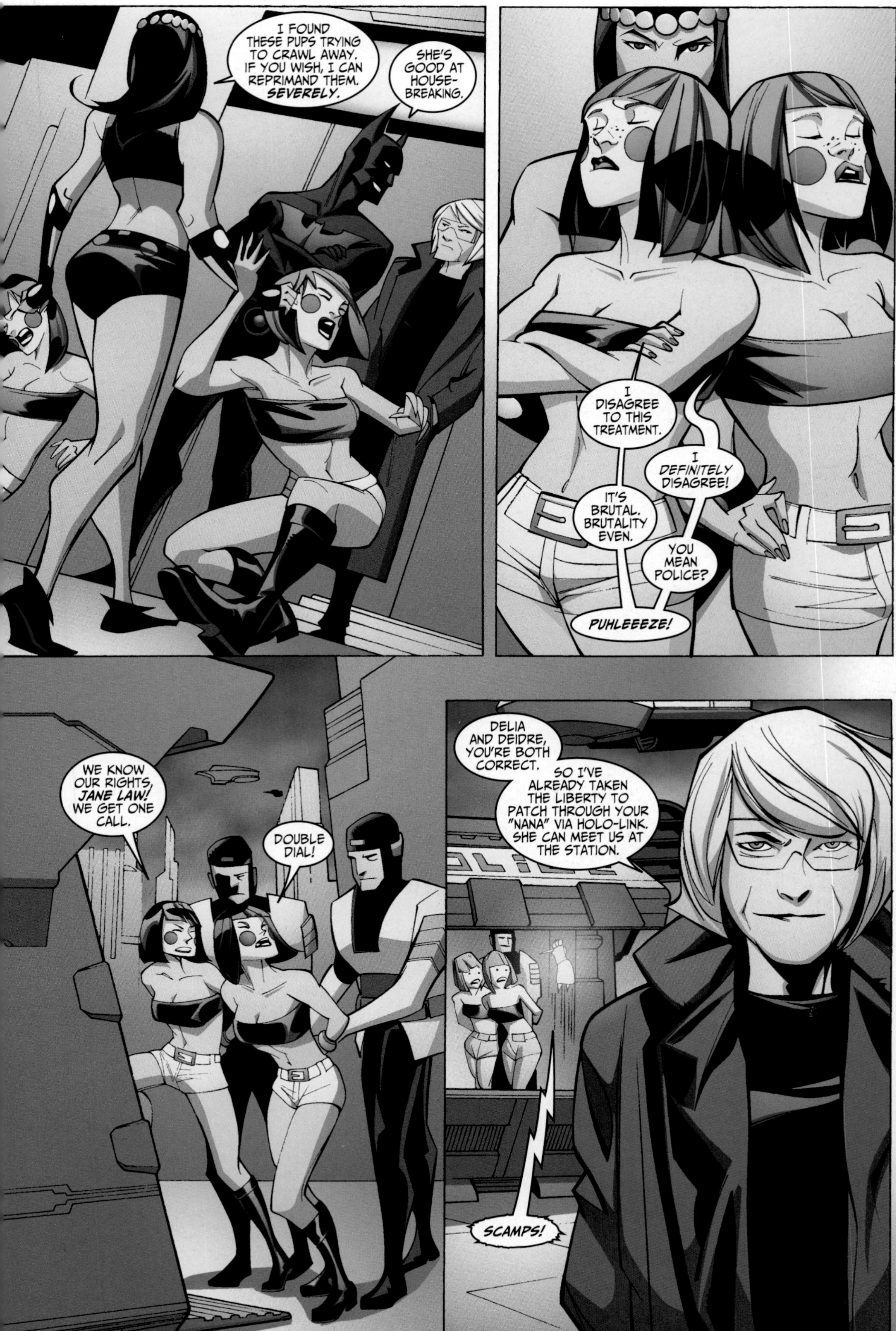
I FOUND THESE PUPS TRYING TO CRAWL AWAY. IF YOU WISH, I CAN REPRIMAND THEM. SEVERELY.
SHE'S GOOD AT HOUSE-BREAKING.
I DISAGREE TO THIS TREATMENT.
I DEFINITELY DISAGREE!
IT'S BRUTAL. BRUTALITY EVEN.
YOU MEAN POLICE?
PUHLEEEZE!
WE KNOW OUR RIGHTS, JANE LAW! WE GET ONE CALL.
DOUBLE DIAL!
DELIA AND DEIDRE, YOU'RE BOTH CORRECT.
SO I'VE ALREADY TAKEN THE LIBERTY TO PATCH THROUGH YOUR "NANA" VIA HOLO-LINK. SHE CAN MEET US AT THE STATION.
SCAMPS!

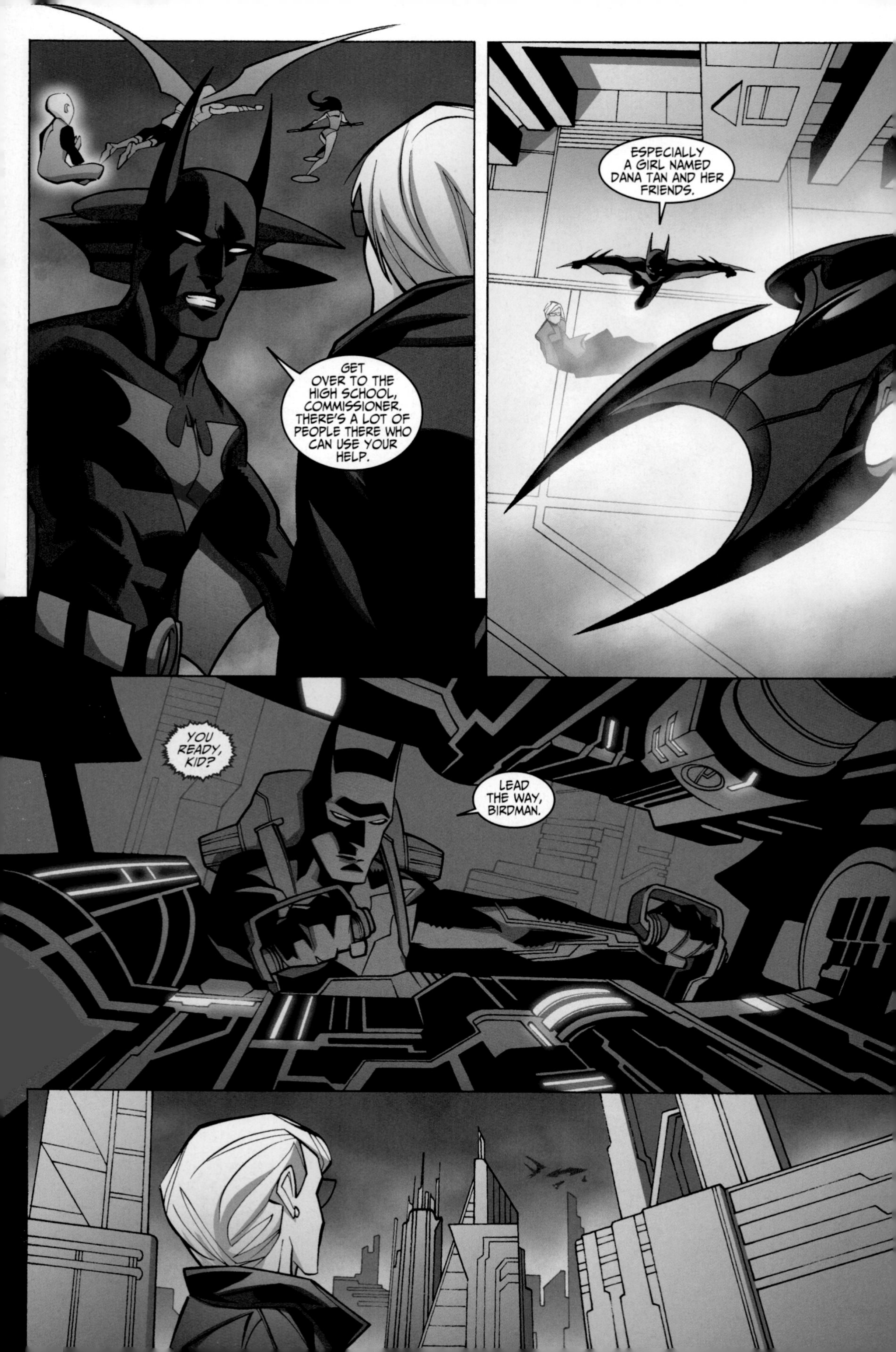
GET OVER TO THE HIGH SCHOOL, COMMISSIONER. THERE'S A LOT OF PEOPLE THERE WHO CAN USE YOUR HELP.
ESPECIALLY A GIRL NAMED DANA TAN AND HER FRIENDS.
YOU READY, KID?
LEAD THE WAY, BIRDMAN.

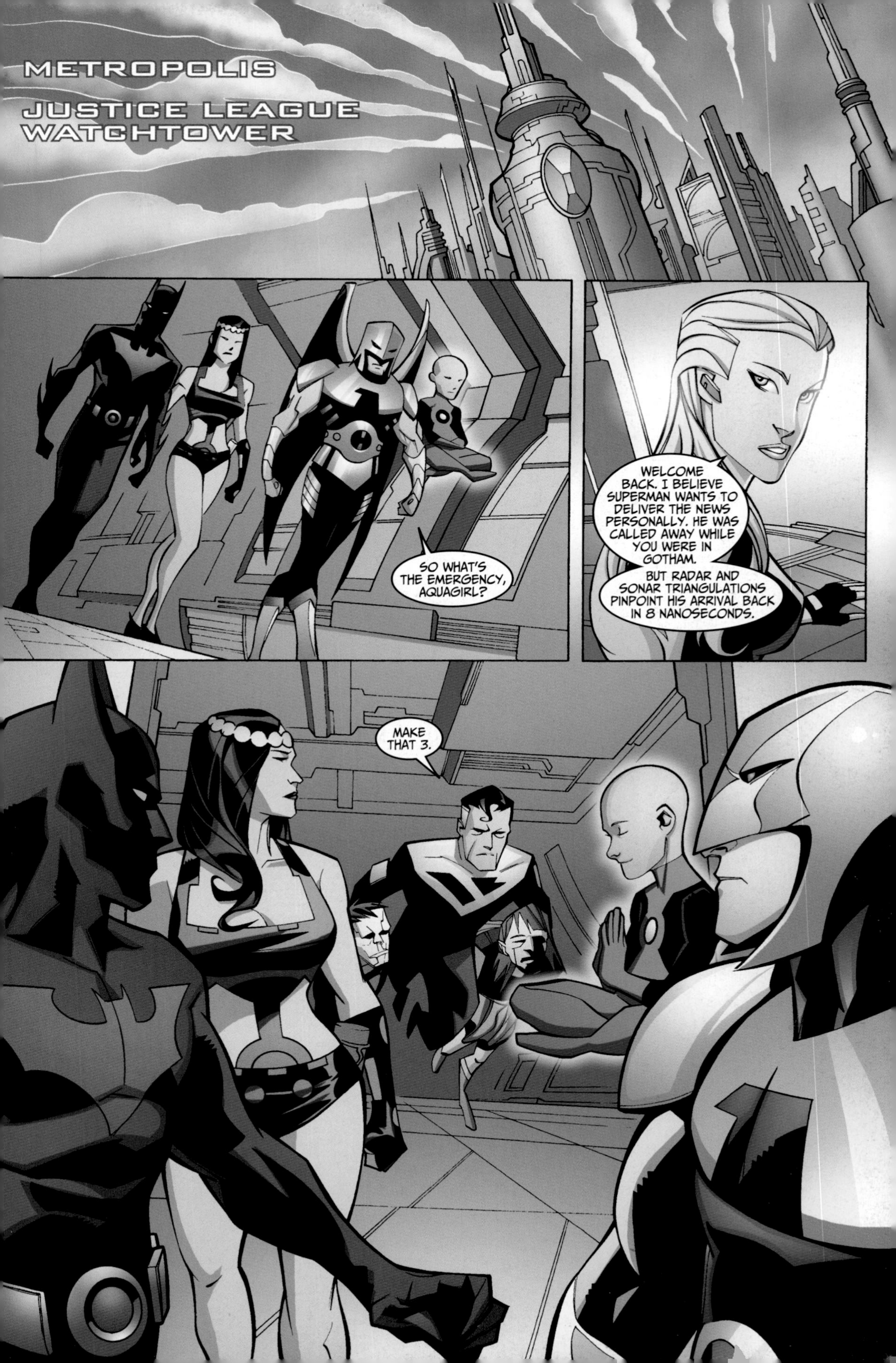
METROPOLIS
JUSTICE LEAGUE WATCHTOWER
SO WHAT'S THE EMERGENCY, AQUAGIRL?
WELCOME BACK. I BELIEVE SUPERMAN WANTS TO DELIVER THE NEWS PERSONALLY. HE WAS CALLED AWAY WHILE YOU WERE IN GOTHAM.
BUT RADAR AND SONAR TRIANGULATIONS PINPOINT HIS ARRIVAL BACK IN 8 NANOSECONDS.
MAKE THAT 3.

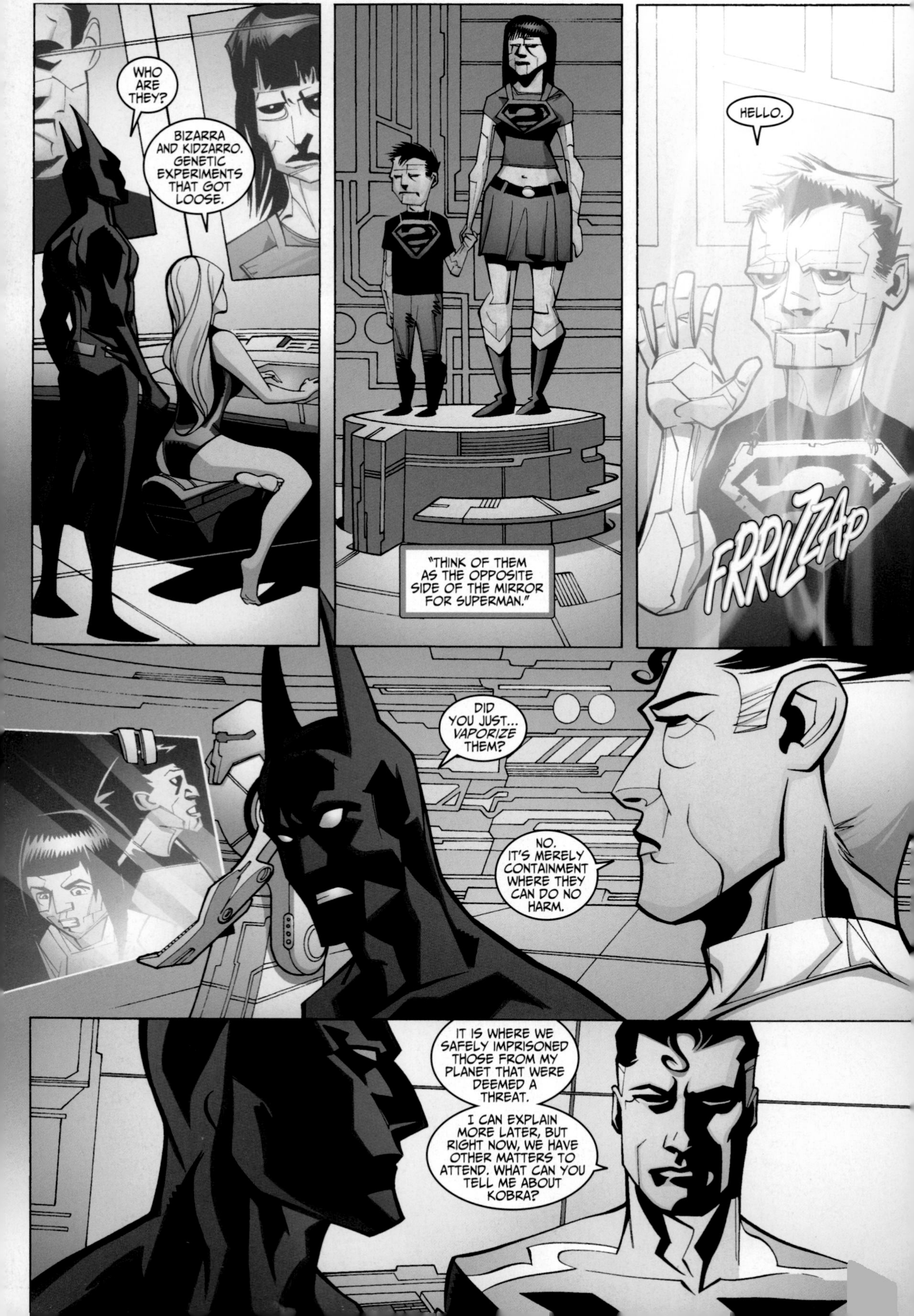
WHO ARE THEY?
BIZARRA AND KIDZARRO. GENETIC EXPERIMENTS THAT GOT LOOSE.
"THINK OF THEM AS THE OPPOSITE SIDE OF THE MIRROR FOR SUPERMAN."
HELLO.
FRRIZZAP
DID YOU JUST... VAPORIZE THEM?
NO. IT'S MERELY CONTAINMENT WHERE THEY CAN DO NO HARM.
IT IS WHERE WE SAFELY IMPRISONED THOSE FROM MY PLANET THAT WERE DEEMED A THREAT.
I CAN EXPLAIN MORE LATER, BUT RIGHT NOW, WE HAVE OTHER MATTERS TO ATTEND. WHAT CAN YOU TELL ME ABOUT KOBRA?

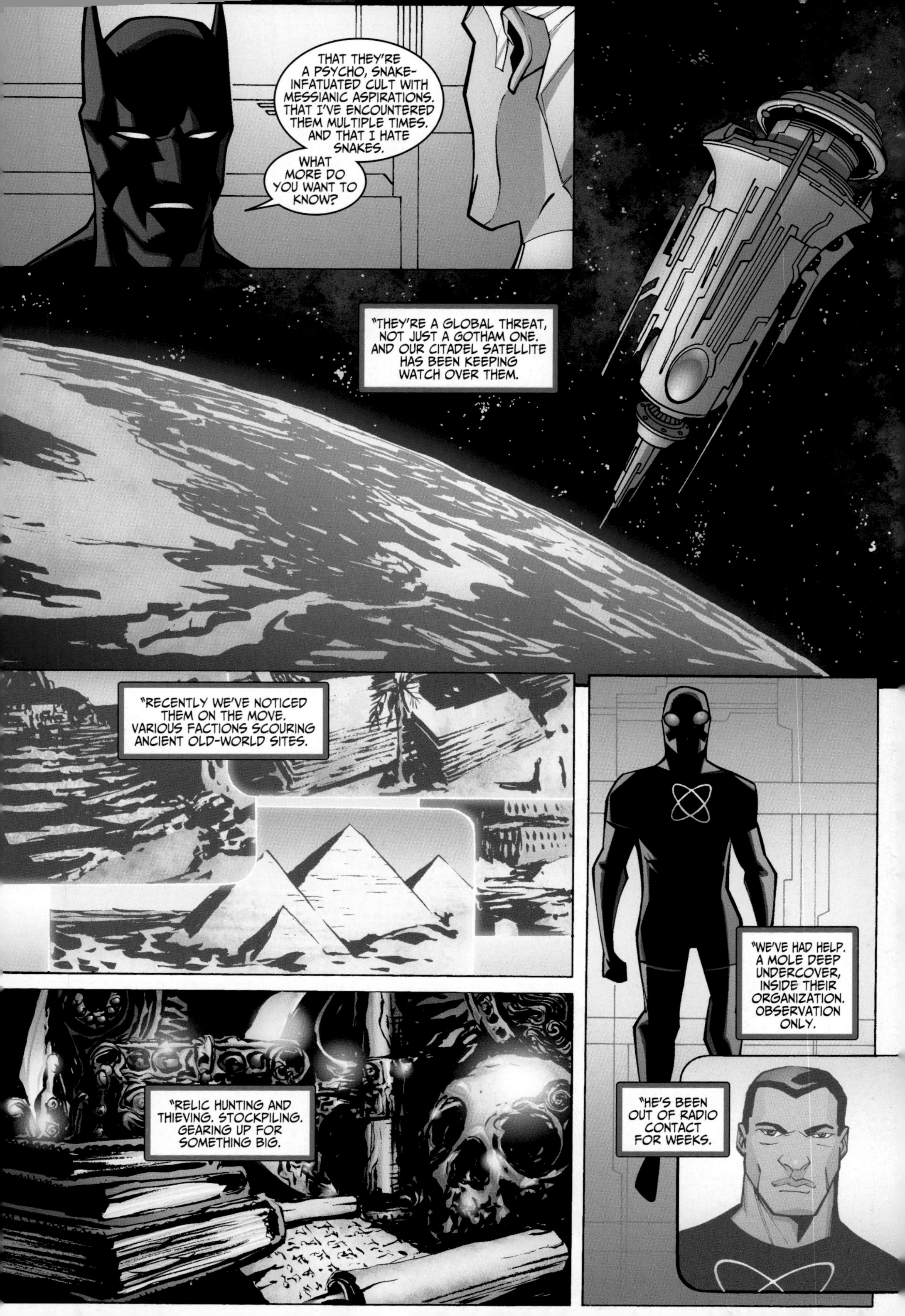
THAT THEY'RE A PSYCHO, SNAKE-INFATUATED CULT WITH MESSIANIC ASPIRATIONS. THAT I'VE ENCOUNTERED THEM MULTIPLE TIMES. AND THAT I HATE SNAKES.
WHAT MORE DO YOU WANT TO KNOW?
"THEY'RE A GLOBAL THREAT, NOT JUST A GOTHAM ONE. AND OUR CITADEL SATELLITE HAS BEEN KEEPING WATCH OVER THEM.
"RECENTLY WE'VE NOTICED THEM ON THE MOVE. VARIOUS FACTIONS SCOURING ANCIENT OLD-WORLD SITES.
"RELIC HUNTING AND THIEVING. STOCKPILING. GEARING UP FOR SOMETHING BIG.
"WE'VE HAD HELP. A MOLE DEEP UNDERCOVER, INSIDE THEIR ORGANIZATION. OBSERVATION ONLY.
"HE'S BEEN OUT OF RADIO CONTACT FOR WEEKS.

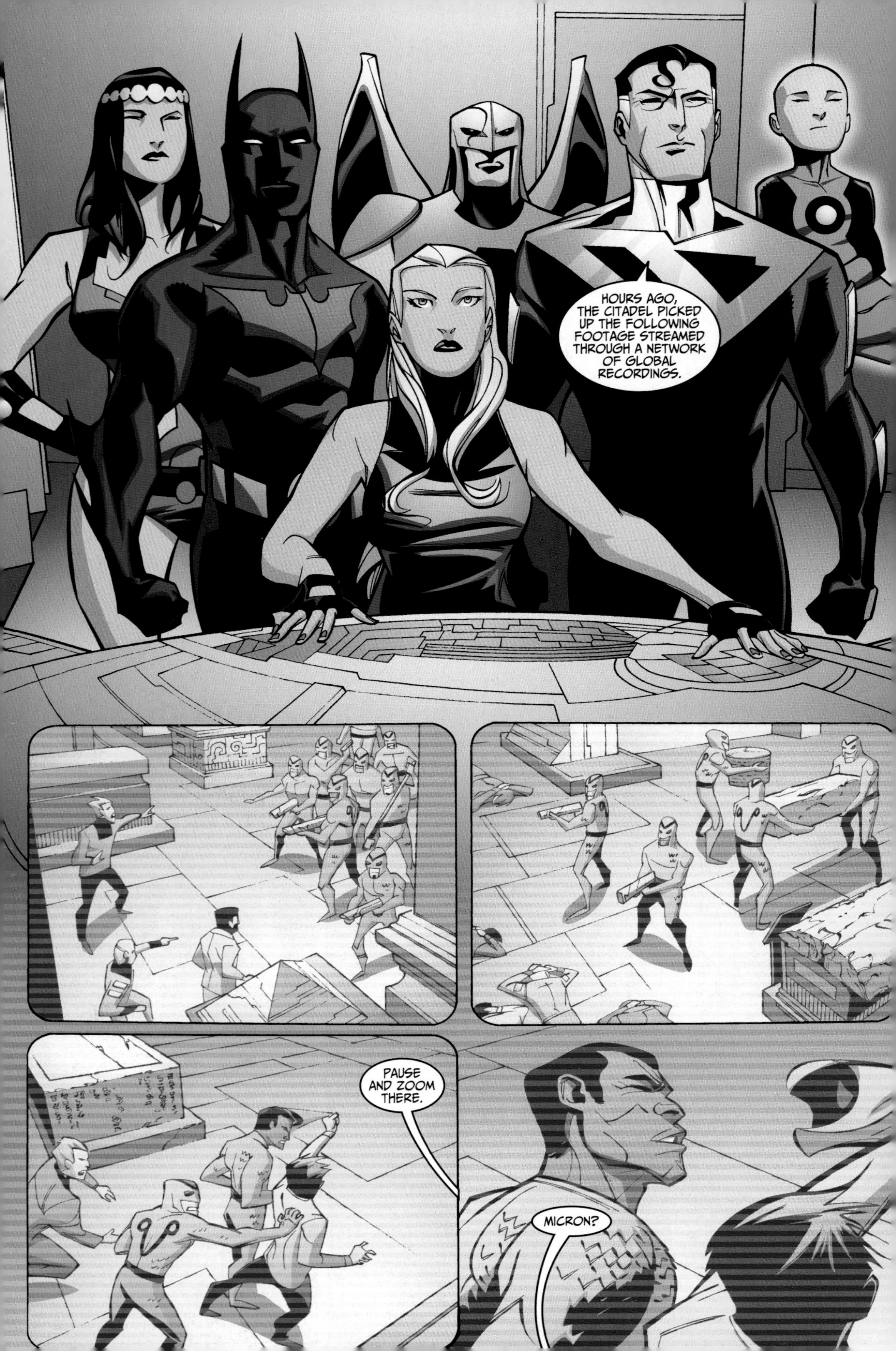
HOURS AGO, THE CITADEL PICKED UP THE FOLLOWING FOOTAGE STREAMED THROUGH A NETWORK OF GLOBAL RECORDINGS.
PAUSE AND ZOOM THERE.
MICRON?

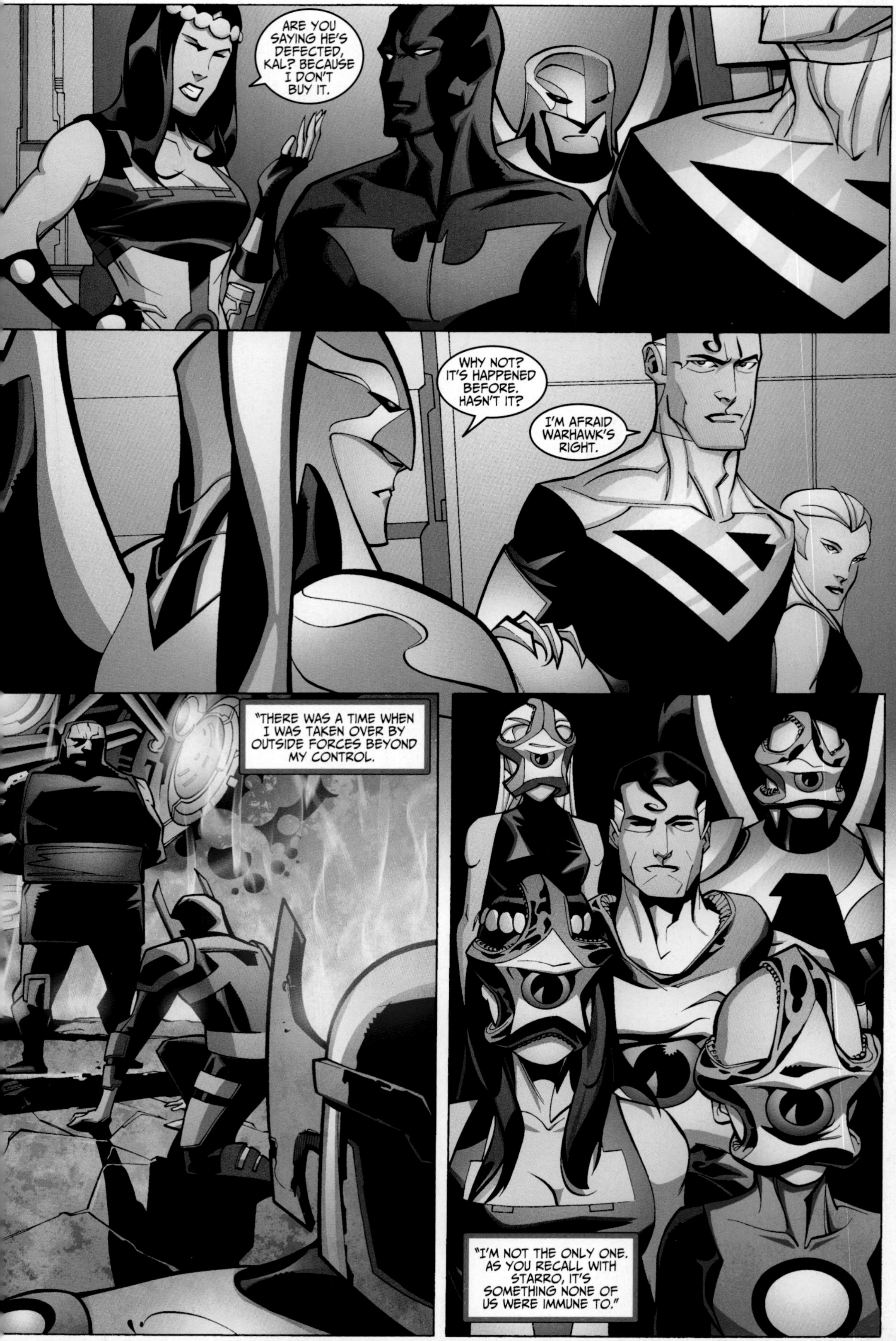
ARE YOU SAYING HE'S DEFECTED, KAL? BECAUSE I DON'T BUY IT.
WHY NOT? IT'S HAPPENED BEFORE. HASN'T IT?
I'M AFRAID WARHAWK'S RIGHT.
"THERE WAS A TIME WHEN I WAS TAKEN OVER BY OUTSIDE FORCES BEYOND MY CONTROL.
"I'M NOT THE ONLY ONE. AS YOU RECALL WITH STARRO, IT'S SOMETHING NONE OF US WERE IMMUNE TO."

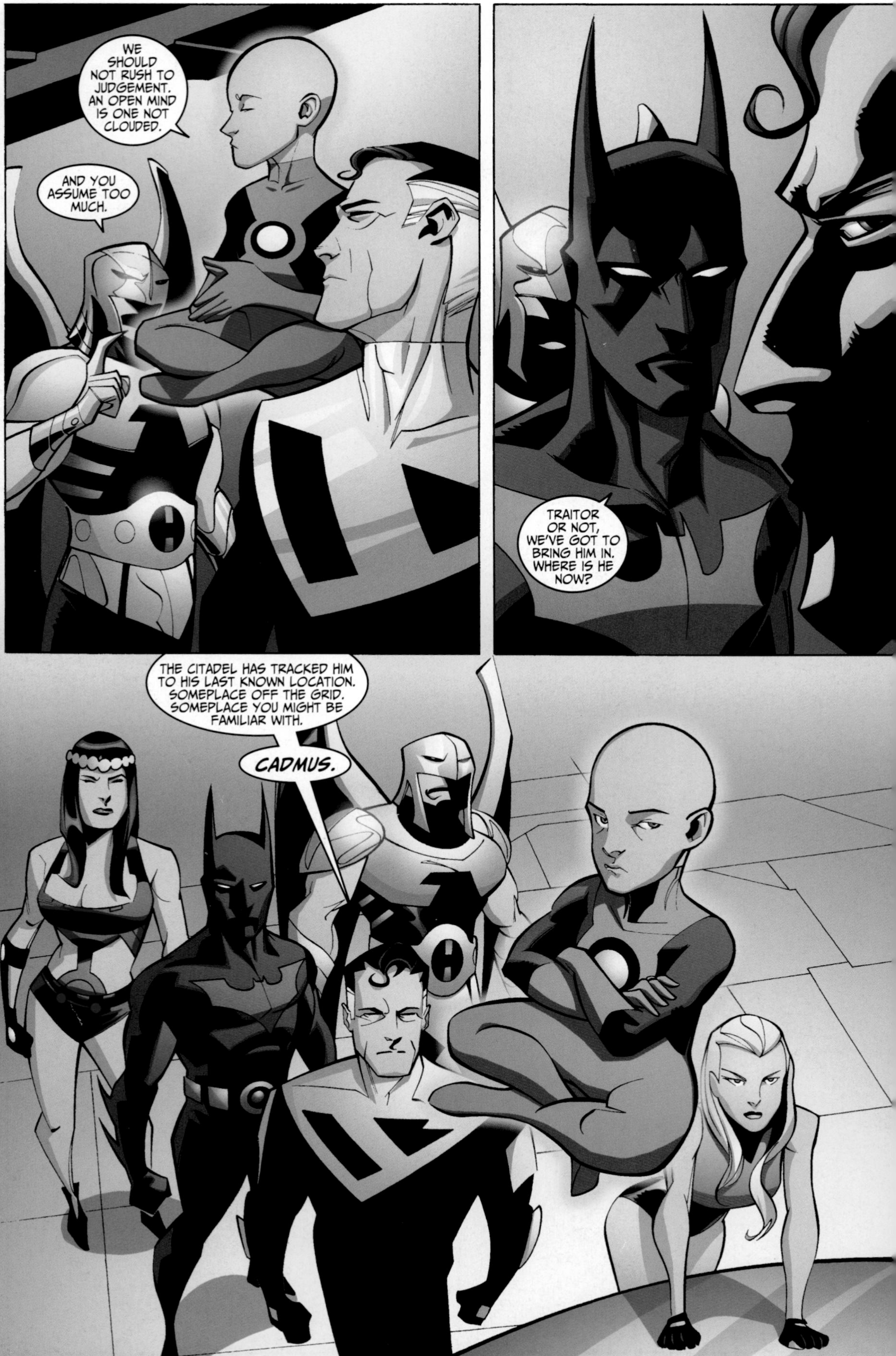
WE SHOULD NOT RUSH TO JUDGEMENT. AN OPEN MIND IS ONE NOT CLOUDED.
AND YOU ASSUME TOO MUCH.
TRAITOR OR NOT, WE'VE GOT TO BRING HIM IN. WHERE IS HE NOW?
THE CITADEL HAS TRACKED HIM TO HIS LAST KNOWN LOCATION. SOMEPLACE OFF THE GRID. SOMEPLACE YOU MIGHT BE FAMILIAR WITH.
CADMUS.

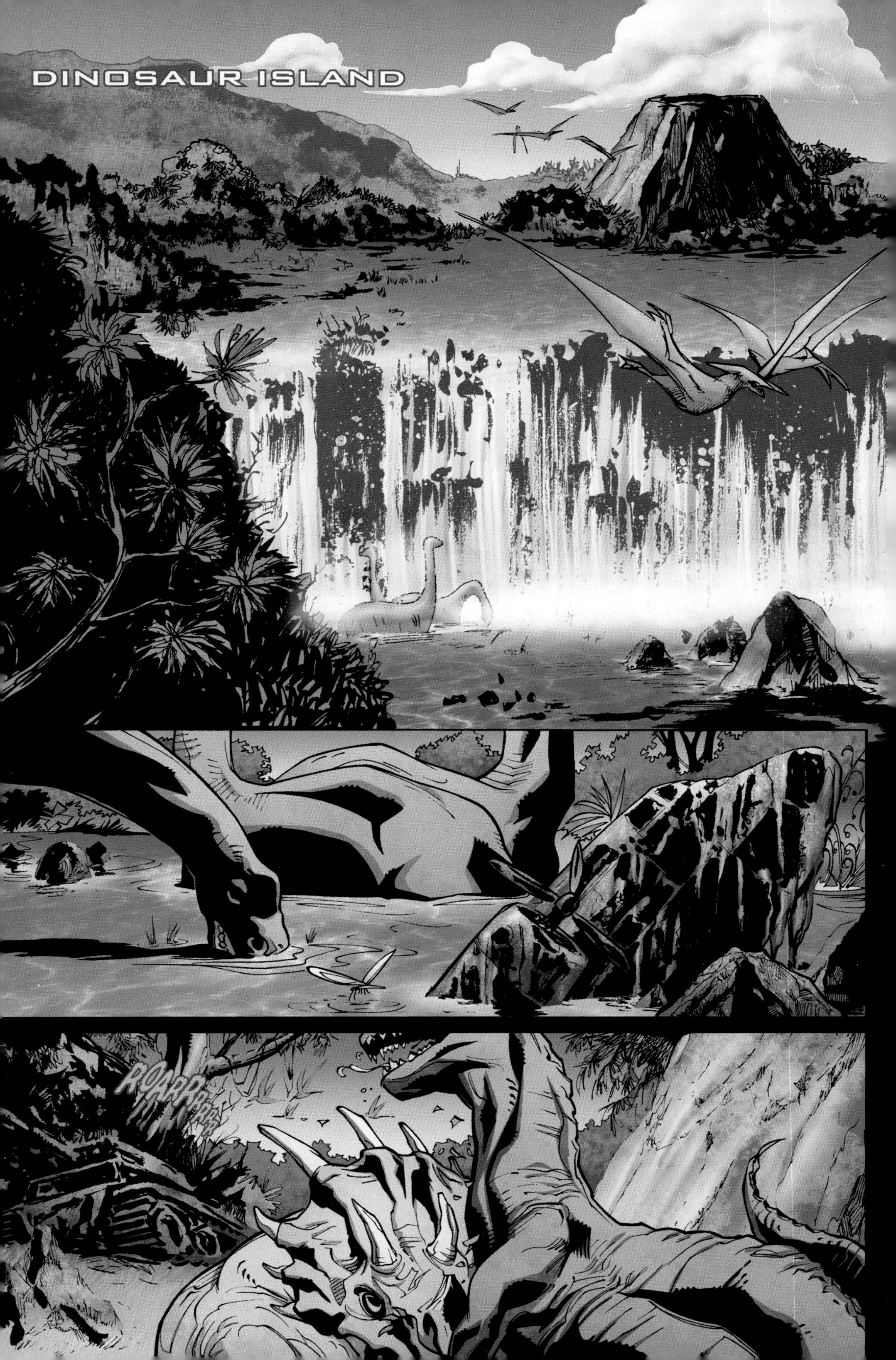
DINOSAUR ISLAND
ROARRRRR

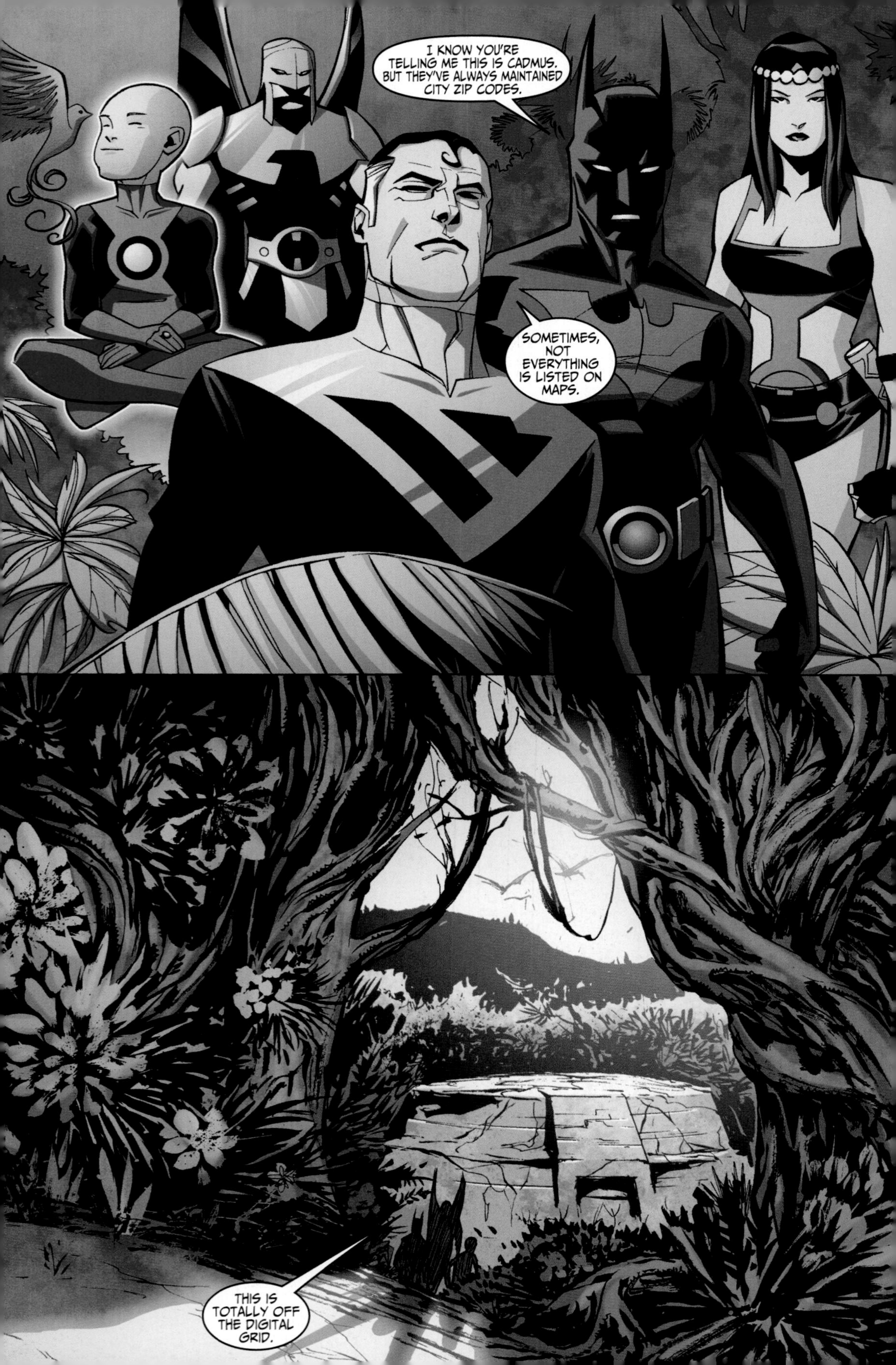
I KNOW YOU'RE TELLING ME THIS IS CADMUS. BUT THEY'VE ALWAYS MAINTAINED CITY ZIP CODES.
SOMETIMES, NOT EVERYTHING IS LISTED ON MAPS.
THIS IS TOTALLY OFF THE DIGITAL GRID.

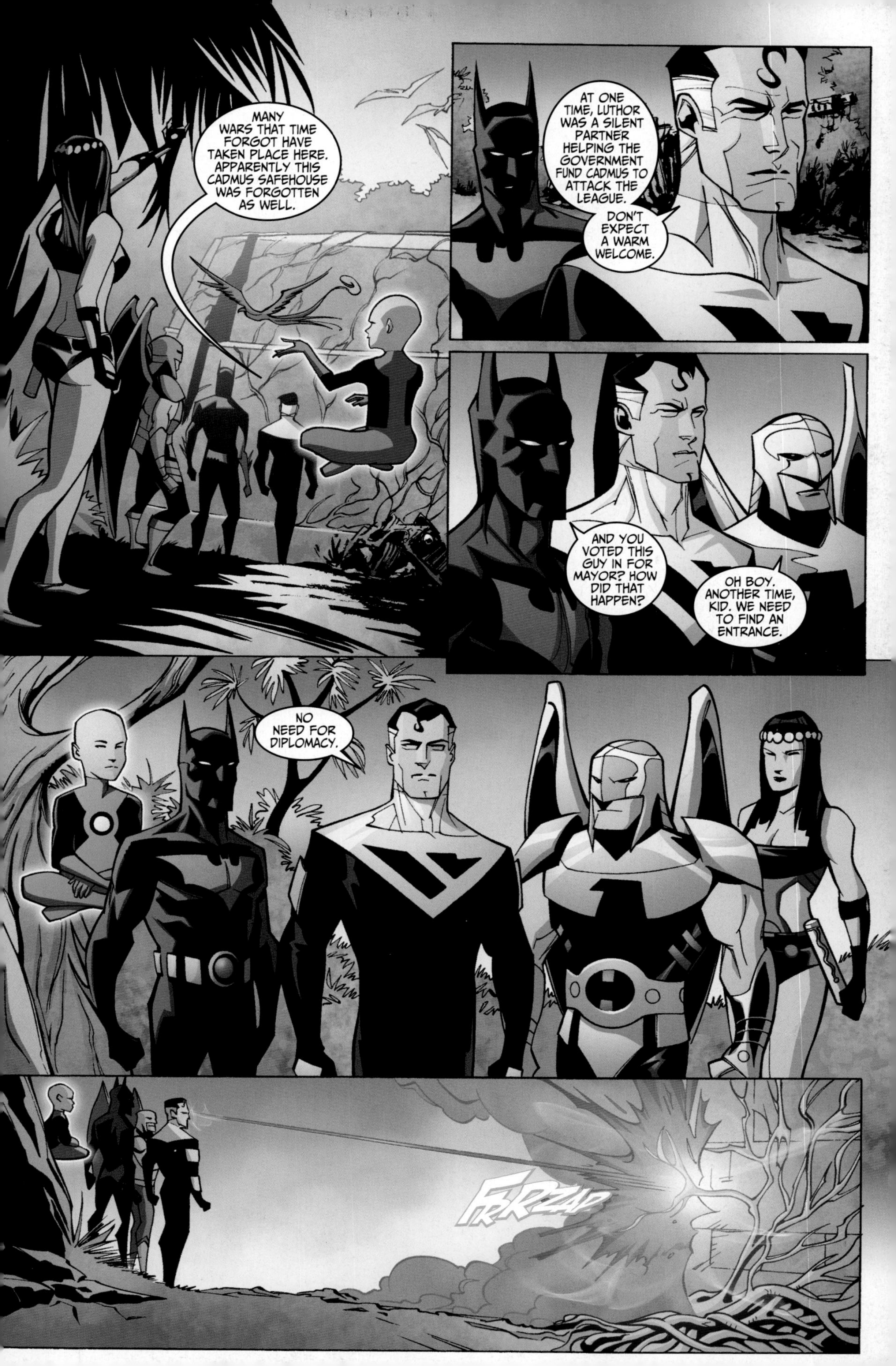
MANY WARS THAT TIME FORGOT HAVE TAKEN PLACE HERE. APPARENTLY THIS CADMUS SAFEHOUSE WAS FORGOTTEN AS WELL.
AT ONE TIME, LUTHOR WAS A SILENT PARTNER HELPING THE GOVERNMENT FUND CADMUS TO ATTACK THE LEAGUE.
DON'T EXPECT A WARM WELCOME.
AND YOU VOTED THIS GUY IN FOR MAYOR? HOW DID THAT HAPPEN?
OH BOY. ANOTHER TIME, KID. WE NEED TO FIND AN ENTRANCE.
NO NEED FOR DIPLOMACY.
FRRZAP

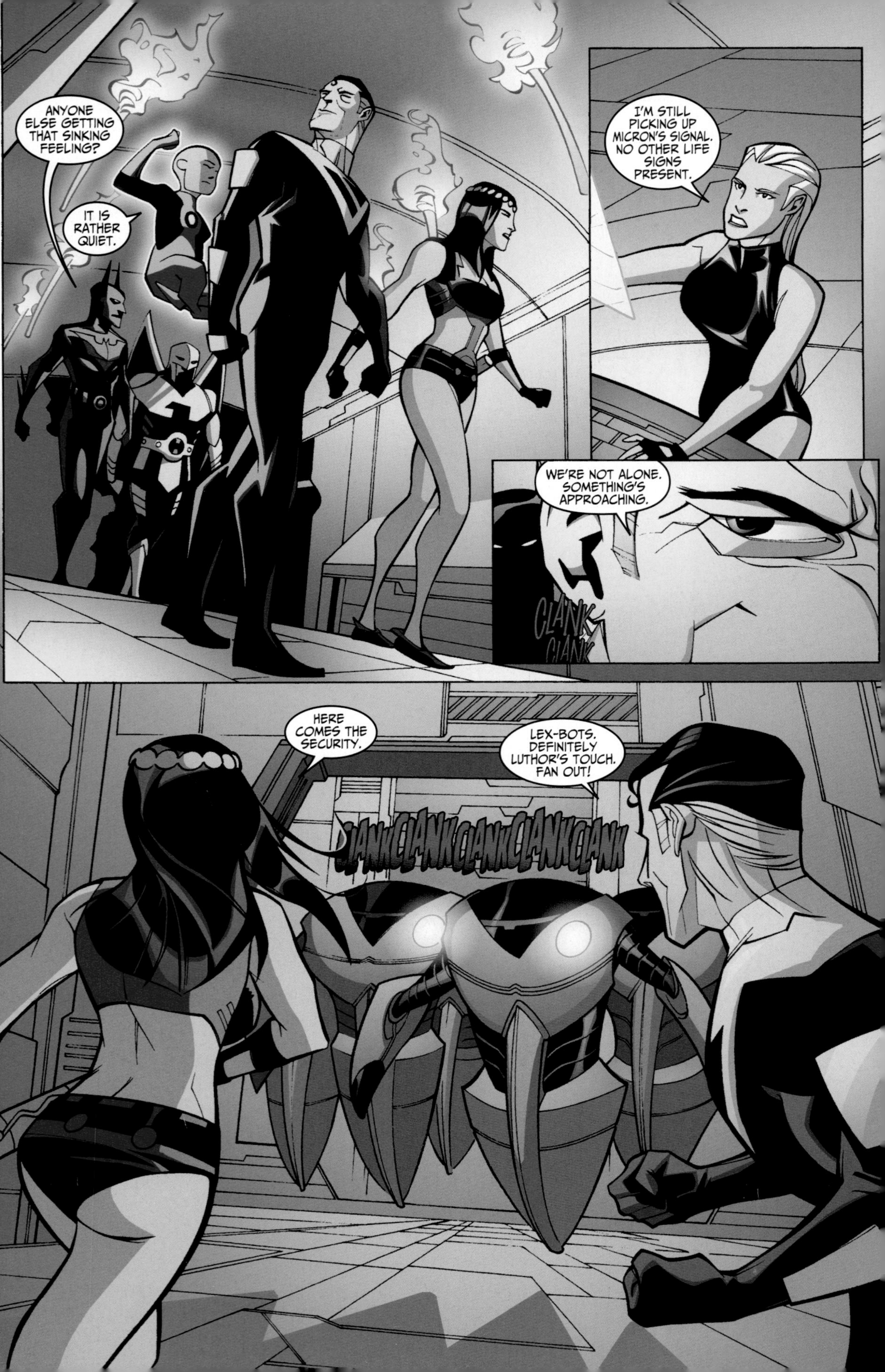

ANYONE ELSE GETTING THAT SINKING FEELING?
IT IS RATHER QUIET.
I'M STILL PICKING UP MICRON'S SIGNAL. NO OTHER LIFE SIGNS PRESENT.
WE'RE NOT ALONE. SOMETHING'S APPROACHING.
CLANK CLANK
HERE COMES THE SECURITY.
LEX-BOTS. DEFINITELY LUTHOR'S TOUCH. FAN OUT!
CLANKCLANKCLANKCLANKCLANK

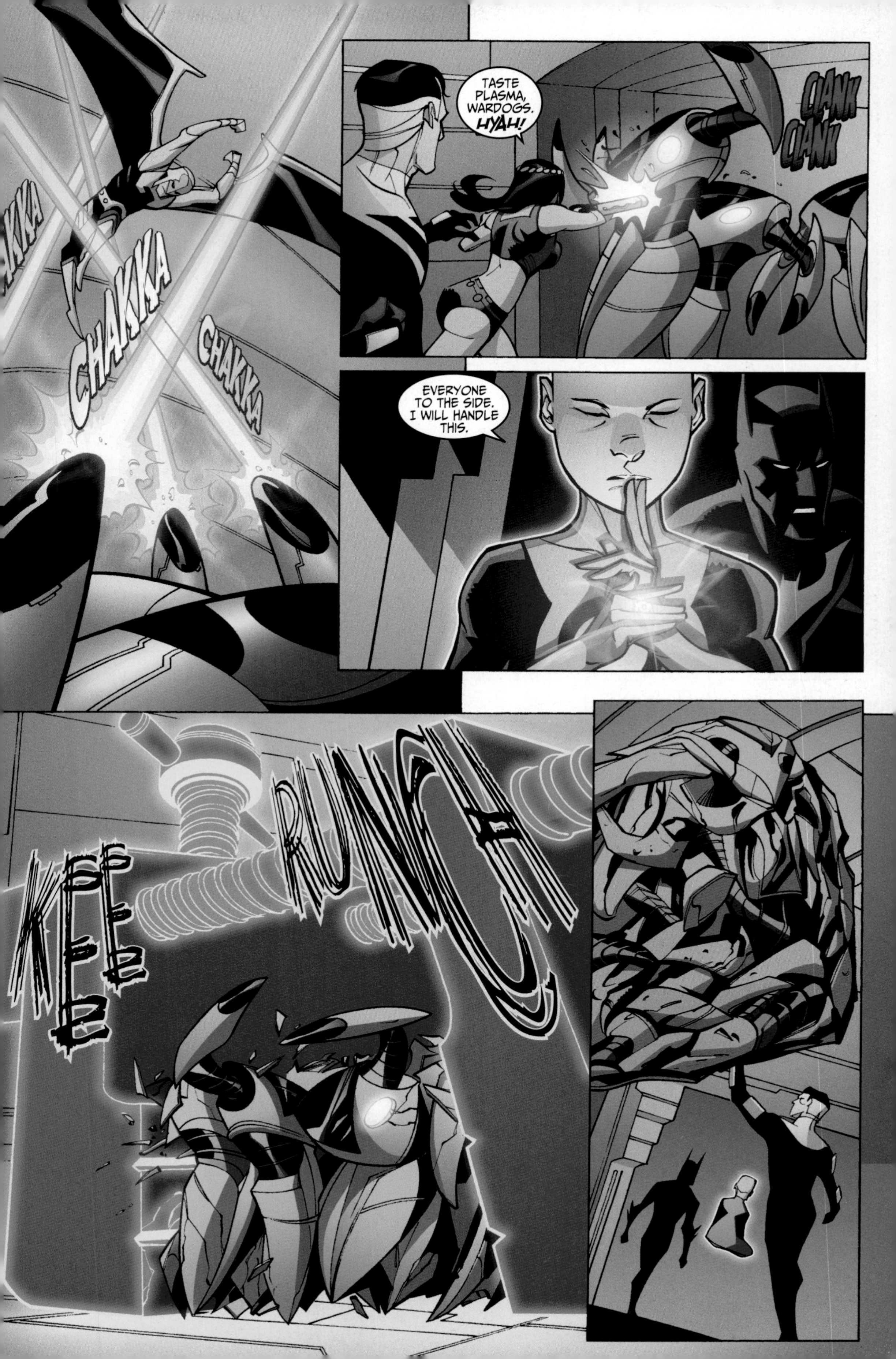
CHAKKA
CHAKKA
CHAKKA
TASTE PLASMA, WARDOGS. HYAH!
CLANK CLANK
EVERYONE TO THE SIDE. I WILL HANDLE THIS.
KEEE
RUNCH

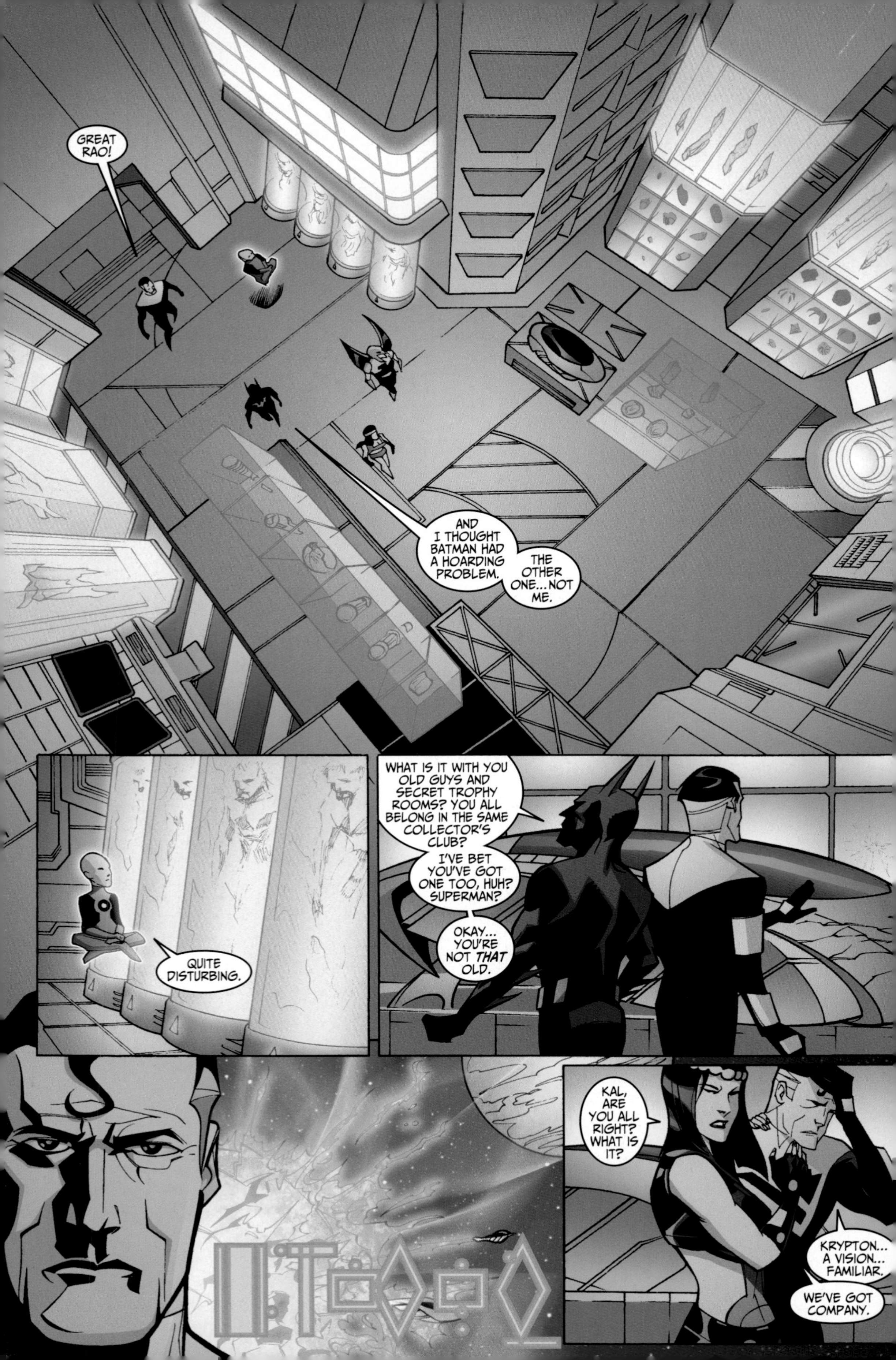
GREAT RAO!
AND I THOUGHT BATMAN HAD A HOARDING PROBLEM.
THE OTHER ONE...NOT ME.
QUITE DISTURBING.
WHAT IS IT WITH YOU OLD GUYS AND SECRET TROPHY ROOMS? YOU ALL BELONG IN THE SAME COLLECTOR'S CLUB?
I'VE BET YOU'VE GOT ONE TOO, HUH? SUPERMAN?
OKAY... YOU'RE NOT *THAT* OLD.
KAL, ARE YOU ALL RIGHT? WHAT IS IT?
KRYPTON... A VISION... FAMILIAR.
WE'VE GOT COMPANY.

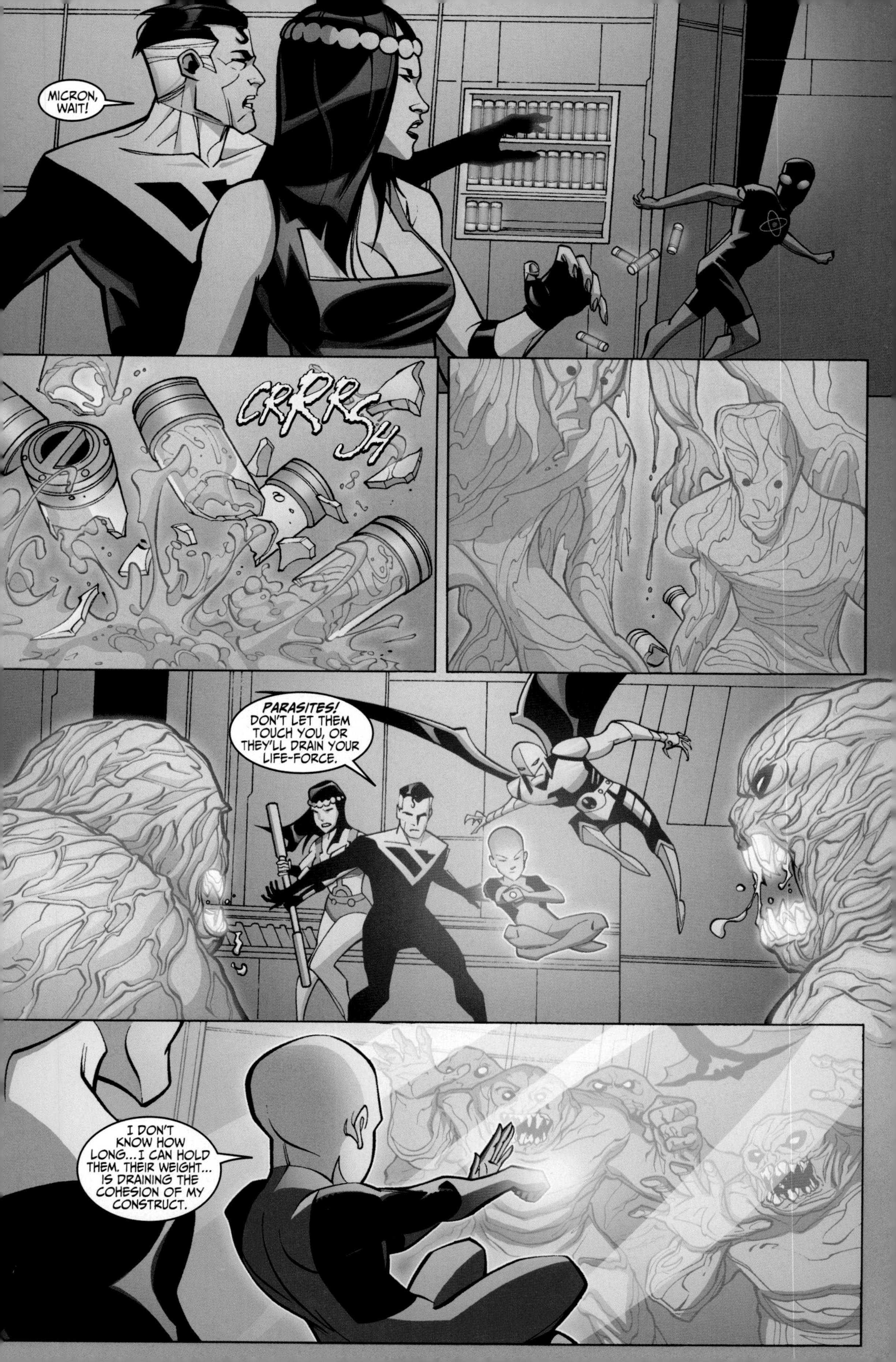
MICRON, WAIT!
CRRRSH
PARASITES! DON'T LET THEM TOUCH YOU, OR THEY'LL DRAIN YOUR LIFE-FORCE.
I DON'T KNOW HOW LONG... I CAN HOLD THEM. THEIR WEIGHT... IS DRAINING THE COHESION OF MY CONSTRUCT.

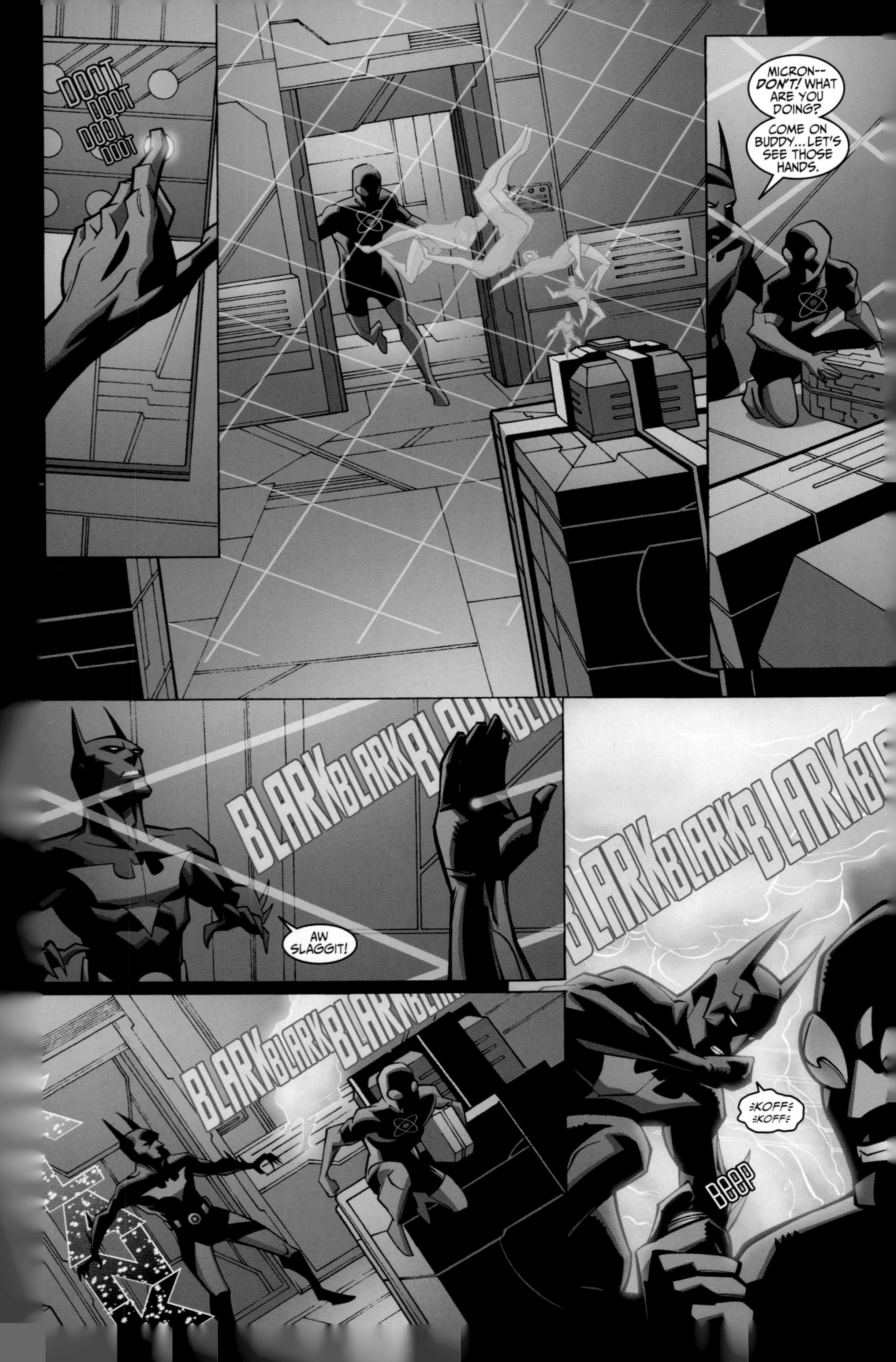
DOOT DOOT DOOT DOOT
MICRON-- DON'T! WHAT ARE YOU DOING?
COME ON BUDDY... LET'S SEE THOSE HANDS.
BLARK BLARK BLARK
AW SLAGGIT!
BLARK BLARK BLARK
BLARK BLARK BLARK
KOFF KOFF
BEEP

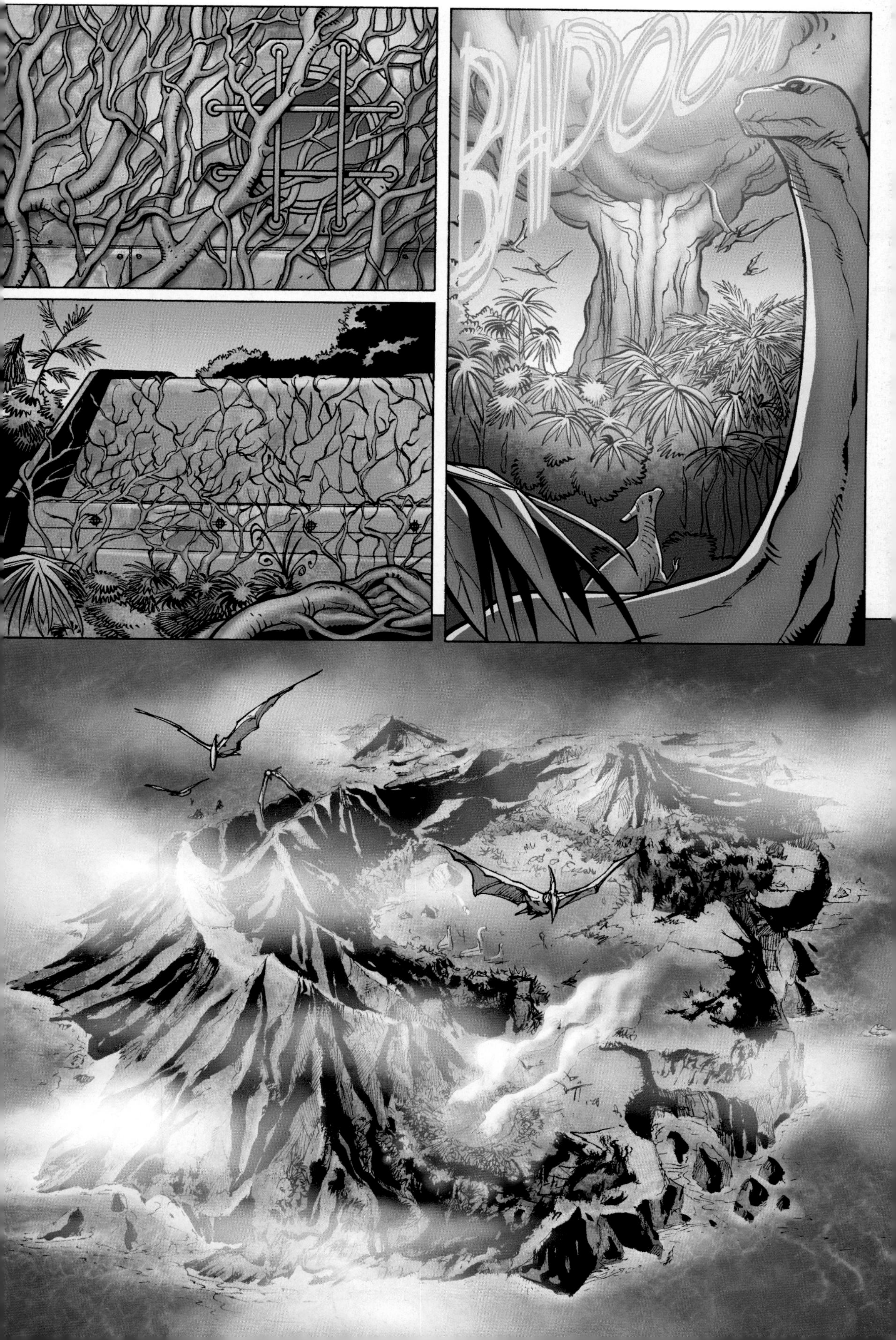
BADOOOM

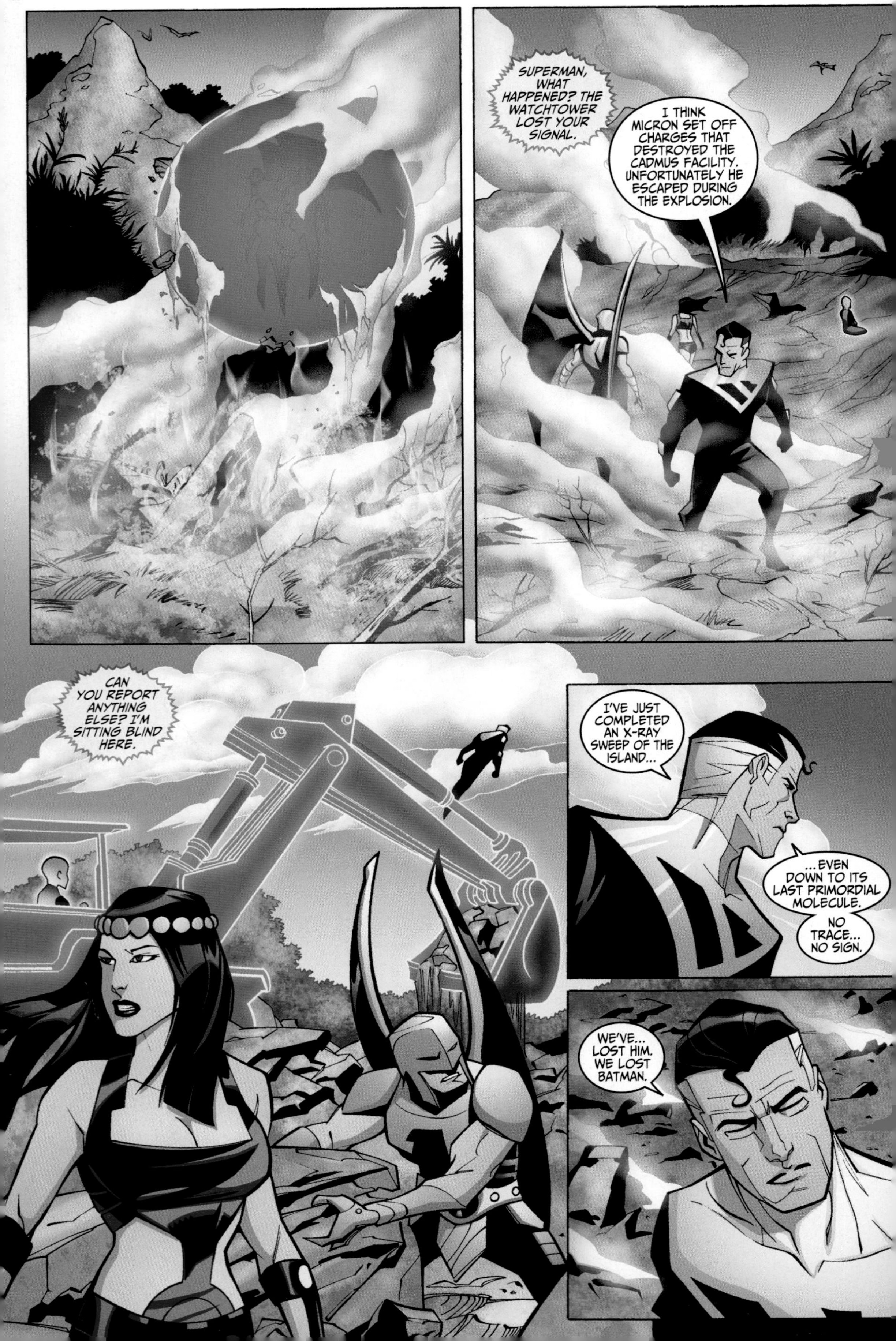
SUPERMAN, WHAT HAPPENED? THE WATCHTOWER LOST YOUR SIGNAL.
I THINK MICRON SET OFF CHARGES THAT DESTROYED THE CADMUS FACILITY. UNFORTUNATELY HE ESCAPED DURING THE EXPLOSION.
CAN YOU REPORT ANYTHING ELSE? I'M SITTING BLIND HERE.
I'VE JUST COMPLETED AN X-RAY SWEEP OF THE ISLAND...
...EVEN DOWN TO ITS LAST PRIMORDIAL MOLECULE.
NO TRACE... NO SIGN.
WE'VE... LOST HIM. WE LOST BATMAN.

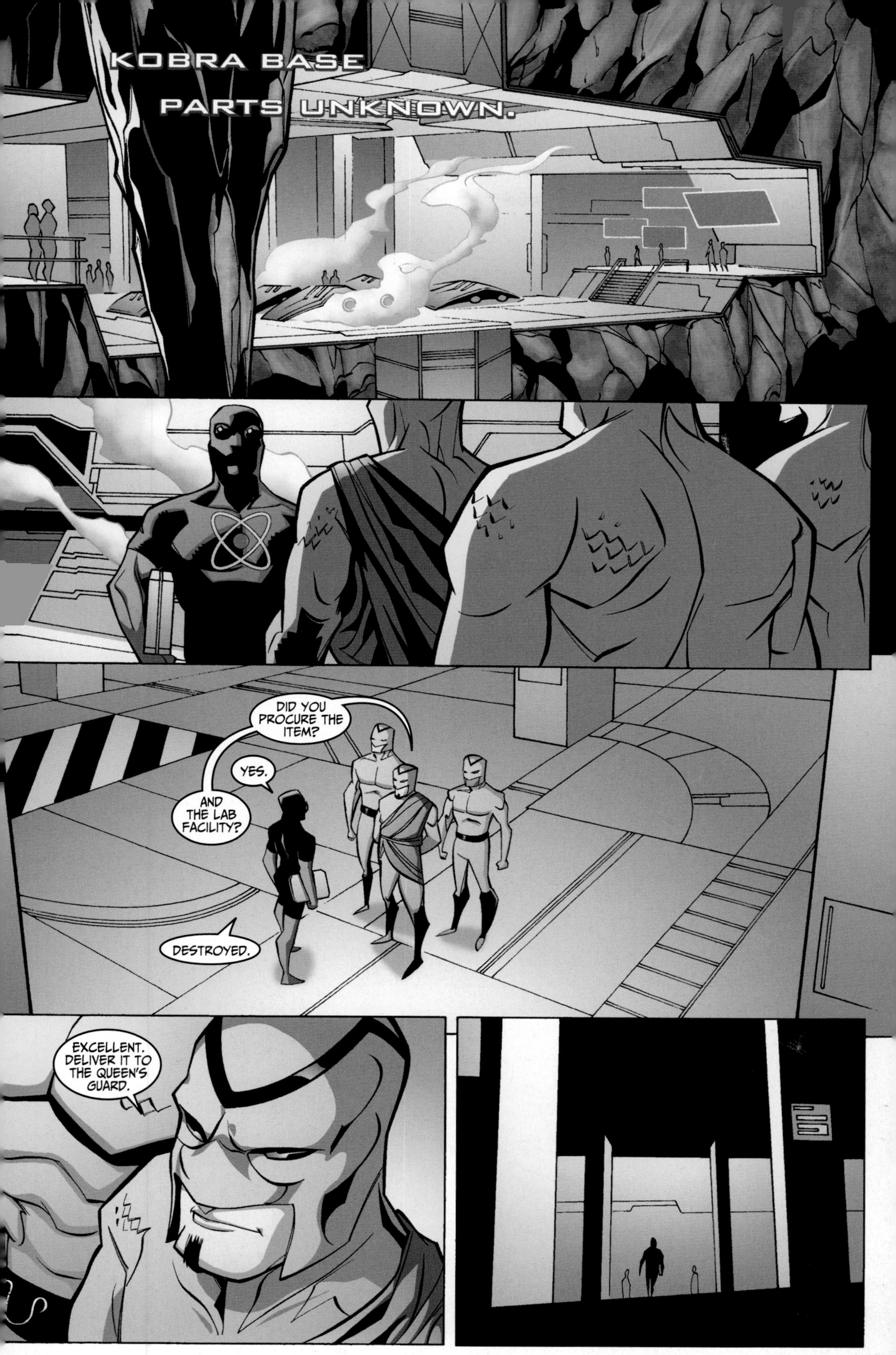
KOBRA BASE
PARTS UNKNOWN.
DID YOU PROCURE THE ITEM?
YES.
AND THE LAB FACILITY?
DESTROYED.
EXCELLENT. DELIVER IT TO THE QUEEN'S GUARD.

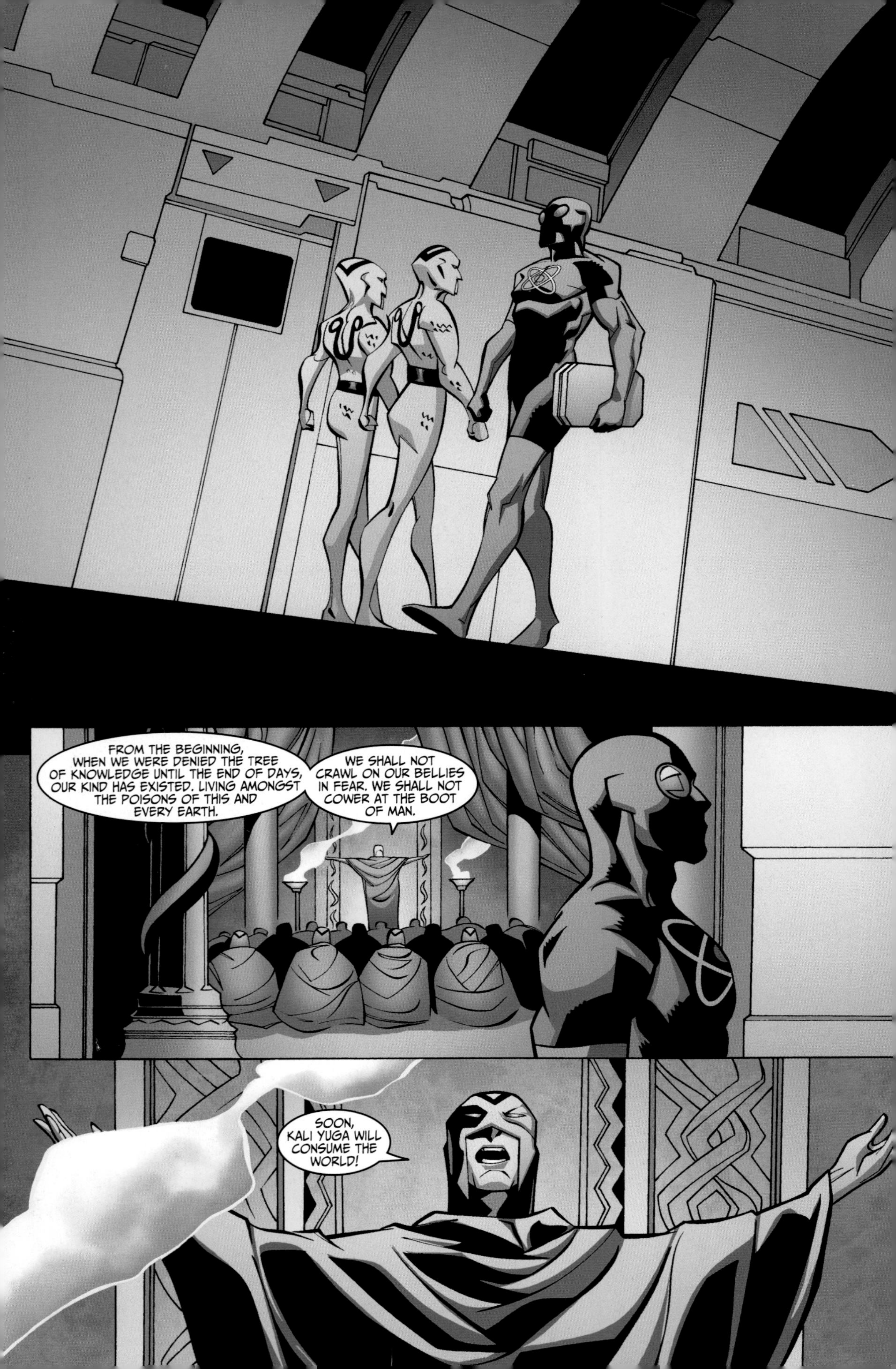
FROM THE BEGINNING, WHEN WE WERE DENIED THE TREE OF KNOWLEDGE UNTIL THE END OF DAYS, OUR KIND HAS EXISTED. LIVING AMONGST THE POISONS OF THIS AND EVERY EARTH.
WE SHALL NOT CRAWL ON OUR BELLIES IN FEAR. WE SHALL NOT COWER AT THE BOOT OF MAN.
SOON, KALI YUGA WILL CONSUME THE WORLD!

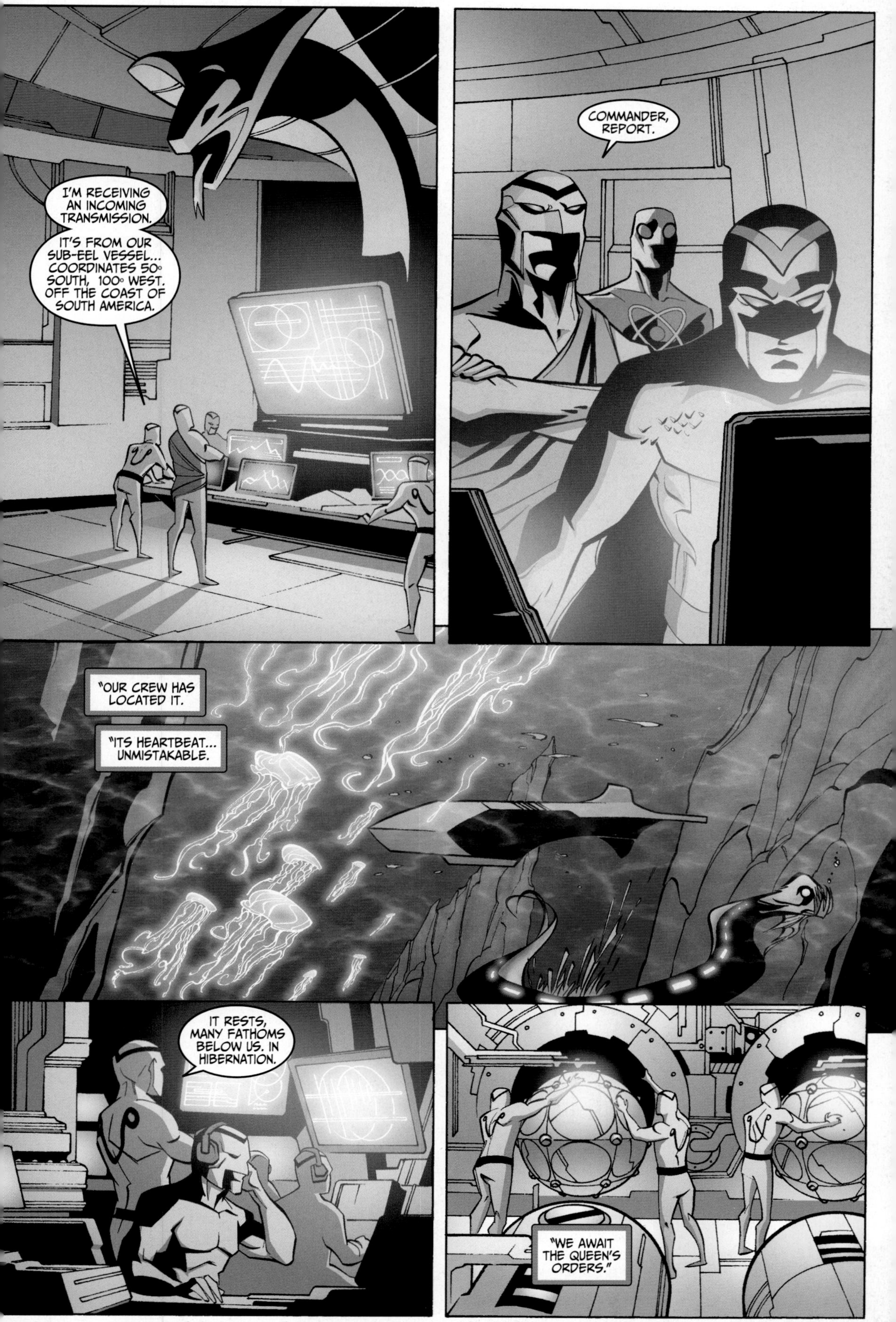
I'M RECEIVING AN INCOMING TRANSMISSION.
IT'S FROM OUR SUB-EEL VESSEL... COORDINATES 50° SOUTH, 100° WEST. OFF THE COAST OF SOUTH AMERICA.
COMMANDER, REPORT.
"OUR CREW HAS LOCATED IT.
"ITS HEARTBEAT... UNMISTAKABLE.
IT RESTS, MANY FATHOMS BELOW US. IN HIBERNATION.
"WE AWAIT THE QUEEN'S ORDERS."

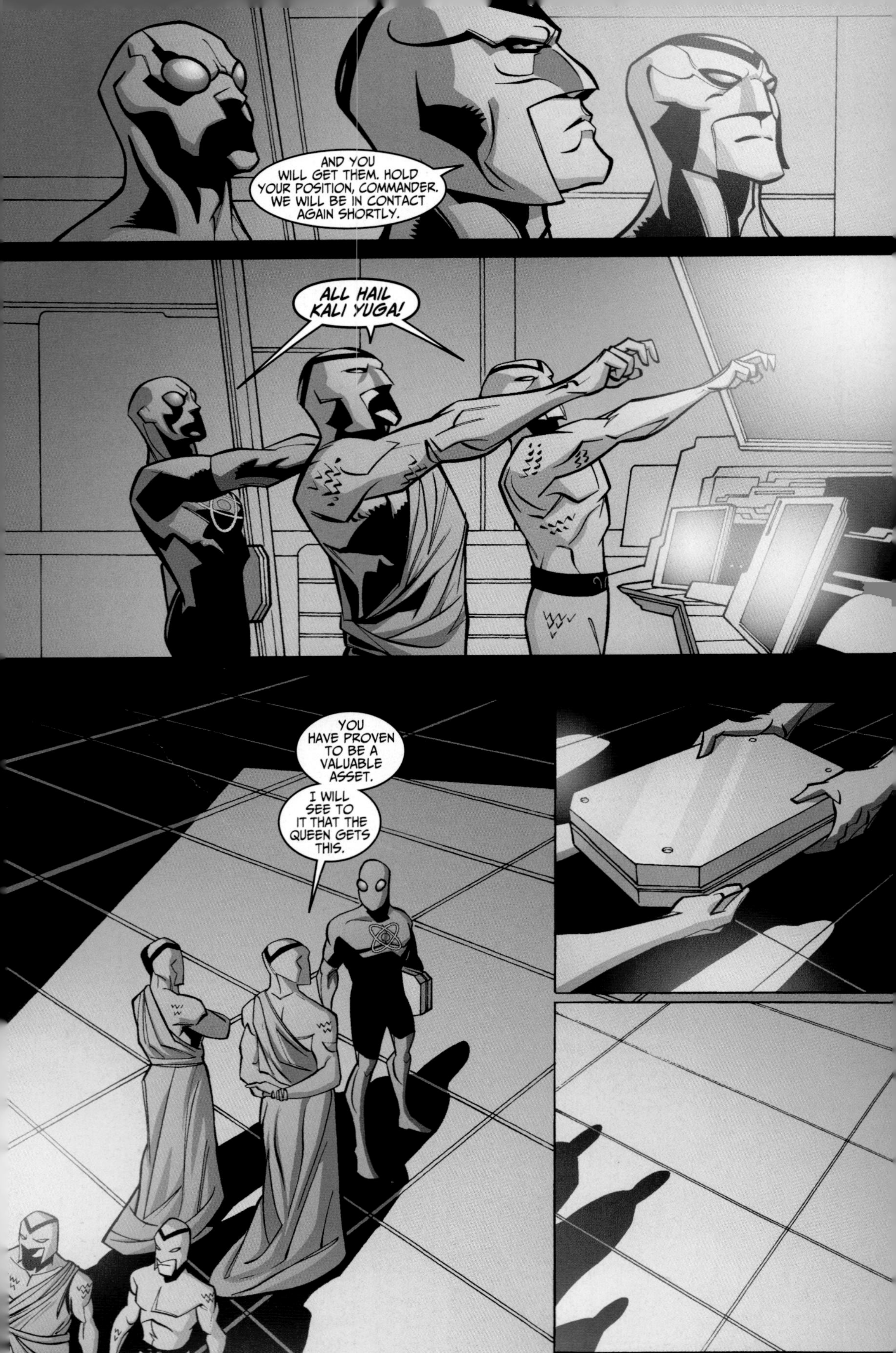
AND YOU WILL GET THEM. HOLD YOUR POSITION, COMMANDER. WE WILL BE IN CONTACT AGAIN SHORTLY.
ALL HAIL KALI YUGA!
YOU HAVE PROVEN TO BE A VALUABLE ASSET.
I WILL SEE TO IT THAT THE QUEEN GETS THIS.

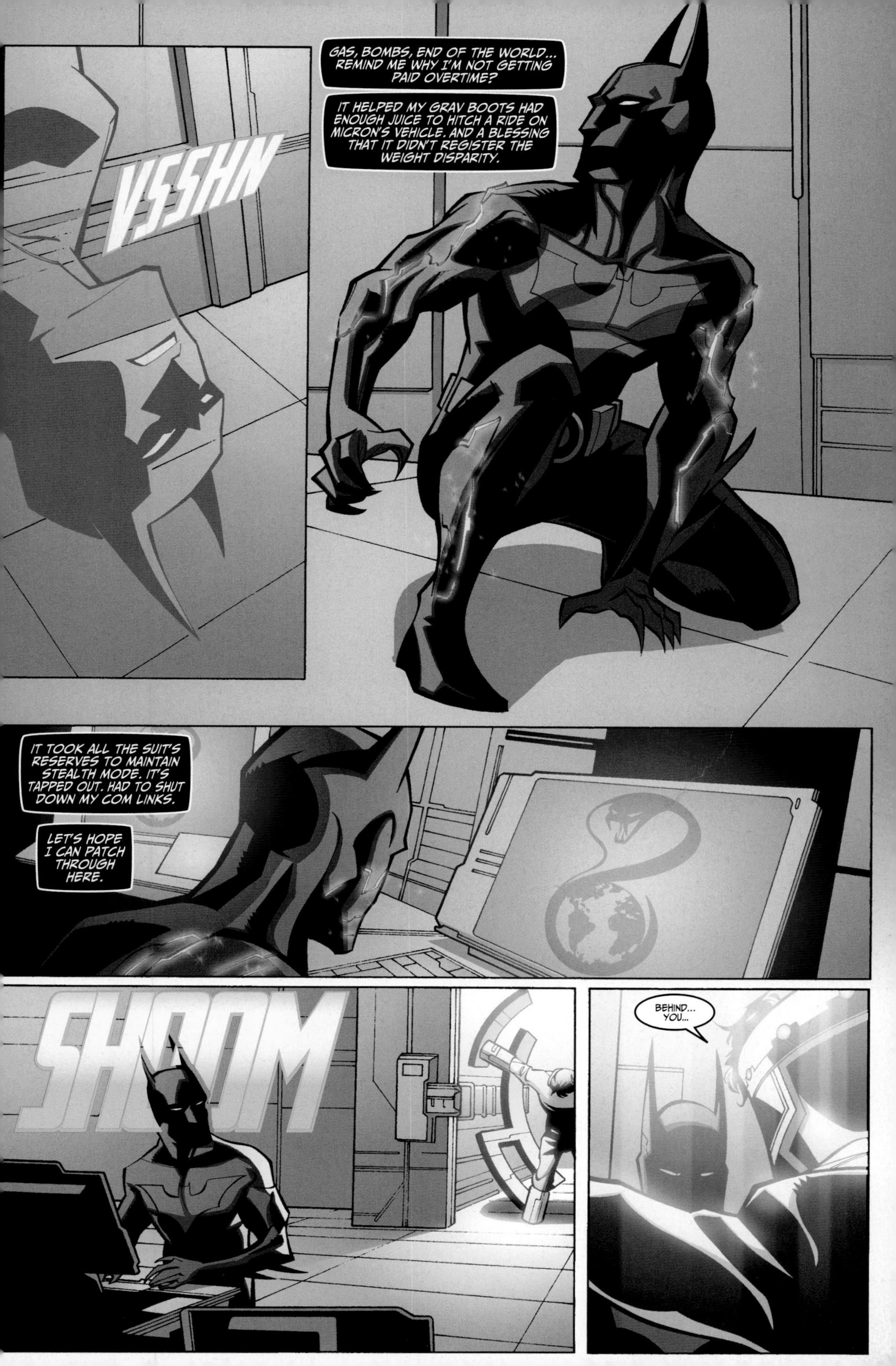
GAS, BOMBS, END OF THE WORLD... REMIND ME WHY I'M NOT GETTING PAID OVERTIME?
IT HELPED MY GRAV BOOTS HAD ENOUGH JUICE TO HITCH A RIDE ON MICRON'S VEHICLE. AND A BLESSING THAT IT DIDN'T REGISTER THE WEIGHT DISPARITY.
VSSHN
IT TOOK ALL THE SUIT'S RESERVES TO MAINTAIN STEALTH MODE. IT'S TAPPED OUT. HAD TO SHUT DOWN MY COM LINKS.
LET'S HOPE I CAN PATCH THROUGH HERE.
SHOOM
BEHIND... YOU...

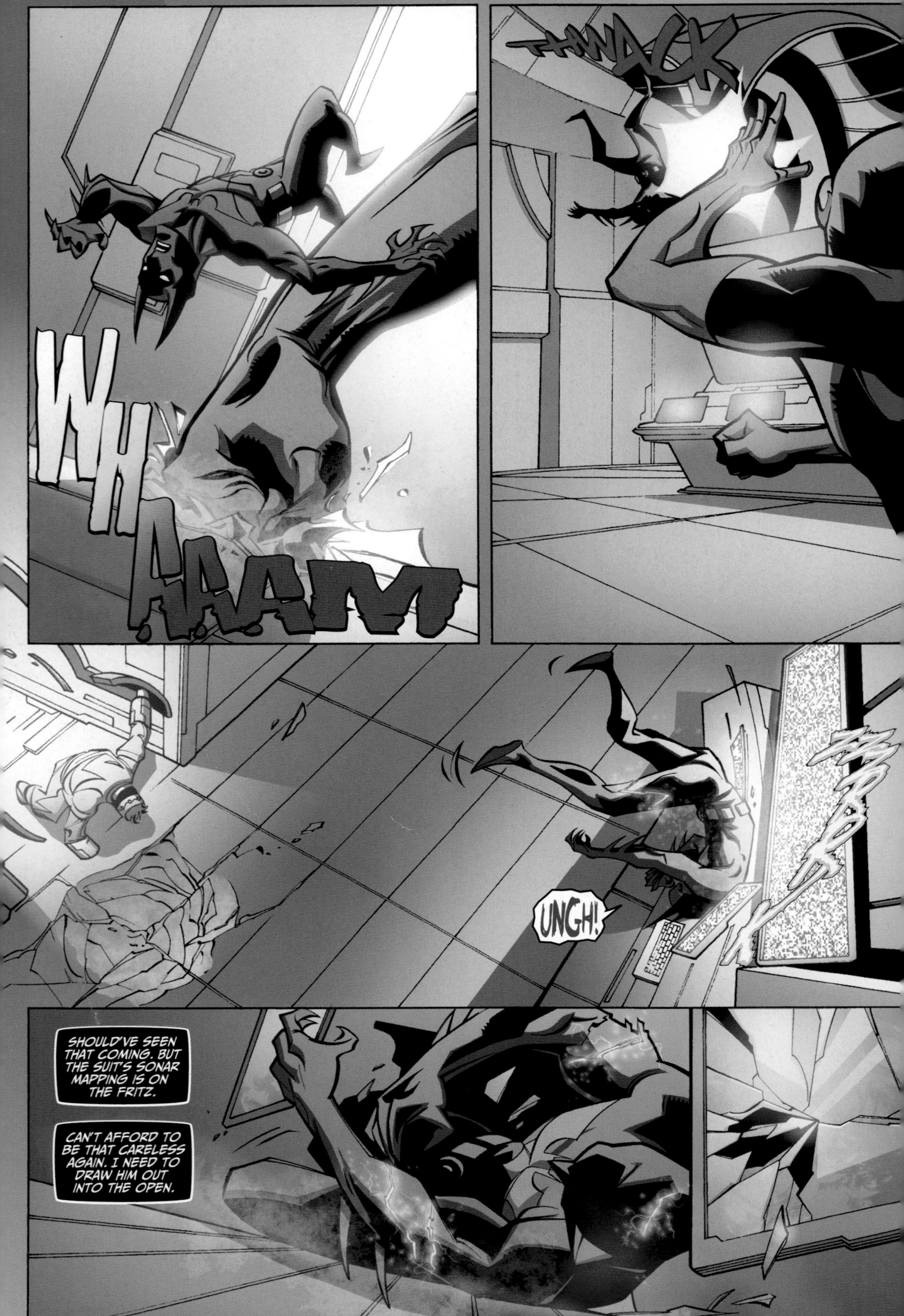
WHAAAM
THWACK
ZZZRRK
UNGH!
SHOULD'VE SEEN THAT COMING. BUT THE SUIT'S SONAR MAPPING IS ON THE FRITZ.
CAN'T AFFORD TO BE THAT CARELESS AGAIN. I NEED TO DRAW HIM OUT INTO THE OPEN.

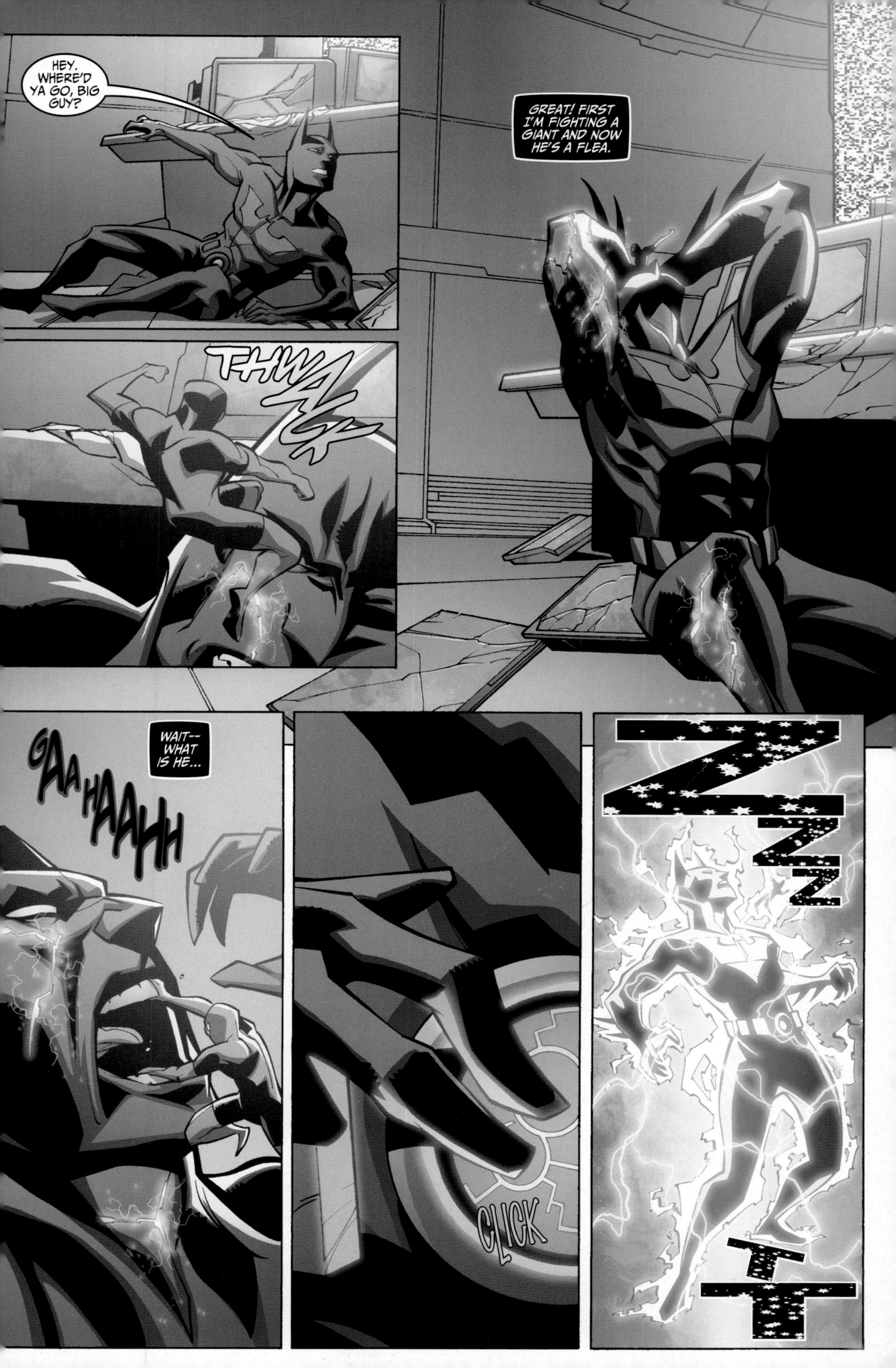
HEY. WHERE'D YA GO, BIG GUY?
GREAT! FIRST I'M FIGHTING A GIANT AND NOW HE'S A FLEA.
THWAK
WAIT-- WHAT IS HE...
GAAHAAAHH
CLICK
ZZZT

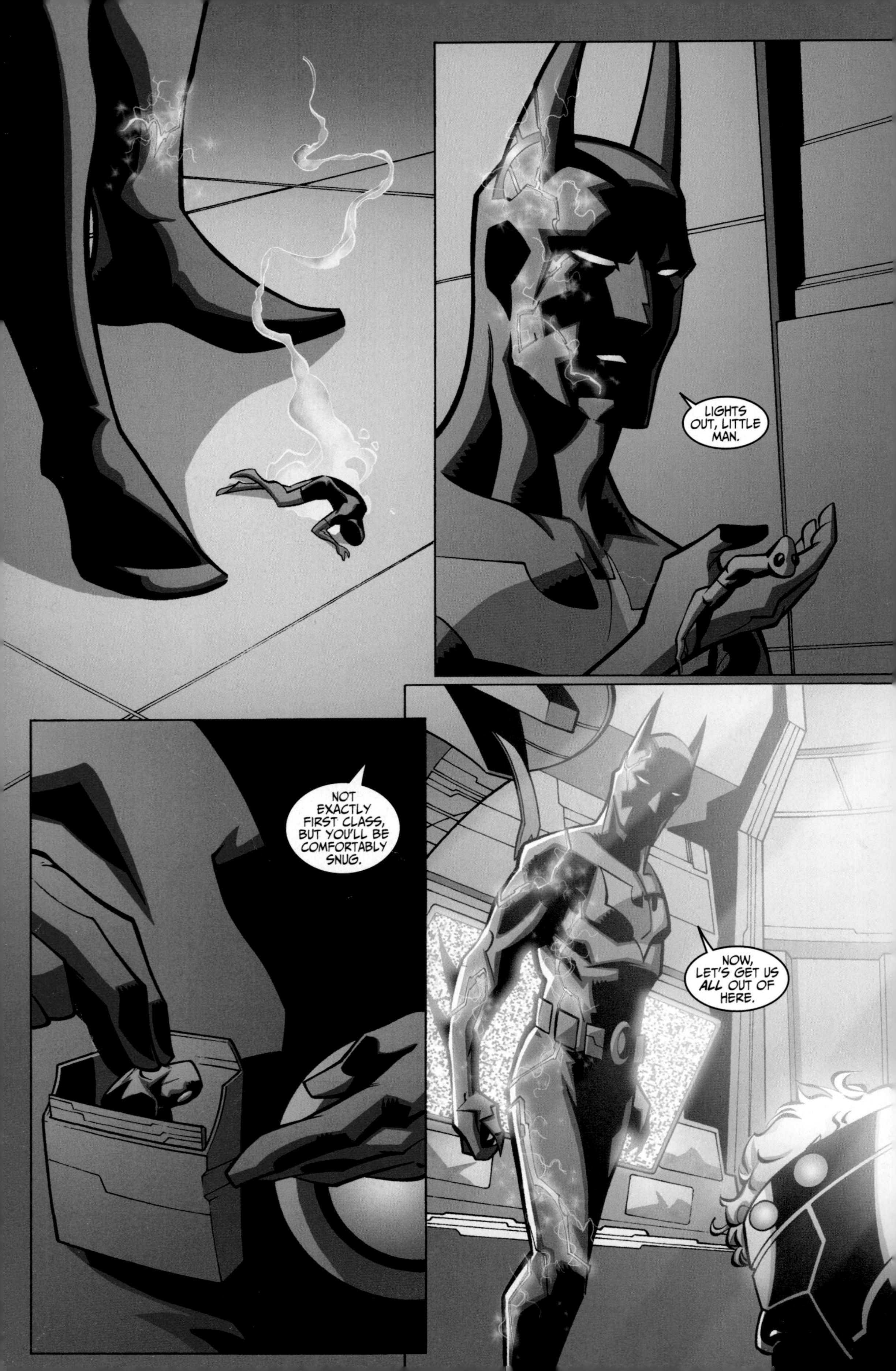
LIGHTS OUT, LITTLE MAN.
NOT EXACTLY FIRST CLASS, BUT YOU'LL BE COMFORTABLY SNUG.
NOW, LET'S GET US ALL OUT OF HERE.

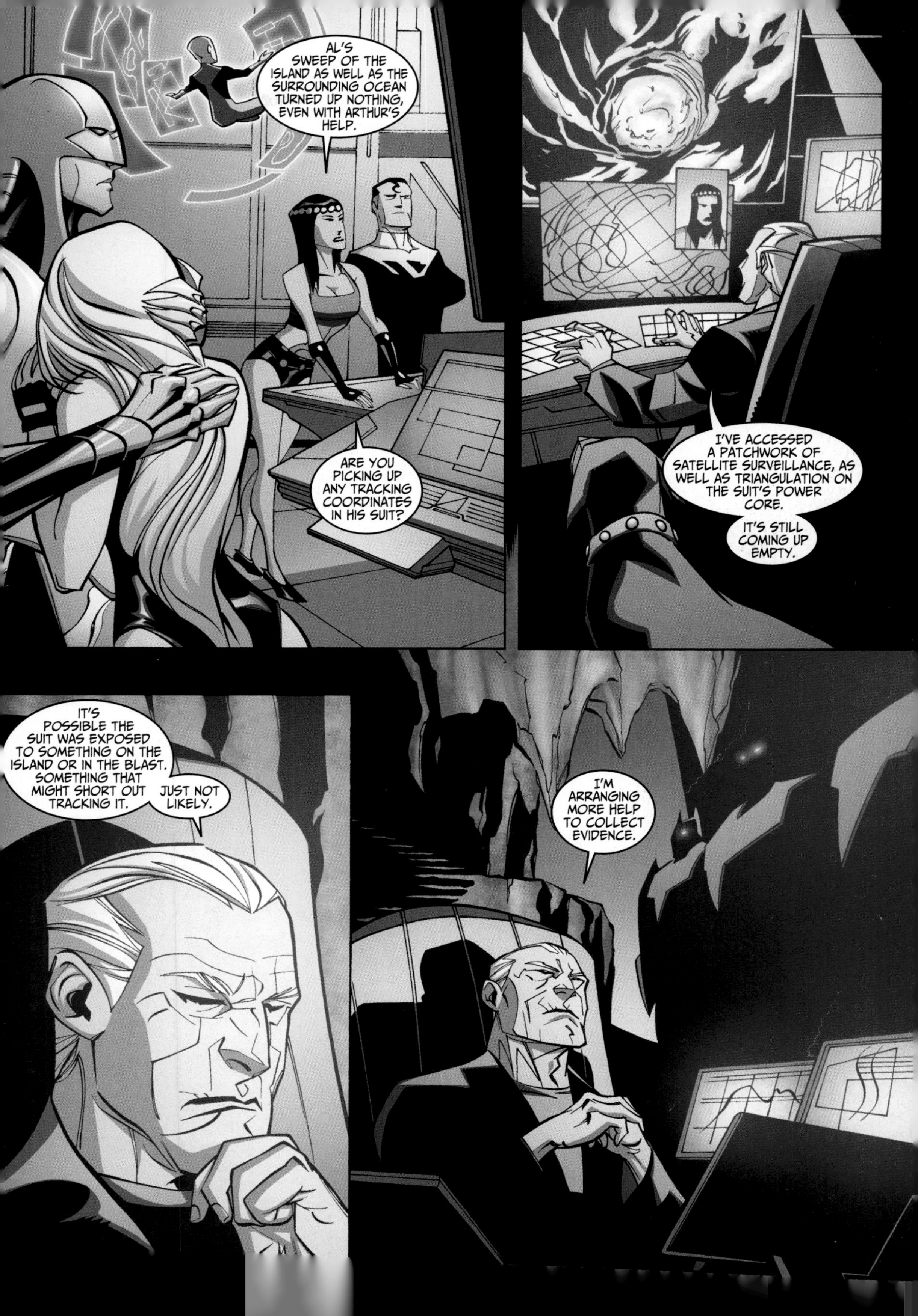
AL'S SWEEP OF THE ISLAND AS WELL AS THE SURROUNDING OCEAN TURNED UP NOTHING, EVEN WITH ARTHUR'S HELP.
ARE YOU PICKING UP ANY TRACKING COORDINATES IN HIS SUIT?
I'VE ACCESSED A PATCHWORK OF SATELLITE SURVEILLANCE, AS WELL AS TRIANGULATION ON THE SUIT'S POWER CORE.
IT'S STILL COMING UP EMPTY.
IT'S POSSIBLE THE SUIT WAS EXPOSED TO SOMETHING ON THE ISLAND OR IN THE BLAST. SOMETHING THAT MIGHT SHORT OUT TRACKING IT.
JUST NOT LIKELY.
I'M ARRANGING MORE HELP TO COLLECT EVIDENCE.

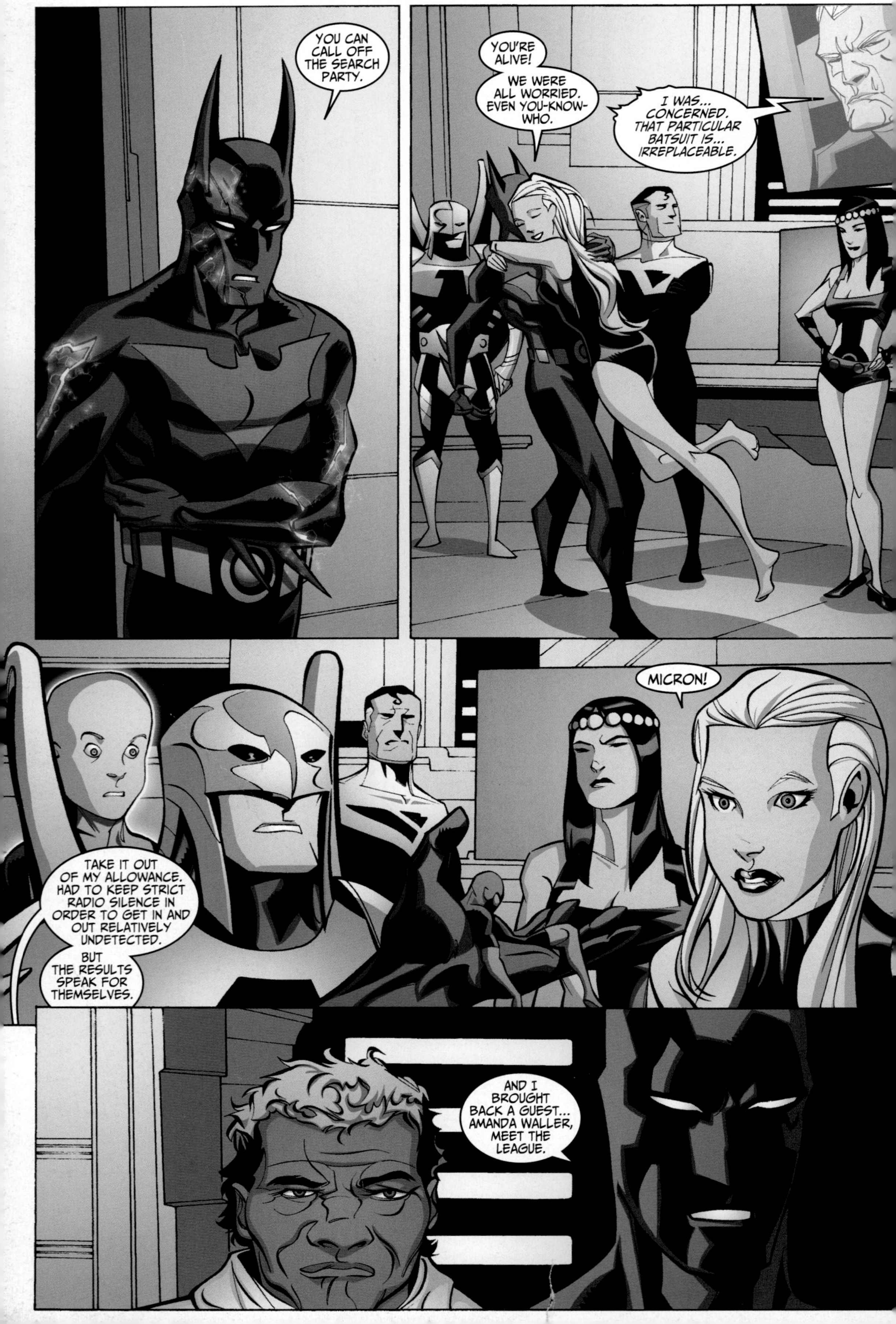
YOU CAN CALL OFF THE SEARCH PARTY.
YOU'RE ALIVE!
WE WERE ALL WORRIED. EVEN YOU-KNOW-WHO.
I WAS... CONCERNED. THAT PARTICULAR BATSUIT IS... IRREPLACEABLE.
TAKE IT OUT OF MY ALLOWANCE. HAD TO KEEP STRICT RADIO SILENCE IN ORDER TO GET IN AND OUT RELATIVELY UNDETECTED.
BUT THE RESULTS SPEAK FOR THEMSELVES.
MICRON!
AND I BROUGHT BACK A GUEST... AMANDA WALLER, MEET THE LEAGUE.

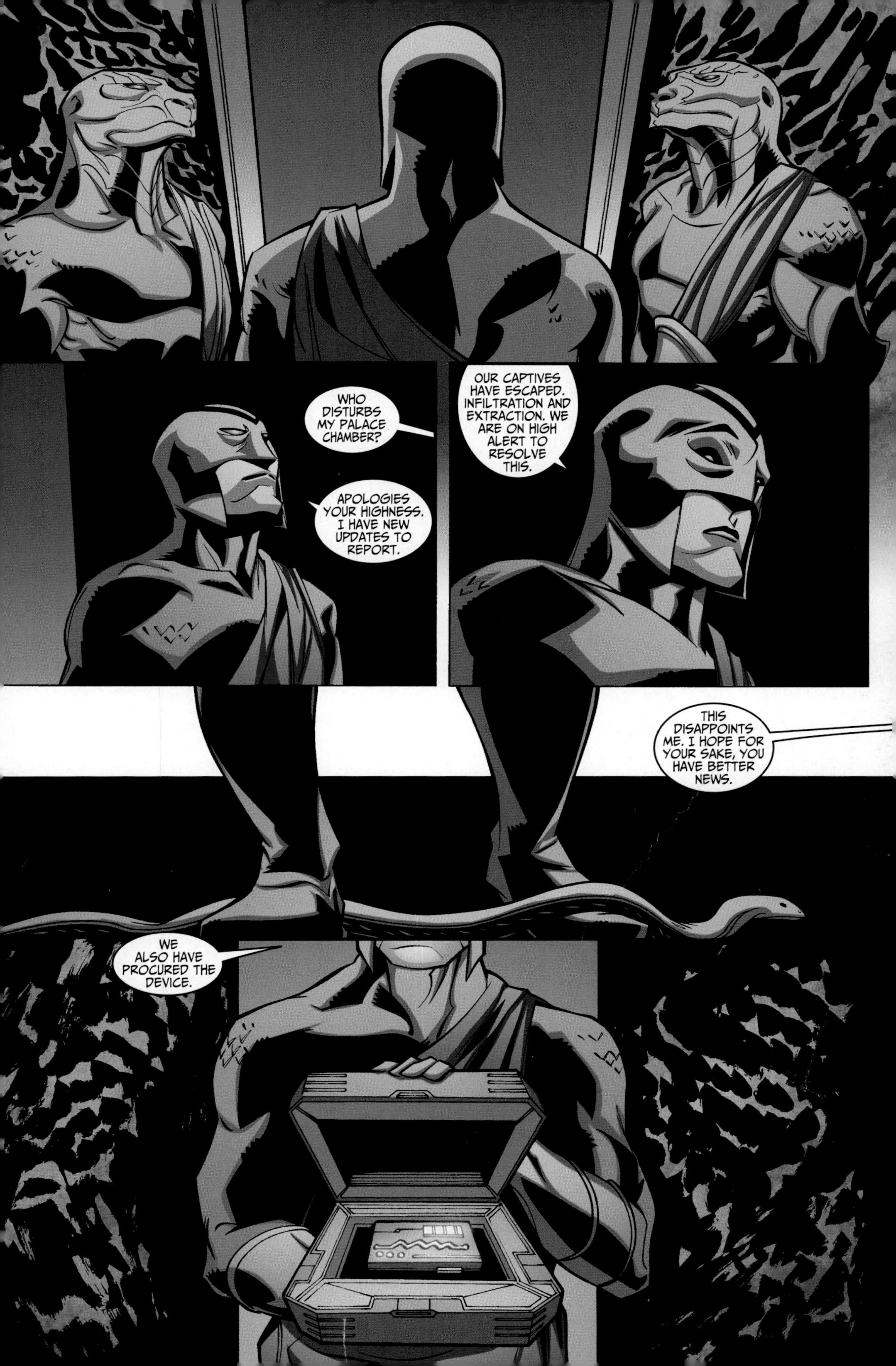
WHO DISTURBS MY PALACE CHAMBER?
APOLOGIES YOUR HIGHNESS. I HAVE NEW UPDATES TO REPORT.
OUR CAPTIVES HAVE ESCAPED. INFILTRATION AND EXTRACTION. WE ARE ON HIGH ALERT TO RESOLVE THIS.
THIS DISAPPOINTS ME. I HOPE FOR YOUR SAKE, YOU HAVE BETTER NEWS.
WE ALSO HAVE PROCURED THE DEVICE.

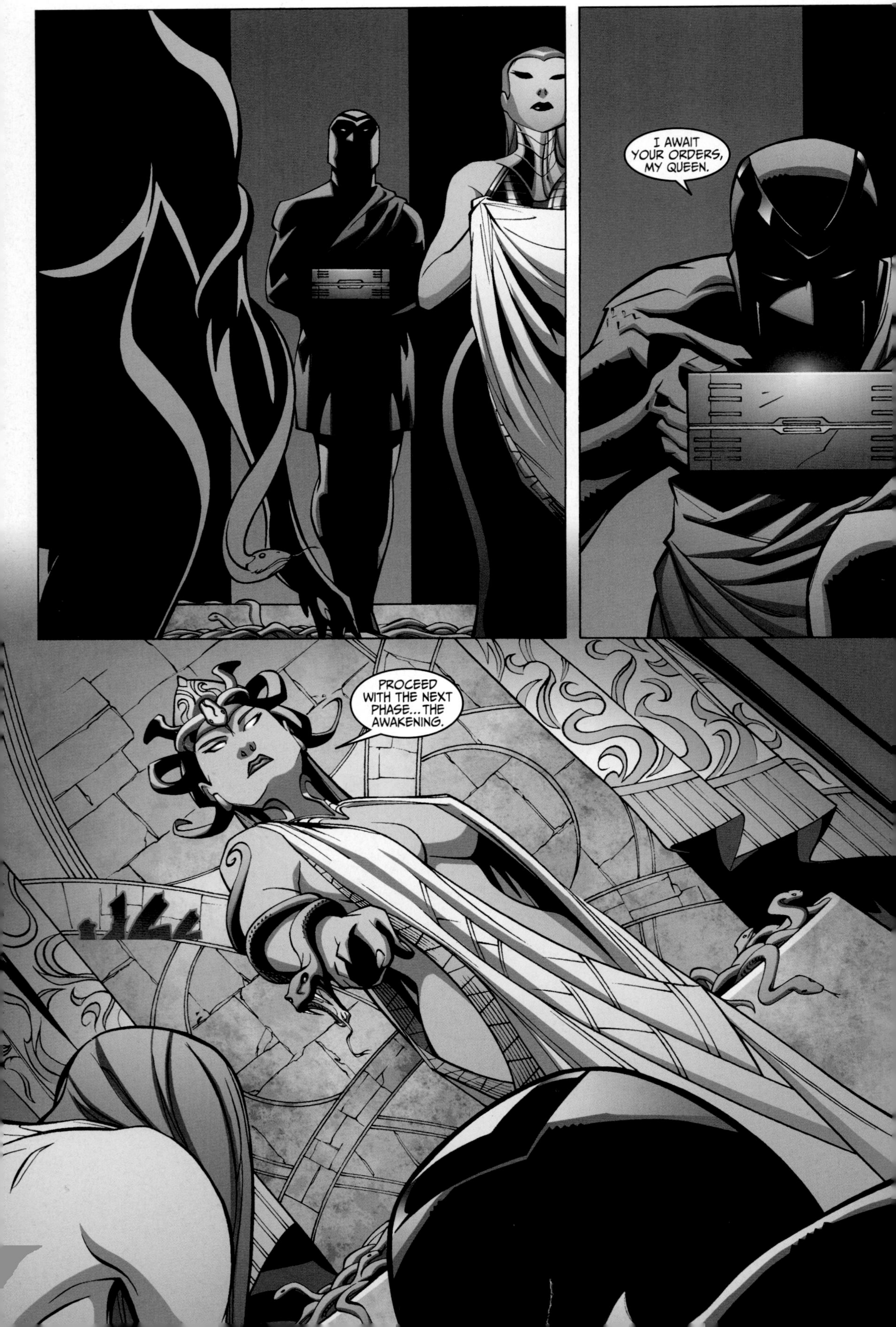
I AWAIT YOUR ORDERS, MY QUEEN.
PROCEED WITH THE NEXT PHASE... THE AWAKENING.

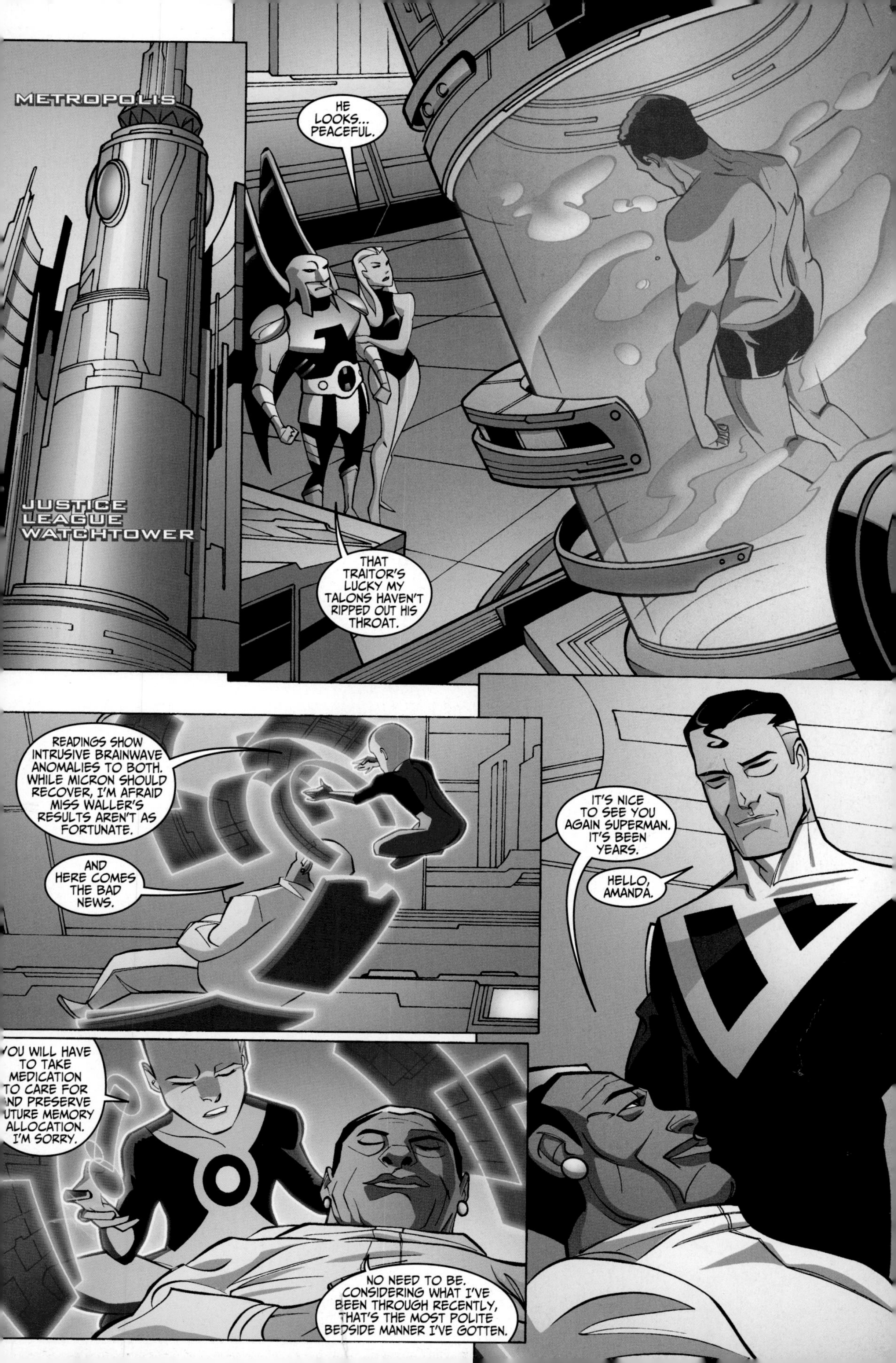
METROPOLIS
JUSTICE LEAGUE WATCHTOWER
HE LOOKS... PEACEFUL.
THAT TRAITOR'S LUCKY MY TALONS HAVEN'T RIPPED OUT HIS THROAT.
READINGS SHOW INTRUSIVE BRAINWAVE ANOMALIES TO BOTH. WHILE MICRON SHOULD RECOVER, I'M AFRAID MISS WALLER'S RESULTS AREN'T AS FORTUNATE.
AND HERE COMES THE BAD NEWS.
OU WILL HAVE TO TAKE MEDICATION TO CARE FOR ND PRESERVE UTURE MEMORY ALLOCATION. I'M SORRY.
NO NEED TO BE. CONSIDERING WHAT I'VE BEEN THROUGH RECENTLY, THAT'S THE MOST POLITE BEDSIDE MANNER I'VE GOTTEN.
IT'S NICE TO SEE YOU AGAIN SUPERMAN. IT'S BEEN YEARS.
HELLO, AMANDA.

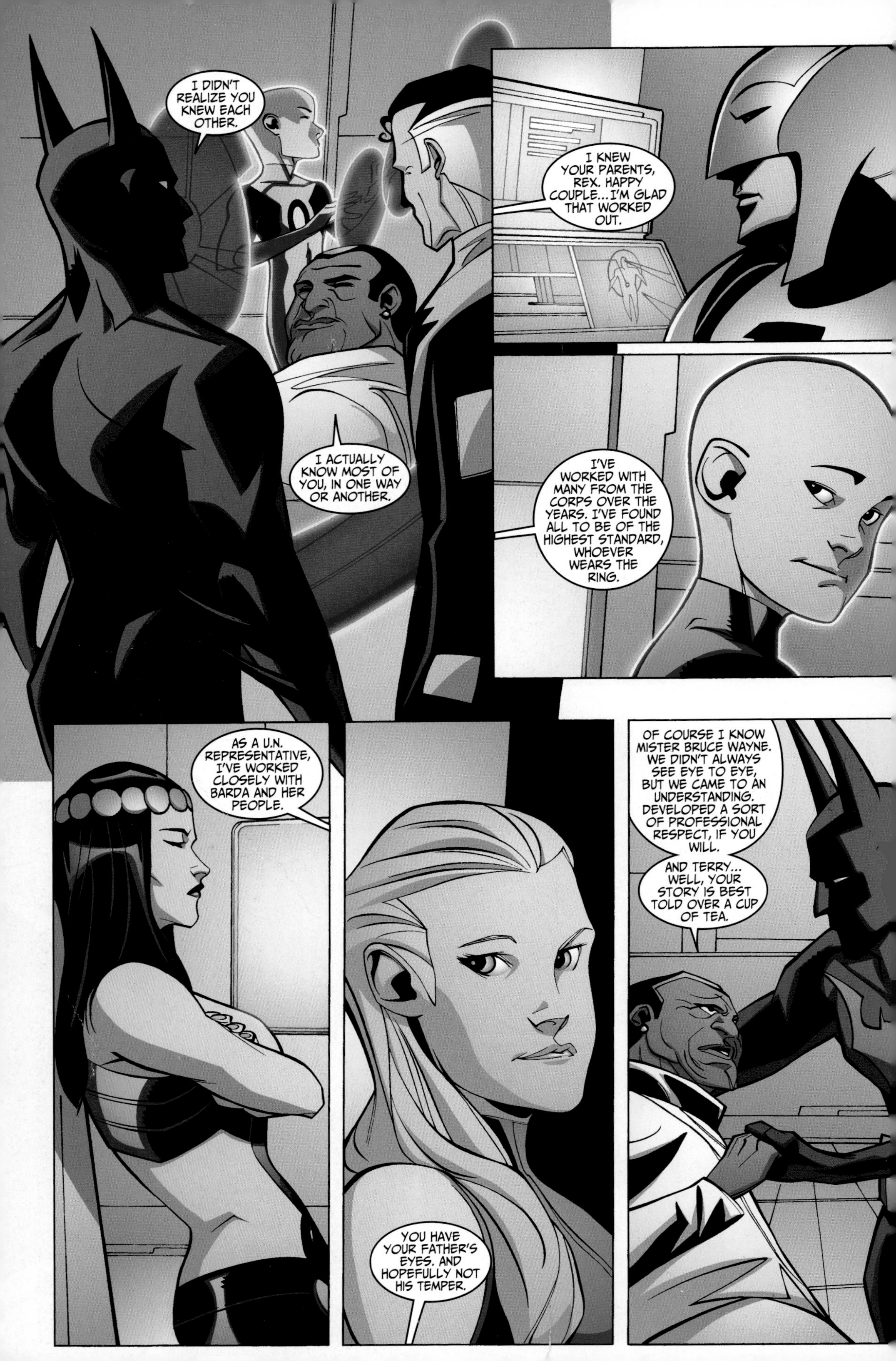

I DIDN'T REALIZE YOU KNEW EACH OTHER.
I KNEW YOUR PARENTS, REX. HAPPY COUPLE...I'M GLAD THAT WORKED OUT.
I ACTUALLY KNOW MOST OF YOU, IN ONE WAY OR ANOTHER.
I'VE WORKED WITH MANY FROM THE CORPS OVER THE YEARS. I'VE FOUND ALL TO BE OF THE HIGHEST STANDARD, WHOEVER WEARS THE RING.
AS A U.N. REPRESENTATIVE, I'VE WORKED CLOSELY WITH BARDA AND HER PEOPLE.
YOU HAVE YOUR FATHER'S EYES. AND HOPEFULLY NOT HIS TEMPER.
OF COURSE I KNOW MISTER BRUCE WAYNE. WE DIDN'T ALWAYS SEE EYE TO EYE, BUT WE CAME TO AN UNDERSTANDING. DEVELOPED A SORT OF PROFESSIONAL RESPECT, IF YOU WILL.
AND TERRY... WELL, YOUR STORY IS BEST TOLD OVER A CUP OF TEA.

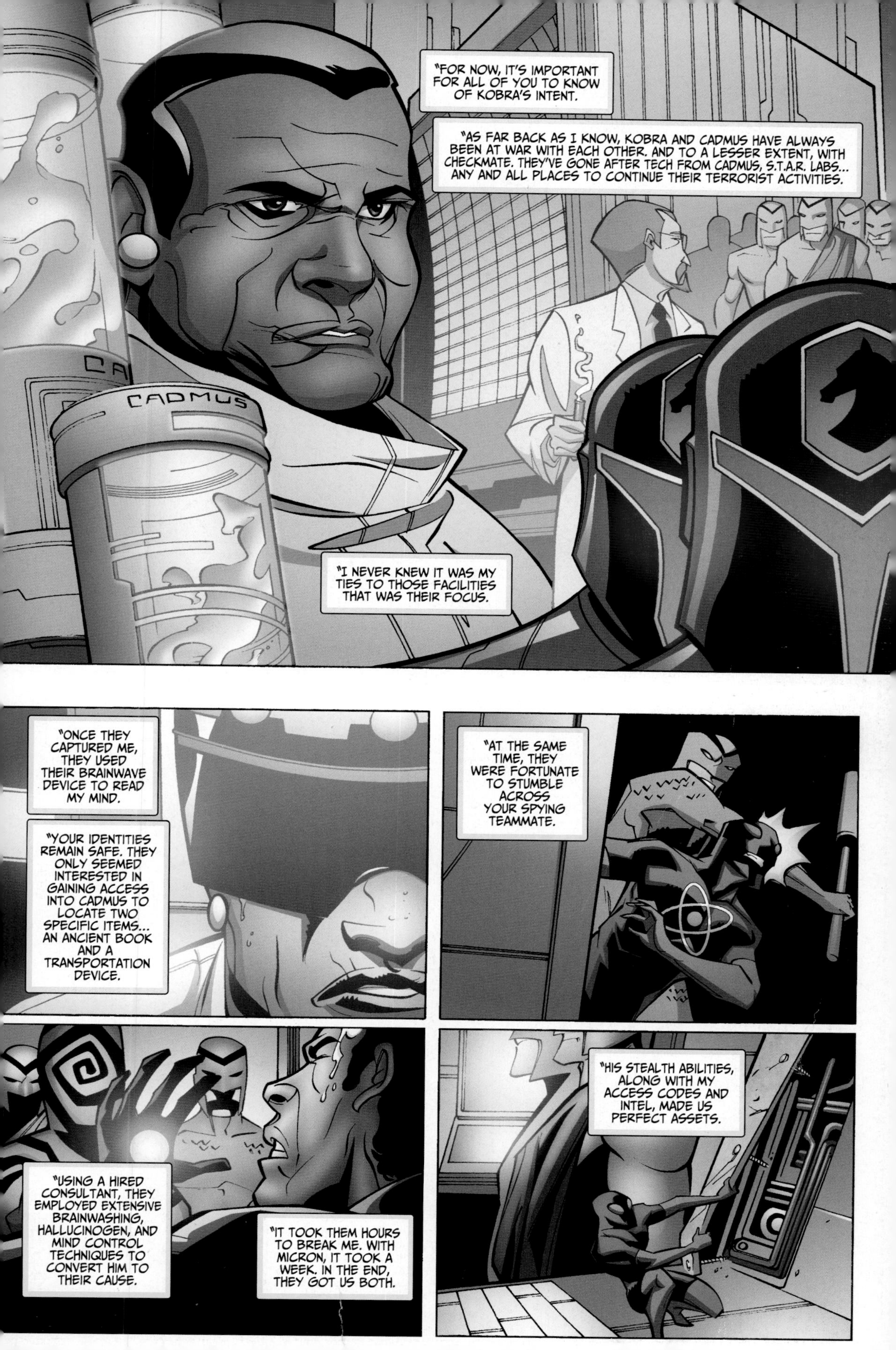
"FOR NOW, IT'S IMPORTANT FOR ALL OF YOU TO KNOW OF KOBRA'S INTENT.
"AS FAR BACK AS I KNOW, KOBRA AND CADMUS HAVE ALWAYS BEEN AT WAR WITH EACH OTHER. AND TO A LESSER EXTENT, WITH CHECKMATE. THEY'VE GONE AFTER TECH FROM CADMUS, S.T.A.R. LABS... ANY AND ALL PLACES TO CONTINUE THEIR TERRORIST ACTIVITIES.
CADMUS
"I NEVER KNEW IT WAS MY TIES TO THOSE FACILITIES THAT WAS THEIR FOCUS.
"ONCE THEY CAPTURED ME, THEY USED THEIR BRAINWAVE DEVICE TO READ MY MIND.
"YOUR IDENTITIES REMAIN SAFE. THEY ONLY SEEMED INTERESTED IN GAINING ACCESS INTO CADMUS TO LOCATE TWO SPECIFIC ITEMS... AN ANCIENT BOOK AND A TRANSPORTATION DEVICE.
"AT THE SAME TIME, THEY WERE FORTUNATE TO STUMBLE ACROSS YOUR SPYING TEAMMATE.
"USING A HIRED CONSULTANT, THEY EMPLOYED EXTENSIVE BRAINWASHING, HALLUCINOGEN, AND MIND CONTROL TECHNIQUES TO CONVERT HIM TO THEIR CAUSE.
"IT TOOK THEM HOURS TO BREAK ME. WITH MICRON, IT TOOK A WEEK. IN THE END, THEY GOT US BOTH.
"HIS STEALTH ABILITIES, ALONG WITH MY ACCESS CODES AND INTEL, MADE US PERFECT ASSETS.

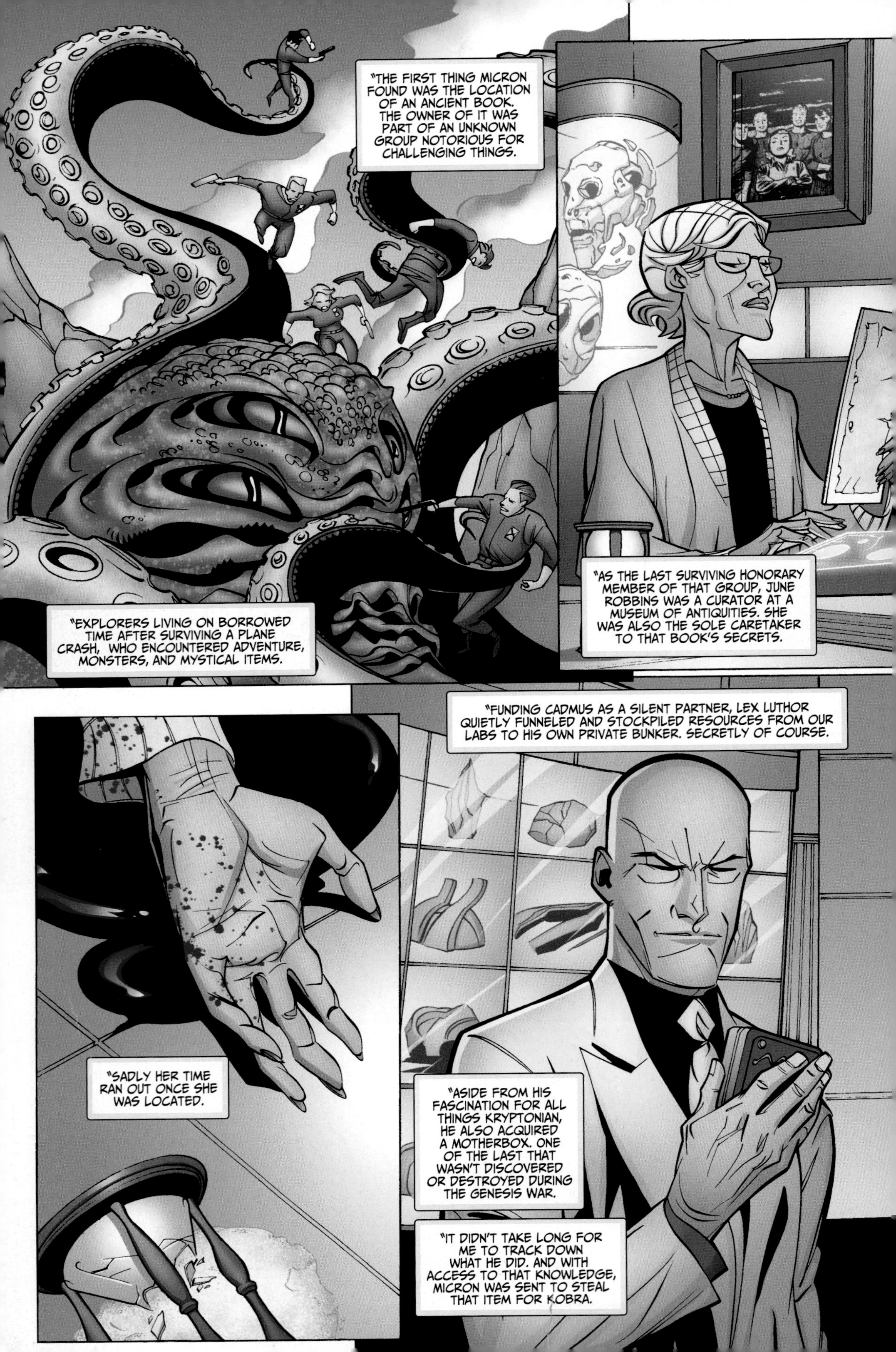
"THE FIRST THING MICRON FOUND WAS THE LOCATION OF AN ANCIENT BOOK. THE OWNER OF IT WAS PART OF AN UNKNOWN GROUP NOTORIOUS FOR CHALLENGING THINGS.
"EXPLORERS LIVING ON BORROWED TIME AFTER SURVIVING A PLANE CRASH, WHO ENCOUNTERED ADVENTURE, MONSTERS, AND MYSTICAL ITEMS.
"AS THE LAST SURVIVING HONORARY MEMBER OF THAT GROUP, JUNE ROBBINS WAS A CURATOR AT A MUSEUM OF ANTIQUITIES. SHE WAS ALSO THE SOLE CARETAKER TO THAT BOOK'S SECRETS.
"SADLY HER TIME RAN OUT ONCE SHE WAS LOCATED.
"FUNDING CADMUS AS A SILENT PARTNER, LEX LUTHOR QUIETLY FUNNELED AND STOCKPILED RESOURCES FROM OUR LABS TO HIS OWN PRIVATE BUNKER. SECRETLY OF COURSE.
"ASIDE FROM HIS FASCINATION FOR ALL THINGS KRYPTONIAN, HE ALSO ACQUIRED A MOTHERBOX. ONE OF THE LAST THAT WASN'T DISCOVERED OR DESTROYED DURING THE GENESIS WAR.
"IT DIDN'T TAKE LONG FOR ME TO TRACK DOWN WHAT HE DID. AND WITH ACCESS TO THAT KNOWLEDGE, MICRON WAS SENT TO STEAL THAT ITEM FOR KOBRA.

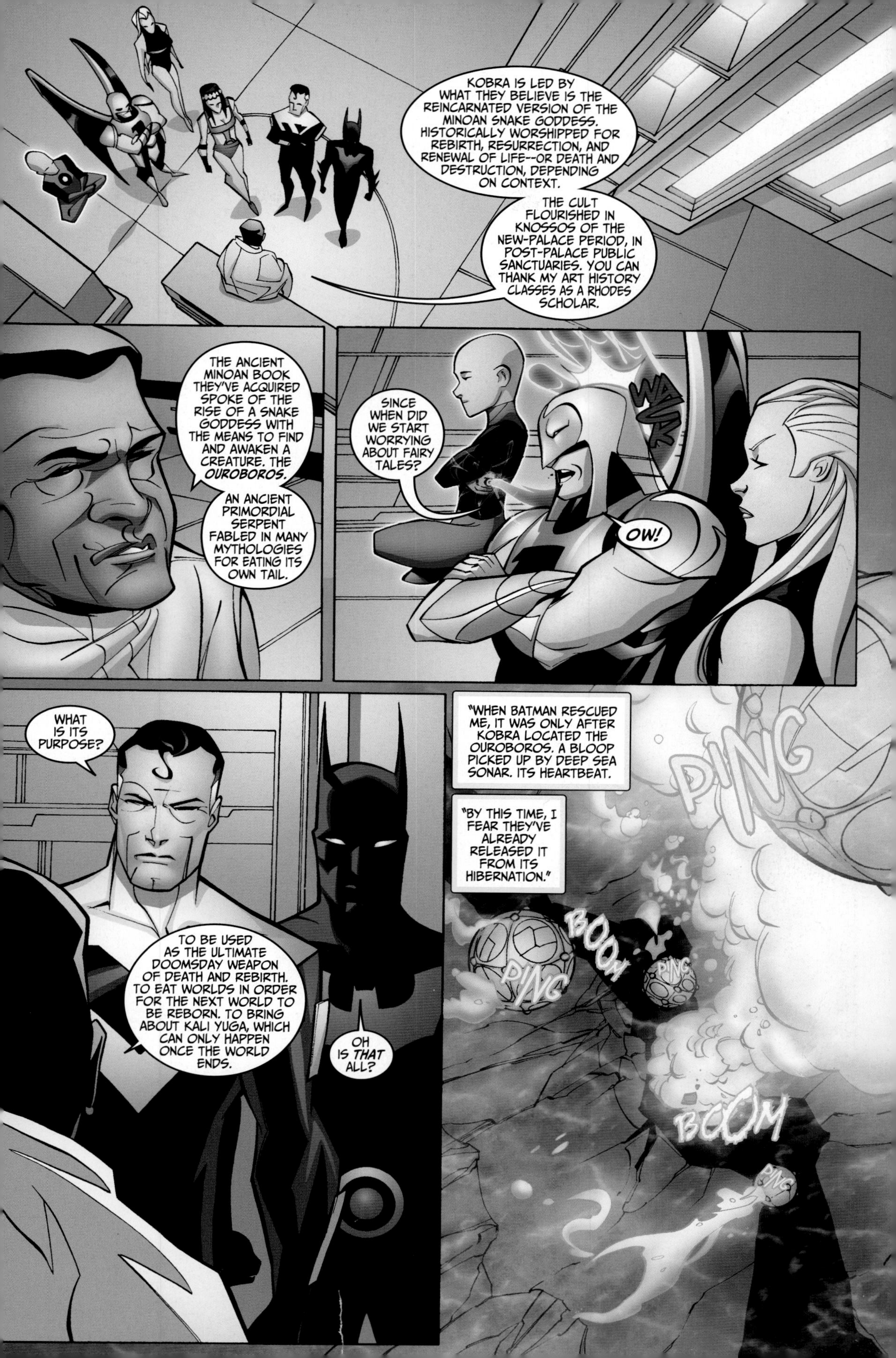
KOBRA IS LED BY WHAT THEY BELIEVE IS THE REINCARNATED VERSION OF THE MINOAN SNAKE GODDESS. HISTORICALLY WORSHIPPED FOR REBIRTH, RESURRECTION, AND RENEWAL OF LIFE--OR DEATH AND DESTRUCTION, DEPENDING ON CONTEXT.
THE CULT FLOURISHED IN KNOSSOS OF THE NEW-PALACE PERIOD, IN POST-PALACE PUBLIC SANCTUARIES. YOU CAN THANK MY ART HISTORY CLASSES AS A RHODES SCHOLAR.
THE ANCIENT MINOAN BOOK THEY'VE ACQUIRED SPOKE OF THE RISE OF A SNAKE GODDESS WITH THE MEANS TO FIND AND AWAKEN A CREATURE. THE *OUROBOROS*.
AN ANCIENT PRIMORDIAL SERPENT FABLED IN MANY MYTHOLOGIES FOR EATING ITS OWN TAIL.
SINCE WHEN DID WE START WORRYING ABOUT FAIRY TALES?
WAK
OW!
WHAT IS ITS PURPOSE?
TO BE USED AS THE ULTIMATE DOOMSDAY WEAPON OF DEATH AND REBIRTH. TO EAT WORLDS IN ORDER FOR THE NEXT WORLD TO BE REBORN. TO BRING ABOUT KALI YUGA, WHICH CAN ONLY HAPPEN ONCE THE WORLD ENDS.
OH IS *THAT* ALL?
"WHEN BATMAN RESCUED ME, IT WAS ONLY AFTER KOBRA LOCATED THE OUROBOROS. A BLOOP PICKED UP BY DEEP SEA SONAR. ITS HEARTBEAT.
"BY THIS TIME, I FEAR THEY'VE ALREADY RELEASED IT FROM ITS HIBERNATION."
PING
BOOM
PING
PING
BOOM
PING

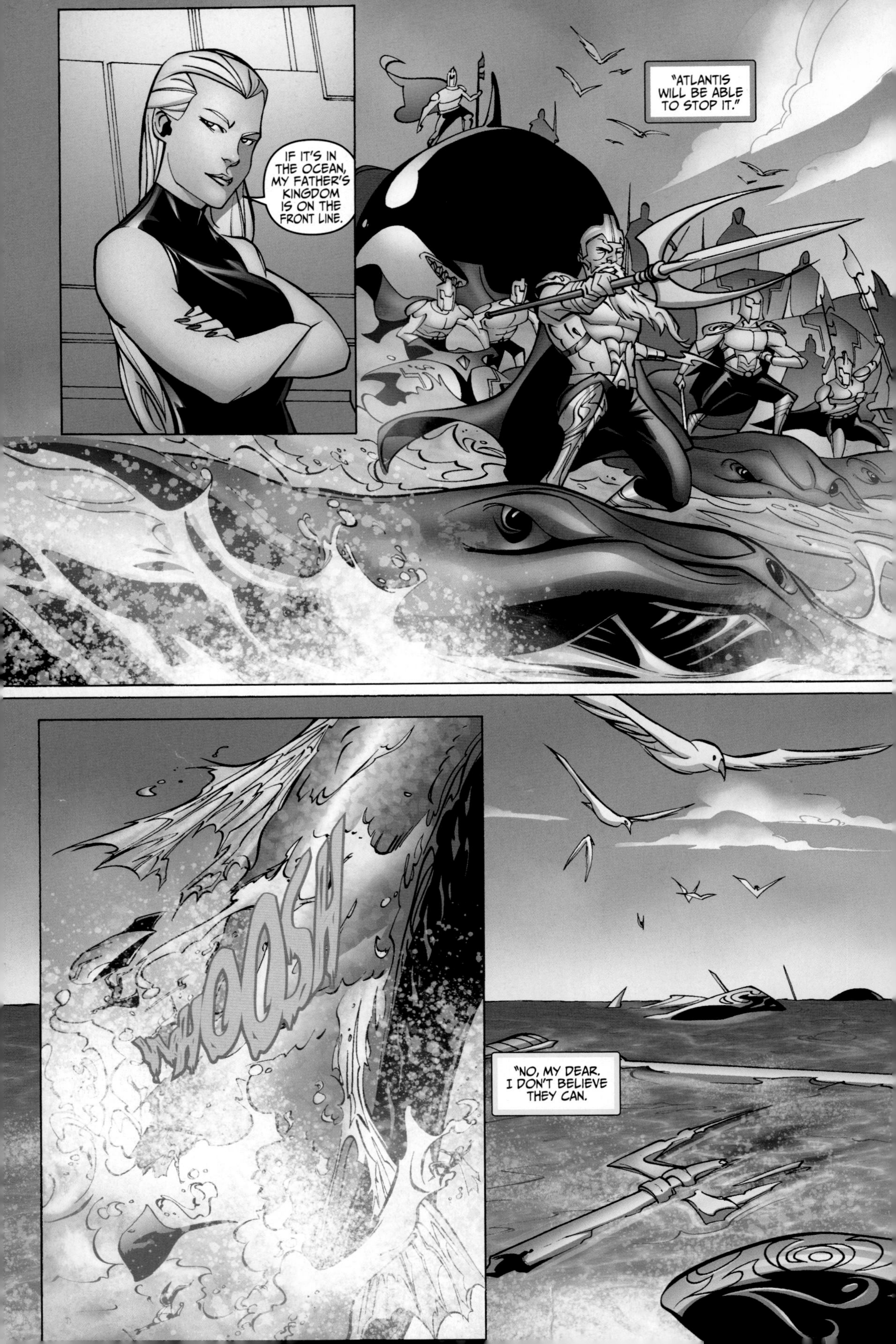
IF IT'S IN THE OCEAN, MY FATHER'S KINGDOM IS ON THE FRONT LINE.
"ATLANTIS WILL BE ABLE TO STOP IT."
WHOOSH
"NO, MY DEAR. I DON'T BELIEVE THEY CAN.

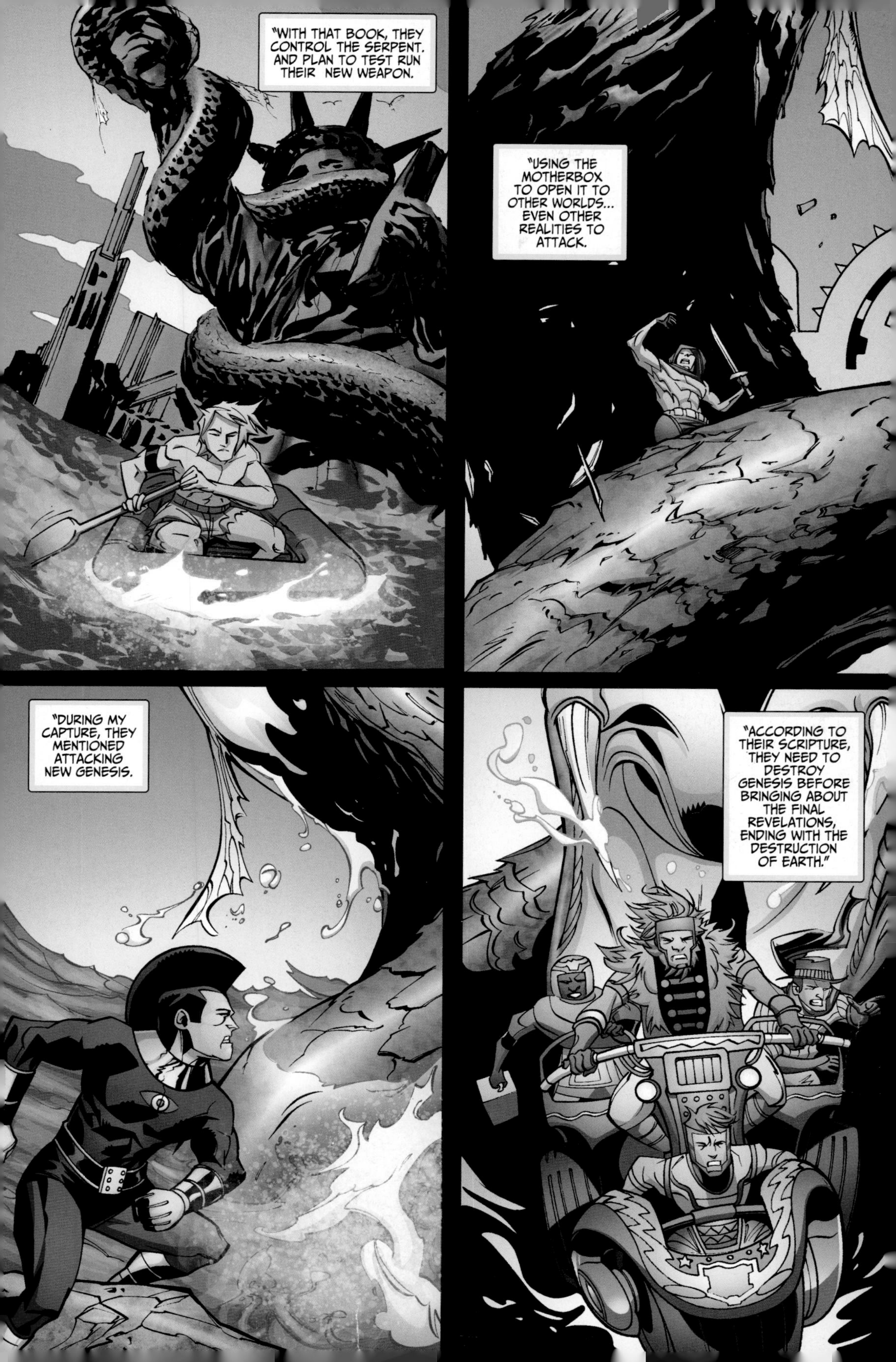
"WITH THAT BOOK, THEY CONTROL THE SERPENT. AND PLAN TO TEST RUN THEIR NEW WEAPON.
"USING THE MOTHERBOX TO OPEN IT TO OTHER WORLDS... EVEN OTHER REALITIES TO ATTACK.
"DURING MY CAPTURE, THEY MENTIONED ATTACKING NEW GENESIS.
"ACCORDING TO THEIR SCRIPTURE, THEY NEED TO DESTROY GENESIS BEFORE BRINGING ABOUT THE FINAL REVELATIONS, ENDING WITH THE DESTRUCTION OF EARTH."

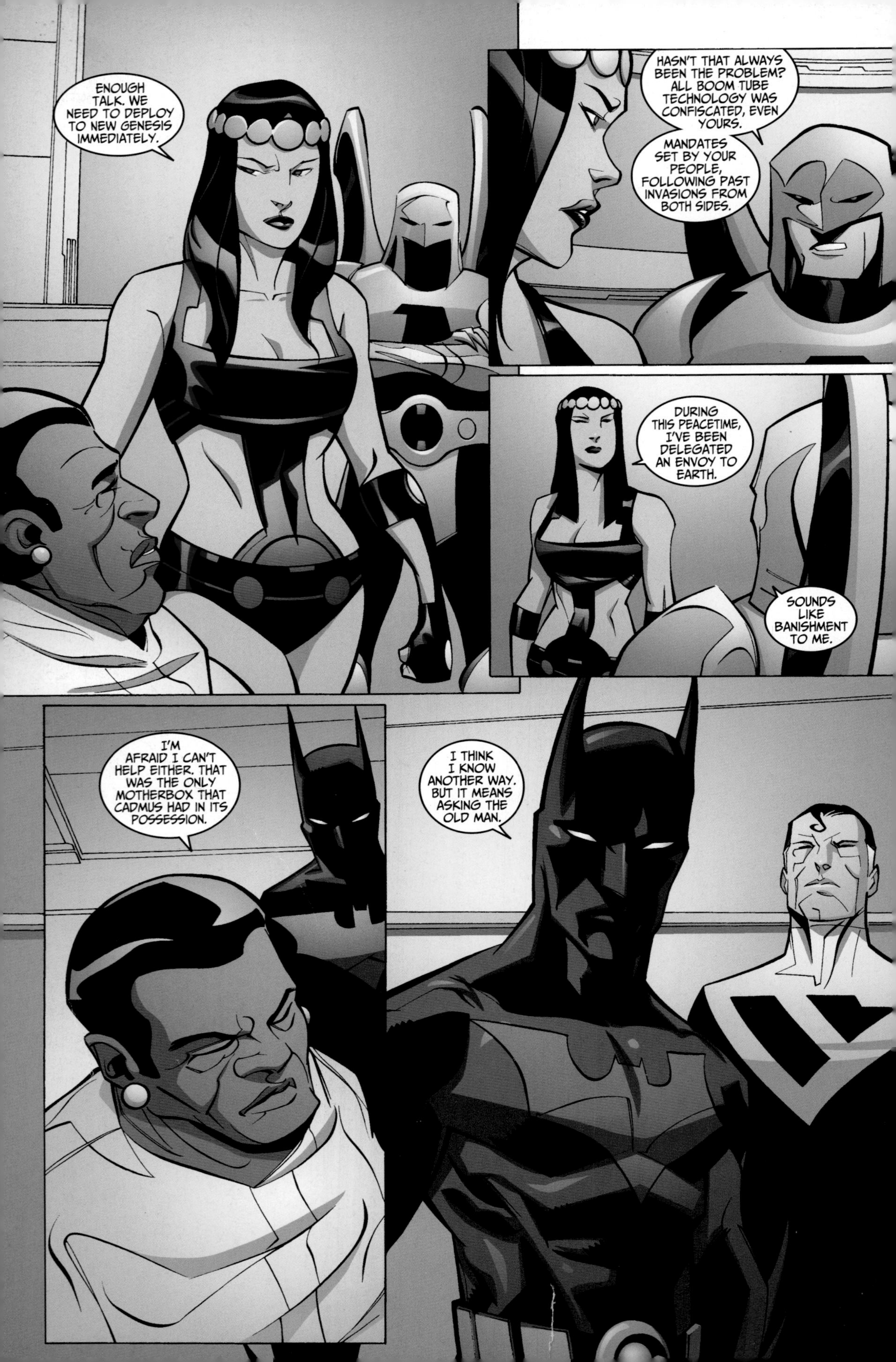
ENOUGH TALK. WE NEED TO DEPLOY TO NEW GENESIS IMMEDIATELY.
HASN'T THAT ALWAYS BEEN THE PROBLEM? ALL BOOM TUBE TECHNOLOGY WAS CONFISCATED, EVEN YOURS.
MANDATES SET BY YOUR PEOPLE, FOLLOWING PAST INVASIONS FROM BOTH SIDES.
DURING THIS PEACETIME, I'VE BEEN DELEGATED AN ENVOY TO EARTH.
SOUNDS LIKE BANISHMENT TO ME.
I'M AFRAID I CAN'T HELP EITHER. THAT WAS THE ONLY MOTHERBOX THAT CADMUS HAD IN ITS POSSESSION.
I THINK I KNOW ANOTHER WAY. BUT IT MEANS ASKING THE OLD MAN.

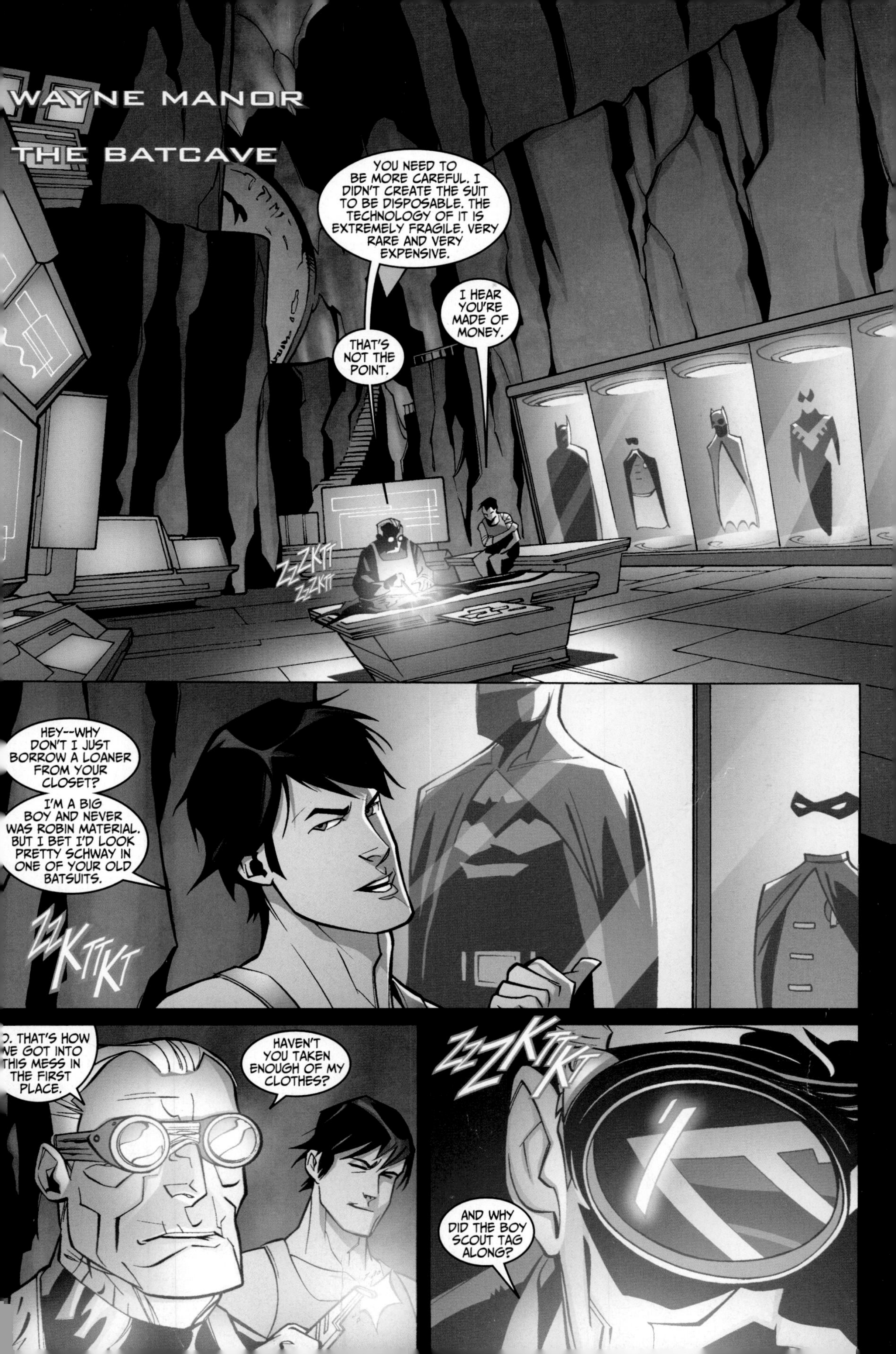
WAYNE MANOR
THE BATCAVE
YOU NEED TO BE MORE CAREFUL. I DIDN'T CREATE THE SUIT TO BE DISPOSABLE. THE TECHNOLOGY OF IT IS EXTREMELY FRAGILE. VERY RARE AND VERY EXPENSIVE.
I HEAR YOU'RE MADE OF MONEY.
THAT'S NOT THE POINT.
ZZZKTT
ZZZKTT
HEY--WHY DON'T I JUST BORROW A LOANER FROM YOUR CLOSET?
I'M A BIG BOY AND NEVER WAS ROBIN MATERIAL. BUT I BET I'D LOOK PRETTY SCHWAY IN ONE OF YOUR OLD BATSUITS.
ZZKTTKT
O. THAT'S HOW WE GOT INTO THIS MESS IN THE FIRST PLACE.
HAVEN'T YOU TAKEN ENOUGH OF MY CLOTHES?
ZZZKTTKT
AND WHY DID THE BOY SCOUT TAG ALONG?

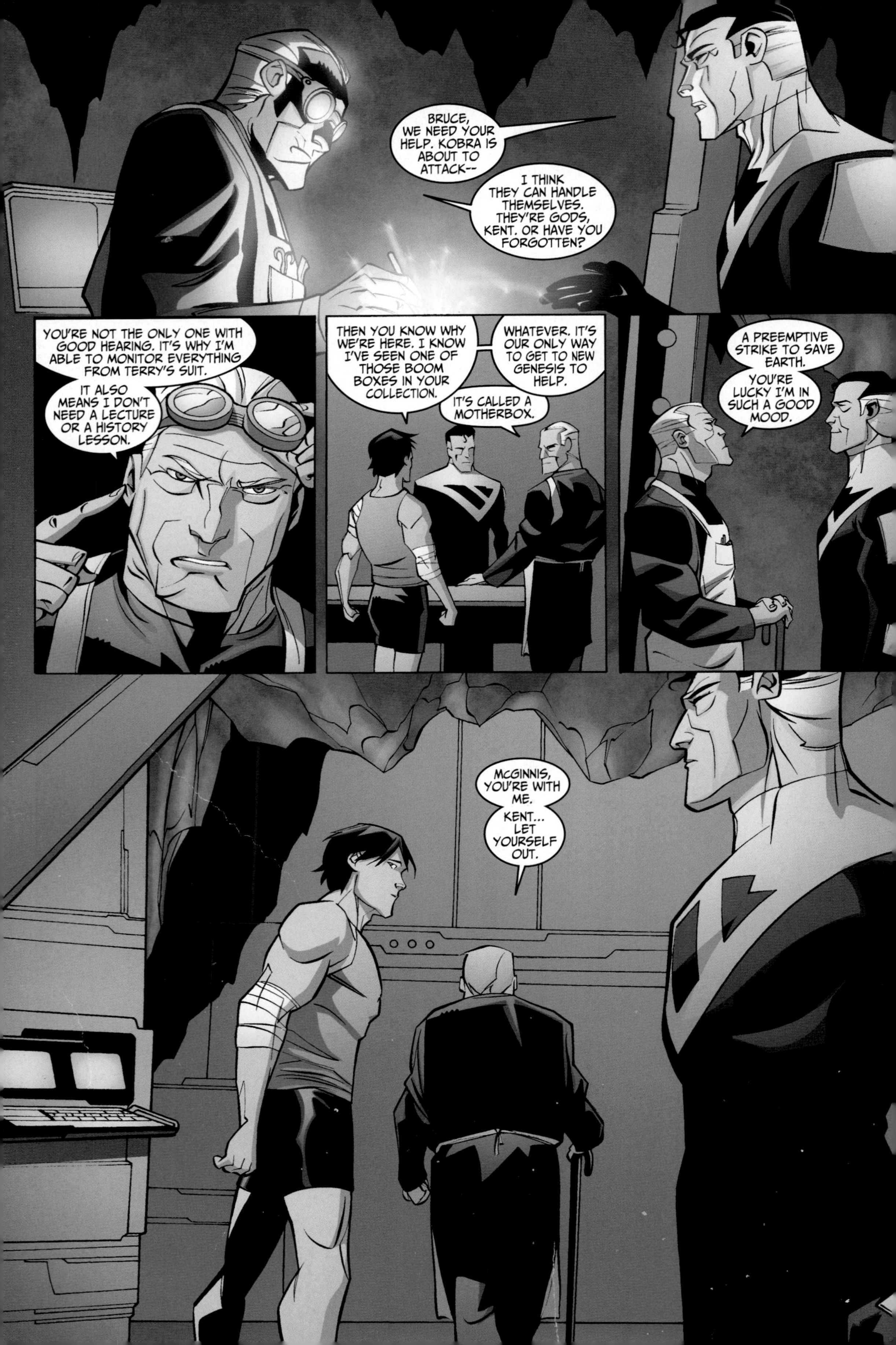
BRUCE, WE NEED YOUR HELP. KOBRA IS ABOUT TO ATTACK--
I THINK THEY CAN HANDLE THEMSELVES. THEY'RE GODS, KENT. OR HAVE YOU FORGOTTEN?
YOU'RE NOT THE ONLY ONE WITH GOOD HEARING. IT'S WHY I'M ABLE TO MONITOR EVERYTHING FROM TERRY'S SUIT.
IT ALSO MEANS I DON'T NEED A LECTURE OR A HISTORY LESSON.
THEN YOU KNOW WHY WE'RE HERE. I KNOW I'VE SEEN ONE OF THOSE BOOM BOXES IN YOUR COLLECTION.
WHATEVER. IT'S OUR ONLY WAY TO GET TO NEW GENESIS TO HELP.
IT'S CALLED A MOTHERBOX.
A PREEMPTIVE STRIKE TO SAVE EARTH.
YOU'RE LUCKY I'M IN SUCH A GOOD MOOD.
MCGINNIS, YOU'RE WITH ME.
KENT... LET YOURSELF OUT.

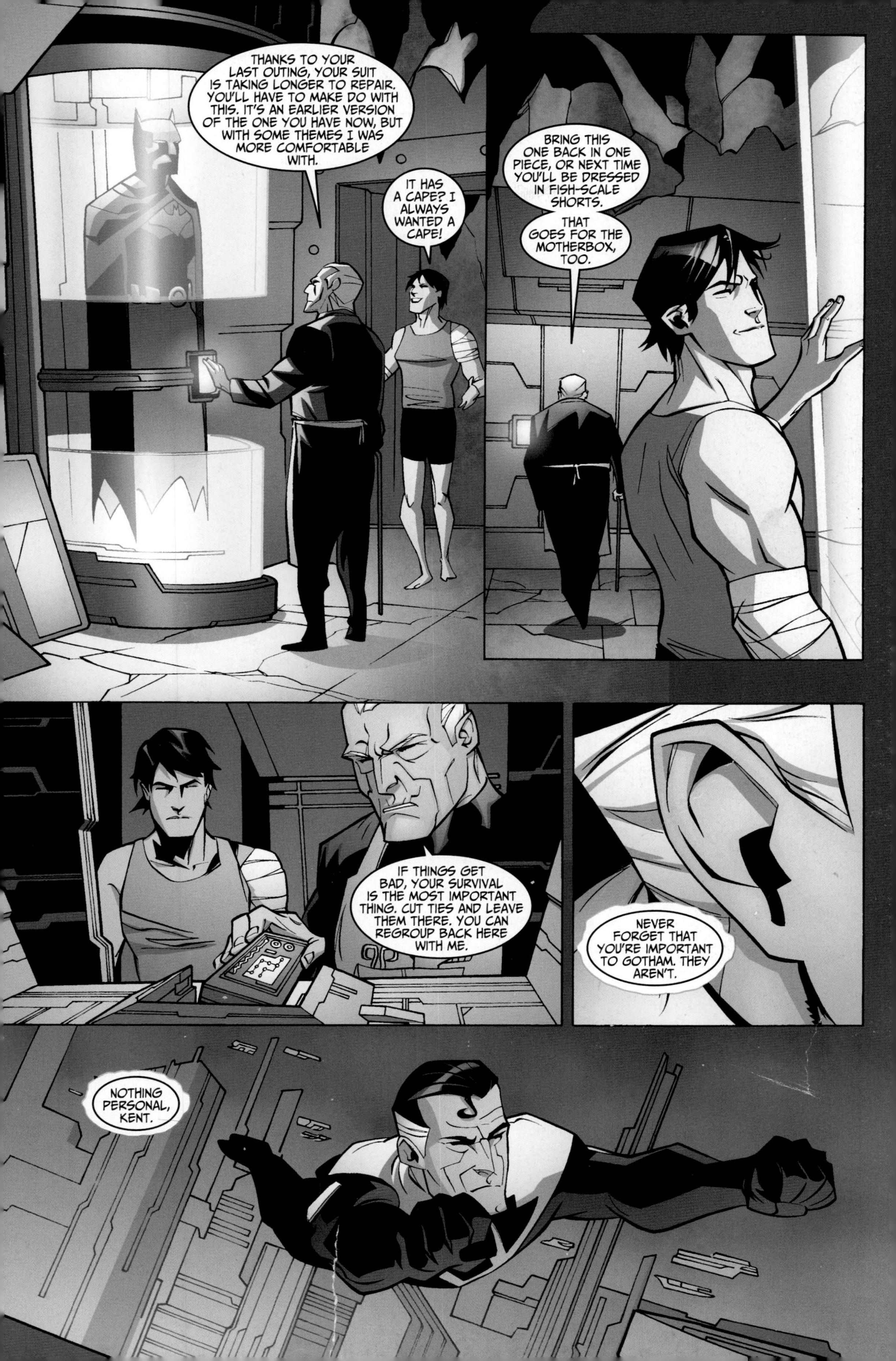
THANKS TO YOUR LAST OUTING, YOUR SUIT IS TAKING LONGER TO REPAIR. YOU'LL HAVE TO MAKE DO WITH THIS. IT'S AN EARLIER VERSION OF THE ONE YOU HAVE NOW, BUT WITH SOME THEMES I WAS MORE COMFORTABLE WITH.
IT HAS A CAPE? I ALWAYS WANTED A CAPE!
BRING THIS ONE BACK IN ONE PIECE, OR NEXT TIME YOU'LL BE DRESSED IN FISH-SCALE SHORTS.
THAT GOES FOR THE MOTHERBOX, TOO.
IF THINGS GET BAD, YOUR SURVIVAL IS THE MOST IMPORTANT THING. CUT TIES AND LEAVE THEM THERE. YOU CAN REGROUP BACK HERE WITH ME.
NEVER FORGET THAT YOU'RE IMPORTANT TO GOTHAM. THEY AREN'T.
NOTHING PERSONAL, KENT.

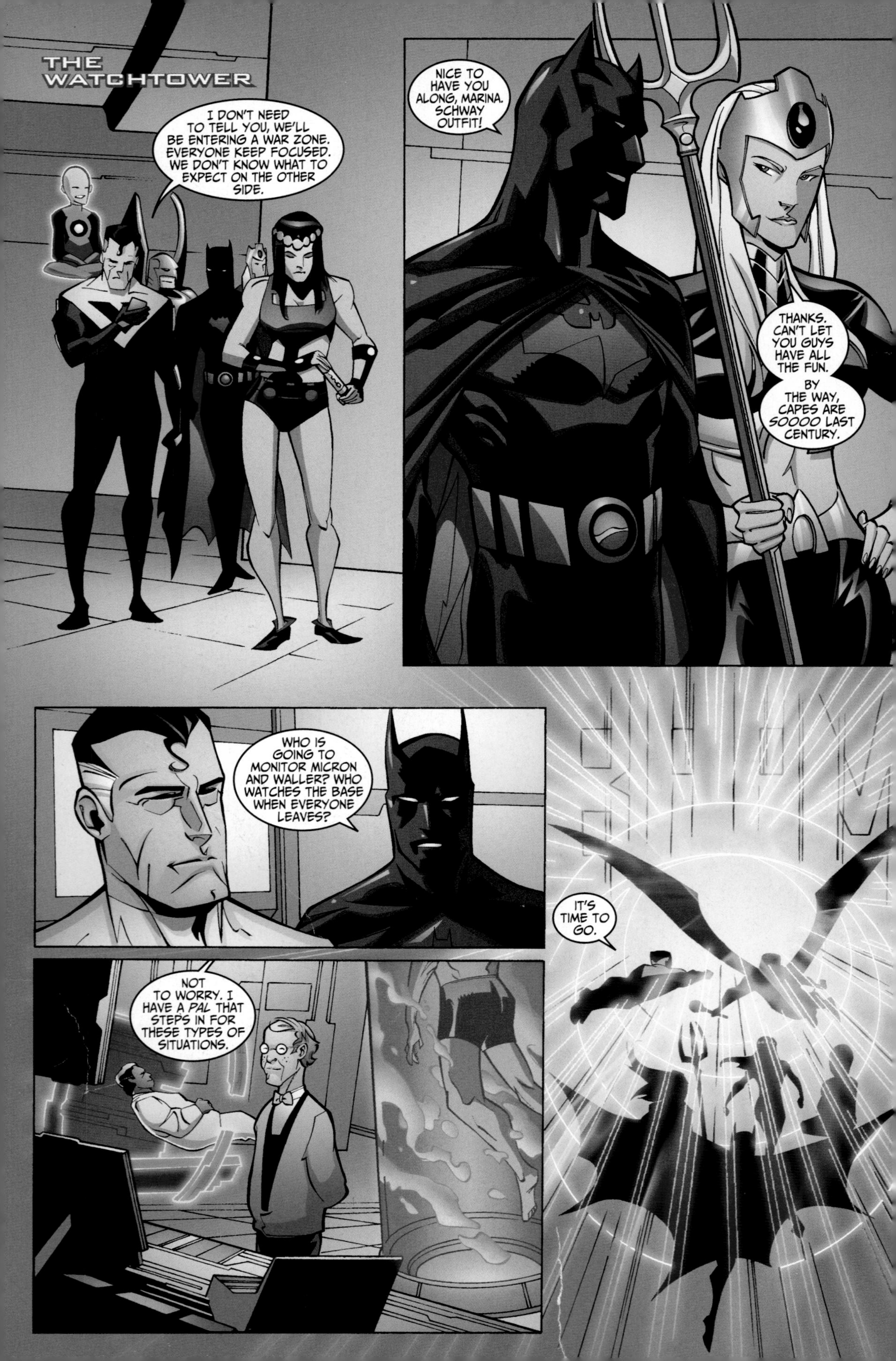
THE WATCHTOWER
I DON'T NEED TO TELL YOU, WE'LL BE ENTERING A WAR ZONE. EVERYONE KEEP FOCUSED. WE DON'T KNOW WHAT TO EXPECT ON THE OTHER SIDE.
NICE TO HAVE YOU ALONG, MARINA. SCHWAY OUTFIT!
THANKS. CAN'T LET YOU GUYS HAVE ALL THE FUN.
BY THE WAY, CAPES ARE SOOOO LAST CENTURY.
WHO IS GOING TO MONITOR MICRON AND WALLER? WHO WATCHES THE BASE WHEN EVERYONE LEAVES?
NOT TO WORRY. I HAVE A *PAL* THAT STEPS IN FOR THESE TYPES OF SITUATIONS.
IT'S TIME TO GO.

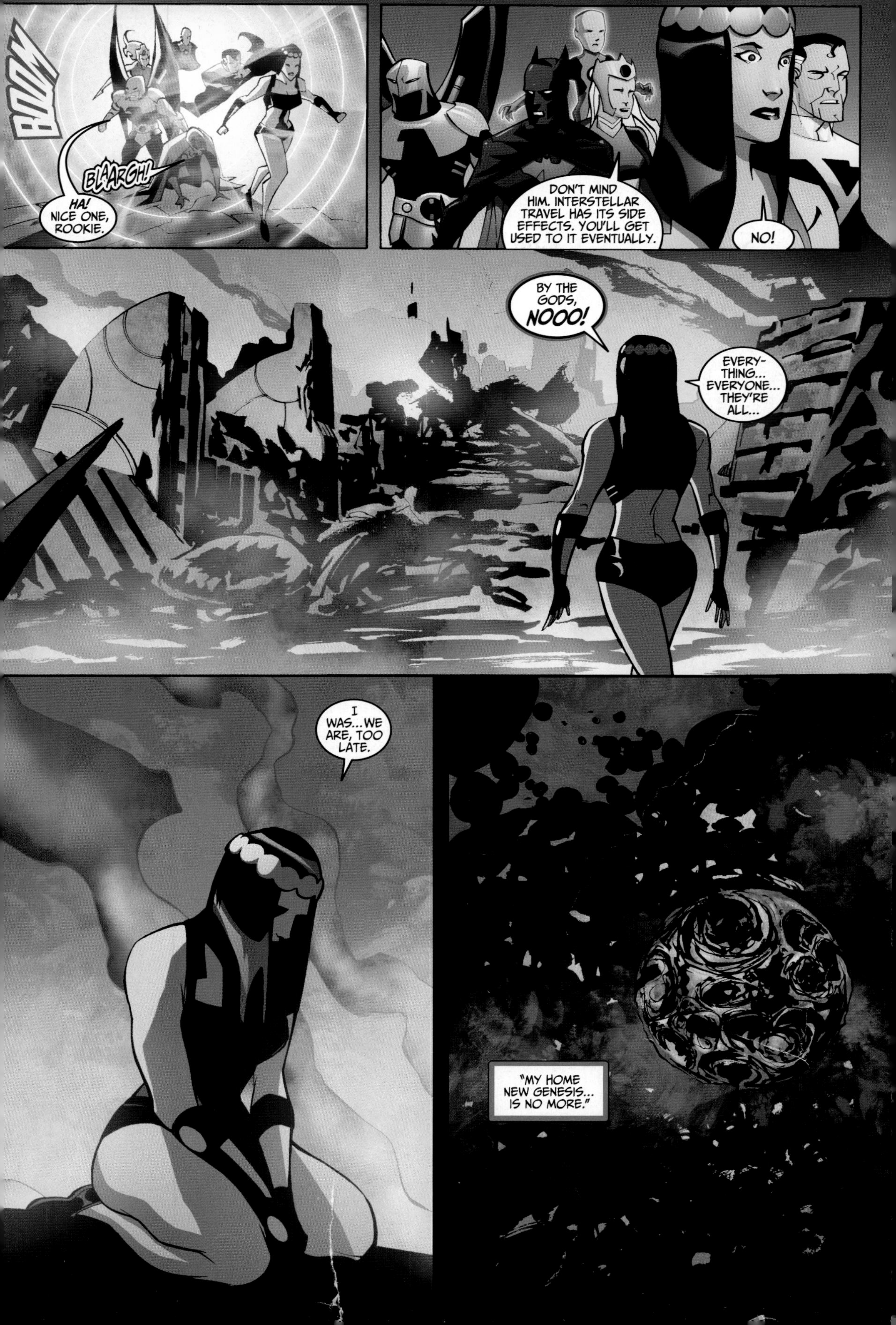
BOOM
BLAARGH!
HA! NICE ONE, ROOKIE.
DON'T MIND HIM. INTERSTELLAR TRAVEL HAS ITS SIDE EFFECTS. YOU'LL GET USED TO IT EVENTUALLY.
NO!
BY THE GODS, NOOO!
EVERY-THING... EVERYONE... THEY'RE ALL...
I WAS...WE ARE, TOO LATE.
"MY HOME NEW GENESIS... IS NO MORE."

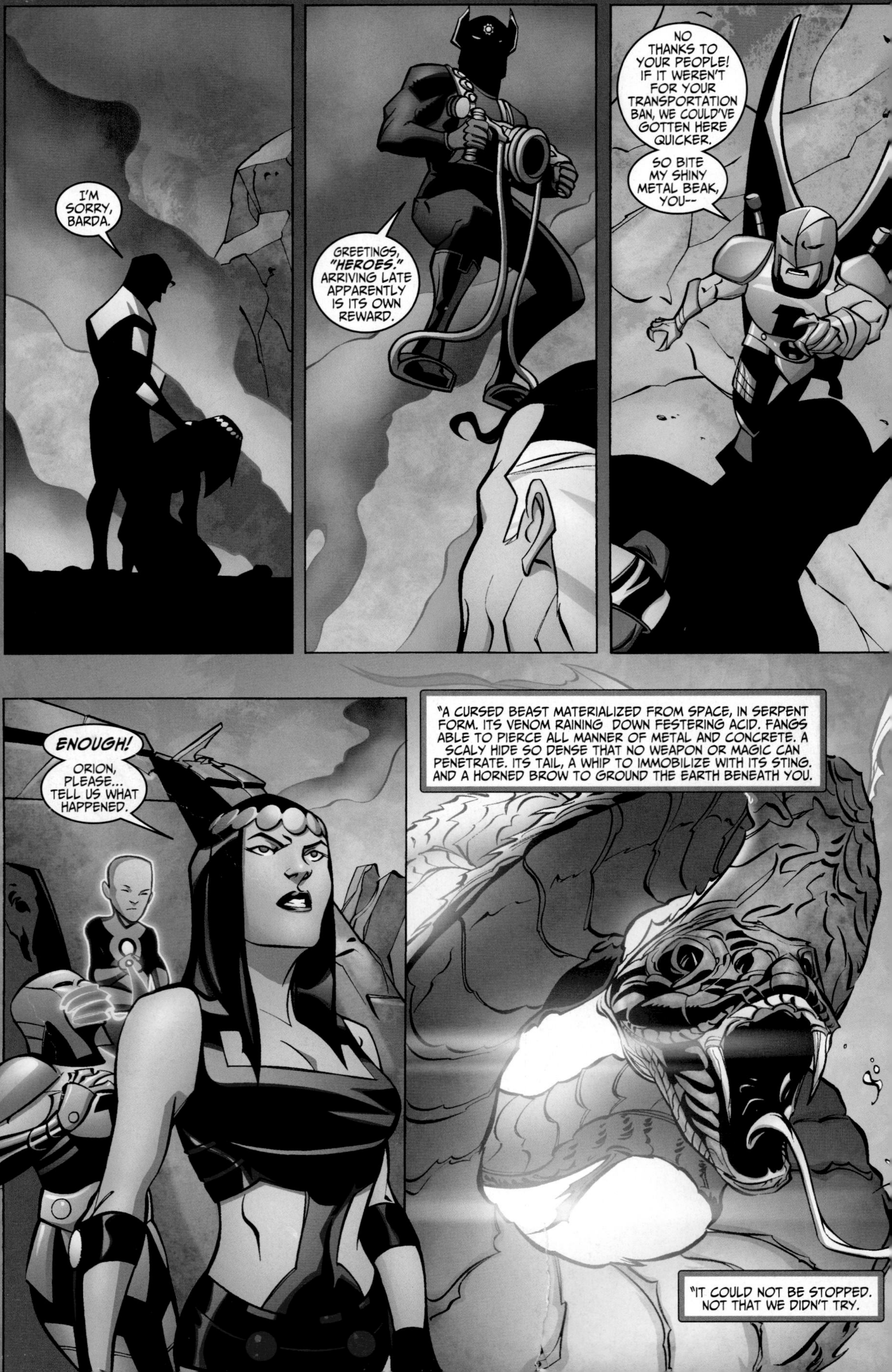
I'M SORRY, BARDA.
GREETINGS, "HEROES." ARRIVING LATE APPARENTLY IS ITS OWN REWARD.
NO THANKS TO YOUR PEOPLE! IF IT WEREN'T FOR YOUR TRANSPORTATION BAN, WE COULD'VE GOTTEN HERE QUICKER.
SO BITE MY SHINY METAL BEAK, YOU--
ENOUGH!
ORION, PLEASE... TELL US WHAT HAPPENED.
"A CURSED BEAST MATERIALIZED FROM SPACE, IN SERPENT FORM. ITS VENOM RAINING DOWN FESTERING ACID. FANGS ABLE TO PIERCE ALL MANNER OF METAL AND CONCRETE. A SCALY HIDE SO DENSE THAT NO WEAPON OR MAGIC CAN PENETRATE. ITS TAIL, A WHIP TO IMMOBILIZE WITH ITS STING. AND A HORNED BROW TO GROUND THE EARTH BENEATH YOU.
"IT COULD NOT BE STOPPED. NOT THAT WE DIDN'T TRY.

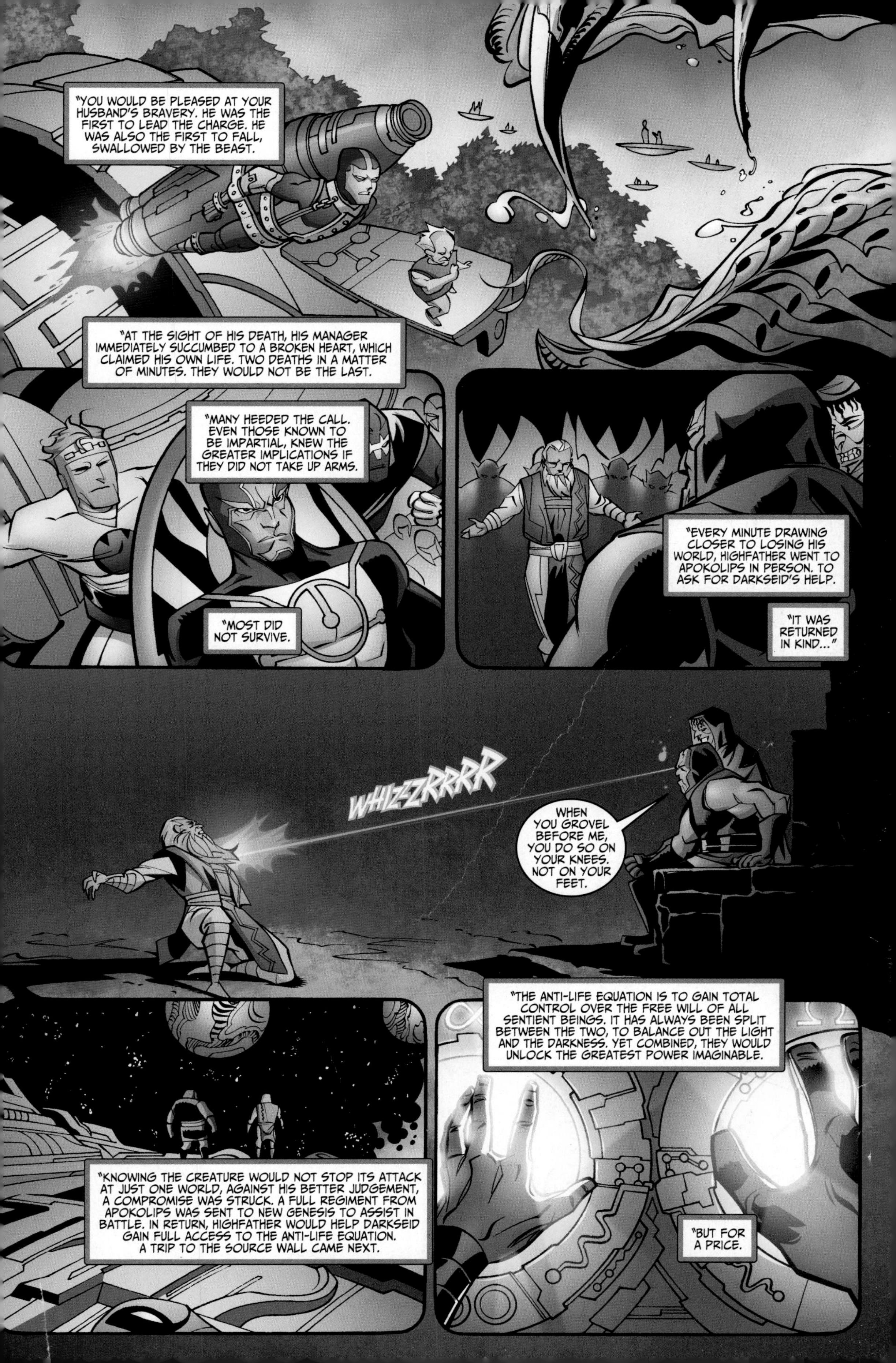
"YOU WOULD BE PLEASED AT YOUR HUSBAND'S BRAVERY. HE WAS THE FIRST TO LEAD THE CHARGE. HE WAS ALSO THE FIRST TO FALL, SWALLOWED BY THE BEAST.
"AT THE SIGHT OF HIS DEATH, HIS MANAGER IMMEDIATELY SUCCUMBED TO A BROKEN HEART, WHICH CLAIMED HIS OWN LIFE. TWO DEATHS IN A MATTER OF MINUTES. THEY WOULD NOT BE THE LAST.
"MANY HEEDED THE CALL. EVEN THOSE KNOWN TO BE IMPARTIAL, KNEW THE GREATER IMPLICATIONS IF THEY DID NOT TAKE UP ARMS.
"MOST DID NOT SURVIVE.
"EVERY MINUTE DRAWING CLOSER TO LOSING HIS WORLD, HIGHFATHER WENT TO APOKOLIPS IN PERSON. TO ASK FOR DARKSEID'S HELP.
"IT WAS RETURNED IN KIND..."
WHIZZZRRRR
WHEN YOU GROVEL BEFORE ME, YOU DO SO ON YOUR KNEES. NOT ON YOUR FEET.
"KNOWING THE CREATURE WOULD NOT STOP ITS ATTACK AT JUST ONE WORLD, AGAINST HIS BETTER JUDGEMENT, A COMPROMISE WAS STRUCK. A FULL REGIMENT FROM APOKOLIPS WAS SENT TO NEW GENESIS TO ASSIST IN BATTLE. IN RETURN, HIGHFATHER WOULD HELP DARKSEID GAIN FULL ACCESS TO THE ANTI-LIFE EQUATION. A TRIP TO THE SOURCE WALL CAME NEXT.
"THE ANTI-LIFE EQUATION IS TO GAIN TOTAL CONTROL OVER THE FREE WILL OF ALL SENTIENT BEINGS. IT HAS ALWAYS BEEN SPLIT BETWEEN THE TWO, TO BALANCE OUT THE LIGHT AND THE DARKNESS. YET COMBINED, THEY WOULD UNLOCK THE GREATEST POWER IMAGINABLE.
"BUT FOR A PRICE.

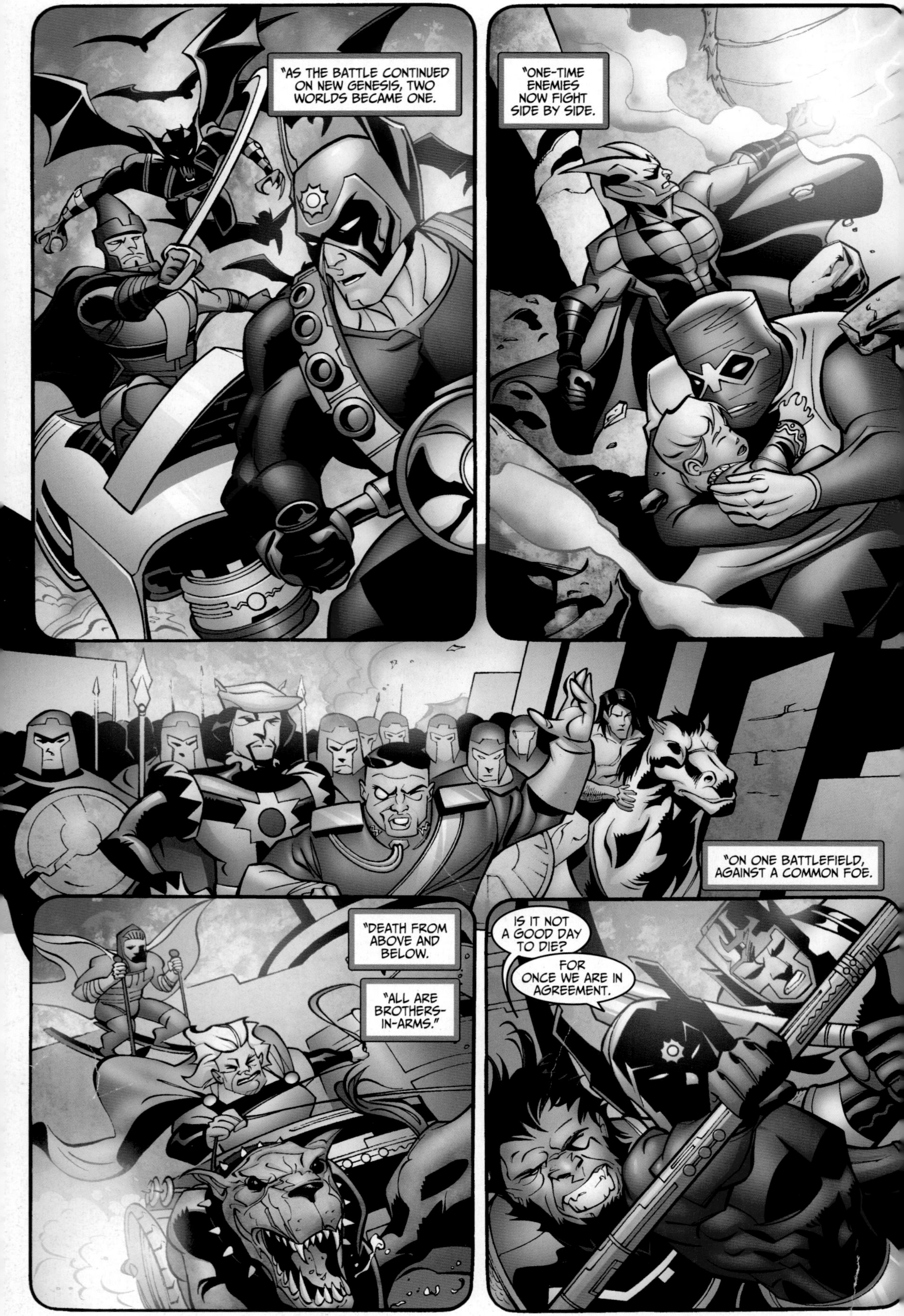
"AS THE BATTLE CONTINUED ON NEW GENESIS, TWO WORLDS BECAME ONE.
"ONE-TIME ENEMIES NOW FIGHT SIDE BY SIDE.
"ON ONE BATTLEFIELD, AGAINST A COMMON FOE.
"DEATH FROM ABOVE AND BELOW.
"ALL ARE BROTHERS-IN-ARMS."
IS IT NOT A GOOD DAY TO DIE?
FOR ONCE WE ARE IN AGREEMENT.

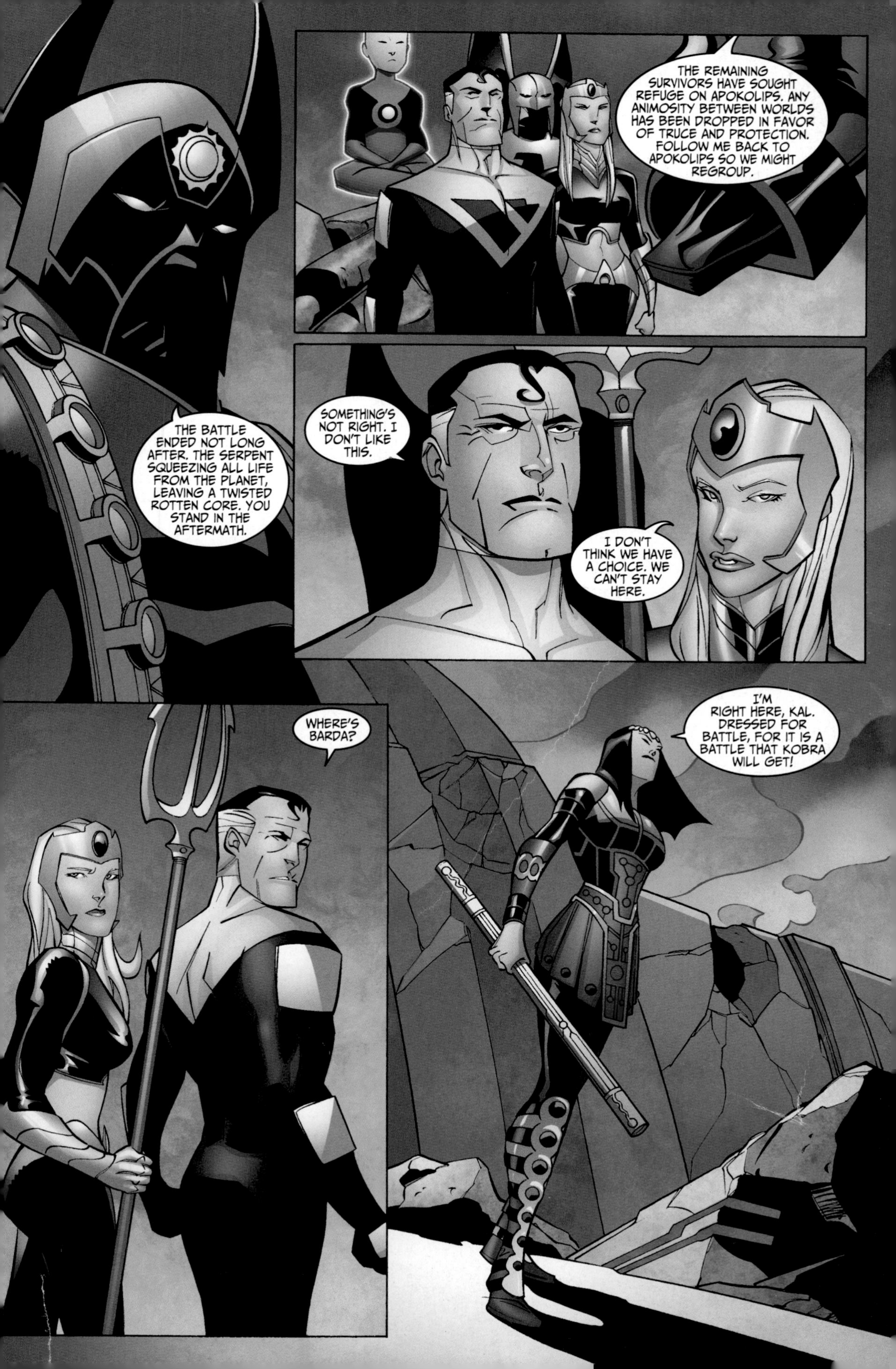
THE REMAINING SURVIVORS HAVE SOUGHT REFUGE ON APOKOLIPS. ANY ANIMOSITY BETWEEN WORLDS HAS BEEN DROPPED IN FAVOR OF TRUCE AND PROTECTION. FOLLOW ME BACK TO APOKOLIPS SO WE MIGHT REGROUP.
THE BATTLE ENDED NOT LONG AFTER. THE SERPENT SQUEEZING ALL LIFE FROM THE PLANET, LEAVING A TWISTED ROTTEN CORE. YOU STAND IN THE AFTERMATH.
SOMETHING'S NOT RIGHT. I DON'T LIKE THIS.
I DON'T THINK WE HAVE A CHOICE. WE CAN'T STAY HERE.
WHERE'S BARDA?
I'M RIGHT HERE, KAL. DRESSED FOR BATTLE, FOR IT IS A BATTLE THAT KOBRA WILL GET!

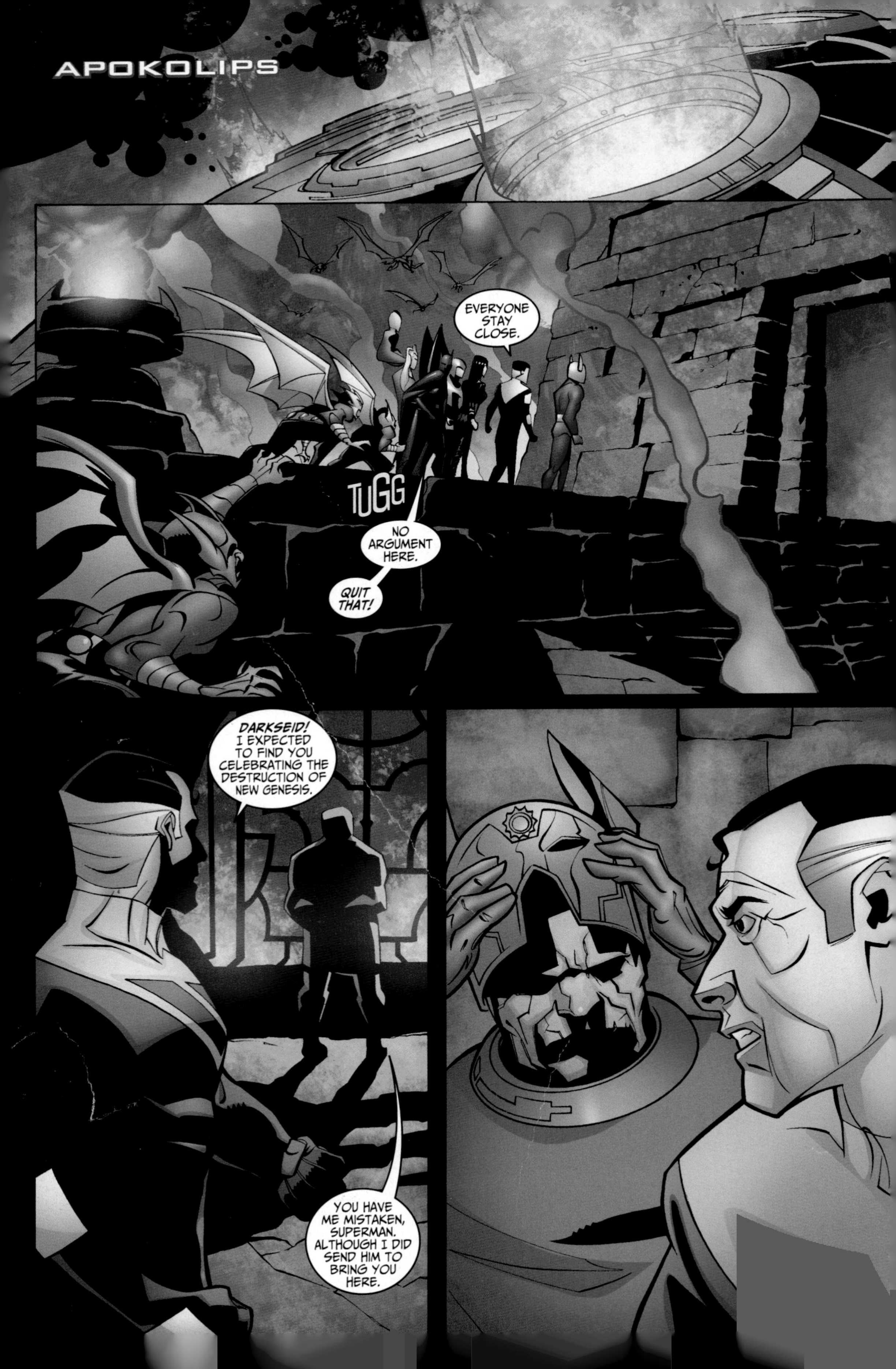
APOKOLIPS
EVERYONE STAY CLOSE.
TUGG
NO ARGUMENT HERE.
QUIT THAT!
DARKSEID! I EXPECTED TO FIND YOU CELEBRATING THE DESTRUCTION OF NEW GENESIS.
YOU HAVE ME MISTAKEN, SUPERMAN. ALTHOUGH I DID SEND HIM TO BRING YOU HERE.

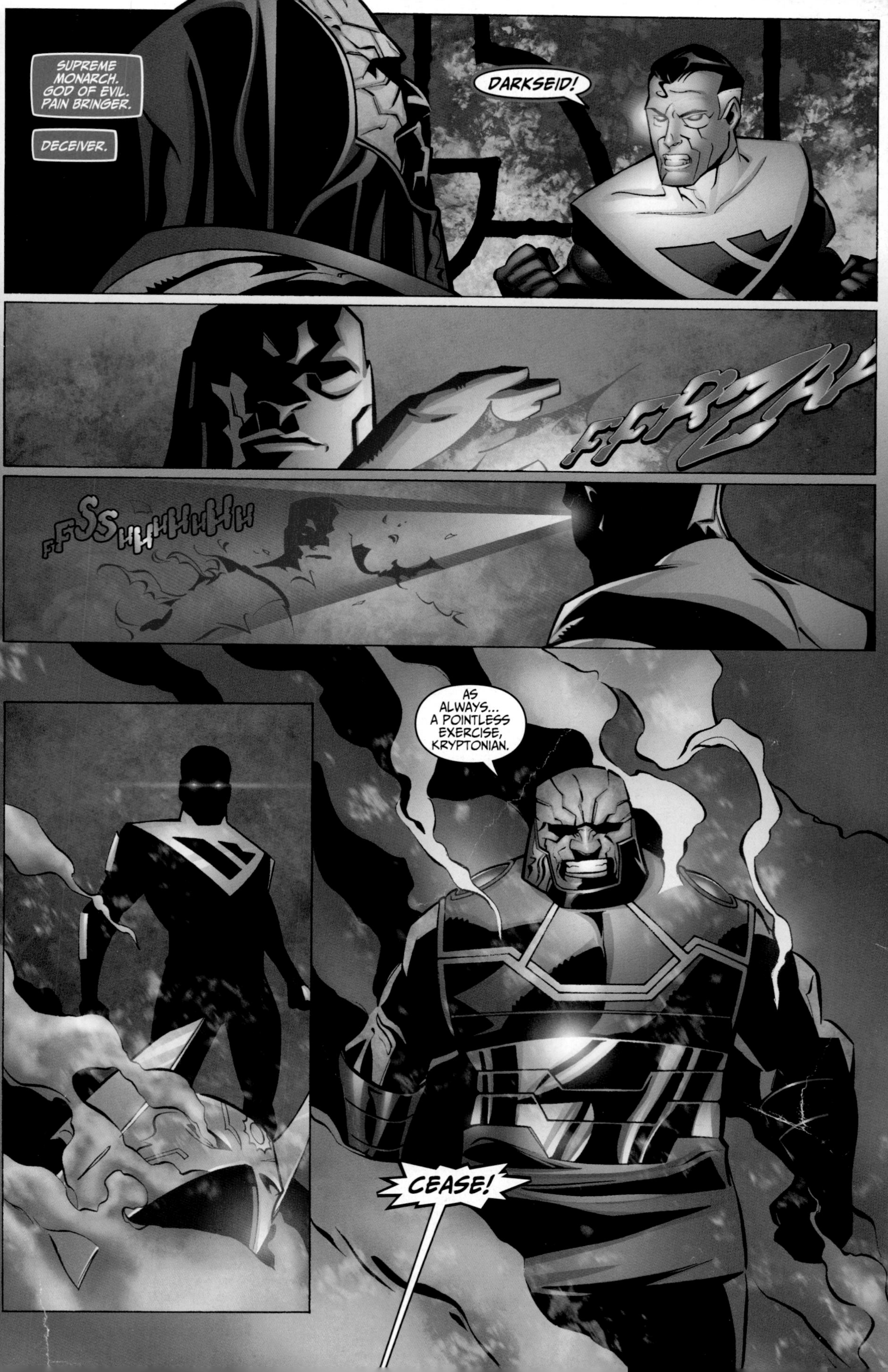
SUPREME MONARCH. GOD OF EVIL. PAIN BRINGER.
DECEIVER.
DARKSEID!
FFRZZAK
FFSSHHHHHHHHH
AS ALWAYS... A POINTLESS EXERCISE, KRYPTONIAN.
CEASE!

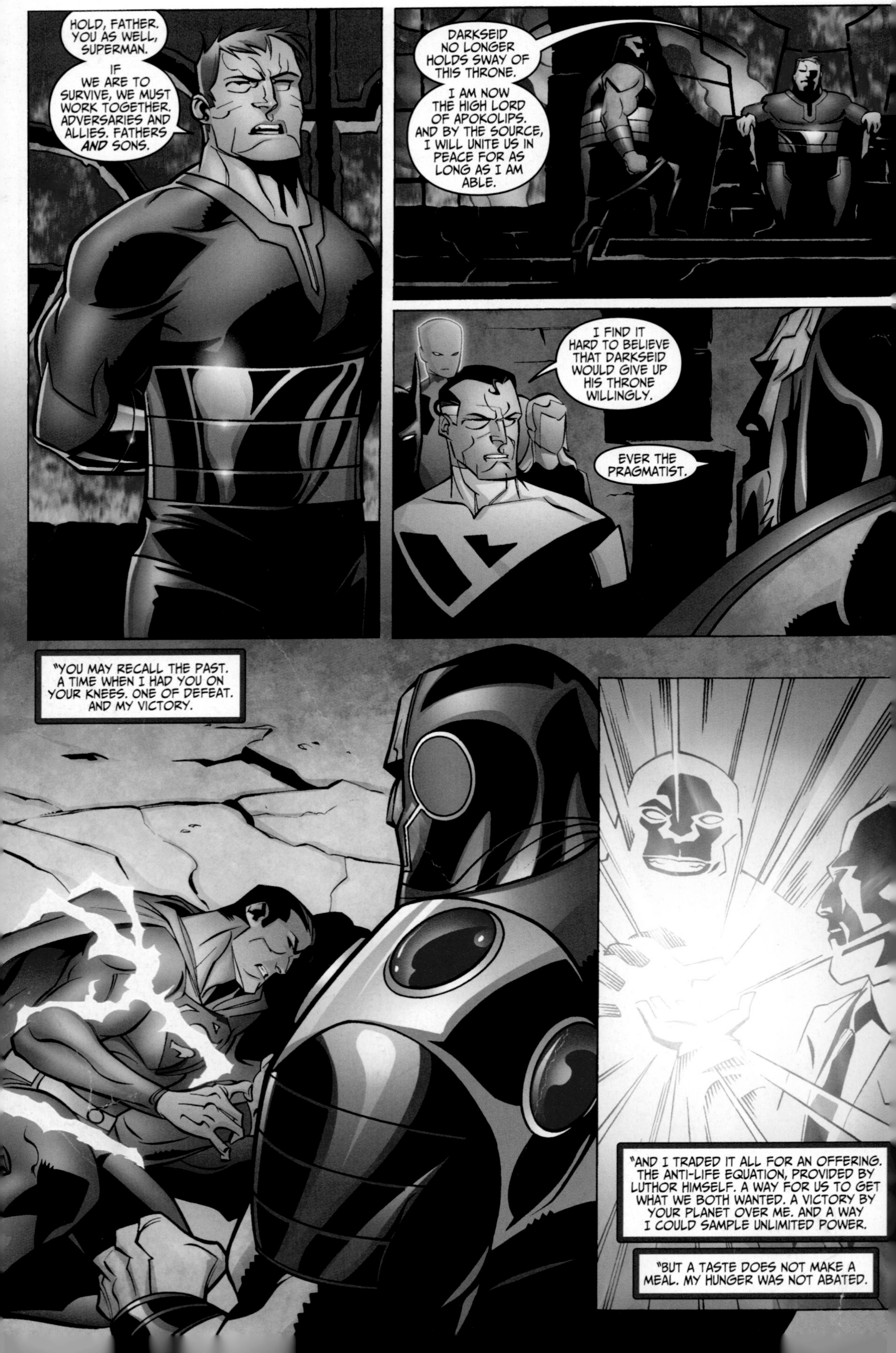
HOLD, FATHER. YOU AS WELL, SUPERMAN.
IF WE ARE TO SURVIVE, WE MUST WORK TOGETHER. ADVERSARIES AND ALLIES. FATHERS AND SONS.
DARKSEID NO LONGER HOLDS SWAY OF THIS THRONE.
I AM NOW THE HIGH LORD OF APOKOLIPS. AND BY THE SOURCE, I WILL UNITE US IN PEACE FOR AS LONG AS I AM ABLE.
I FIND IT HARD TO BELIEVE THAT DARKSEID WOULD GIVE UP HIS THRONE WILLINGLY.
EVER THE PRAGMATIST.
"YOU MAY RECALL THE PAST. A TIME WHEN I HAD YOU ON YOUR KNEES. ONE OF DEFEAT. AND MY VICTORY.
"AND I TRADED IT ALL FOR AN OFFERING. THE ANTI-LIFE EQUATION, PROVIDED BY LUTHOR HIMSELF. A WAY FOR US TO GET WHAT WE BOTH WANTED. A VICTORY BY YOUR PLANET OVER ME. AND A WAY I COULD SAMPLE UNLIMITED POWER.
"BUT A TASTE DOES NOT MAKE A MEAL. MY HUNGER WAS NOT ABATED.

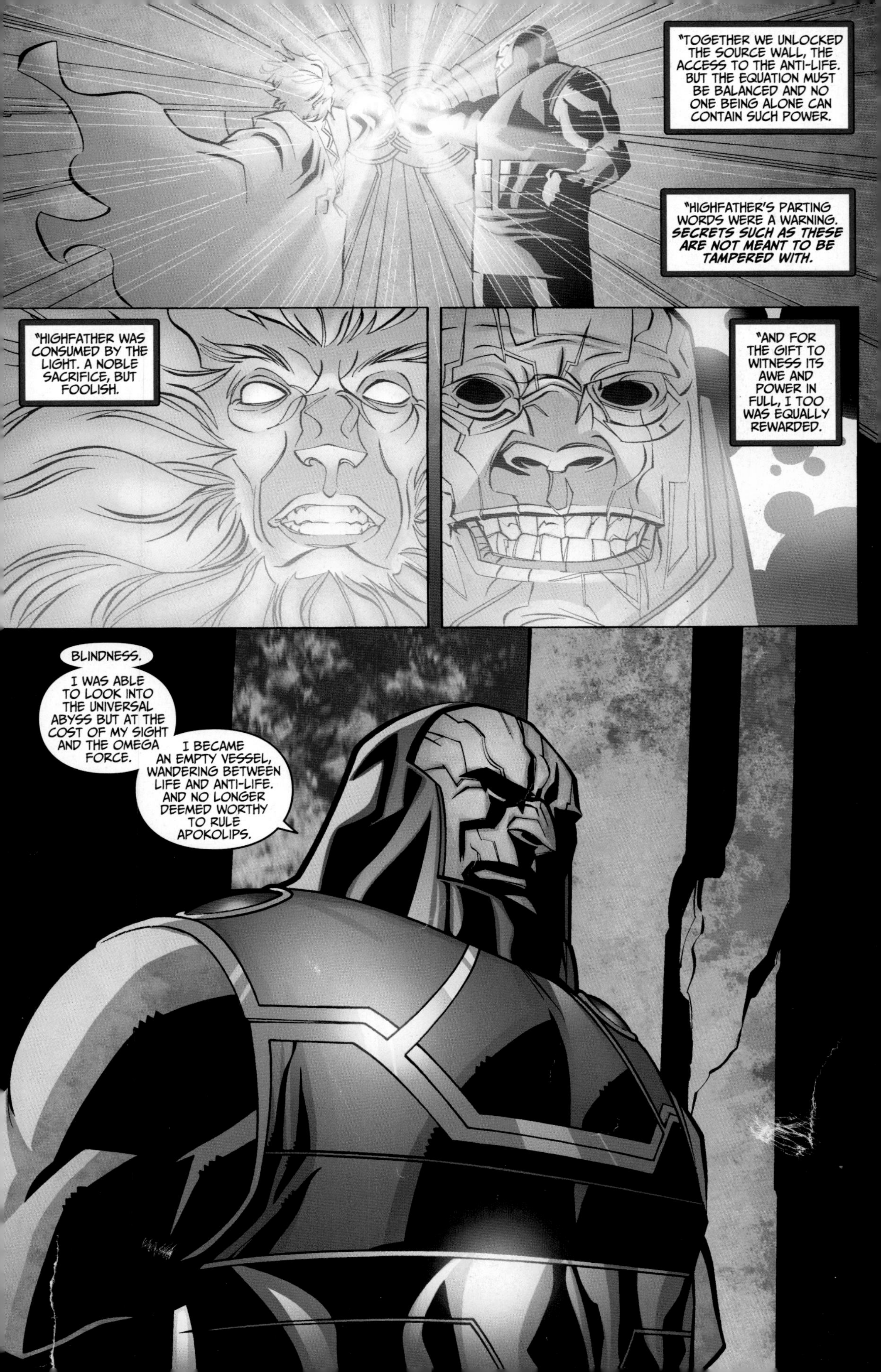
"TOGETHER WE UNLOCKED THE SOURCE WALL, THE ACCESS TO THE ANTI-LIFE. BUT THE EQUATION MUST BE BALANCED AND NO ONE BEING ALONE CAN CONTAIN SUCH POWER.
"HIGHFATHER'S PARTING WORDS WERE A WARNING. SECRETS SUCH AS THESE ARE NOT MEANT TO BE TAMPERED WITH.
"HIGHFATHER WAS CONSUMED BY THE LIGHT. A NOBLE SACRIFICE, BUT FOOLISH.
"AND FOR THE GIFT TO WITNESS ITS AWE AND POWER IN FULL, I TOO WAS EQUALLY REWARDED.
BLINDNESS.
I WAS ABLE TO LOOK INTO THE UNIVERSAL ABYSS BUT AT THE COST OF MY SIGHT AND THE OMEGA FORCE.
I BECAME AN EMPTY VESSEL, WANDERING BETWEEN LIFE AND ANTI-LIFE. AND NO LONGER DEEMED WORTHY TO RULE APOKOLIPS.

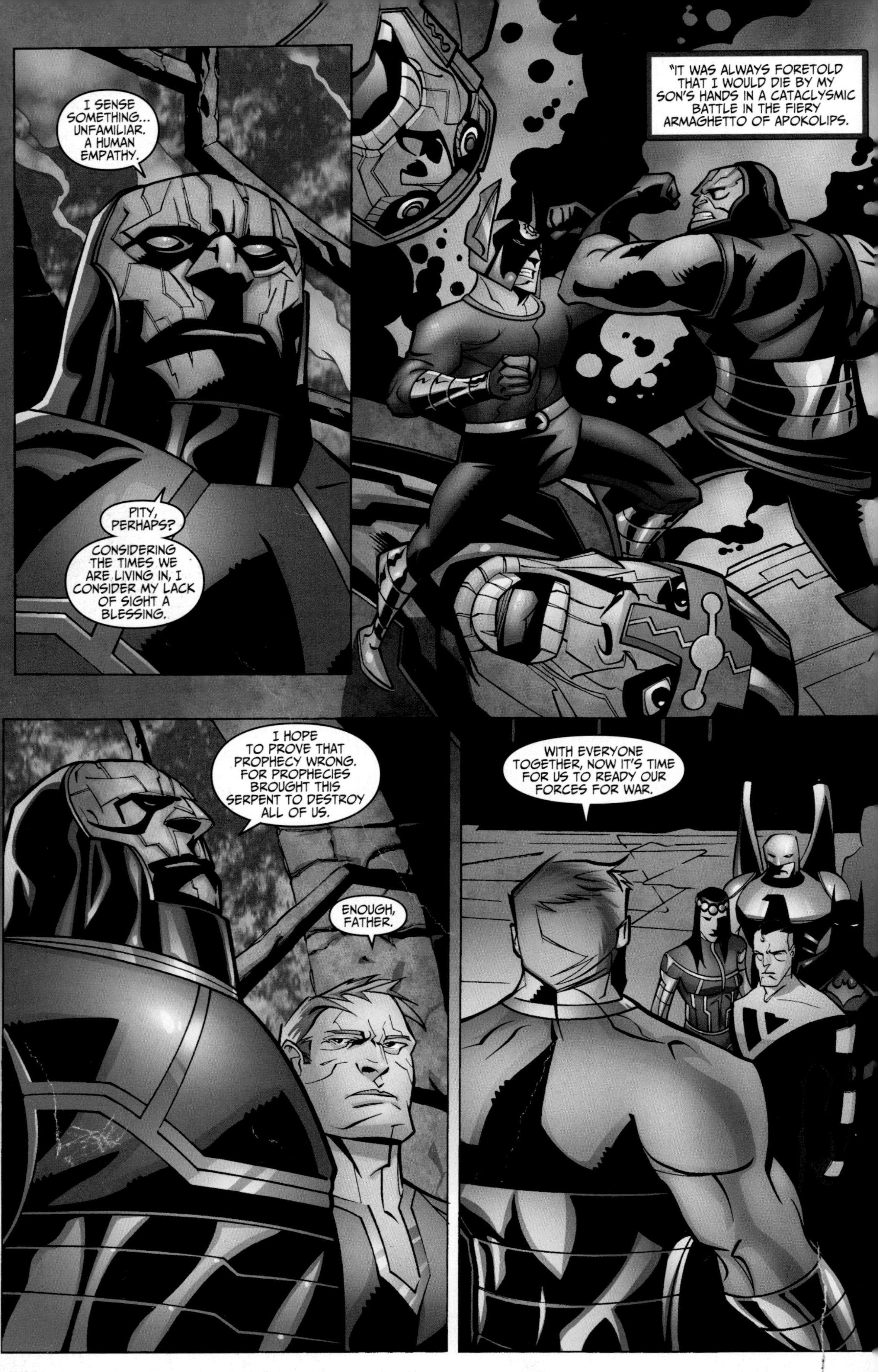
I SENSE SOMETHING... UNFAMILIAR. A HUMAN EMPATHY.
PITY, PERHAPS?
CONSIDERING THE TIMES WE ARE LIVING IN, I CONSIDER MY LACK OF SIGHT A BLESSING.
"IT WAS ALWAYS FORETOLD THAT I WOULD DIE BY MY SON'S HANDS IN A CATACLYSMIC BATTLE IN THE FIERY ARMAGHETTO OF APOKOLIPS.
I HOPE TO PROVE THAT PROPHECY WRONG. FOR PROPHECIES BROUGHT THIS SERPENT TO DESTROY ALL OF US.
ENOUGH, FATHER.
WITH EVERYONE TOGETHER, NOW IT'S TIME FOR US TO READY OUR FORCES FOR WAR.

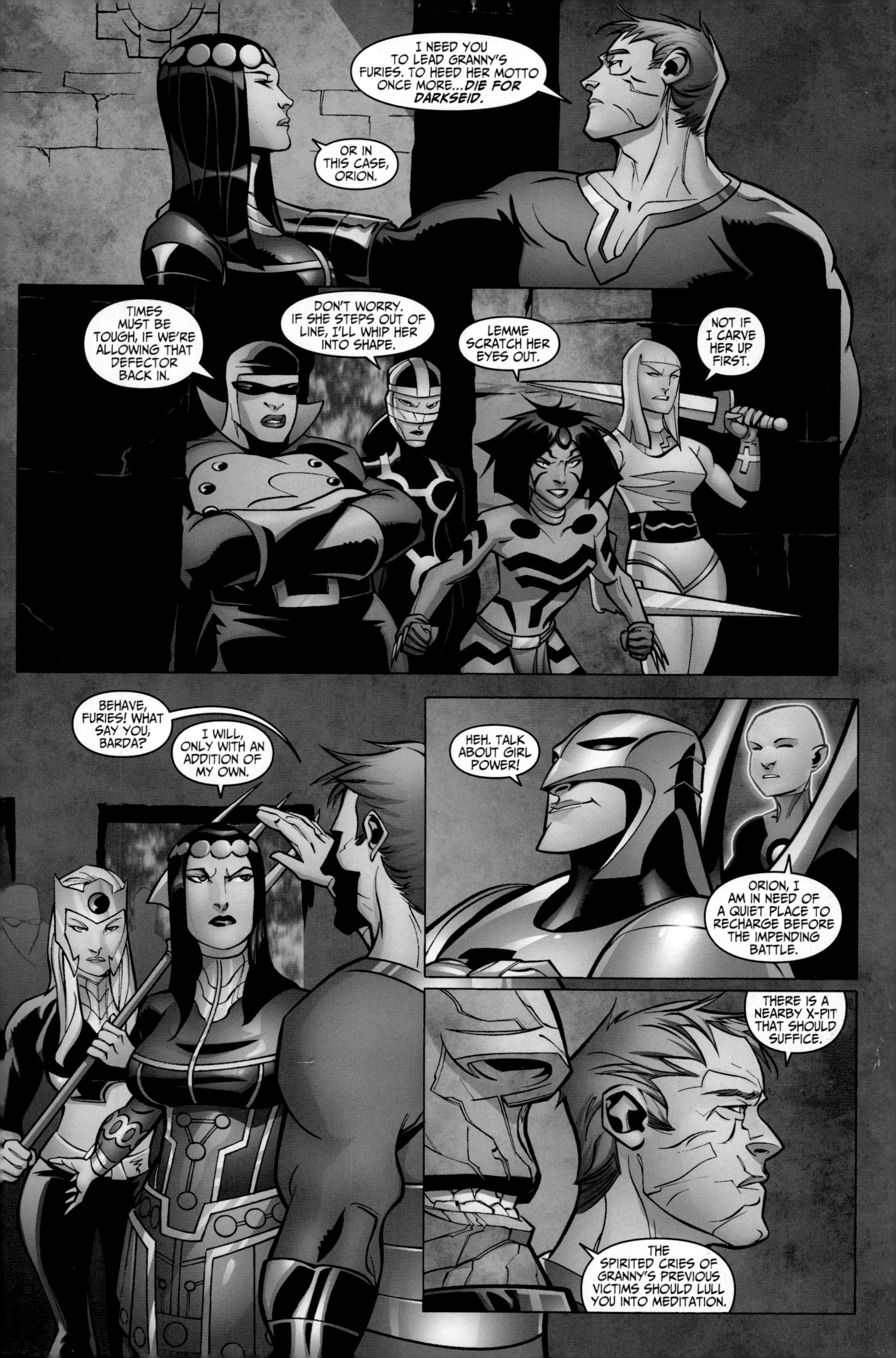
I NEED YOU TO LEAD GRANNY'S FURIES. TO HEED HER MOTTO ONCE MORE...DIE FOR DARKSEID.
OR IN THIS CASE, ORION.
TIMES MUST BE TOUGH, IF WE'RE ALLOWING THAT DEFECTOR BACK IN.
DON'T WORRY. IF SHE STEPS OUT OF LINE, I'LL WHIP HER INTO SHAPE.
LEMME SCRATCH HER EYES OUT.
NOT IF I CARVE HER UP FIRST.
BEHAVE, FURIES! WHAT SAY YOU, BARDA?
I WILL, ONLY WITH AN ADDITION OF MY OWN.
HEH. TALK ABOUT GIRL POWER!
ORION, I AM IN NEED OF A QUIET PLACE TO RECHARGE BEFORE THE IMPENDING BATTLE.
THERE IS A NEARBY X-PIT THAT SHOULD SUFFICE.
THE SPIRITED CRIES OF GRANNY'S PREVIOUS VICTIMS SHOULD LULL YOU INTO MEDITATION.

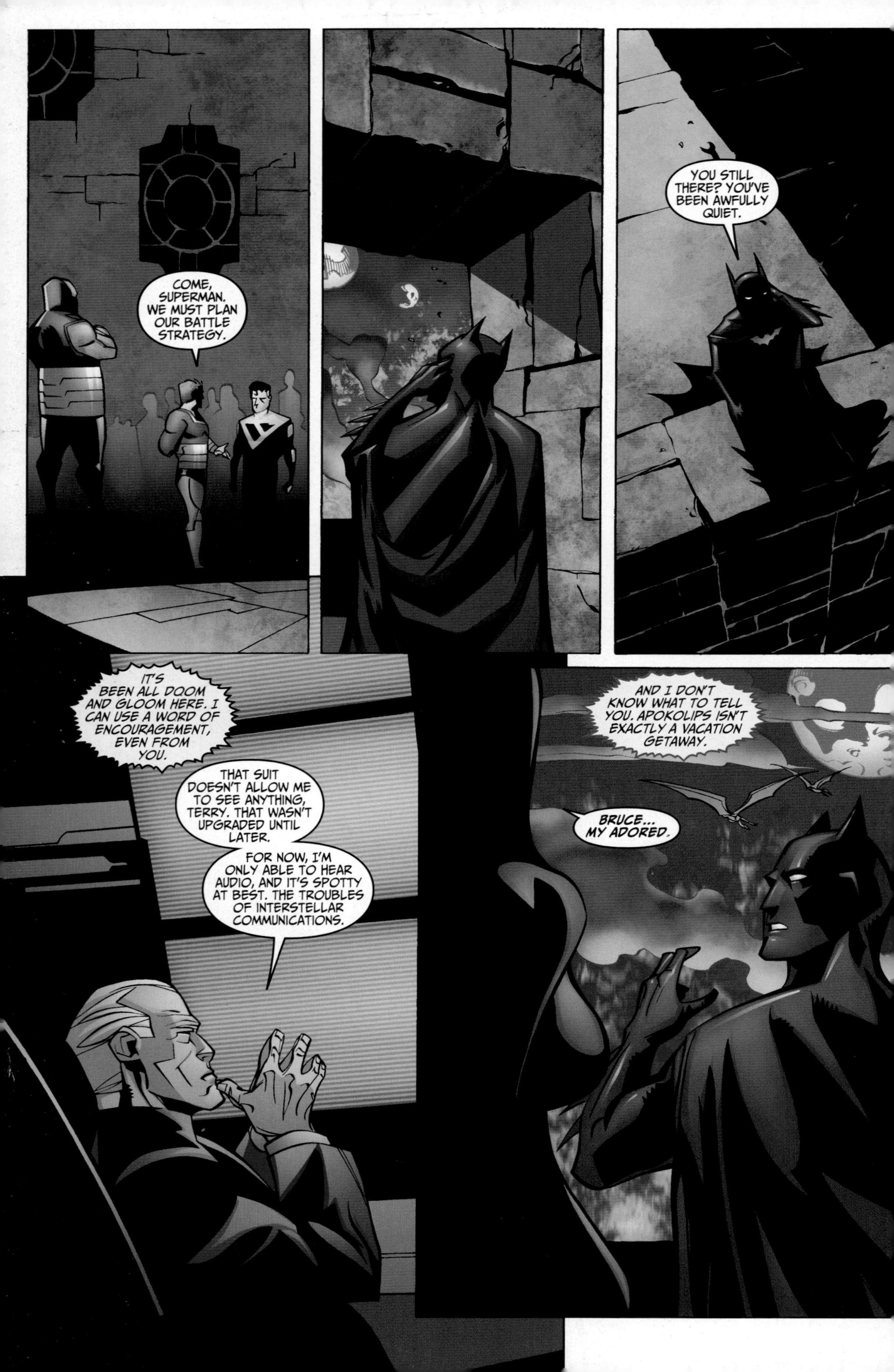
COME, SUPERMAN. WE MUST PLAN OUR BATTLE STRATEGY.
YOU STILL THERE? YOU'VE BEEN AWFULLY QUIET.
IT'S BEEN ALL DOOM AND GLOOM HERE. I CAN USE A WORD OF ENCOURAGEMENT, EVEN FROM YOU.
THAT SUIT DOESN'T ALLOW ME TO SEE ANYTHING, TERRY. THAT WASN'T UPGRADED UNTIL LATER.
FOR NOW, I'M ONLY ABLE TO HEAR AUDIO, AND IT'S SPOTTY AT BEST. THE TROUBLES OF INTERSTELLAR COMMUNICATIONS.
AND I DON'T KNOW WHAT TO TELL YOU. APOKOLIPS ISN'T EXACTLY A VACATION GETAWAY.
BRUCE... MY ADORED.

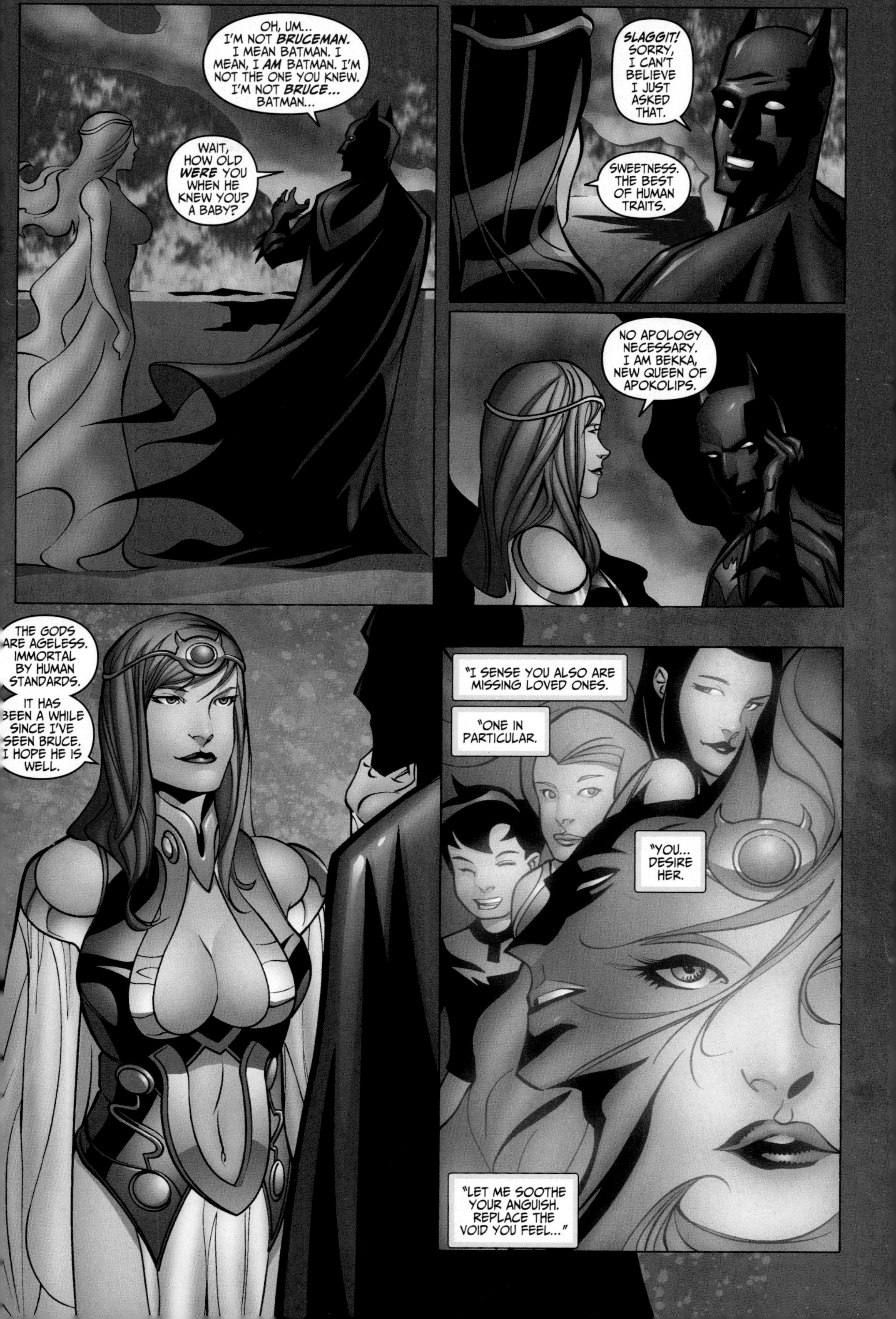

OH, UM... I'M NOT **BRUCEMAN.** I MEAN BATMAN. I MEAN, I ***AM*** BATMAN. I'M NOT THE ONE YOU KNEW. I'M NOT ***BRUCE...*** BATMAN...
WAIT, HOW OLD ***WERE*** YOU WHEN HE KNEW YOU? A BABY?
SLAGGIT! SORRY, I CAN'T BELIEVE I JUST ASKED THAT.
SWEETNESS. THE BEST OF HUMAN TRAITS.
NO APOLOGY NECESSARY. I AM BEKKA, NEW QUEEN OF APOKOLIPS.
THE GODS ARE AGELESS. IMMORTAL BY HUMAN STANDARDS.
IT HAS BEEN A WHILE SINCE I'VE SEEN BRUCE. I HOPE HE IS WELL.
"I SENSE YOU ALSO ARE MISSING LOVED ONES.
"ONE IN PARTICULAR.
"YOU... DESIRE HER.
"LET ME SOOTHE YOUR ANGUISH. REPLACE THE VOID YOU FEEL..."

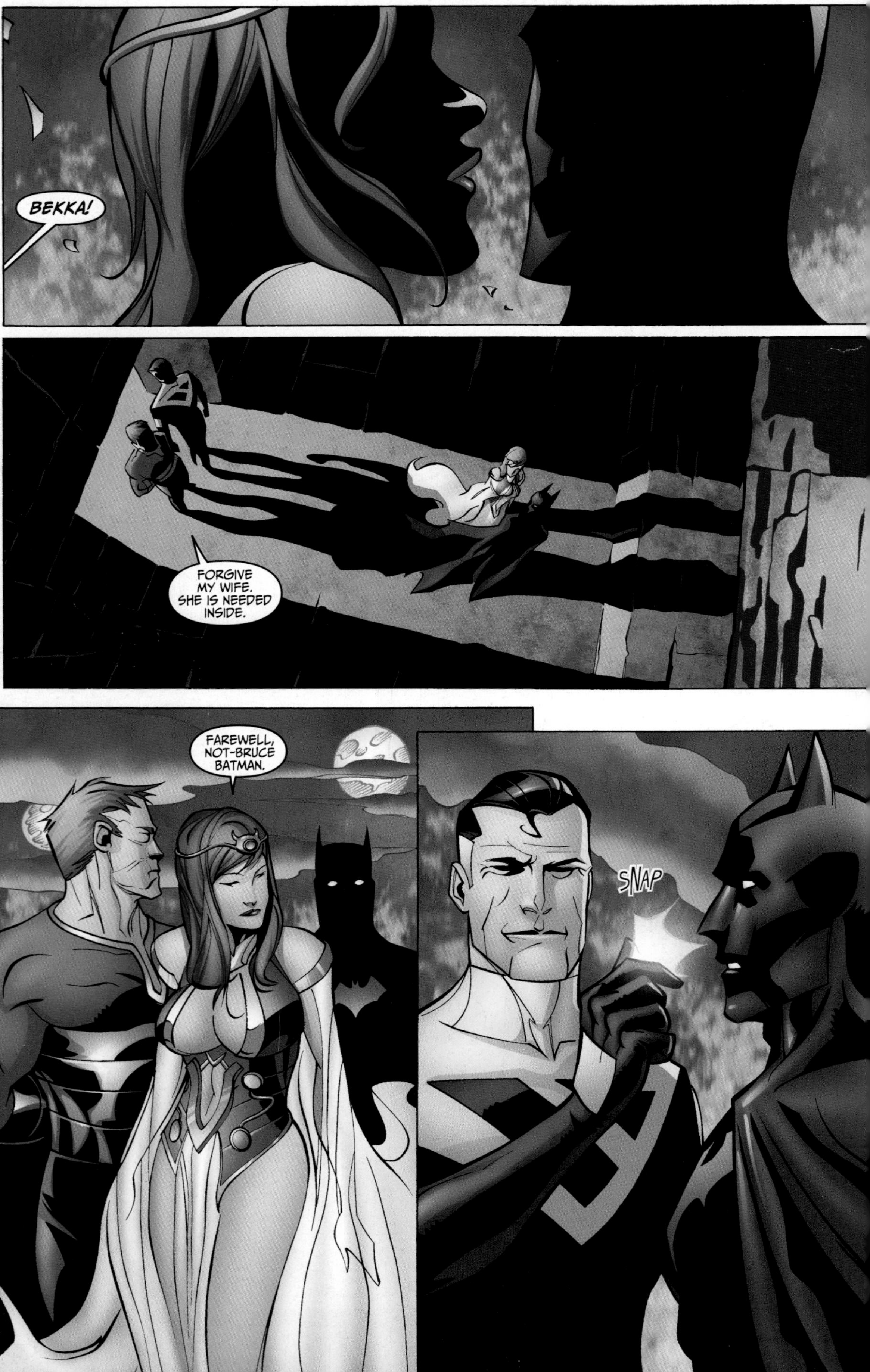
BEKKA!
FORGIVE MY WIFE. SHE IS NEEDED INSIDE.
FAREWELL, NOT-BRUCE BATMAN.
SNAP

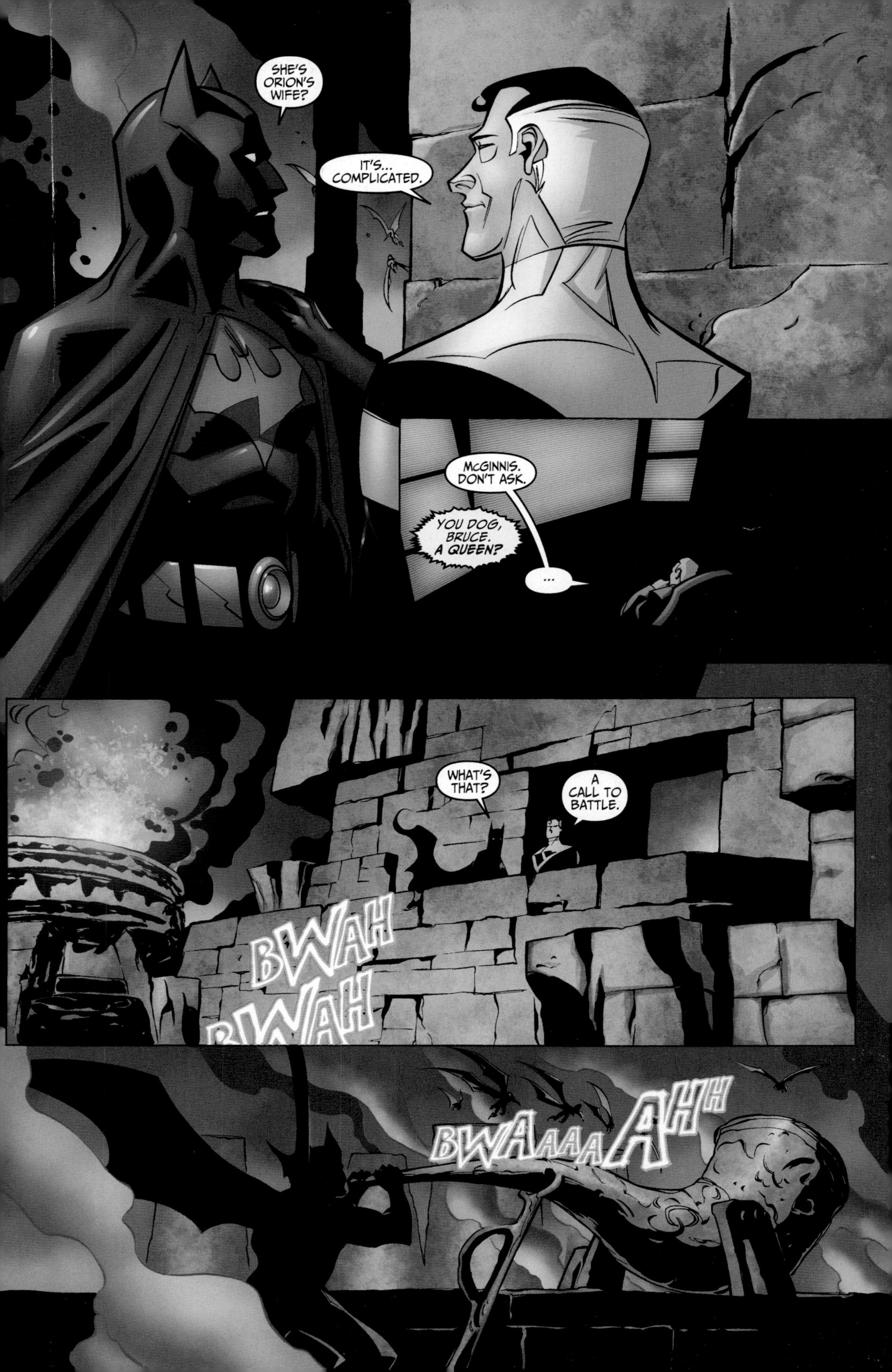
SHE'S ORION'S WIFE?
IT'S... COMPLICATED.
McGINNIS. DON'T ASK.
YOU DOG, BRUCE. A QUEEN?
...
WHAT'S THAT?
A CALL TO BATTLE.
BWAH
BWAH
BWAAAAAHH

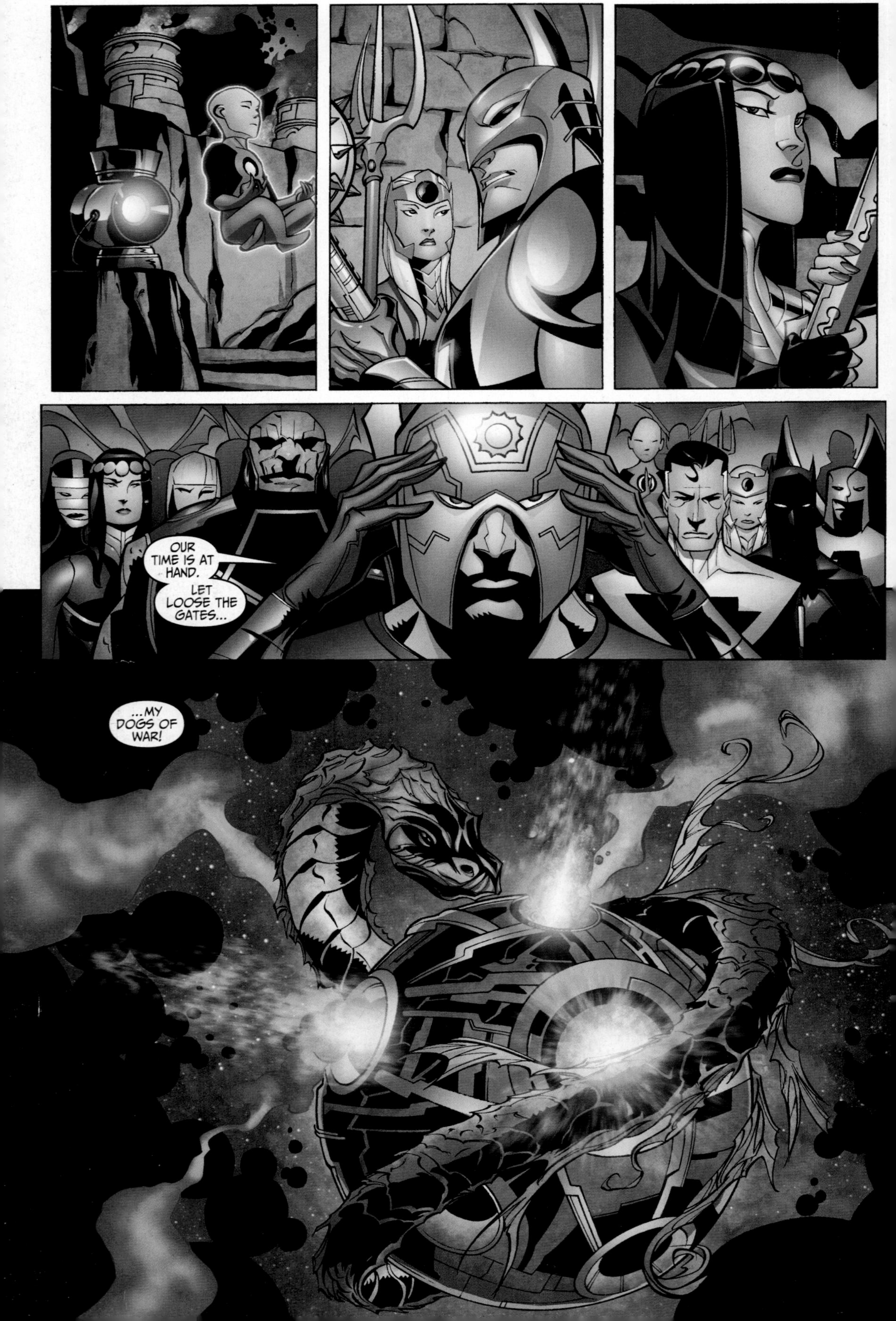
OUR TIME IS AT HAND.
LET LOOSE THE GATES...
...MY DOGS OF WAR!

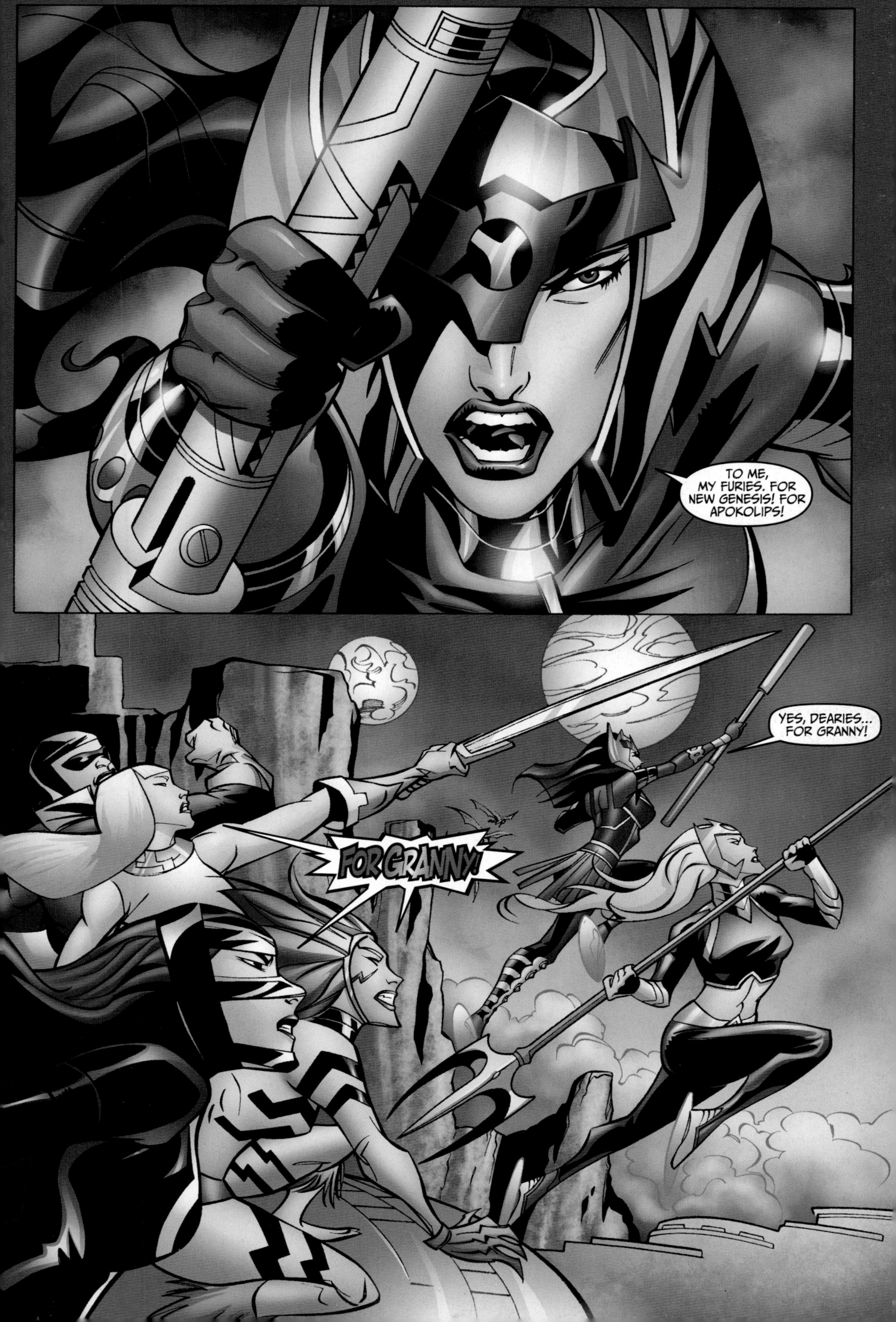
TO ME, MY FURIES. FOR NEW GENESIS! FOR APOKOLIPS!
YES, DEARIES... FOR GRANNY!
FOR GRANNY!

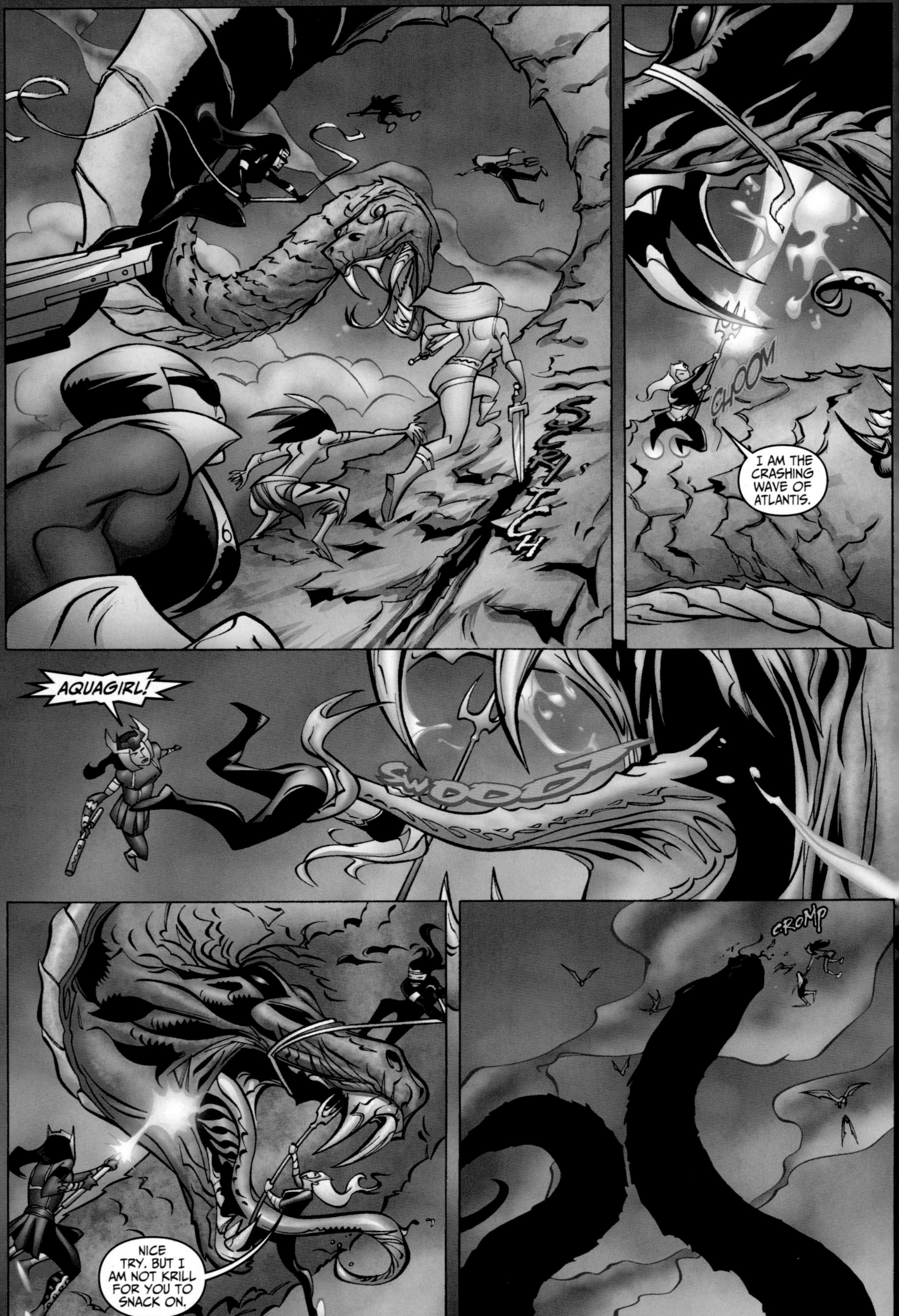
SCHLITCH
CHOOM
I AM THE CRASHING WAVE OF ATLANTIS.
AQUAGIRL!
SWOOOO
NICE TRY. BUT I AM NOT KRILL FOR YOU TO SNACK ON.
CROMP

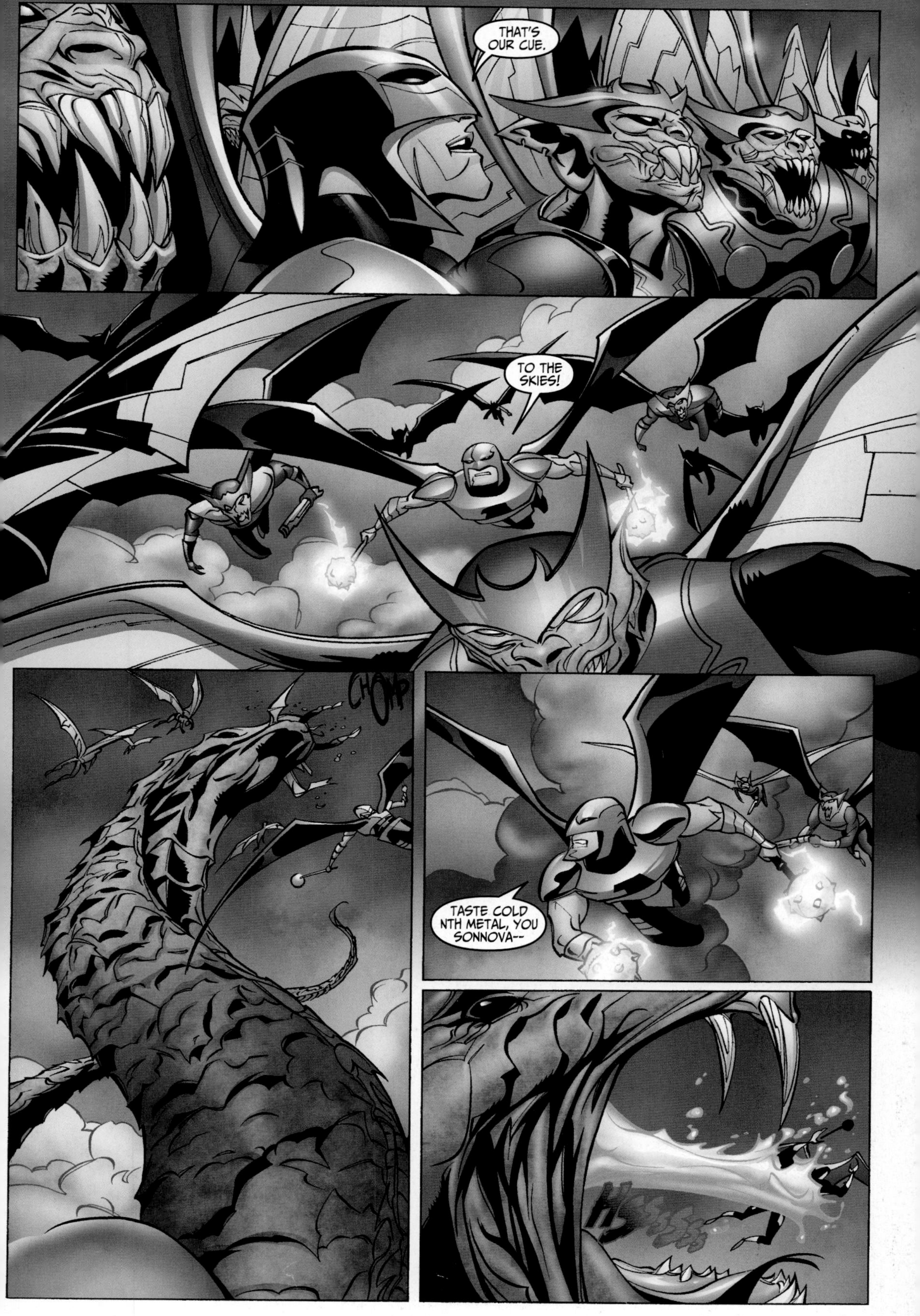
THAT'S OUR CUE.
TO THE SKIES!
CHOMP
TASTE COLD NTH METAL, YOU SONNOVA--

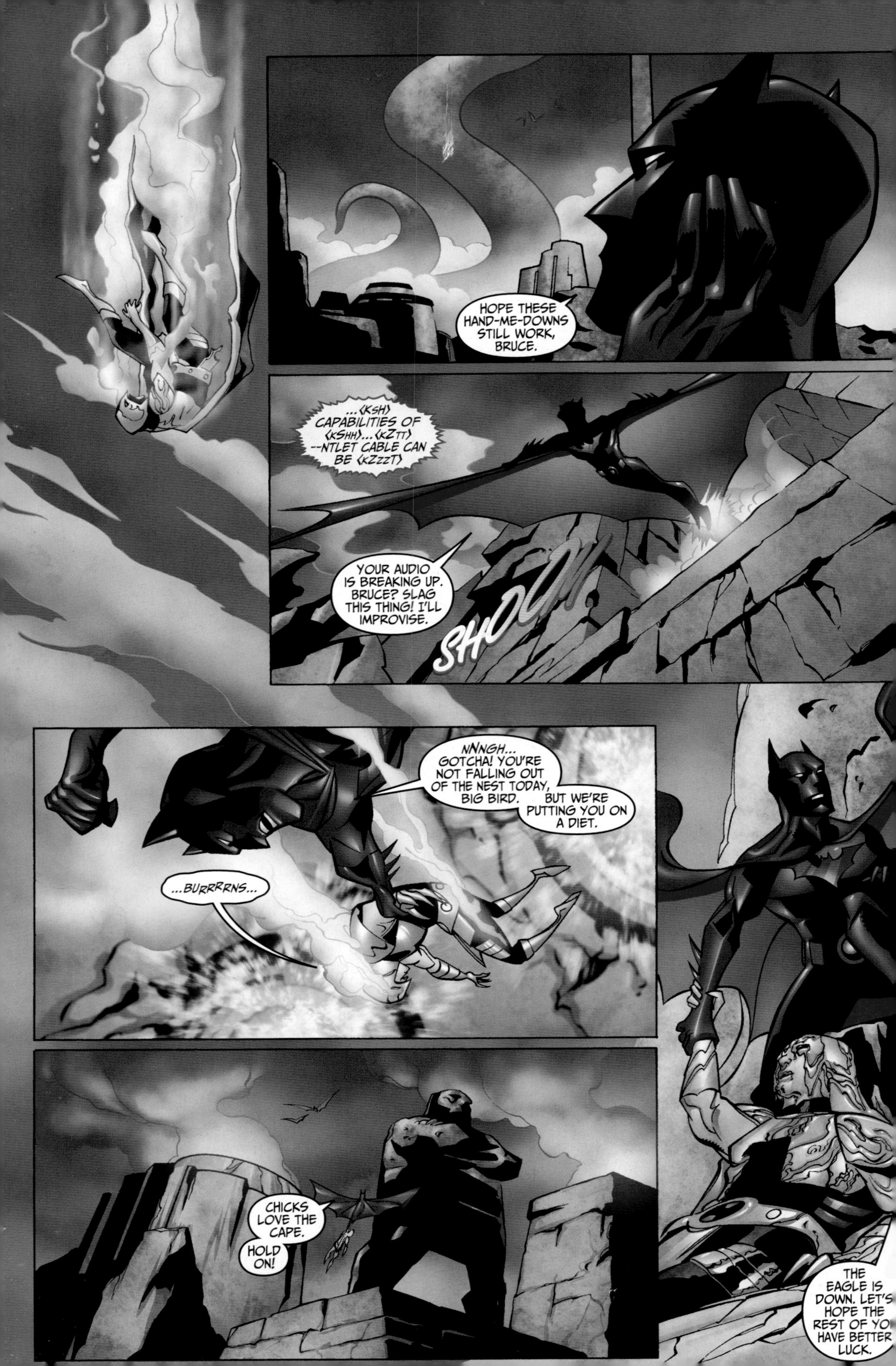
HOPE THESE HAND-ME-DOWNS STILL WORK, BRUCE.
...⟨KSH⟩ CAPABILITIES OF ⟨KSHH⟩...⟨KZTT⟩ --NTLET CABLE CAN BE ⟨KZZZT⟩
YOUR AUDIO IS BREAKING UP. BRUCE? SLAG THIS THING! I'LL IMPROVISE.
SHOOM
NNNGH... GOTCHA! YOU'RE NOT FALLING OUT OF THE NEST TODAY, BIG BIRD.
BUT WE'RE PUTTING YOU ON A DIET.
...BURRRRNS...
CHICKS LOVE THE CAPE.
HOLD ON!
THE EAGLE IS DOWN. LET'S HOPE THE REST OF YO HAVE BETTER LUCK.

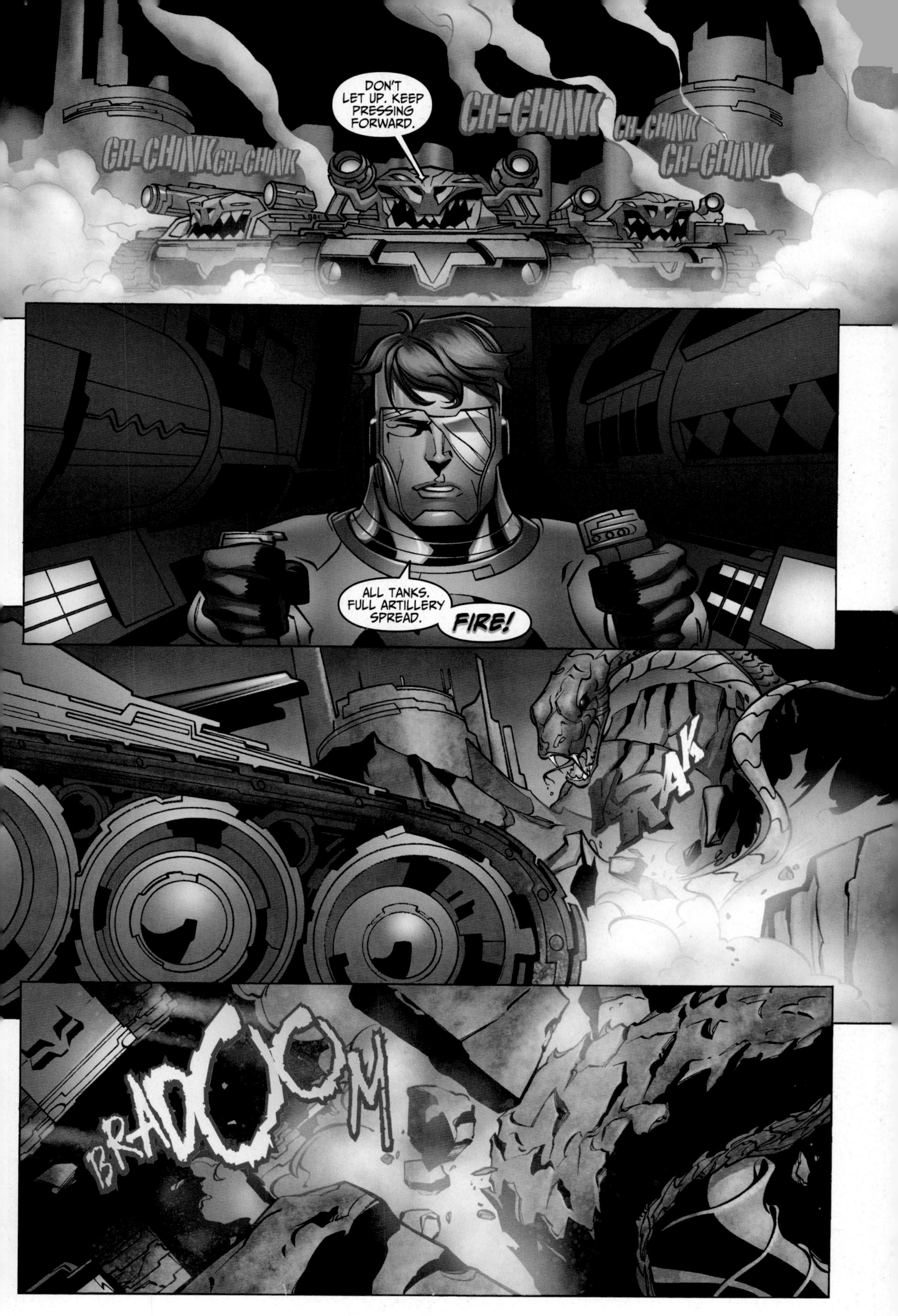
DON'T LET UP. KEEP PRESSING FORWARD.
CH-CHINK
CH-CHINK
CH-CHINK
CH-CHINK
CH-CHINK
ALL TANKS. FULL ARTILLERY SPREAD.
FIRE!
KRAK
BRADOOM

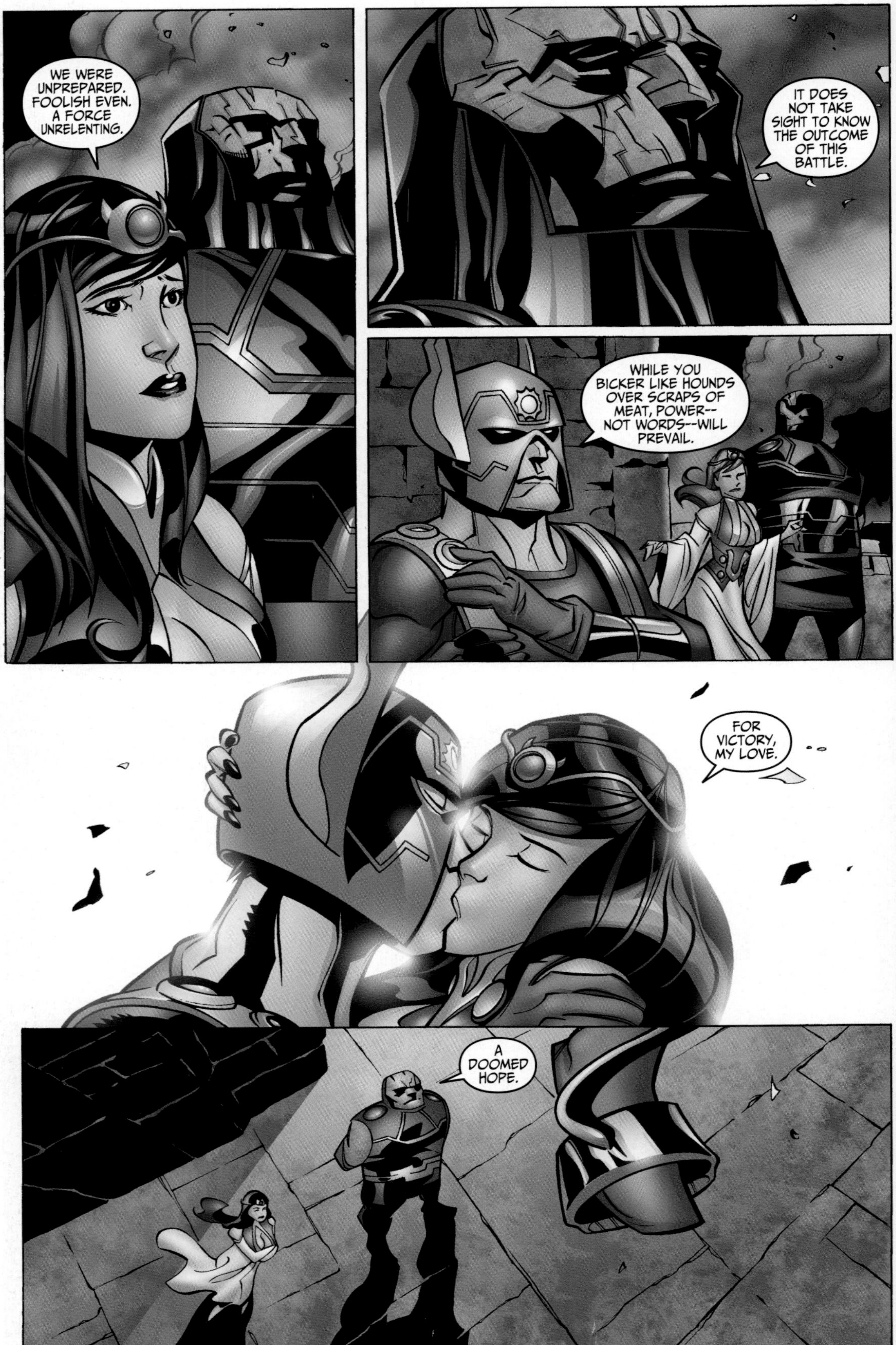
WE WERE UNPREPARED. FOOLISH EVEN. A FORCE UNRELENTING.
IT DOES NOT TAKE SIGHT TO KNOW THE OUTCOME OF THIS BATTLE.
WHILE YOU BICKER LIKE HOUNDS OVER SCRAPS OF MEAT, POWER-- NOT WORDS--WILL PREVAIL.
FOR VICTORY, MY LOVE.
A DOOMED HOPE.

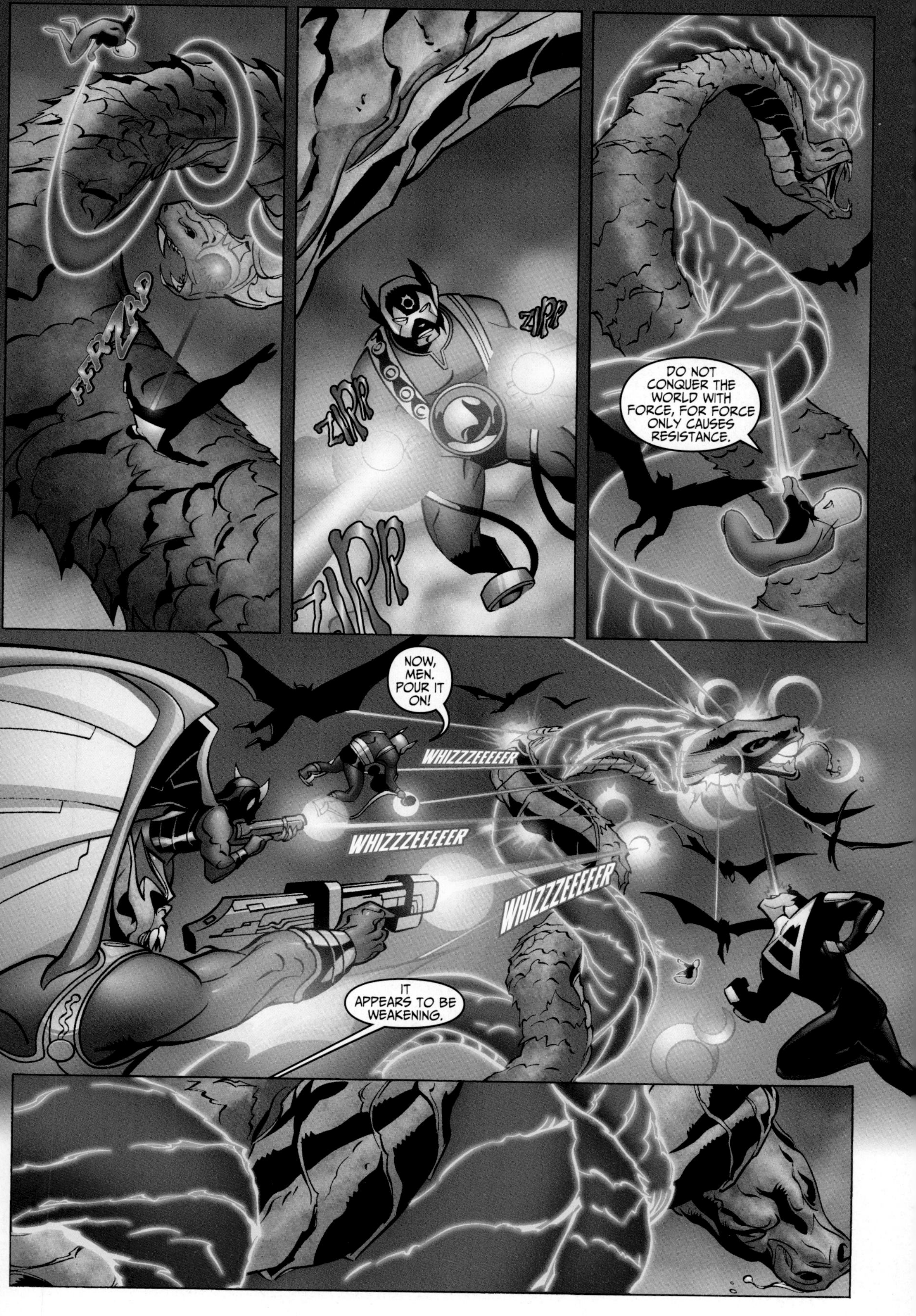

FFFRZAP
ZIPP
ZIPP
ZIPP
DO NOT CONQUER THE WORLD WITH FORCE, FOR FORCE ONLY CAUSES RESISTANCE.
NOW, MEN. POUR IT ON!
WHIZZZEEEEER
WHIZZZEEEEER
WHIZZZEEEEER
IT APPEARS TO BE WEAKENING.

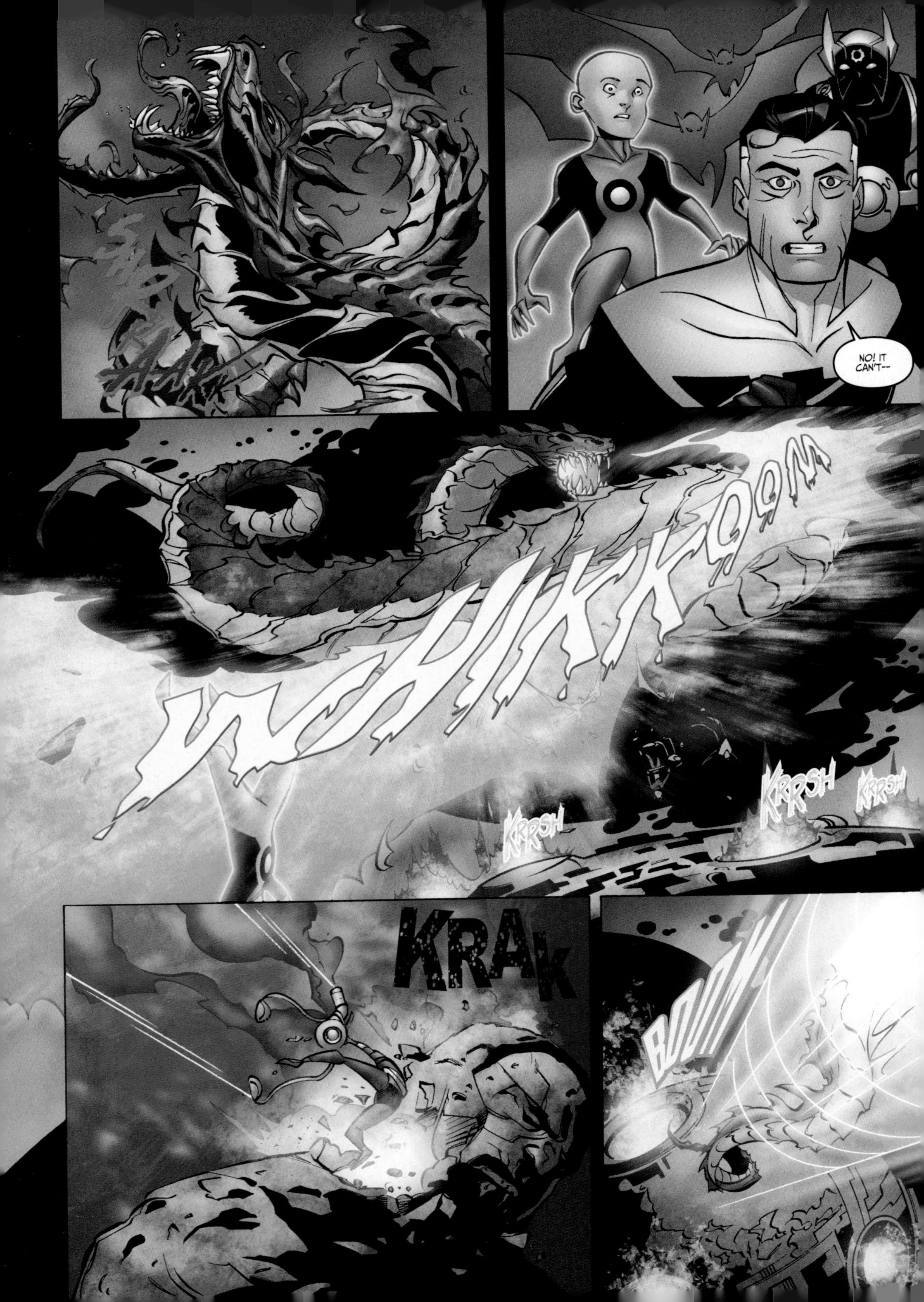
NO! IT CAN'T--
KRRSH
KRRSH
KRRSH
KRAK
BOOM

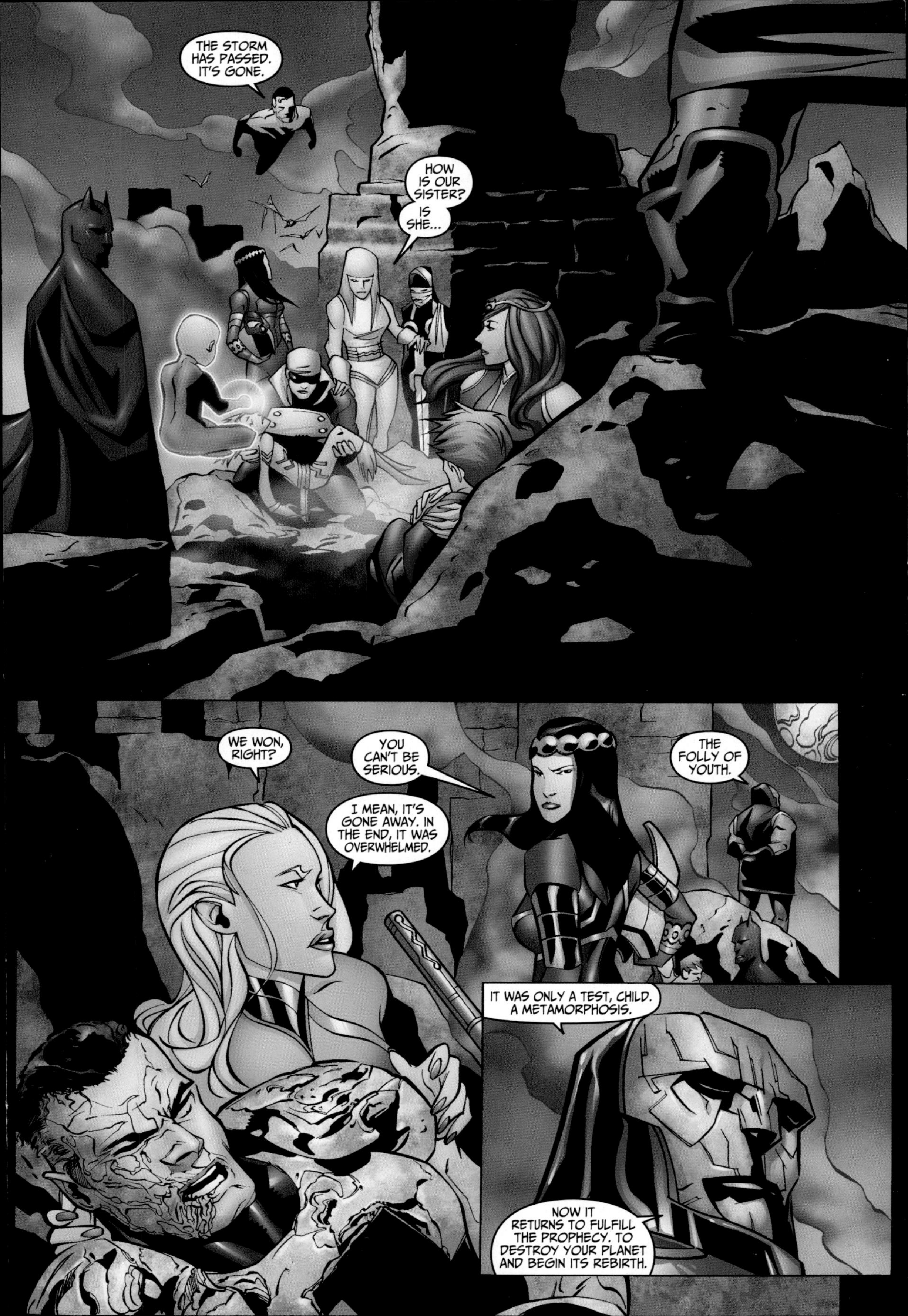
THE STORM HAS PASSED. IT'S GONE.
HOW IS OUR SISTER? IS SHE...
WE WON, RIGHT?
YOU CAN'T BE SERIOUS.
I MEAN, IT'S GONE AWAY. IN THE END, IT WAS OVERWHELMED.
THE FOLLY OF YOUTH.
IT WAS ONLY A TEST, CHILD. A METAMORPHOSIS.
NOW IT RETURNS TO FULFILL THE PROPHECY. TO DESTROY YOUR PLANET AND BEGIN ITS REBIRTH.

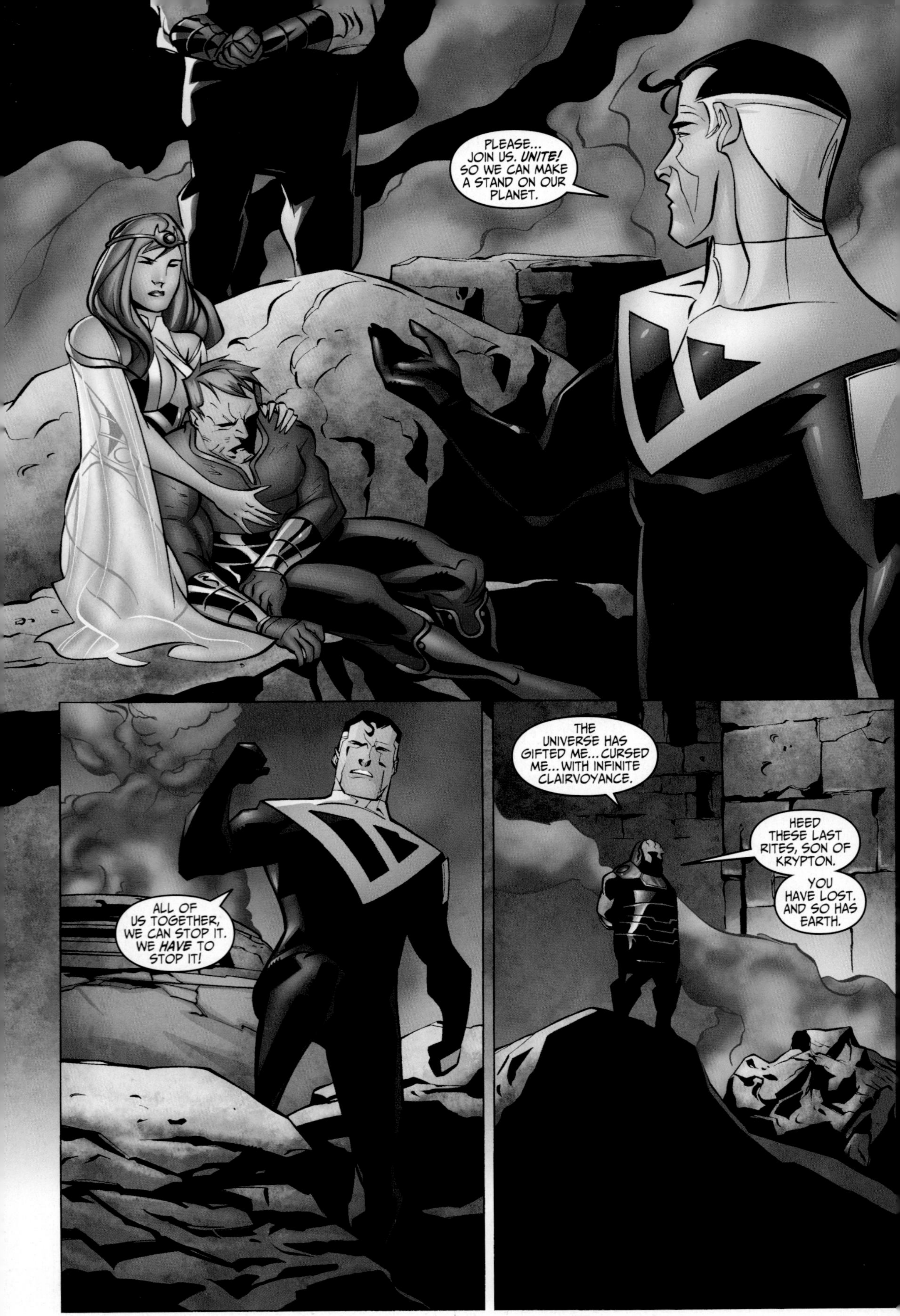
PLEASE... JOIN US. UNITE! SO WE CAN MAKE A STAND ON OUR PLANET.
ALL OF US TOGETHER, WE CAN STOP IT. WE HAVE TO STOP IT!
THE UNIVERSE HAS GIFTED ME...CURSED ME...WITH INFINITE CLAIRVOYANCE.
HEED THESE LAST RITES, SON OF KRYPTON.
YOU HAVE LOST. AND SO HAS EARTH.

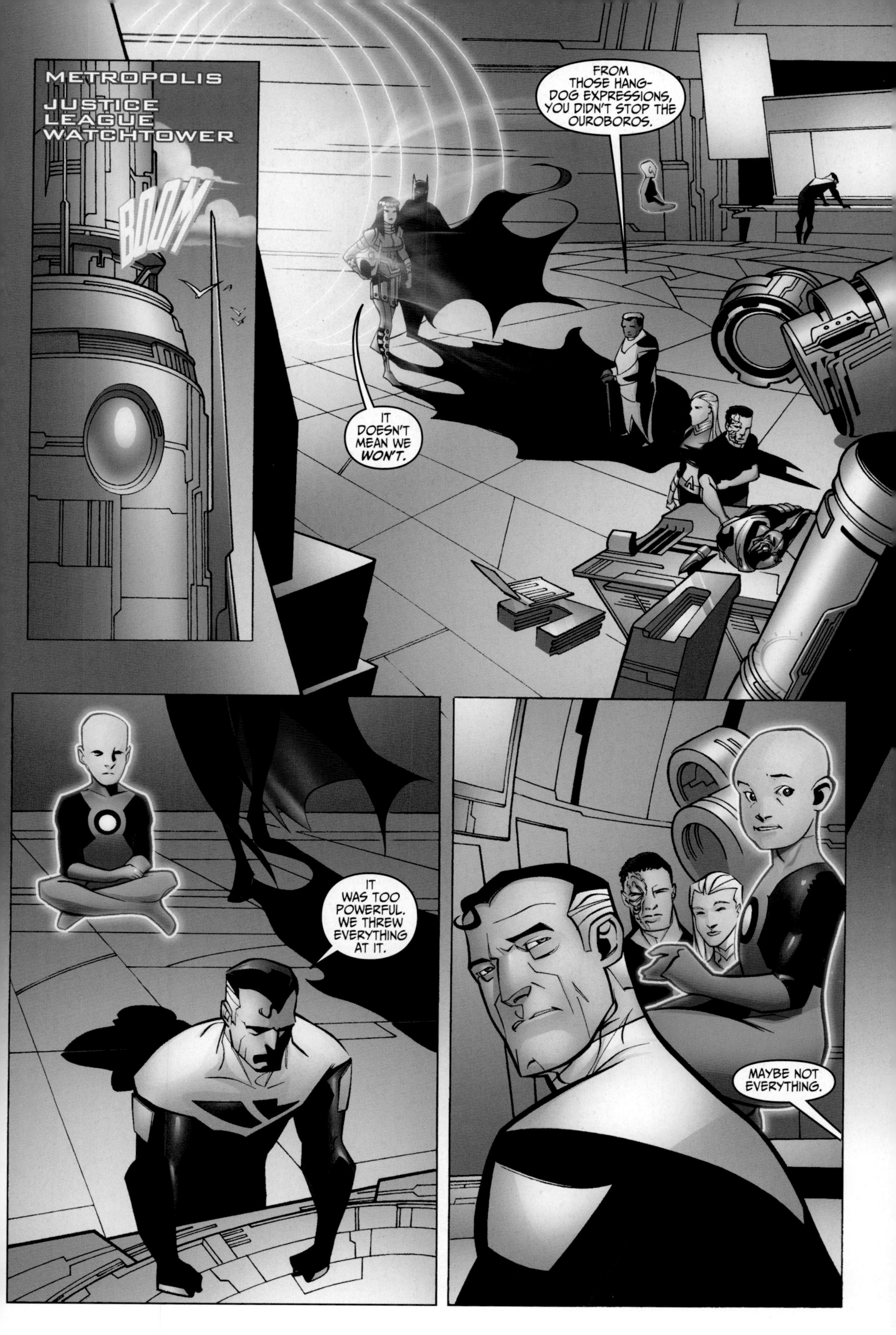
METROPOLIS
JUSTICE LEAGUE WATCHTOWER
BOOM
FROM THOSE HANG-DOG EXPRESSIONS, YOU DIDN'T STOP THE OUROBOROS.
IT DOESN'T MEAN WE *WON'T*.
IT WAS TOO POWERFUL. WE THREW EVERYTHING AT IT.
MAYBE NOT EVERYTHING.

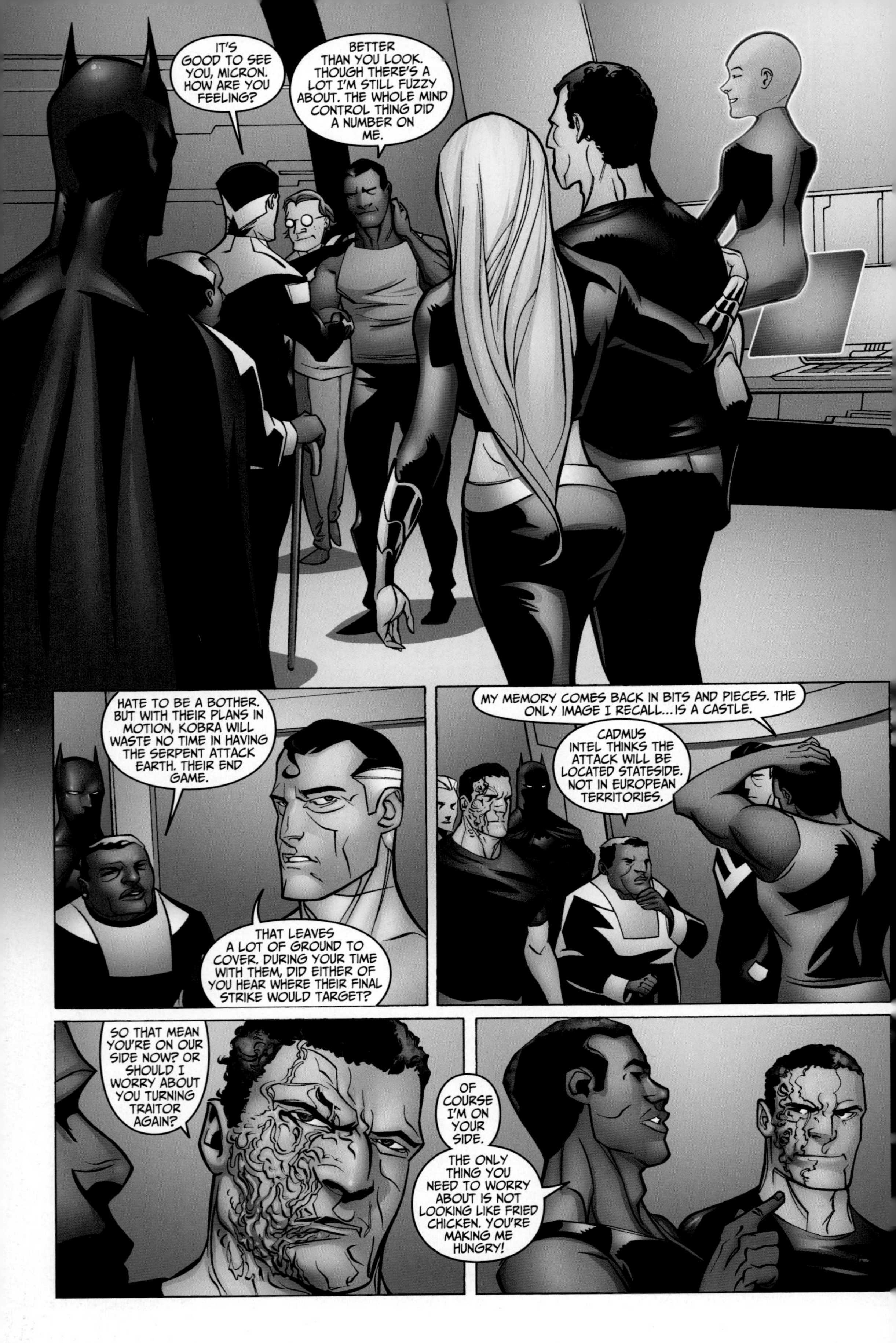
IT'S GOOD TO SEE YOU, MICRON. HOW ARE YOU FEELING?
BETTER THAN YOU LOOK. THOUGH THERE'S A LOT I'M STILL FUZZY ABOUT. THE WHOLE MIND CONTROL THING DID A NUMBER ON ME.
HATE TO BE A BOTHER. BUT WITH THEIR PLANS IN MOTION, KOBRA WILL WASTE NO TIME IN HAVING THE SERPENT ATTACK EARTH. THEIR END GAME.
THAT LEAVES A LOT OF GROUND TO COVER. DURING YOUR TIME WITH THEM, DID EITHER OF YOU HEAR WHERE THEIR FINAL STRIKE WOULD TARGET?
MY MEMORY COMES BACK IN BITS AND PIECES. THE ONLY IMAGE I RECALL... IS A CASTLE.
CADMUS INTEL THINKS THE ATTACK WILL BE LOCATED STATESIDE. NOT IN EUROPEAN TERRITORIES.
SO THAT MEAN YOU'RE ON OUR SIDE NOW? OR SHOULD I WORRY ABOUT YOU TURNING TRAITOR AGAIN?
OF COURSE I'M ON YOUR SIDE.
THE ONLY THING YOU NEED TO WORRY ABOUT IS NOT LOOKING LIKE FRIED CHICKEN. YOU'RE MAKING ME HUNGRY!

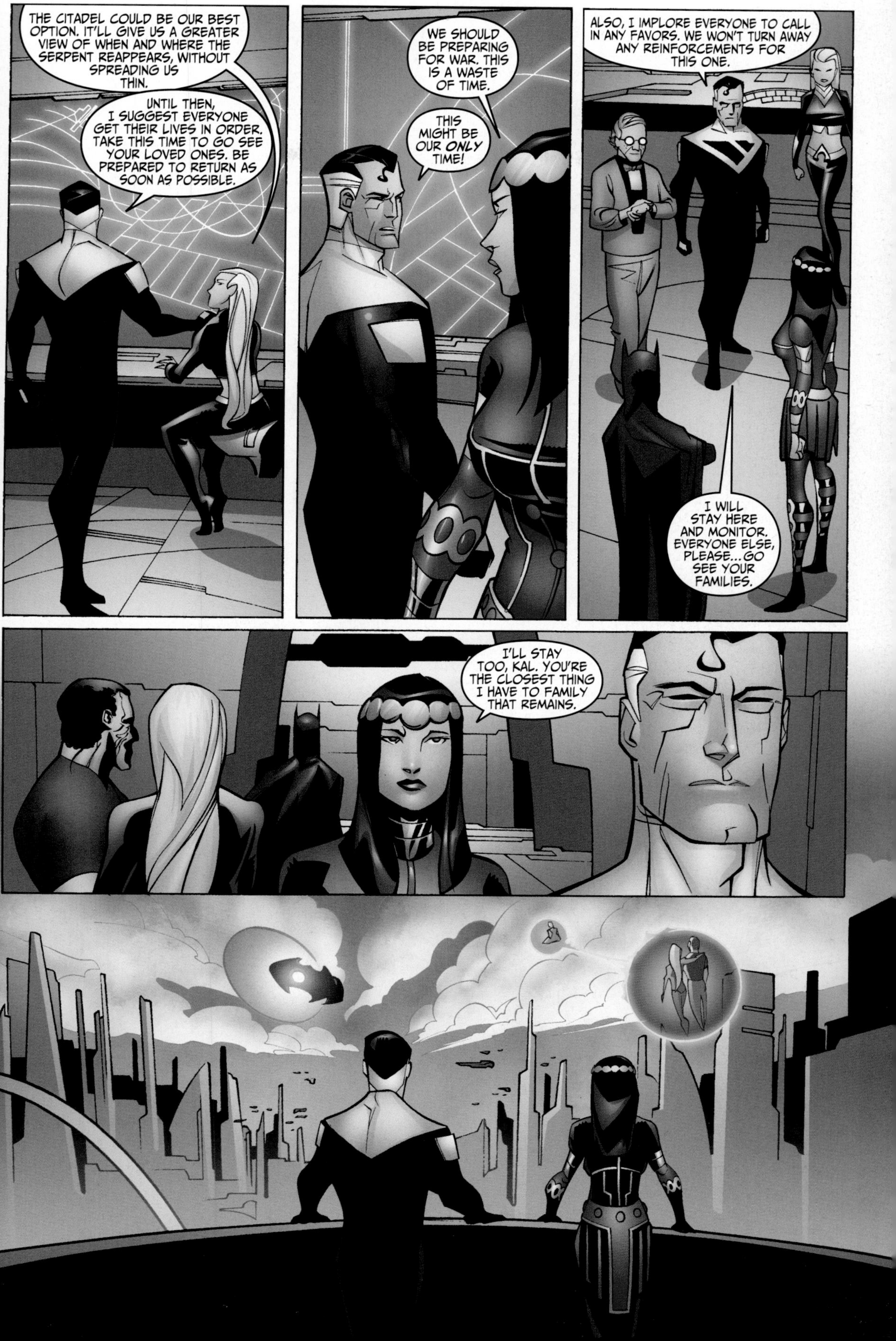
THE CITADEL COULD BE OUR BEST OPTION. IT'LL GIVE US A GREATER VIEW OF WHEN AND WHERE THE SERPENT REAPPEARS, WITHOUT SPREADING US THIN.
UNTIL THEN, I SUGGEST EVERYONE GET THEIR LIVES IN ORDER. TAKE THIS TIME TO GO SEE YOUR LOVED ONES. BE PREPARED TO RETURN AS SOON AS POSSIBLE.
WE SHOULD BE PREPARING FOR WAR. THIS IS A WASTE OF TIME.
THIS MIGHT BE OUR *ONLY* TIME!
ALSO, I IMPLORE EVERYONE TO CALL IN ANY FAVORS. WE WON'T TURN AWAY ANY REINFORCEMENTS FOR THIS ONE.
I WILL STAY HERE AND MONITOR. EVERYONE ELSE, PLEASE...GO SEE YOUR FAMILIES.
I'LL STAY TOO, KAL. YOU'RE THE CLOSEST THING I HAVE TO FAMILY THAT REMAINS.

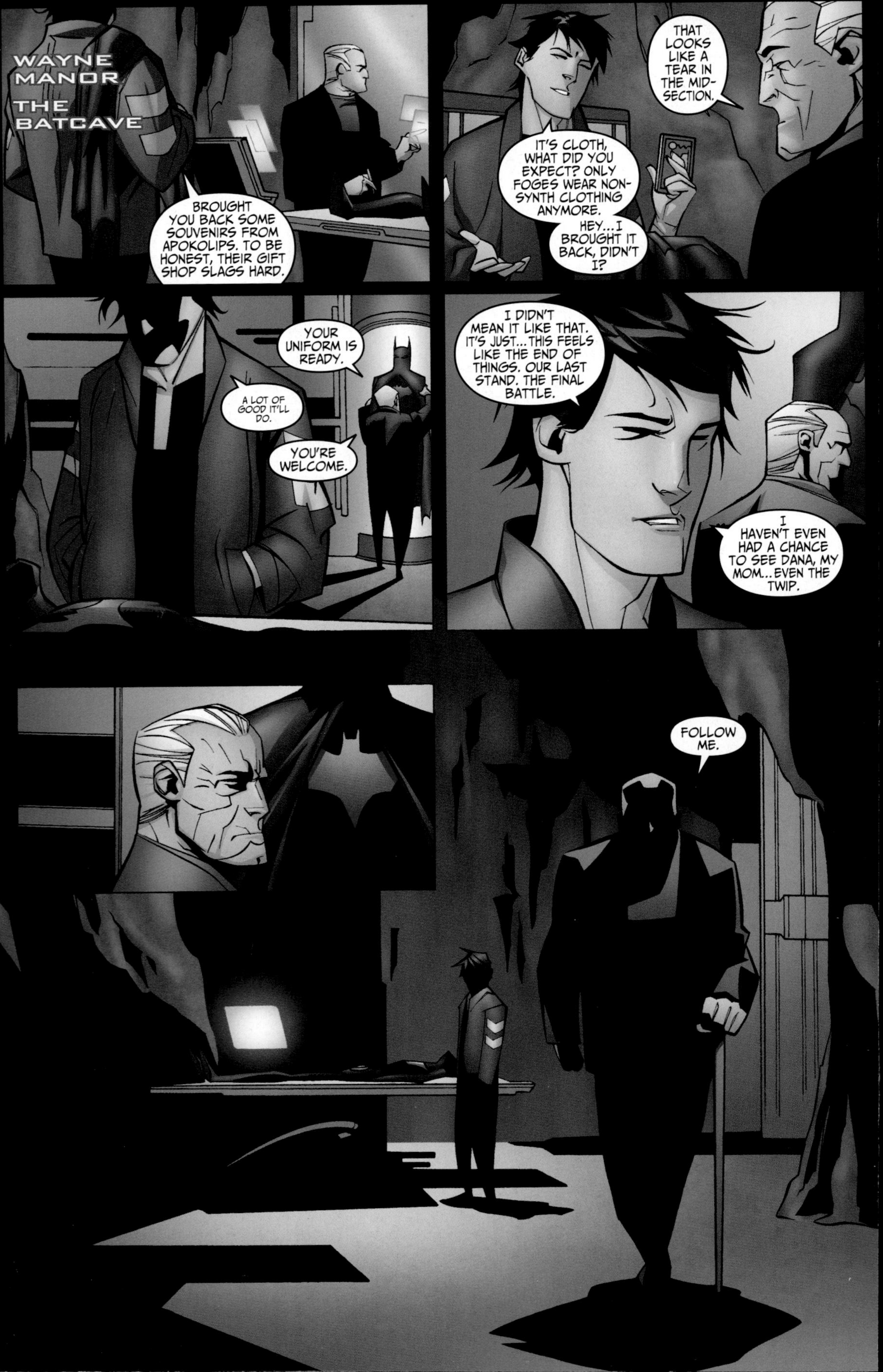
WAYNE MANOR
THE BATCAVE
BROUGHT YOU BACK SOME SOUVENIRS FROM APOKOLIPS. TO BE HONEST, THEIR GIFT SHOP SLAGS HARD.
THAT LOOKS LIKE A TEAR IN THE MID-SECTION.
IT'S CLOTH, WHAT DID YOU EXPECT? ONLY FOGES WEAR NON-SYNTH CLOTHING ANYMORE.
HEY... I BROUGHT IT BACK, DIDN'T I?
YOUR UNIFORM IS READY.
A LOT OF GOOD IT'LL DO.
YOU'RE WELCOME.
I DIDN'T MEAN IT LIKE THAT. IT'S JUST... THIS FEELS LIKE THE END OF THINGS. OUR LAST STAND. THE FINAL BATTLE.
I HAVEN'T EVEN HAD A CHANCE TO SEE DANA, MY MOM... EVEN THE TWIP.
FOLLOW ME.

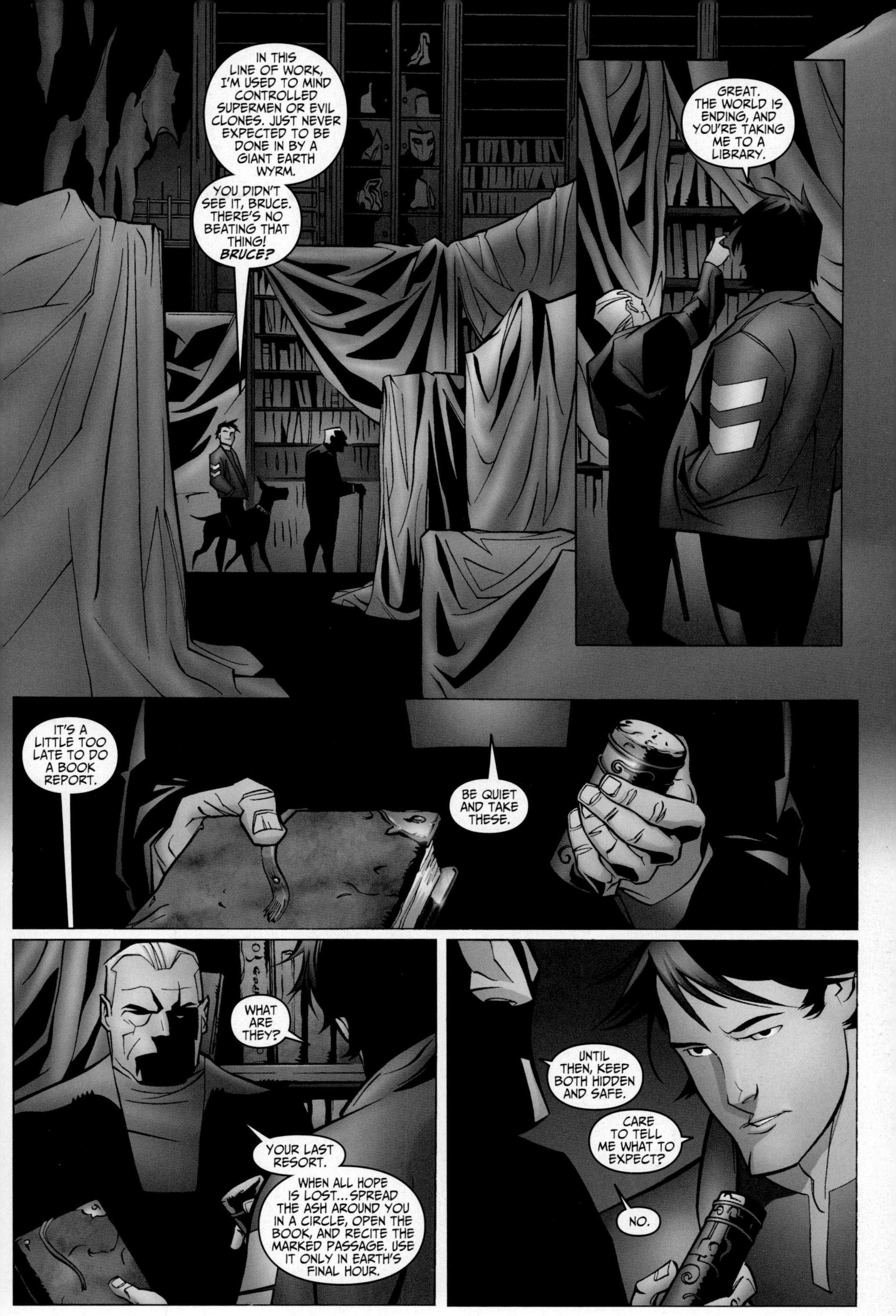
IN THIS LINE OF WORK, I'M USED TO MIND CONTROLLED SUPERMEN OR EVIL CLONES. JUST NEVER EXPECTED TO BE DONE IN BY A GIANT EARTH WYRM.
YOU DIDN'T SEE IT, BRUCE. THERE'S NO BEATING THAT THING! BRUCE?
GREAT. THE WORLD IS ENDING, AND YOU'RE TAKING ME TO A LIBRARY.
IT'S A LITTLE TOO LATE TO DO A BOOK REPORT.
BE QUIET AND TAKE THESE.
WHAT ARE THEY?
YOUR LAST RESORT.
WHEN ALL HOPE IS LOST... SPREAD THE ASH AROUND YOU IN A CIRCLE, OPEN THE BOOK, AND RECITE THE MARKED PASSAGE. USE IT ONLY IN EARTH'S FINAL HOUR.
UNTIL THEN, KEEP BOTH HIDDEN AND SAFE.
CARE TO TELL ME WHAT TO EXPECT?
NO.

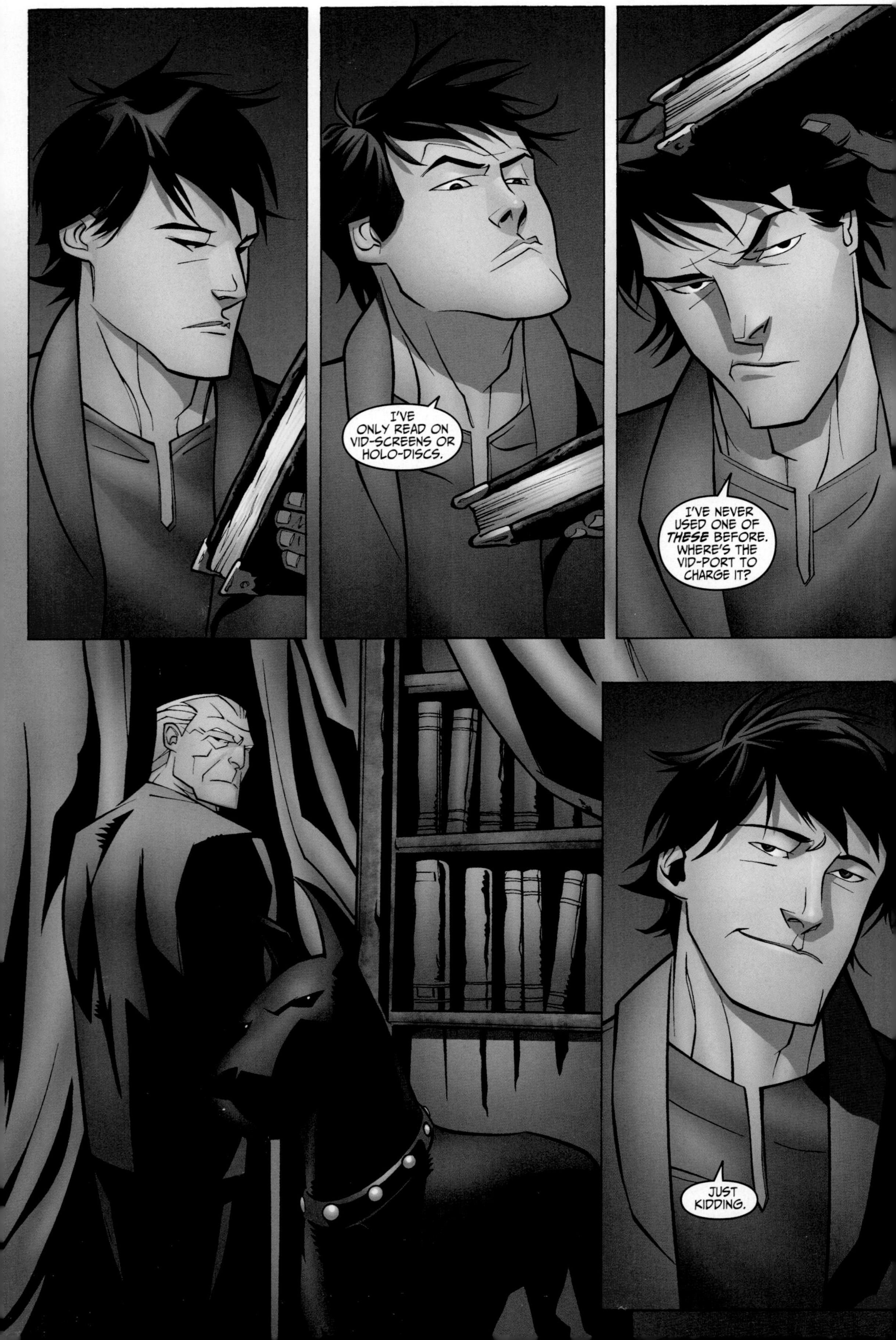
I'VE ONLY READ ON VID-SCREENS OR HOLO-DISCS.
I'VE NEVER USED ONE OF *THESE* BEFORE. WHERE'S THE VID-PORT TO CHARGE IT?
JUST KIDDING.

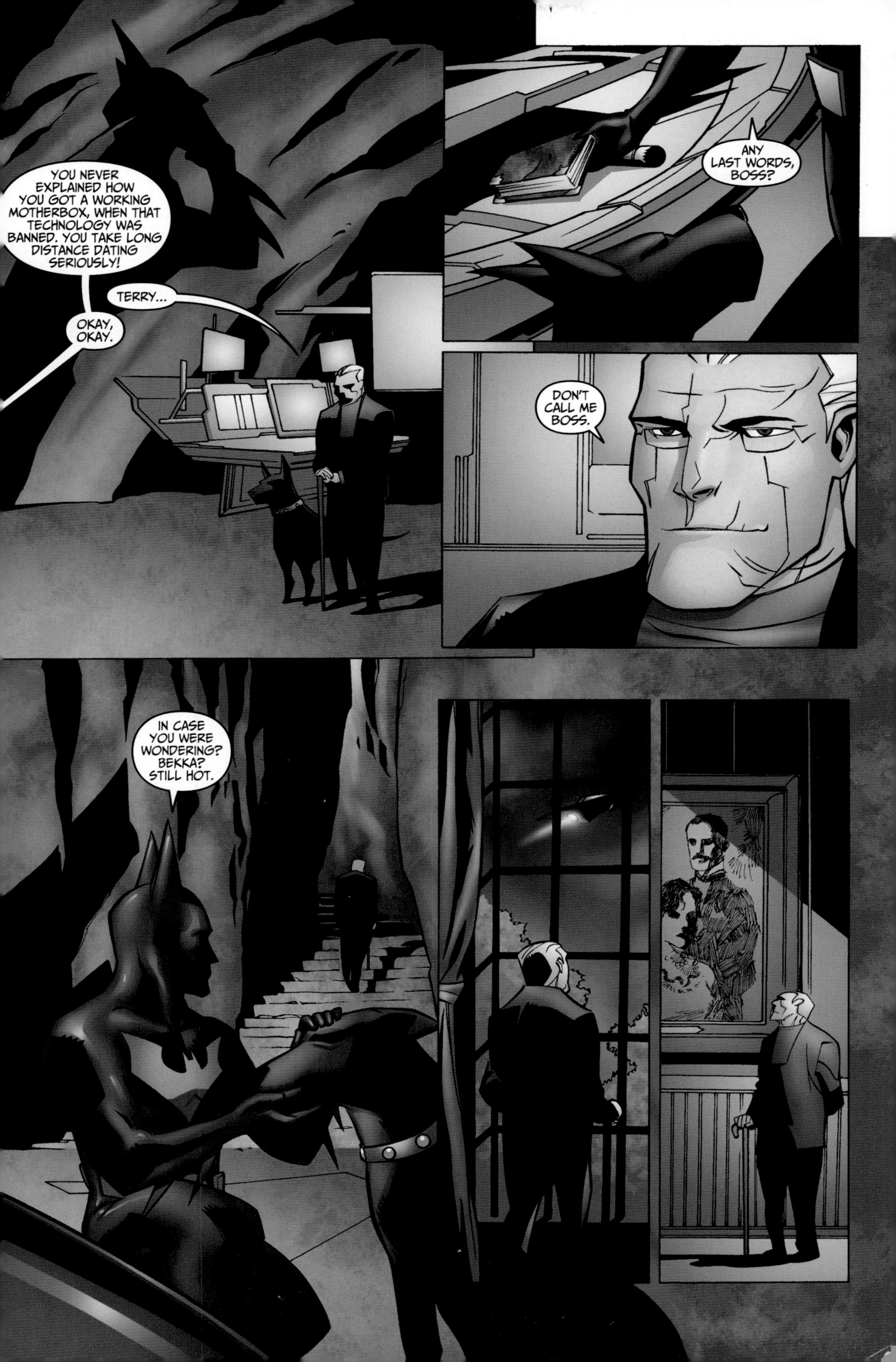
YOU NEVER EXPLAINED HOW YOU GOT A WORKING MOTHERBOX, WHEN THAT TECHNOLOGY WAS BANNED. YOU TAKE LONG DISTANCE DATING SERIOUSLY!
TERRY...
OKAY, OKAY.
ANY LAST WORDS, BOSS?
DON'T CALL ME BOSS.
IN CASE YOU WERE WONDERING? BEKKA? STILL HOT.

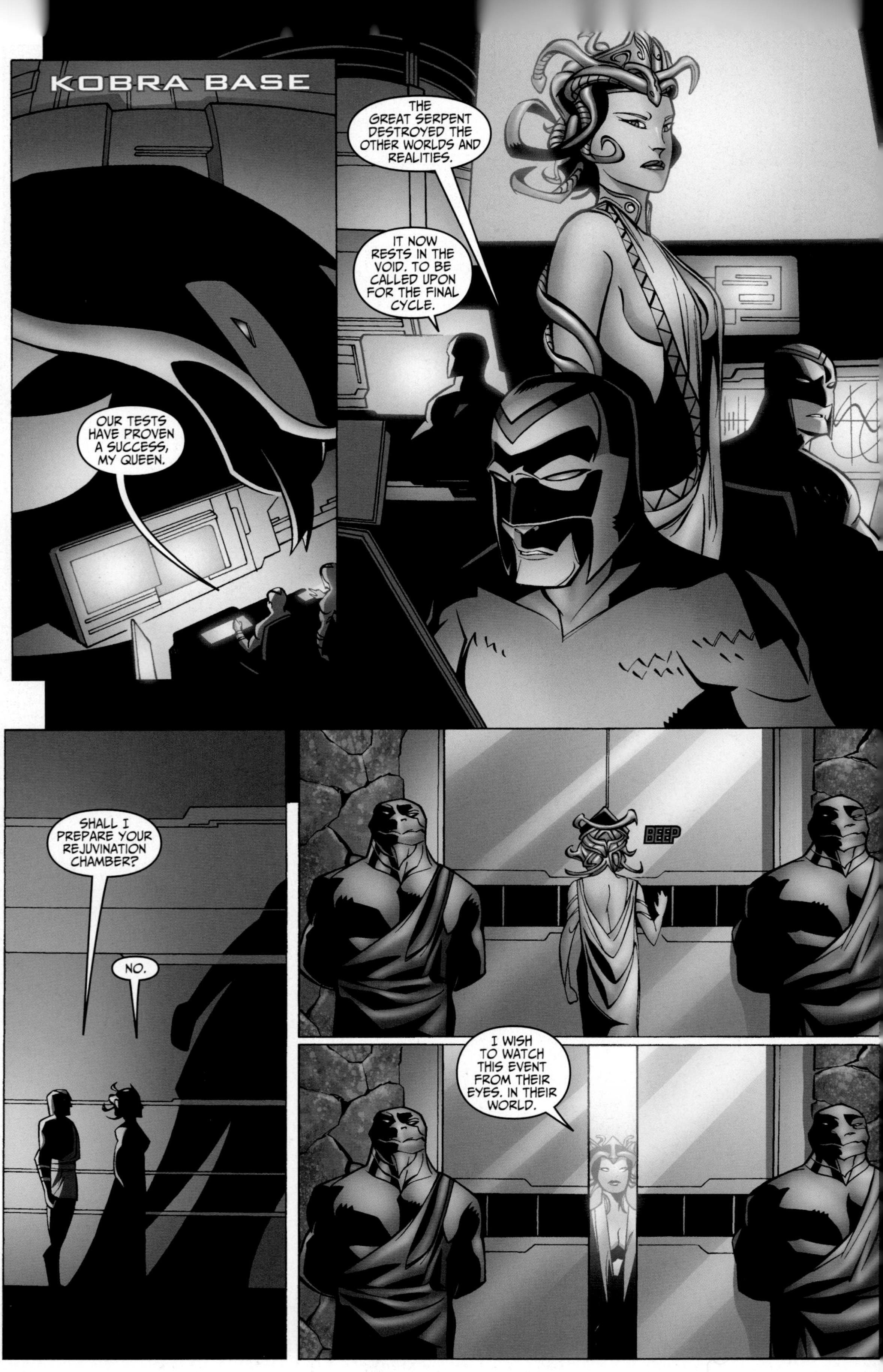
KOBRA BASE
OUR TESTS HAVE PROVEN A SUCCESS, MY QUEEN.
THE GREAT SERPENT DESTROYED THE OTHER WORLDS AND REALITIES.
IT NOW RESTS IN THE VOID. TO BE CALLED UPON FOR THE FINAL CYCLE.
SHALL I PREPARE YOUR REJUVINATION CHAMBER?
NO.
BEEP
I WISH TO WATCH THIS EVENT FROM THEIR EYES. IN THEIR WORLD.

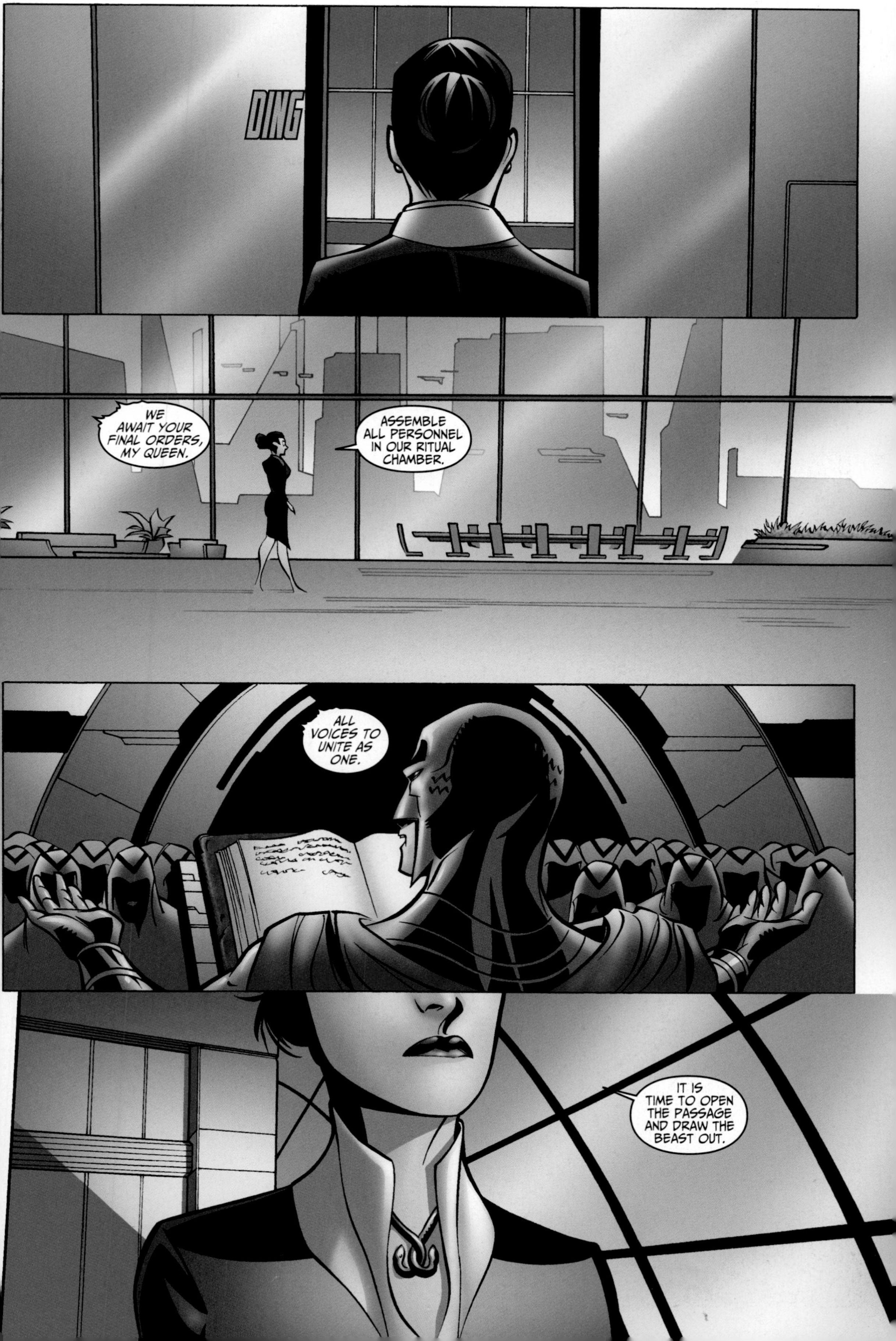
DING
WE AWAIT YOUR FINAL ORDERS, MY QUEEN.
ASSEMBLE ALL PERSONNEL IN OUR RITUAL CHAMBER.
ALL VOICES TO UNITE AS ONE.
IT IS TIME TO OPEN THE PASSAGE AND DRAW THE BEAST OUT.

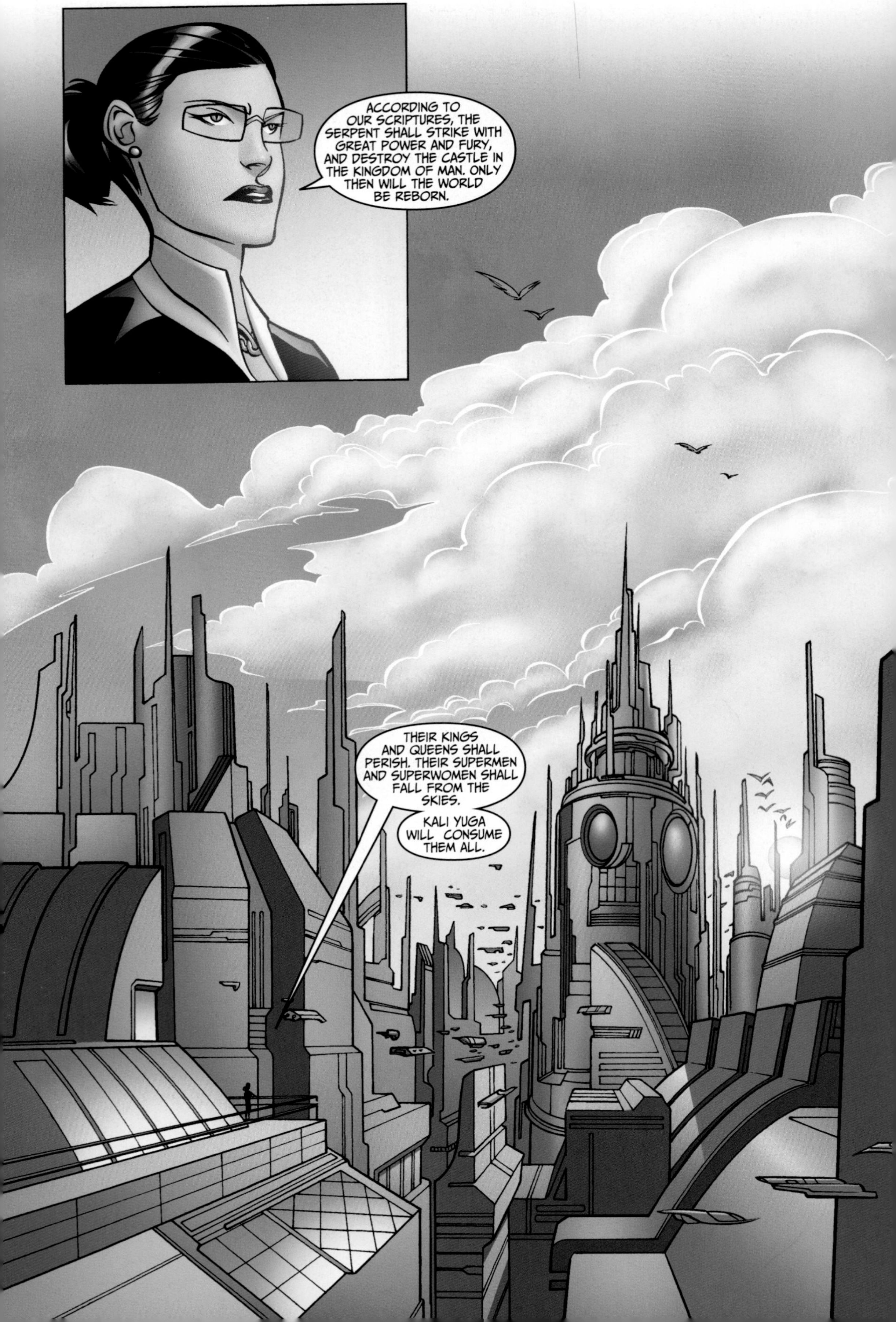
ACCORDING TO OUR SCRIPTURES, THE SERPENT SHALL STRIKE WITH GREAT POWER AND FURY, AND DESTROY THE CASTLE IN THE KINGDOM OF MAN. ONLY THEN WILL THE WORLD BE REBORN.
THEIR KINGS AND QUEENS SHALL PERISH. THEIR SUPERMEN AND SUPERWOMEN SHALL FALL FROM THE SKIES.
KALI YUGA WILL CONSUME THEM ALL.

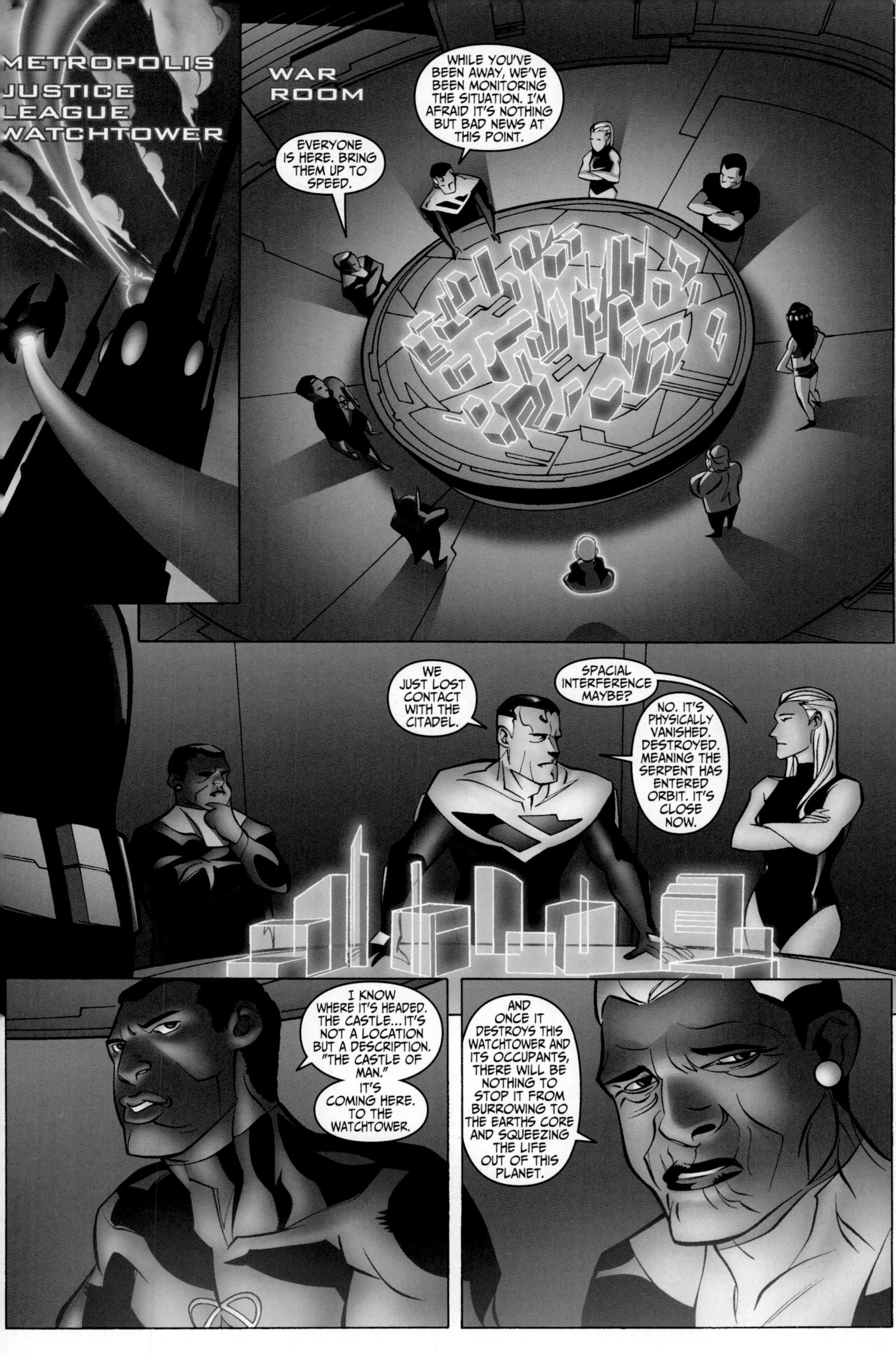
METROPOLIS
JUSTICE LEAGUE WATCHTOWER
WAR ROOM
WHILE YOU'VE BEEN AWAY, WE'VE BEEN MONITORING THE SITUATION. I'M AFRAID IT'S NOTHING BUT BAD NEWS AT THIS POINT.
EVERYONE IS HERE. BRING THEM UP TO SPEED.
WE JUST LOST CONTACT WITH THE CITADEL.
SPACIAL INTERFERENCE MAYBE?
NO. IT'S PHYSICALLY VANISHED. DESTROYED. MEANING THE SERPENT HAS ENTERED ORBIT. IT'S CLOSE NOW.
I KNOW WHERE IT'S HEADED. THE CASTLE... IT'S NOT A LOCATION BUT A DESCRIPTION. "THE CASTLE OF MAN."
IT'S COMING HERE. TO THE WATCHTOWER.
AND ONCE IT DESTROYS THIS WATCHTOWER AND ITS OCCUPANTS, THERE WILL BE NOTHING TO STOP IT FROM BURROWING TO THE EARTHS CORE AND SQUEEZING THE LIFE OUT OF THIS PLANET.

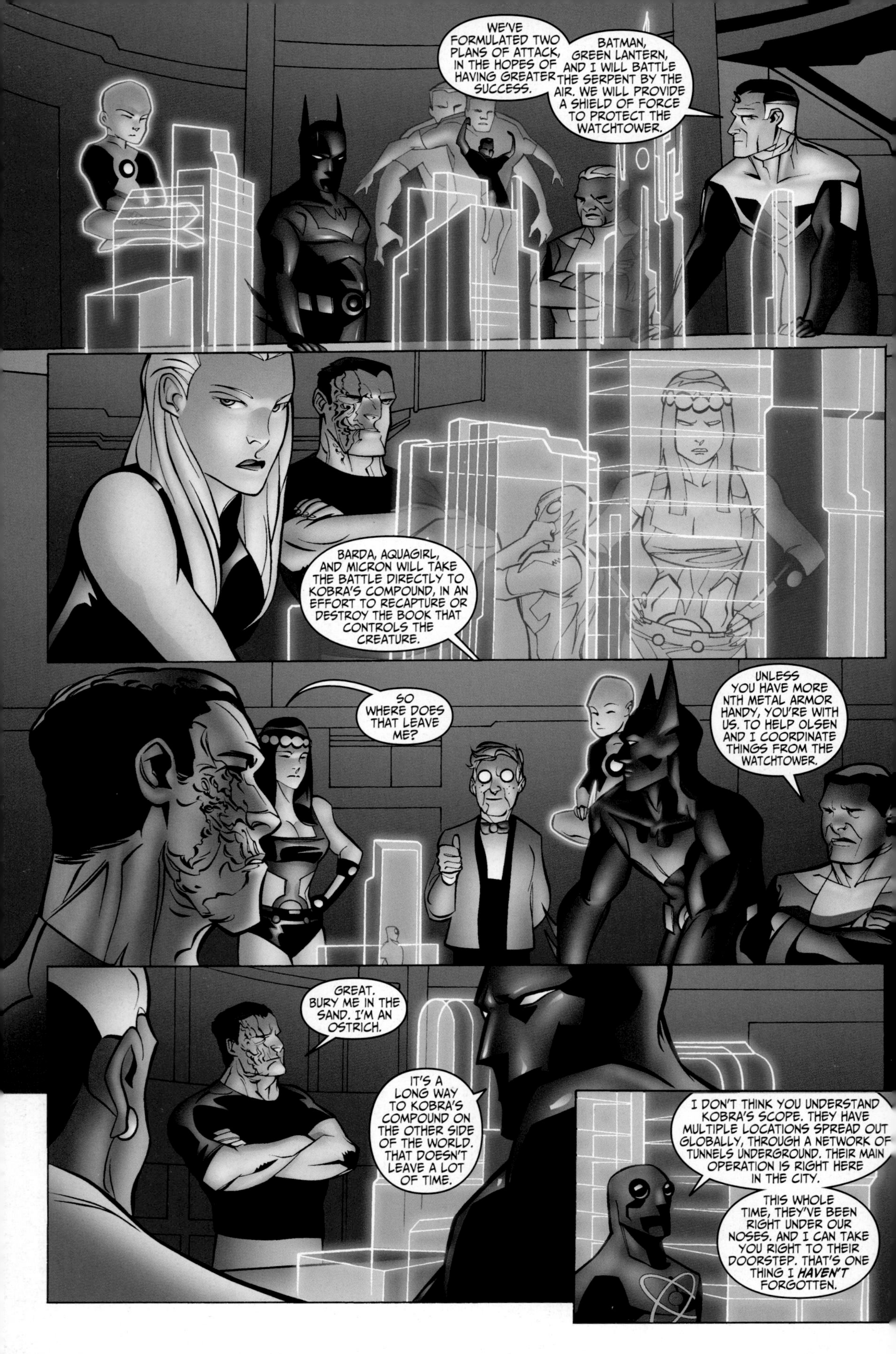

WE'VE FORMULATED TWO PLANS OF ATTACK, IN THE HOPES OF HAVING GREATER SUCCESS.
BATMAN, GREEN LANTERN, AND I WILL BATTLE THE SERPENT BY THE AIR. WE WILL PROVIDE A SHIELD OF FORCE TO PROTECT THE WATCHTOWER.
BARDA, AQUAGIRL, AND MICRON WILL TAKE THE BATTLE DIRECTLY TO KOBRA'S COMPOUND, IN AN EFFORT TO RECAPTURE OR DESTROY THE BOOK THAT CONTROLS THE CREATURE.
SO WHERE DOES THAT LEAVE ME?
UNLESS YOU HAVE MORE NTH METAL ARMOR HANDY, YOU'RE WITH US. TO HELP OLSEN AND I COORDINATE THINGS FROM THE WATCHTOWER.
GREAT. BURY ME IN THE SAND. I'M AN OSTRICH.
IT'S A LONG WAY TO KOBRA'S COMPOUND ON THE OTHER SIDE OF THE WORLD. THAT DOESN'T LEAVE A LOT OF TIME.
I DON'T THINK YOU UNDERSTAND KOBRA'S SCOPE. THEY HAVE MULTIPLE LOCATIONS SPREAD OUT GLOBALLY, THROUGH A NETWORK OF TUNNELS UNDERGROUND. THEIR MAIN OPERATION IS RIGHT HERE IN THE CITY.
THIS WHOLE TIME, THEY'VE BEEN RIGHT UNDER OUR NOSES. AND I CAN TAKE YOU RIGHT TO THEIR DOORSTEP. THAT'S ONE THING I HAVEN'T FORGOTTEN.

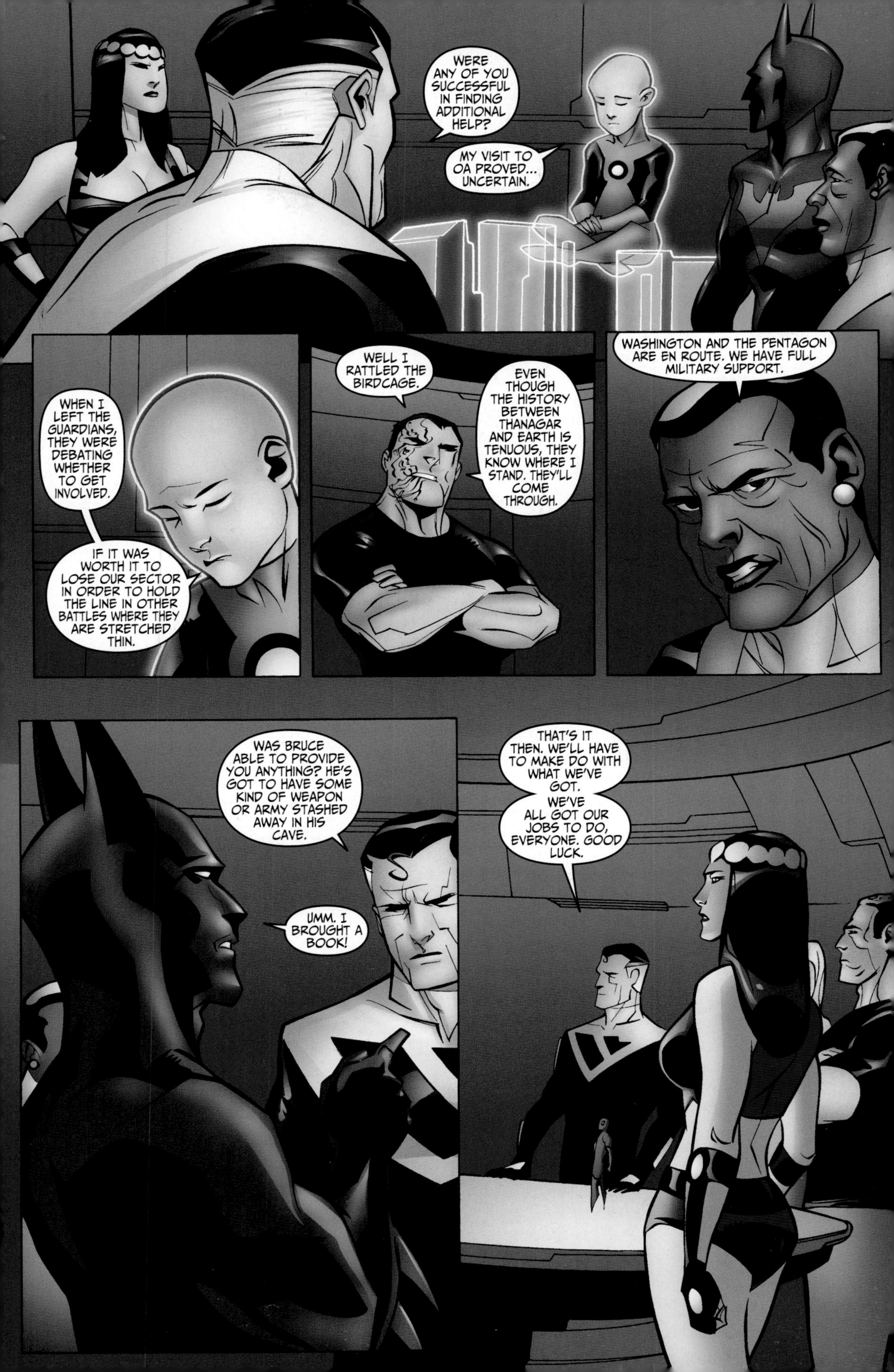
WERE ANY OF YOU SUCCESSFUL IN FINDING ADDITIONAL HELP?
MY VISIT TO OA PROVED... UNCERTAIN.
WHEN I LEFT THE GUARDIANS, THEY WERE DEBATING WHETHER TO GET INVOLVED.
IF IT WAS WORTH IT TO LOSE OUR SECTOR IN ORDER TO HOLD THE LINE IN OTHER BATTLES WHERE THEY ARE STRETCHED THIN.
WELL I RATTLED THE BIRDCAGE.
EVEN THOUGH THE HISTORY BETWEEN THANAGAR AND EARTH IS TENUOUS, THEY KNOW WHERE I STAND. THEY'LL COME THROUGH.
WASHINGTON AND THE PENTAGON ARE EN ROUTE. WE HAVE FULL MILITARY SUPPORT.
WAS BRUCE ABLE TO PROVIDE YOU ANYTHING? HE'S GOT TO HAVE SOME KIND OF WEAPON OR ARMY STASHED AWAY IN HIS CAVE.
UMM. I BROUGHT A BOOK!
THAT'S IT THEN. WE'LL HAVE TO MAKE DO WITH WHAT WE'VE GOT.
WE'VE ALL GOT OUR JOBS TO DO, EVERYONE. GOOD LUCK.

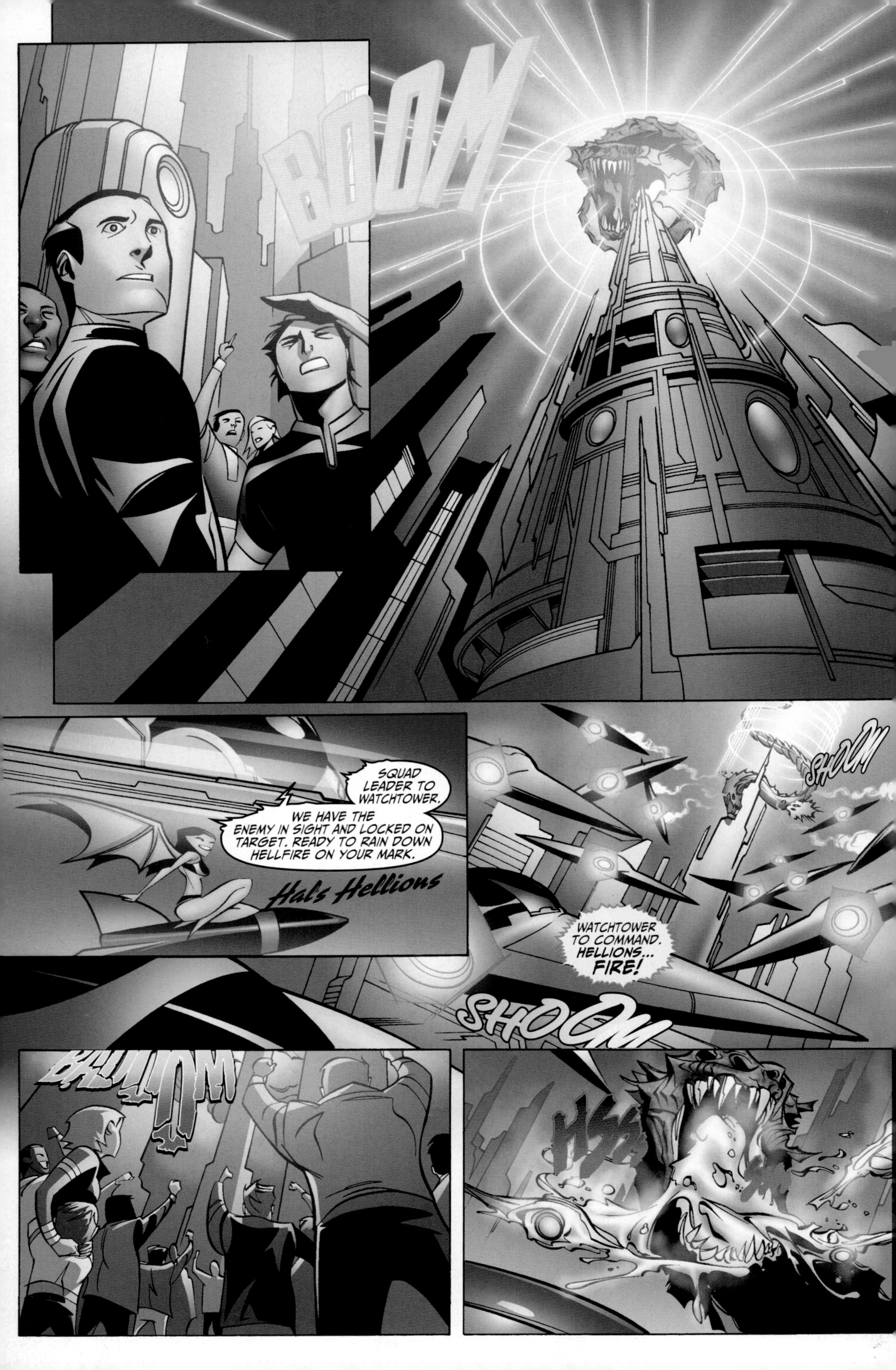
BOOM
SQUAD LEADER TO WATCHTOWER.
WE HAVE THE ENEMY IN SIGHT AND LOCKED ON TARGET. READY TO RAIN DOWN HELLFIRE ON YOUR MARK.
Hal's Hellions
SHOOM
WATCHTOWER TO COMMAND. HELLIONS... FIRE!
SHOOM

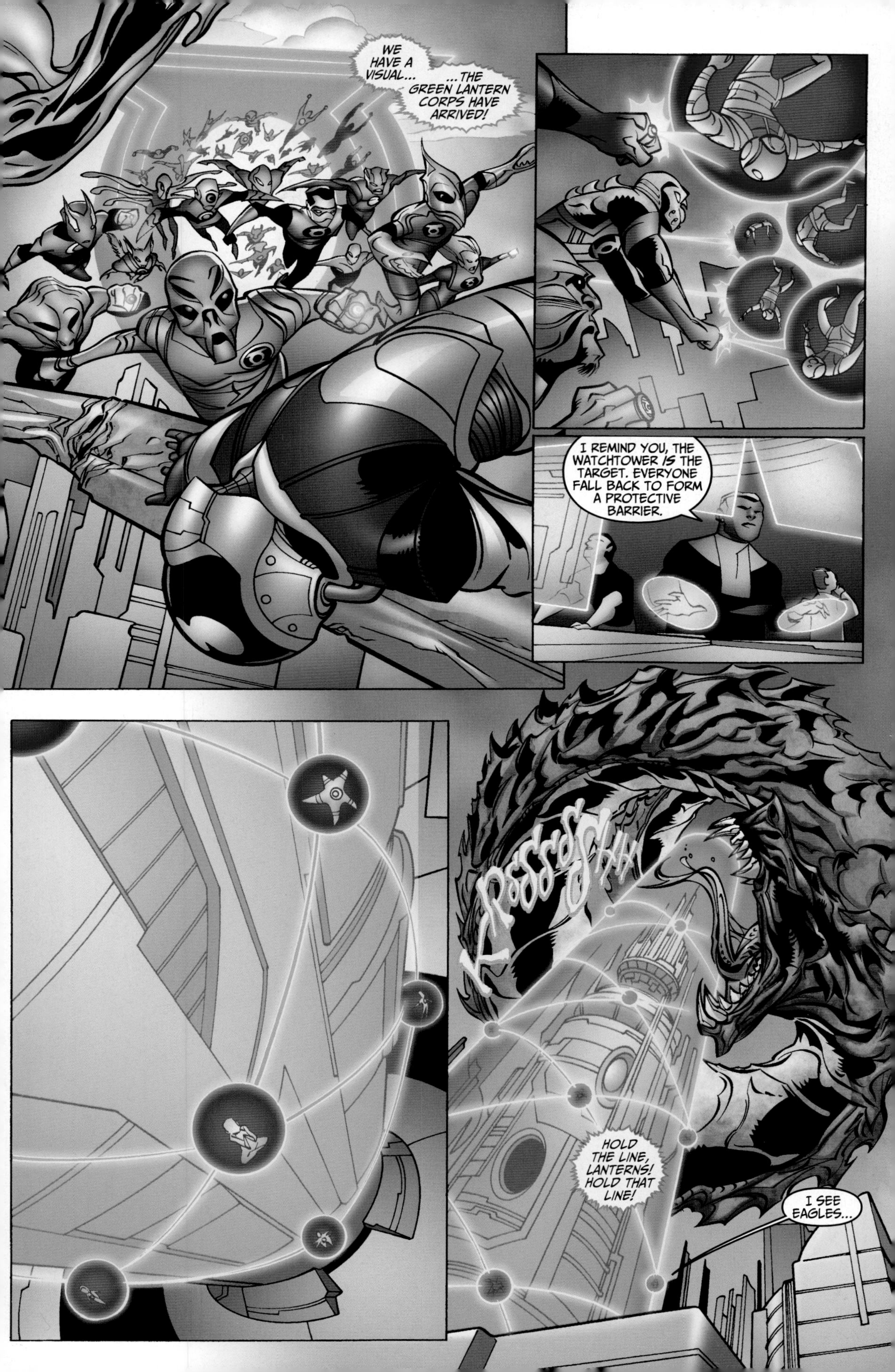
WE HAVE A VISUAL...
...THE GREEN LANTERN CORPS HAVE ARRIVED!
I REMIND YOU, THE WATCHTOWER IS THE TARGET. EVERYONE FALL BACK TO FORM A PROTECTIVE BARRIER.
KRSSSSHH
HOLD THE LINE, LANTERNS! HOLD THAT LINE!
I SEE EAGLES...

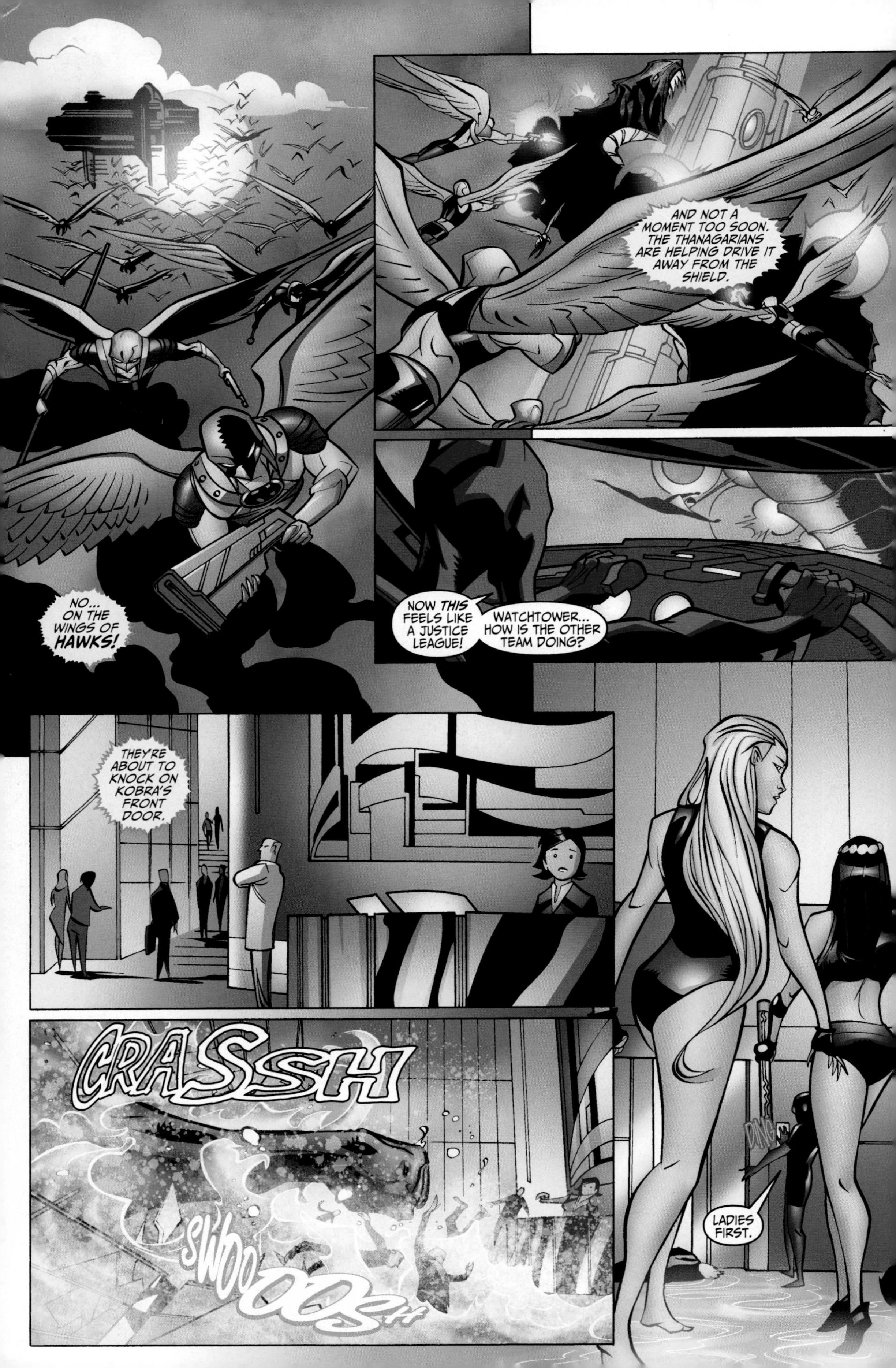
NO... ON THE WINGS OF HAWKS!
AND NOT A MOMENT TOO SOON. THE THANAGARIANS ARE HELPING DRIVE IT AWAY FROM THE SHIELD.
NOW THIS FEELS LIKE A JUSTICE LEAGUE!
WATCHTOWER... HOW IS THE OTHER TEAM DOING?
THEY'RE ABOUT TO KNOCK ON KOBRA'S FRONT DOOR.
CRASSSH
SWOOOOSH
DING
LADIES FIRST.

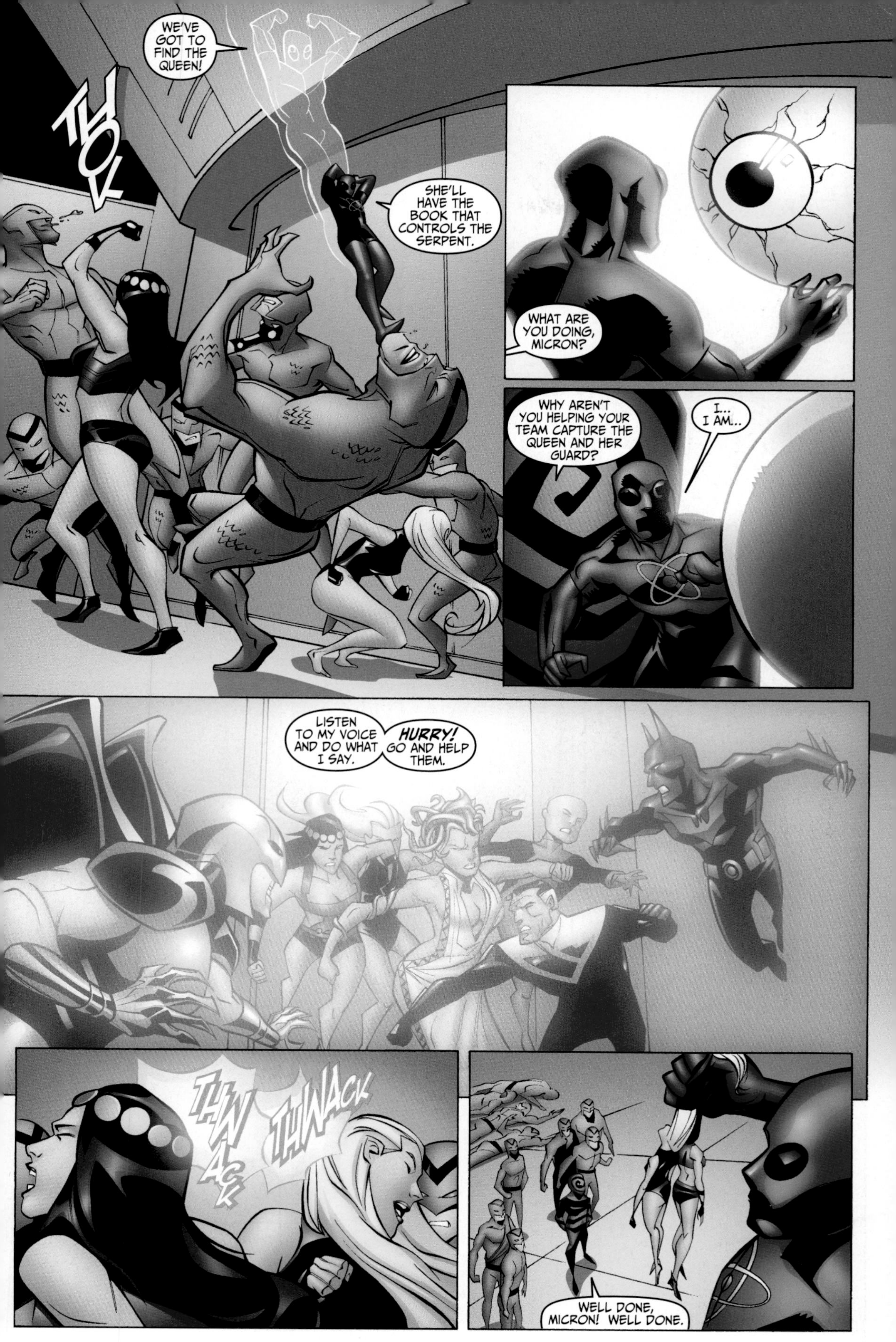
WE'VE GOT TO FIND THE QUEEN!
THOK
SHE'LL HAVE THE BOOK THAT CONTROLS THE SERPENT.
WHAT ARE YOU DOING, MICRON?
WHY AREN'T YOU HELPING YOUR TEAM CAPTURE THE QUEEN AND HER GUARD?
I... I AM...
LISTEN TO MY VOICE AND DO WHAT I SAY.
HURRY! GO AND HELP THEM.
THWACK
THWACK
WELL DONE, MICRON! WELL DONE.

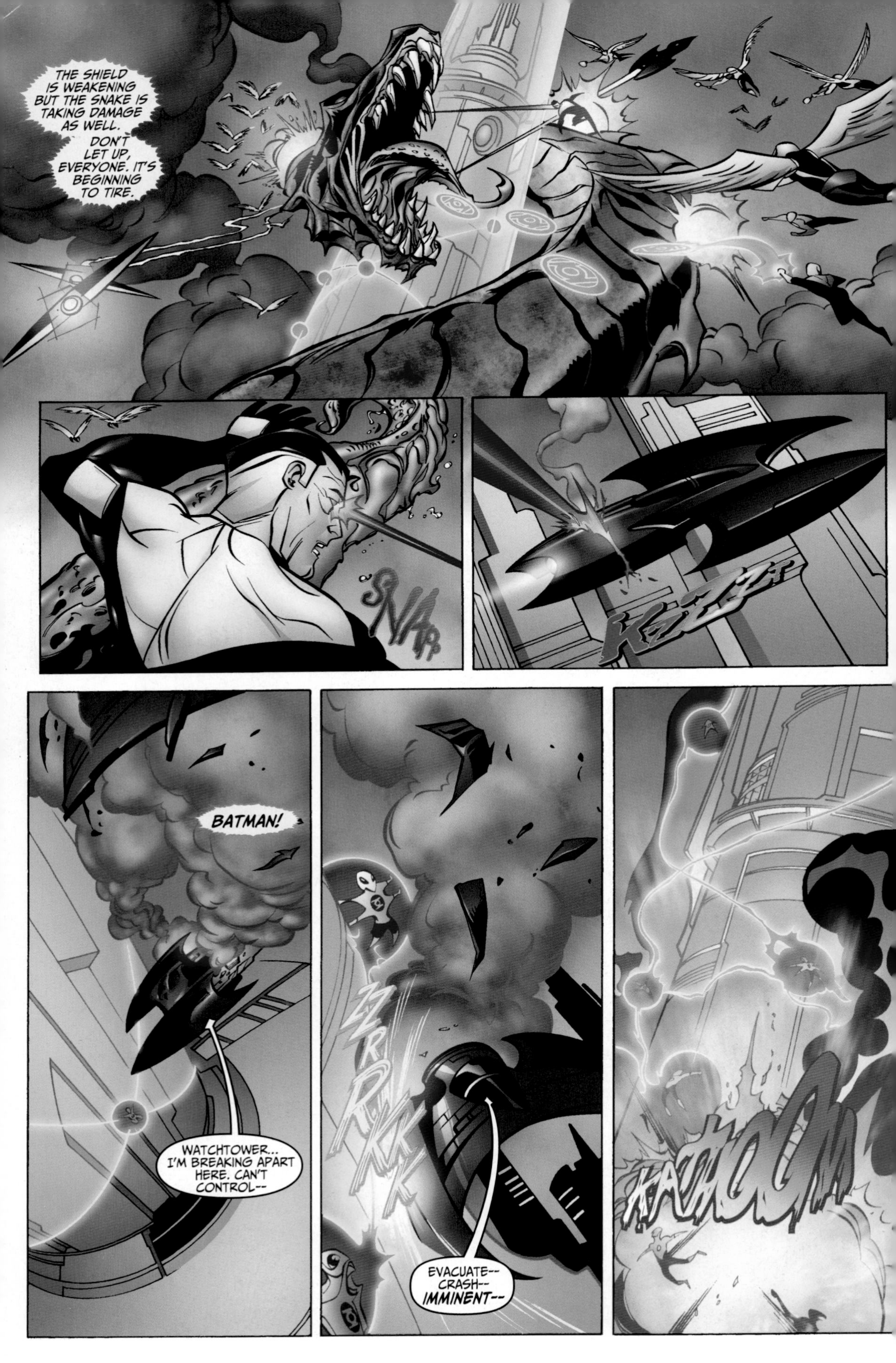
THE SHIELD IS WEAKENING BUT THE SNAKE IS TAKING DAMAGE AS WELL.
DON'T LET UP, EVERYONE. IT'S BEGINNING TO TIRE.
SNARR
KZZZZT
BATMAN!
WATCHTOWER... I'M BREAKING APART HERE. CAN'T CONTROL--
ZZRRKK
EVACUATE-- CRASH-- IMMINENT--
KATHOOM

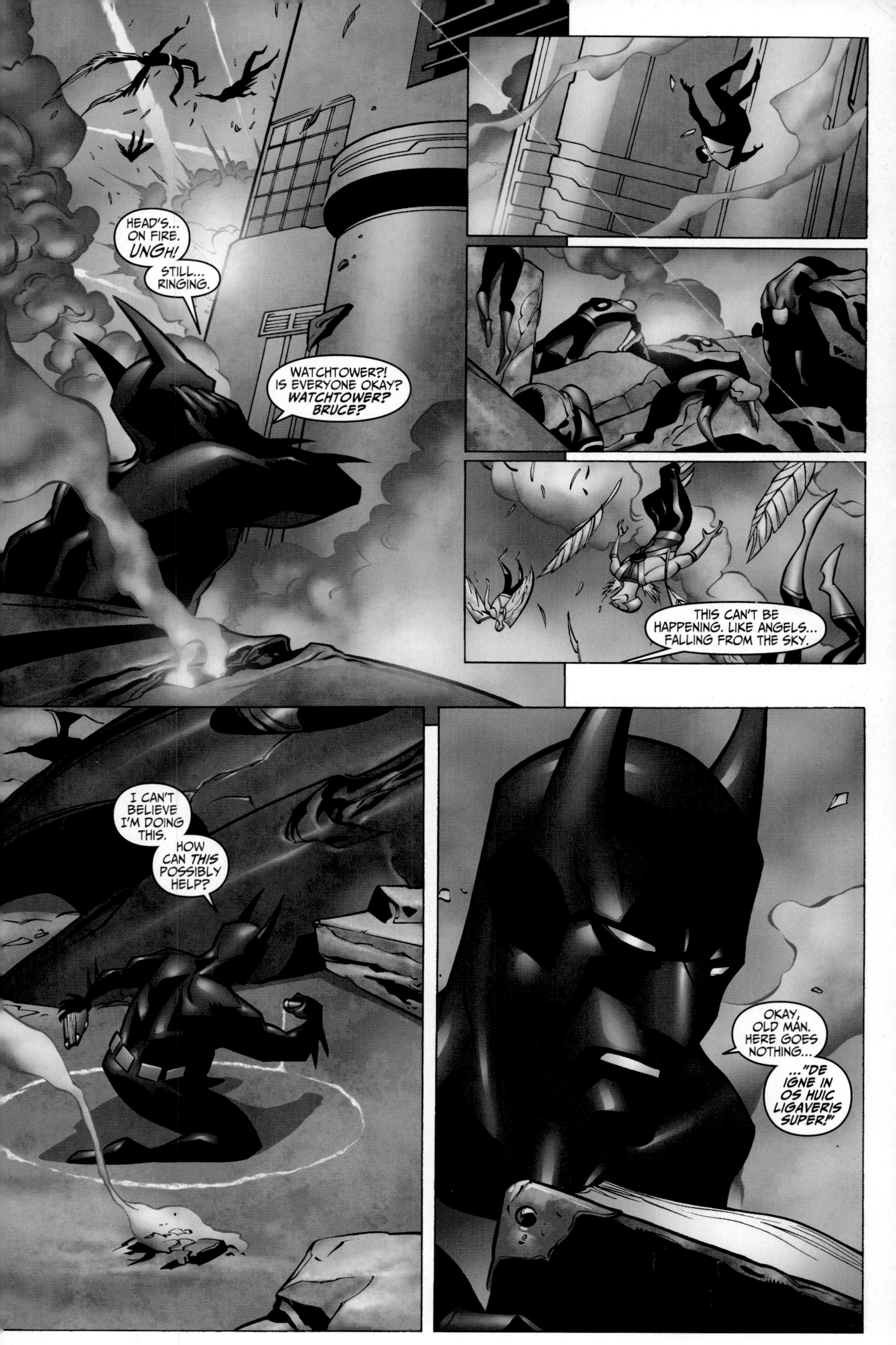
HEAD'S... ON FIRE. UNGH!
STILL... RINGING.
WATCHTOWER?! IS EVERYONE OKAY? WATCHTOWER? BRUCE?
THIS CAN'T BE HAPPENING. LIKE ANGELS... FALLING FROM THE SKY.
I CAN'T BELIEVE I'M DOING THIS.
HOW CAN THIS POSSIBLY HELP?
OKAY, OLD MAN. HERE GOES NOTHING...
..."DE IGNE IN OS HUIC LIGAVERIS SUPER!"

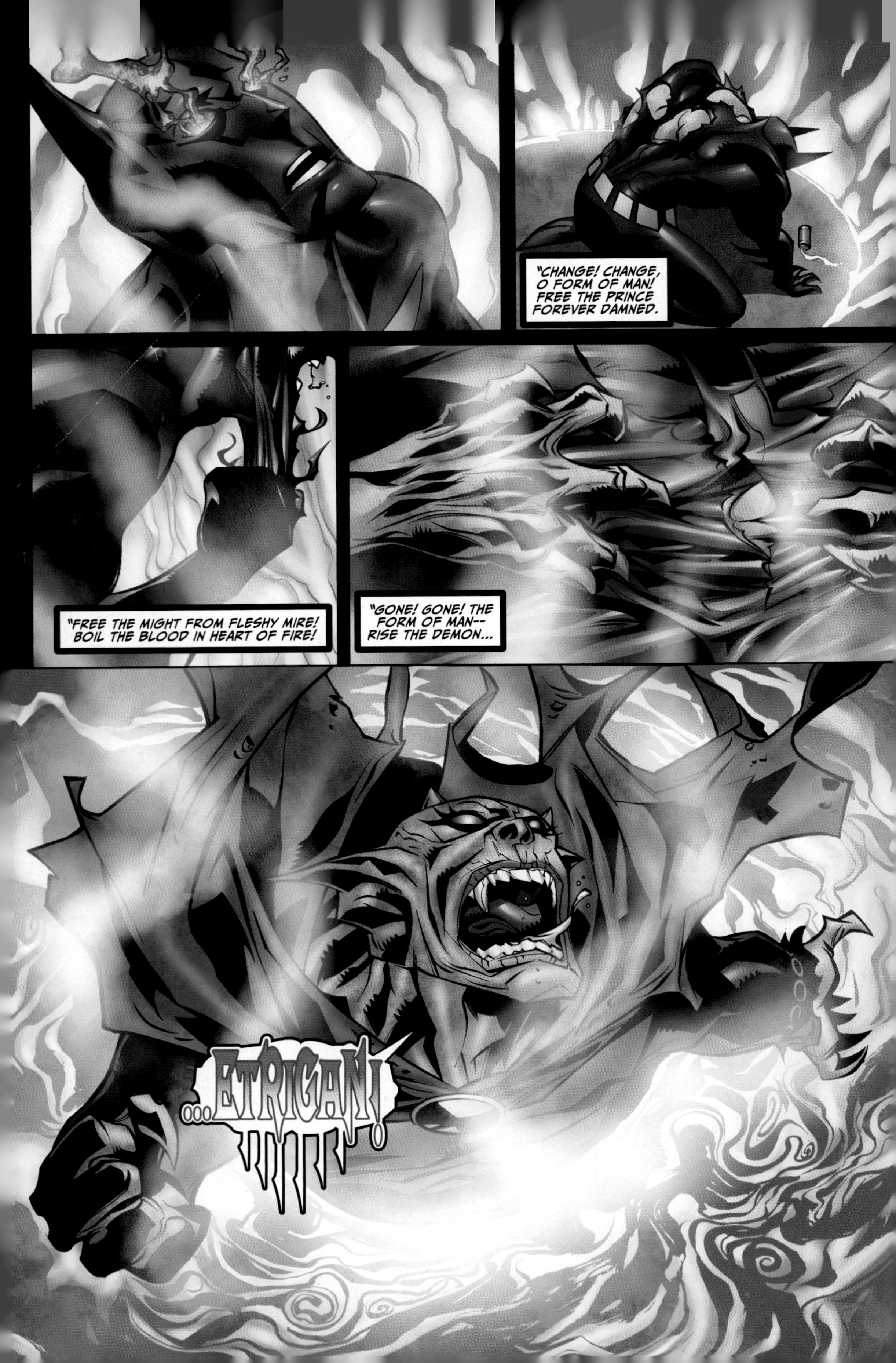

"CHANGE! CHANGE, O FORM OF MAN! FREE THE PRINCE FOREVER DAMNED.
"FREE THE MIGHT FROM FLESHY MIRE! BOIL THE BLOOD IN HEART OF FIRE!
"GONE! GONE! THE FORM OF MAN-- RISE THE DEMON...
...ETRIGAN!

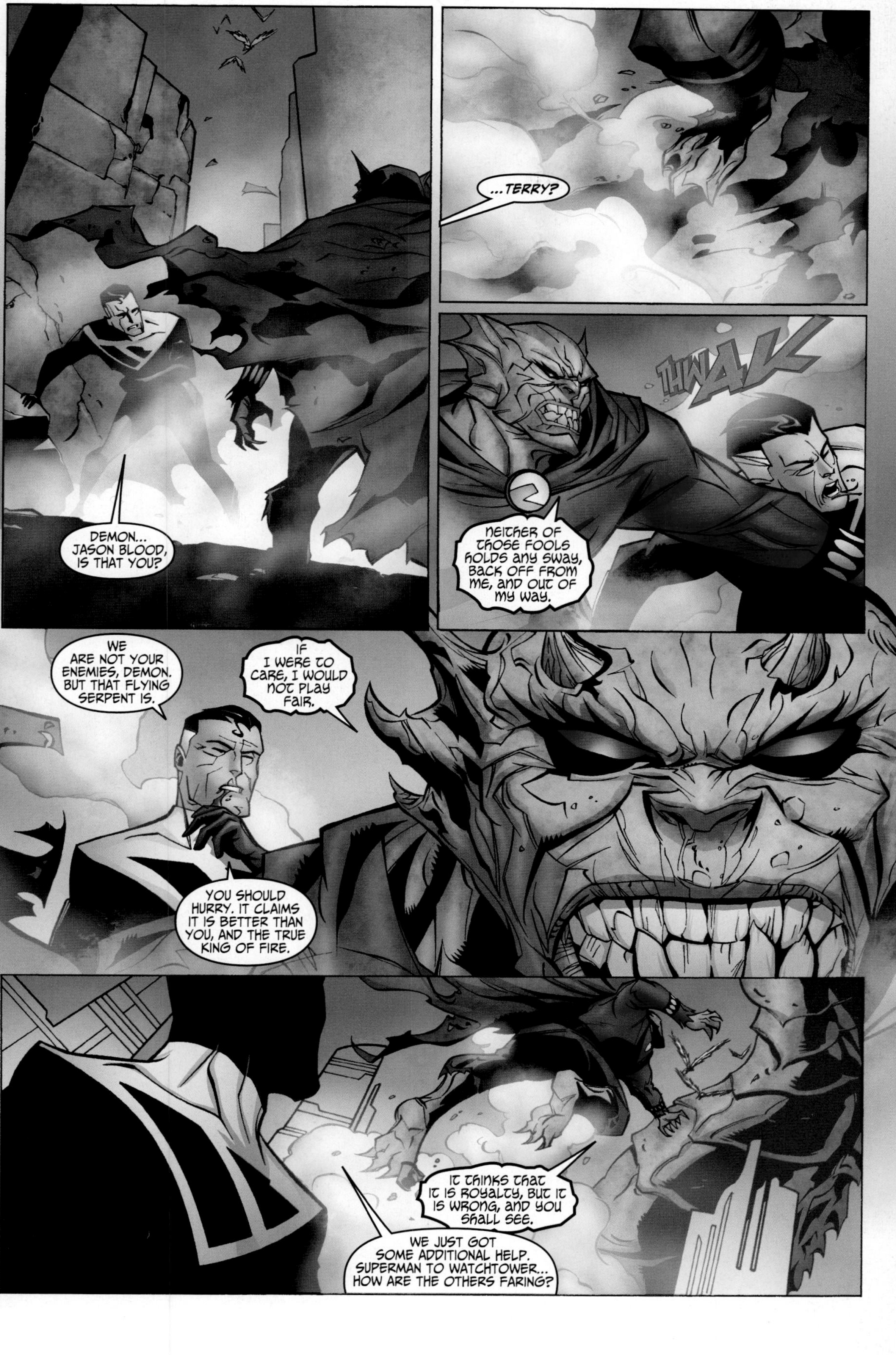
DEMON... JASON BLOOD, IS THAT YOU?
...TERRY?
THWAK
NEITHER OF THOSE FOOLS HOLDS ANY SWAY, BACK OFF FROM ME, AND OUT OF MY WAY.
WE ARE NOT YOUR ENEMIES, DEMON. BUT THAT FLYING SERPENT IS.
IF I WERE TO CARE, I WOULD NOT PLAY FAIR.
YOU SHOULD HURRY. IT CLAIMS IT IS BETTER THAN YOU, AND THE TRUE KING OF FIRE.
IT THINKS THAT IT IS ROYALTY, BUT IT IS WRONG, AND YOU SHALL SEE.
WE JUST GOT SOME ADDITIONAL HELP. SUPERMAN TO WATCHTOWER... HOW ARE THE OTHERS FARING?

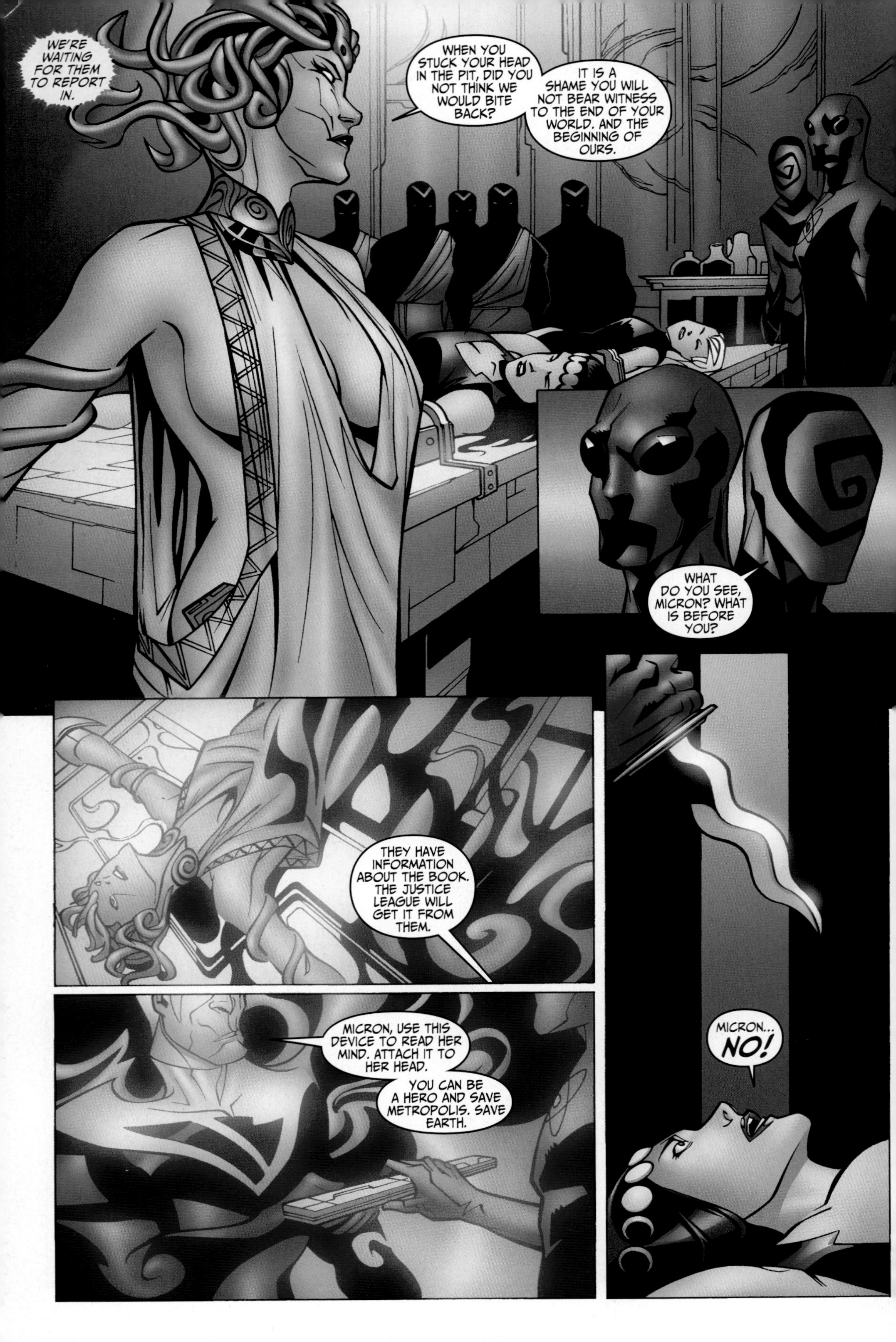
WE'RE WAITING FOR THEM TO REPORT IN.
WHEN YOU STUCK YOUR HEAD IN THE PIT, DID YOU NOT THINK WE WOULD BITE BACK?
IT IS A SHAME YOU WILL NOT BEAR WITNESS TO THE END OF YOUR WORLD. AND THE BEGINNING OF OURS.
WHAT DO YOU SEE, MICRON? WHAT IS BEFORE YOU?
THEY HAVE INFORMATION ABOUT THE BOOK. THE JUSTICE LEAGUE WILL GET IT FROM THEM.
MICRON, USE THIS DEVICE TO READ HER MIND. ATTACH IT TO HER HEAD.
YOU CAN BE A HERO AND SAVE METROPOLIS. SAVE EARTH.
MICRON... NO!

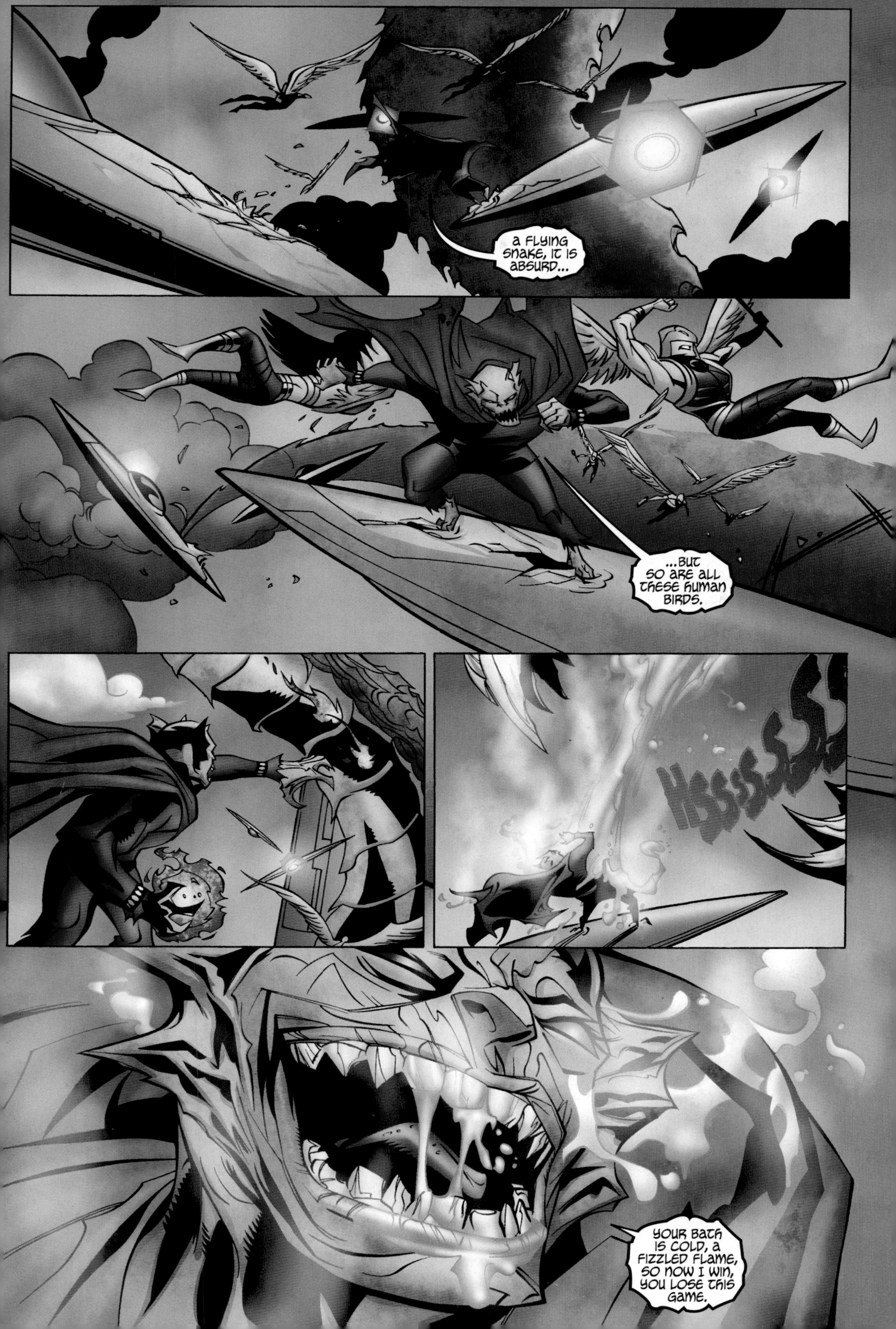
a FLYING SNAKE, IT IS ABSURD...
...BUT SO ARE ALL THESE HUMAN BIRDS.
HSSSSSS
YOUR BATH IS COLD, A FIZZLED FLAME, SO NOW I WIN, YOU LOSE THIS GAME.

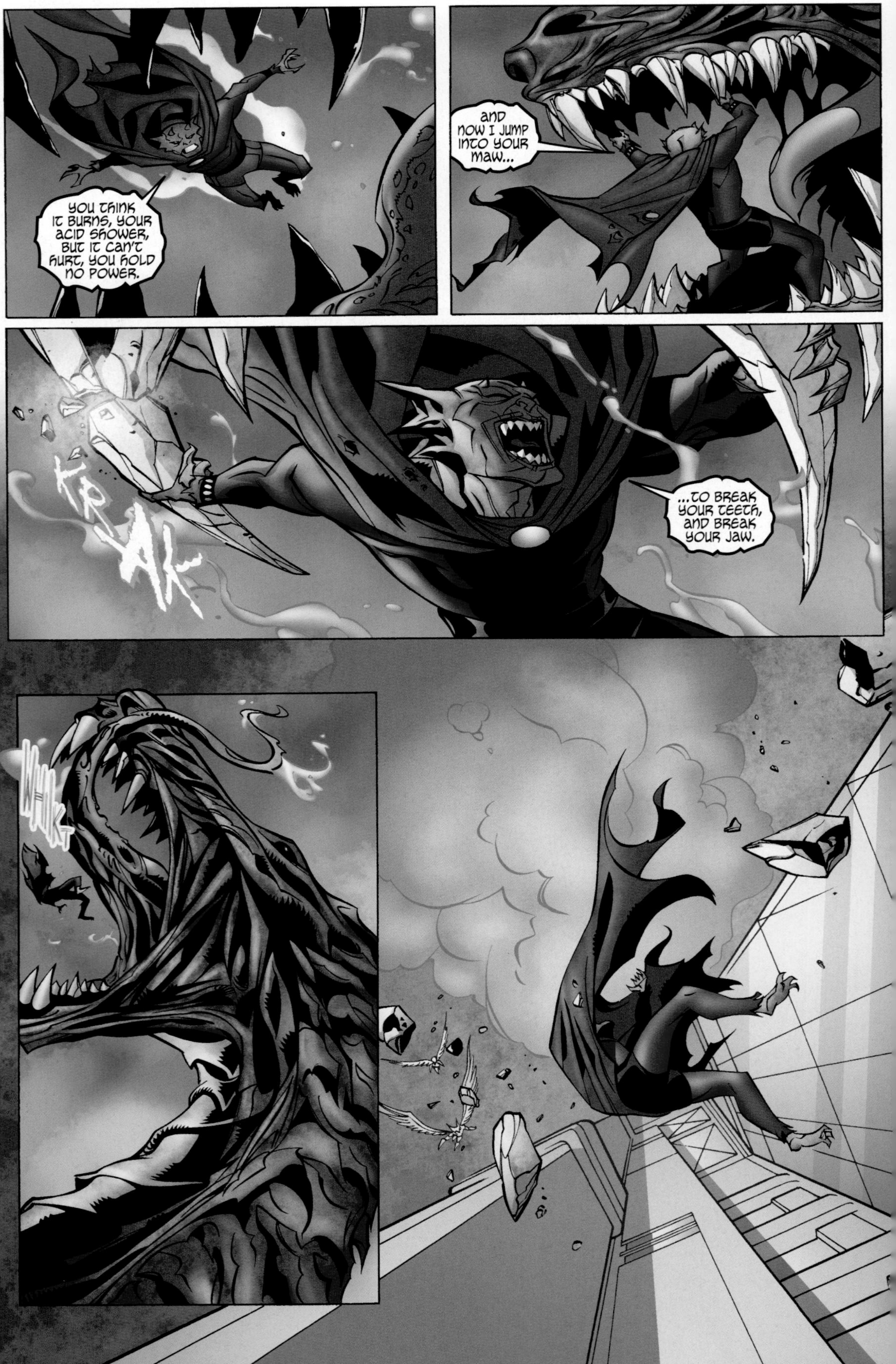
YOU THINK IT BURNS, YOUR ACID SHOWER, BUT IT CAN'T HURT, YOU HOLD NO POWER.
AND NOW I JUMP INTO YOUR MAW...
KRAK
...TO BREAK YOUR TEETH, AND BREAK YOUR JAW.
WHHK

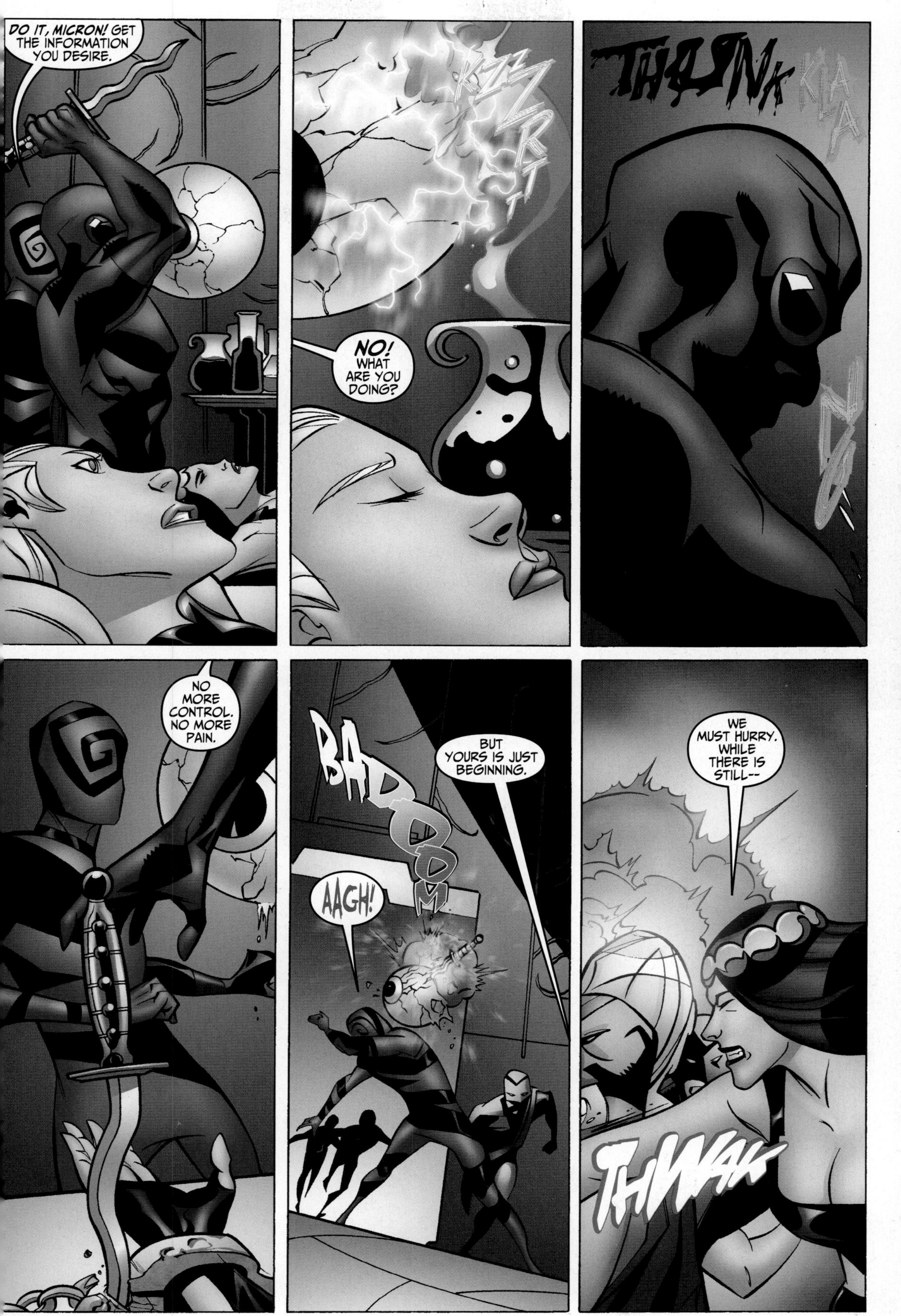

DO IT, MICRON! GET THE INFORMATION YOU DESIRE.
NO! WHAT ARE YOU DOING?
NO MORE CONTROL. NO MORE PAIN.
BADOOM
BUT YOURS IS JUST BEGINNING.
AAGH!
WE MUST HURRY. WHILE THERE IS STILL--
THWAK

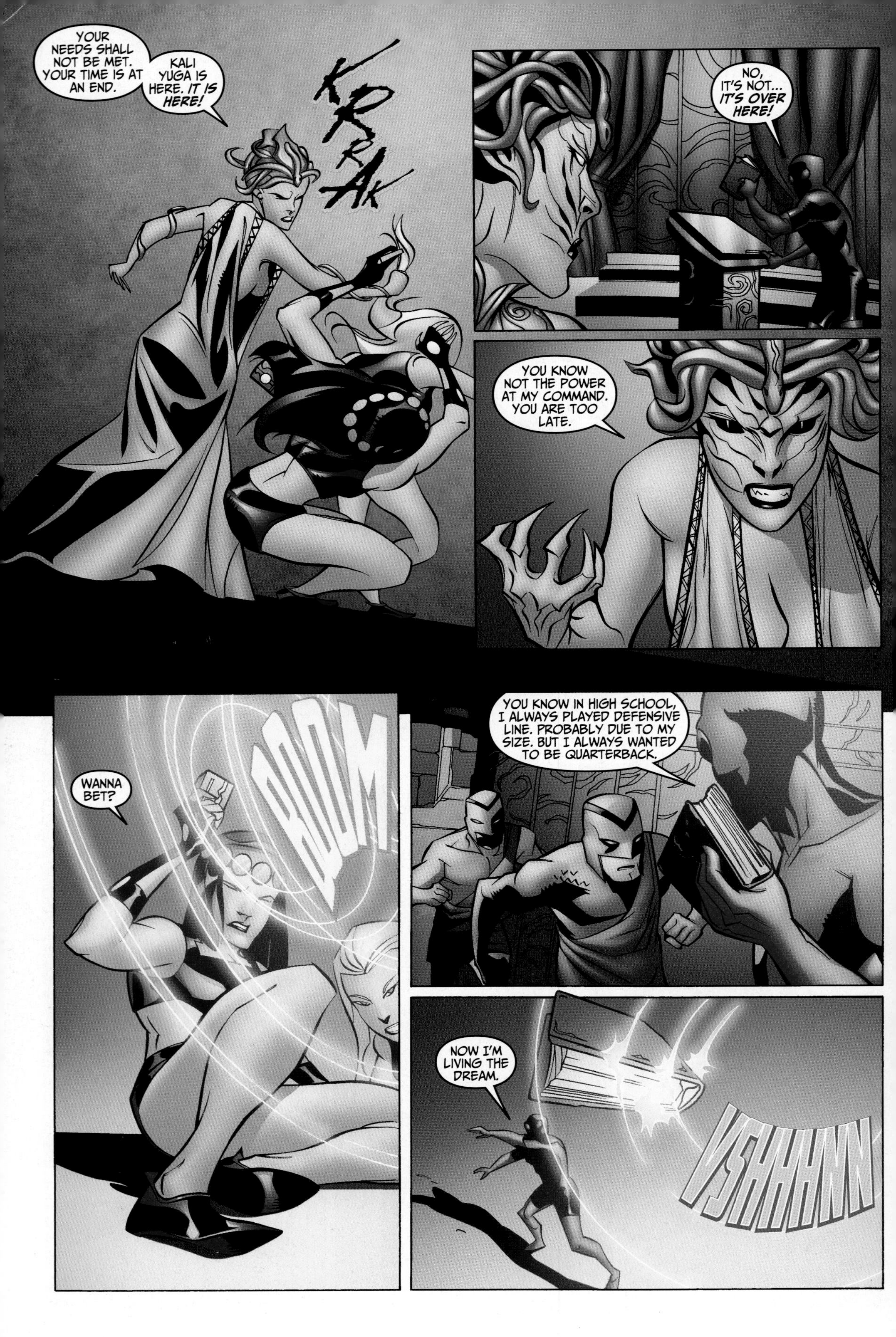
YOUR NEEDS SHALL NOT BE MET. YOUR TIME IS AT AN END.
KALI YUGA IS HERE. IT IS HERE!
KRRAK
NO, IT'S NOT... IT'S OVER HERE!
YOU KNOW NOT THE POWER AT MY COMMAND. YOU ARE TOO LATE.
WANNA BET?
BOOM
YOU KNOW IN HIGH SCHOOL, I ALWAYS PLAYED DEFENSIVE LINE. PROBABLY DUE TO MY SIZE. BUT I ALWAYS WANTED TO BE QUARTERBACK.
NOW I'M LIVING THE DREAM.
VSHHHNN

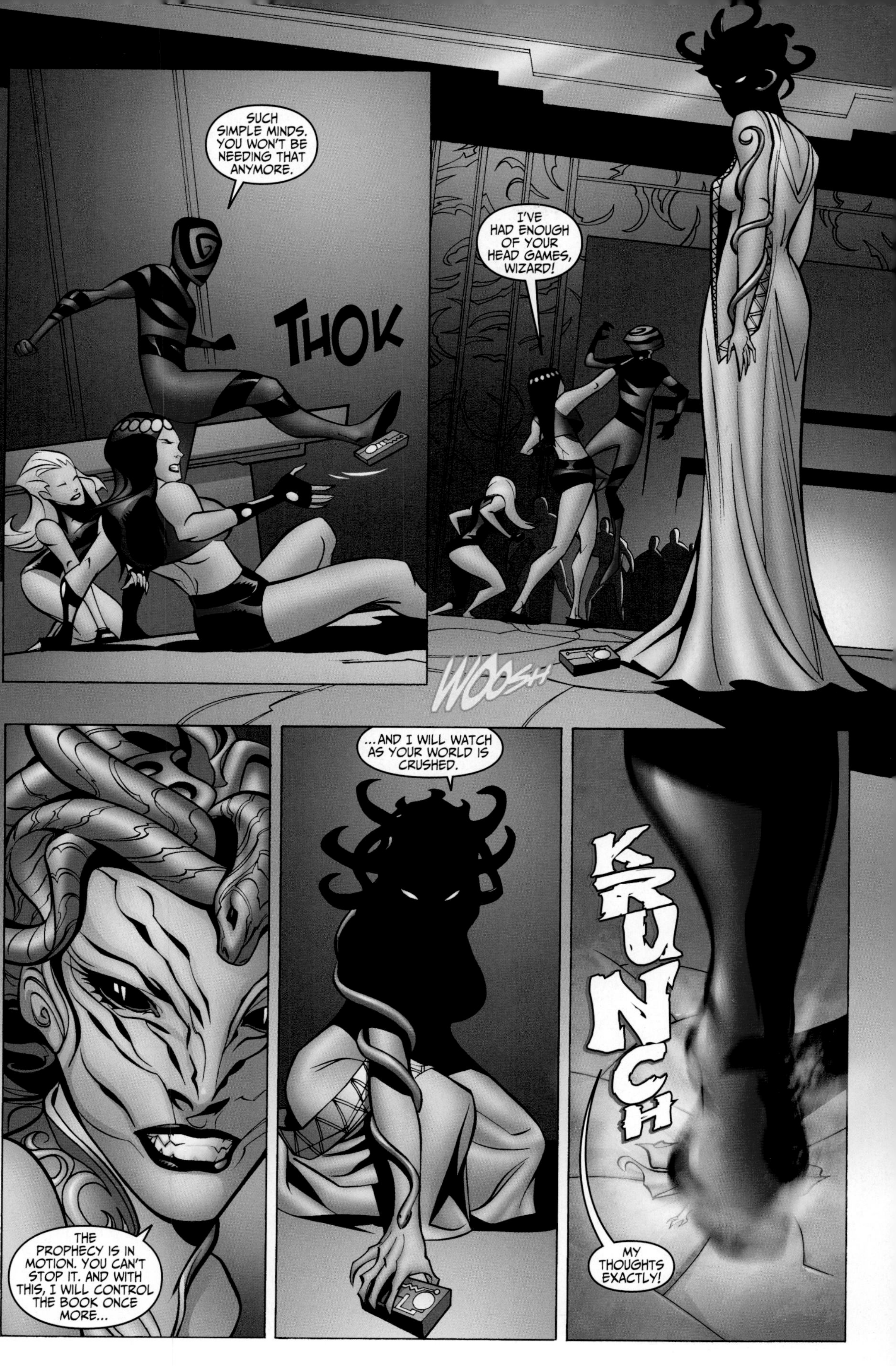
SUCH SIMPLE MINDS. YOU WON'T BE NEEDING THAT ANYMORE.
THOK
I'VE HAD ENOUGH OF YOUR HEAD GAMES, WIZARD!
WOOSH
THE PROPHECY IS IN MOTION. YOU CAN'T STOP IT. AND WITH THIS, I WILL CONTROL THE BOOK ONCE MORE...
...AND I WILL WATCH AS YOUR WORLD IS CRUSHED.
KRUNCH
MY THOUGHTS EXACTLY!

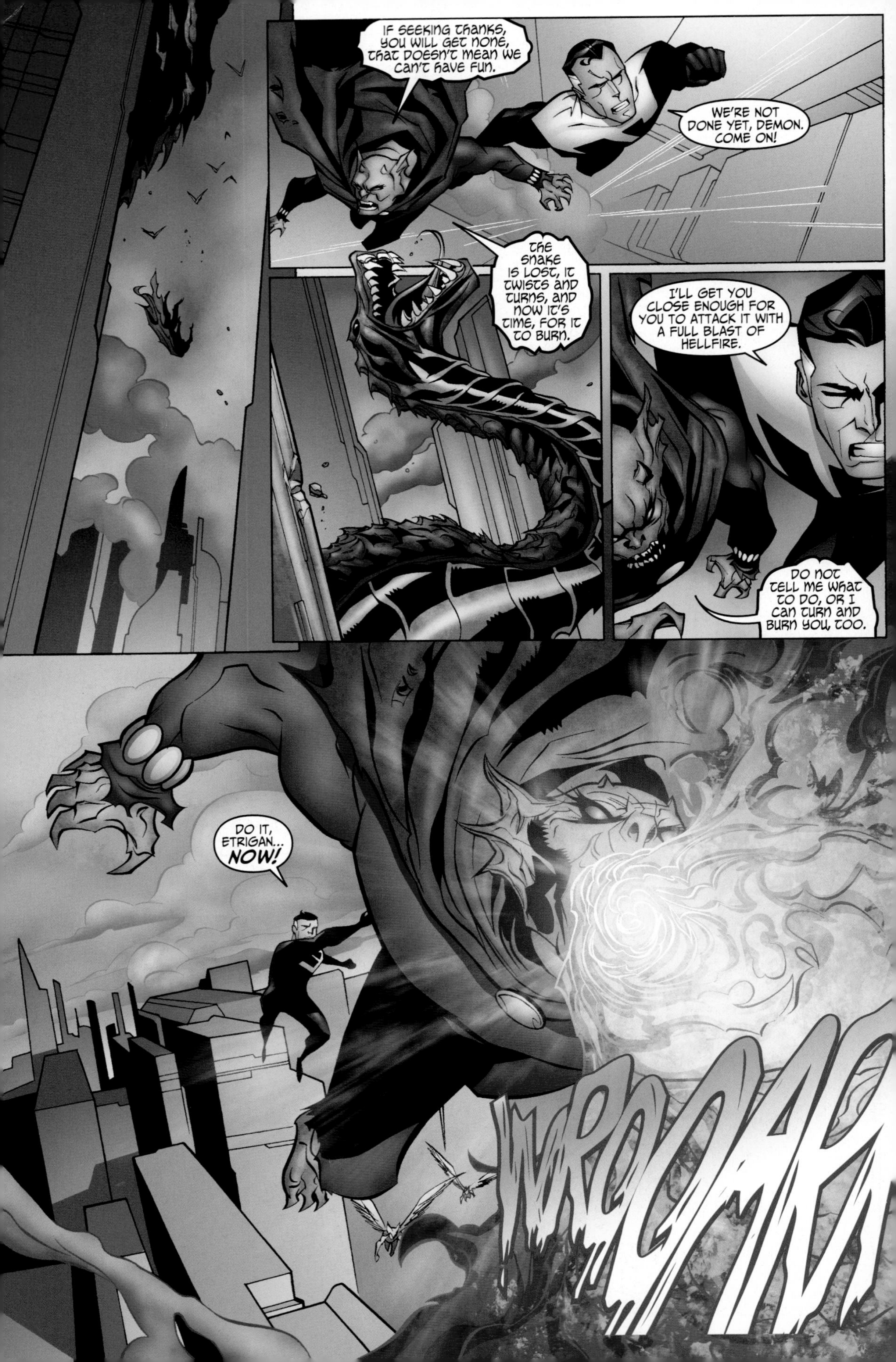
IF SEEKING THANKS, YOU WILL GET NONE, THAT DOESN'T MEAN WE CAN'T HAVE FUN.
WE'RE NOT DONE YET, DEMON. COME ON!
THE SNAKE IS LOST, IT TWISTS AND TURNS, AND NOW IT'S TIME, FOR IT TO BURN.
I'LL GET YOU CLOSE ENOUGH FOR YOU TO ATTACK IT WITH A FULL BLAST OF HELLFIRE.
DO NOT TELL ME WHAT TO DO, OR I CAN TURN AND BURN YOU, TOO.
DO IT, ETRIGAN... NOW!
WROOAH

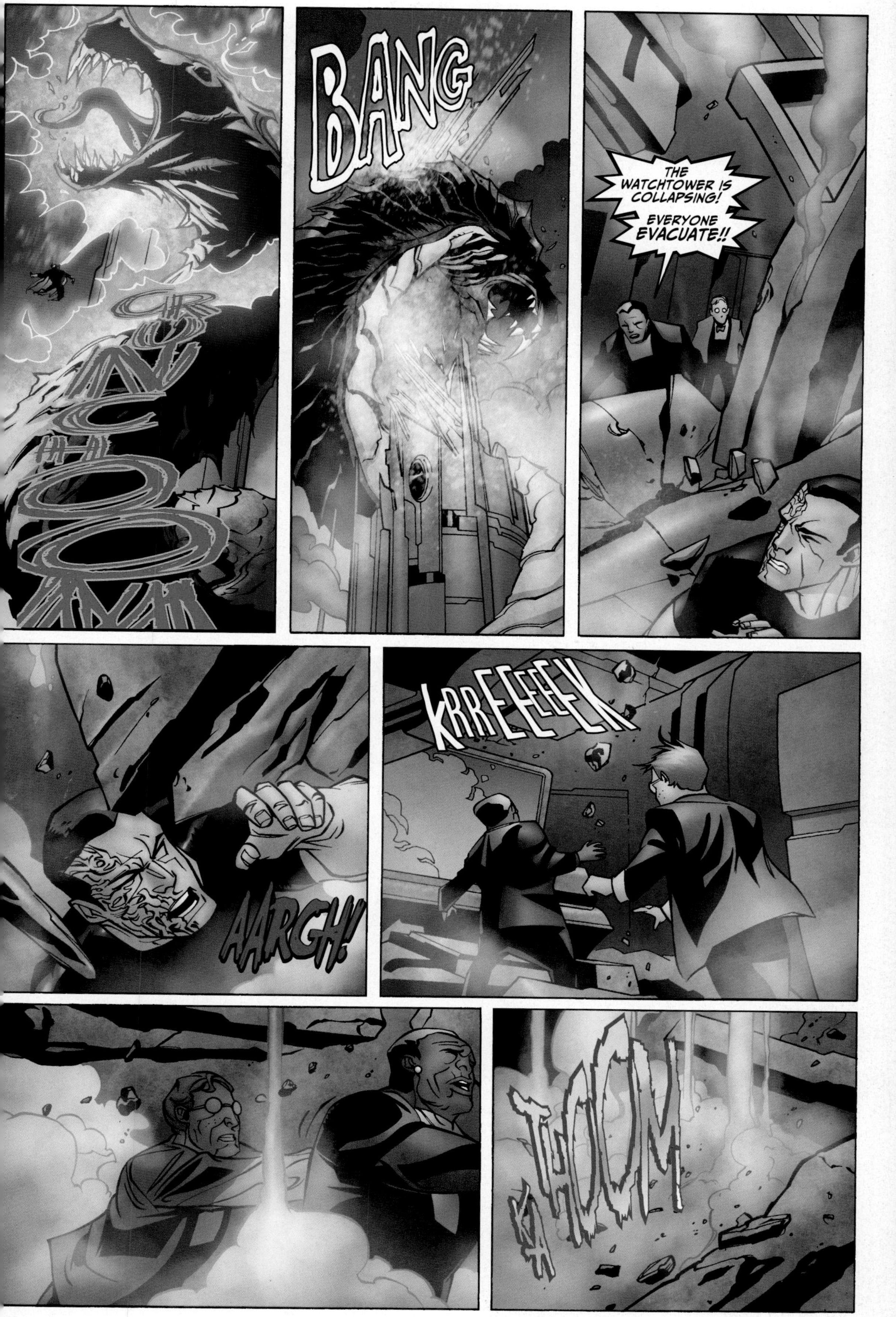
BANG
THE WATCHTOWER IS COLLAPSING!
EVERYONE EVACUATE!!
AARGH!
KRREEEEEK
THOOM

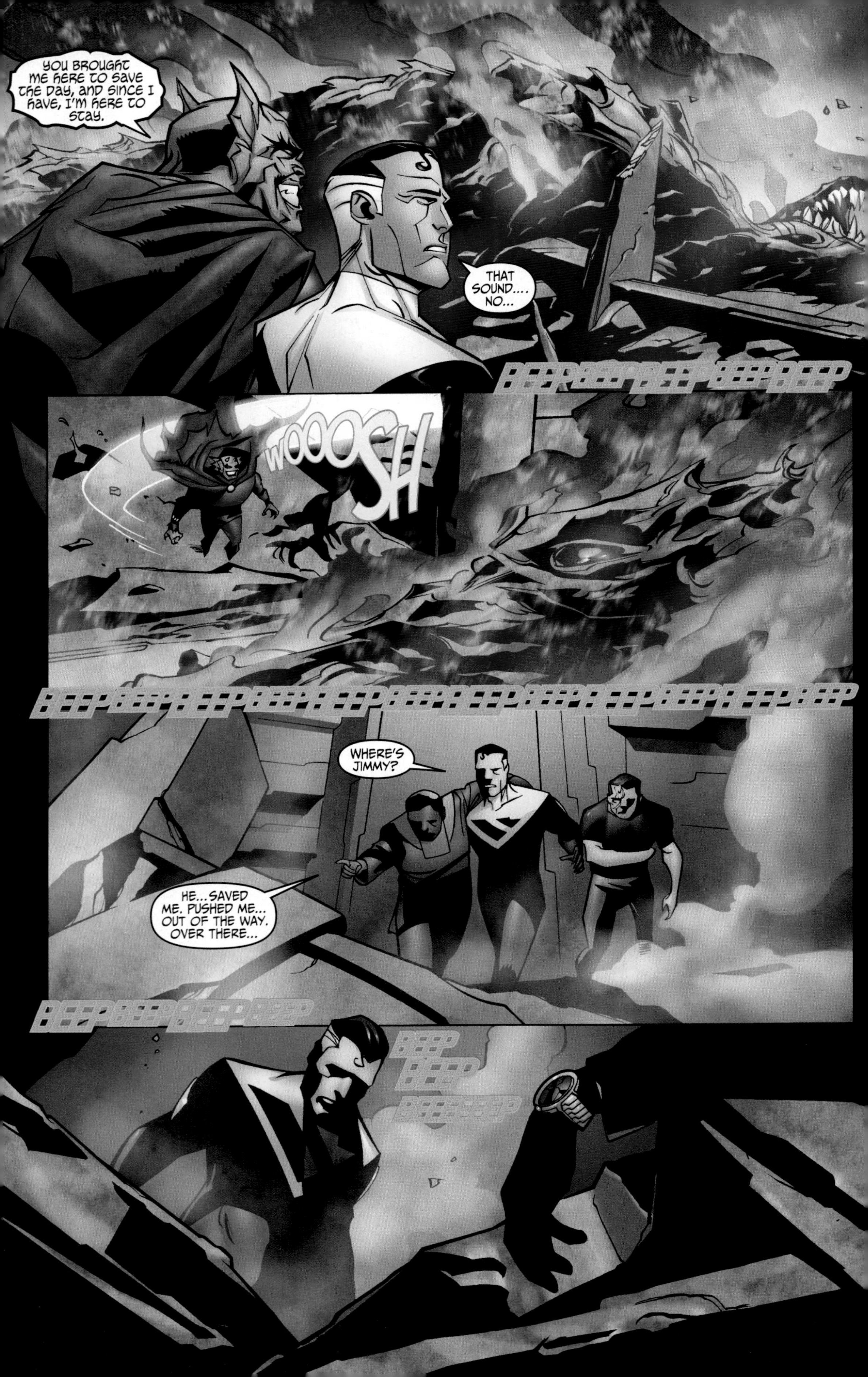
YOU BROUGHT ME HERE TO SAVE THE DAY, AND SINCE I HAVE, I'M HERE TO STAY.
THAT SOUND.... NO...
BEEP BEEP BEEP BEEP BEEP
WOOOSH
BEEP BEEP BEEP BEEP BEEP BEEP BEEP BEEP BEEP BEEP BEEP BEEP BEEP
WHERE'S JIMMY?
HE...SAVED ME. PUSHED ME... OUT OF THE WAY. OVER THERE...
BEEP BEEP BEEP BEEP
BEEP
BEEP
BEEEEEEP

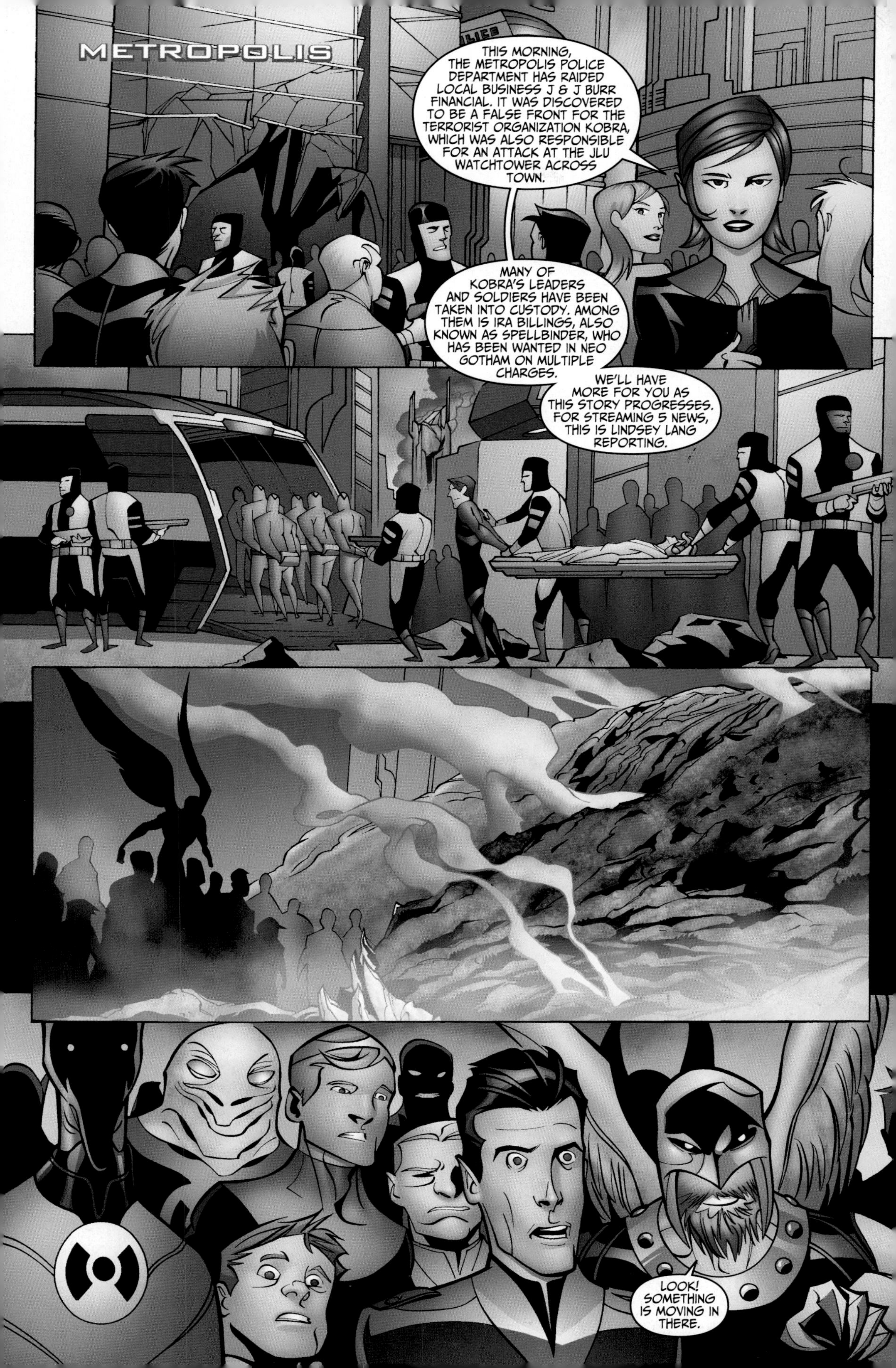
METROPOLIS
THIS MORNING, THE METROPOLIS POLICE DEPARTMENT HAS RAIDED LOCAL BUSINESS J & J BURR FINANCIAL. IT WAS DISCOVERED TO BE A FALSE FRONT FOR THE TERRORIST ORGANIZATION KOBRA, WHICH WAS ALSO RESPONSIBLE FOR AN ATTACK AT THE JLU WATCHTOWER ACROSS TOWN.
MANY OF KOBRA'S LEADERS AND SOLDIERS HAVE BEEN TAKEN INTO CUSTODY. AMONG THEM IS IRA BILLINGS, ALSO KNOWN AS SPELLBINDER, WHO HAS BEEN WANTED IN NEO GOTHAM ON MULTIPLE CHARGES.
WE'LL HAVE MORE FOR YOU AS THIS STORY PROGRESSES. FOR STREAMING 5 NEWS, THIS IS LINDSEY LANG REPORTING.
LOOK! SOMETHING IS MOVING IN THERE.

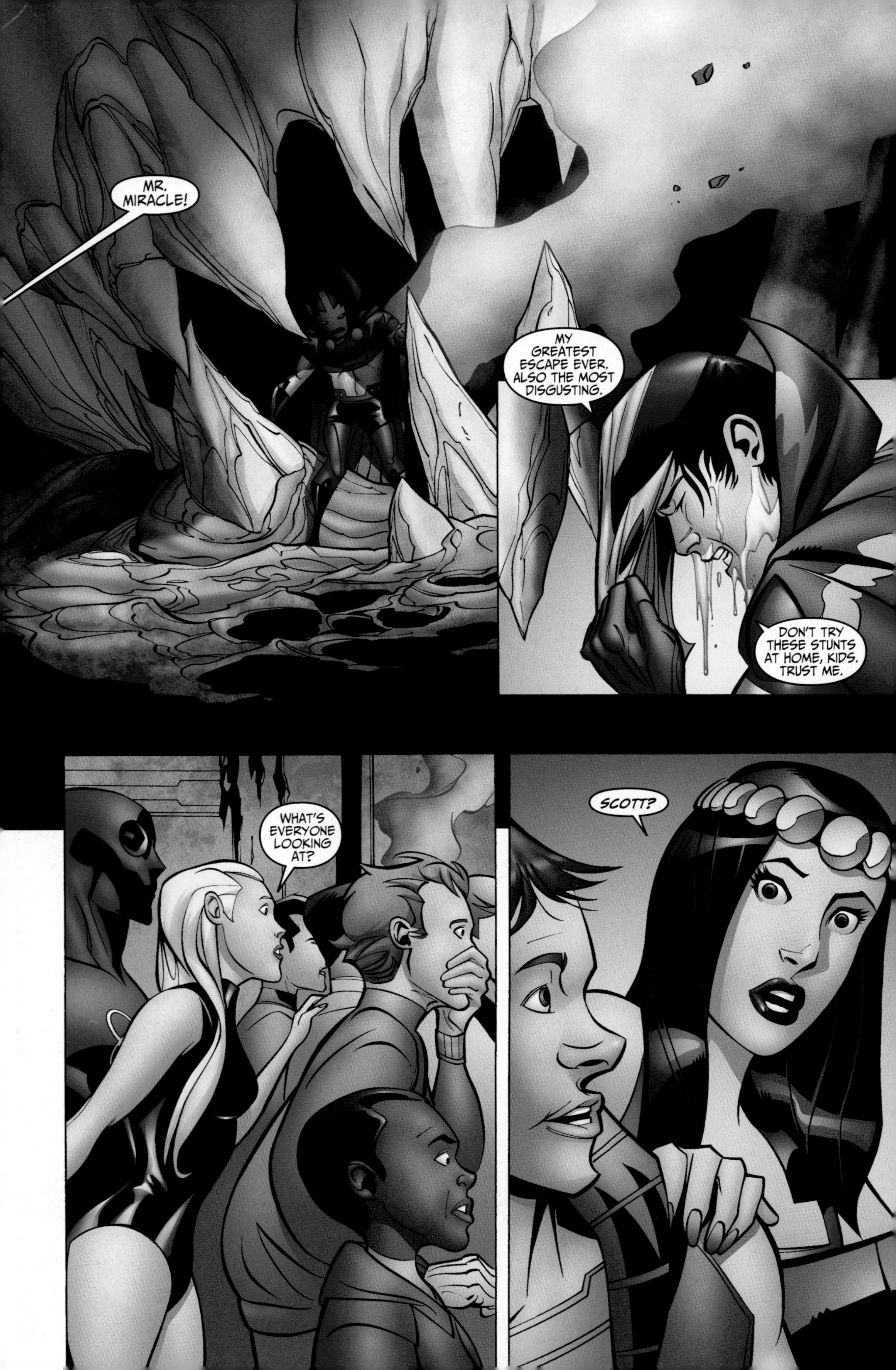
MR. MIRACLE!
MY GREATEST ESCAPE EVER. ALSO THE MOST DISGUSTING.
DON'T TRY THESE STUNTS AT HOME, KIDS. TRUST ME.
WHAT'S EVERYONE LOOKING AT?
SCOTT?

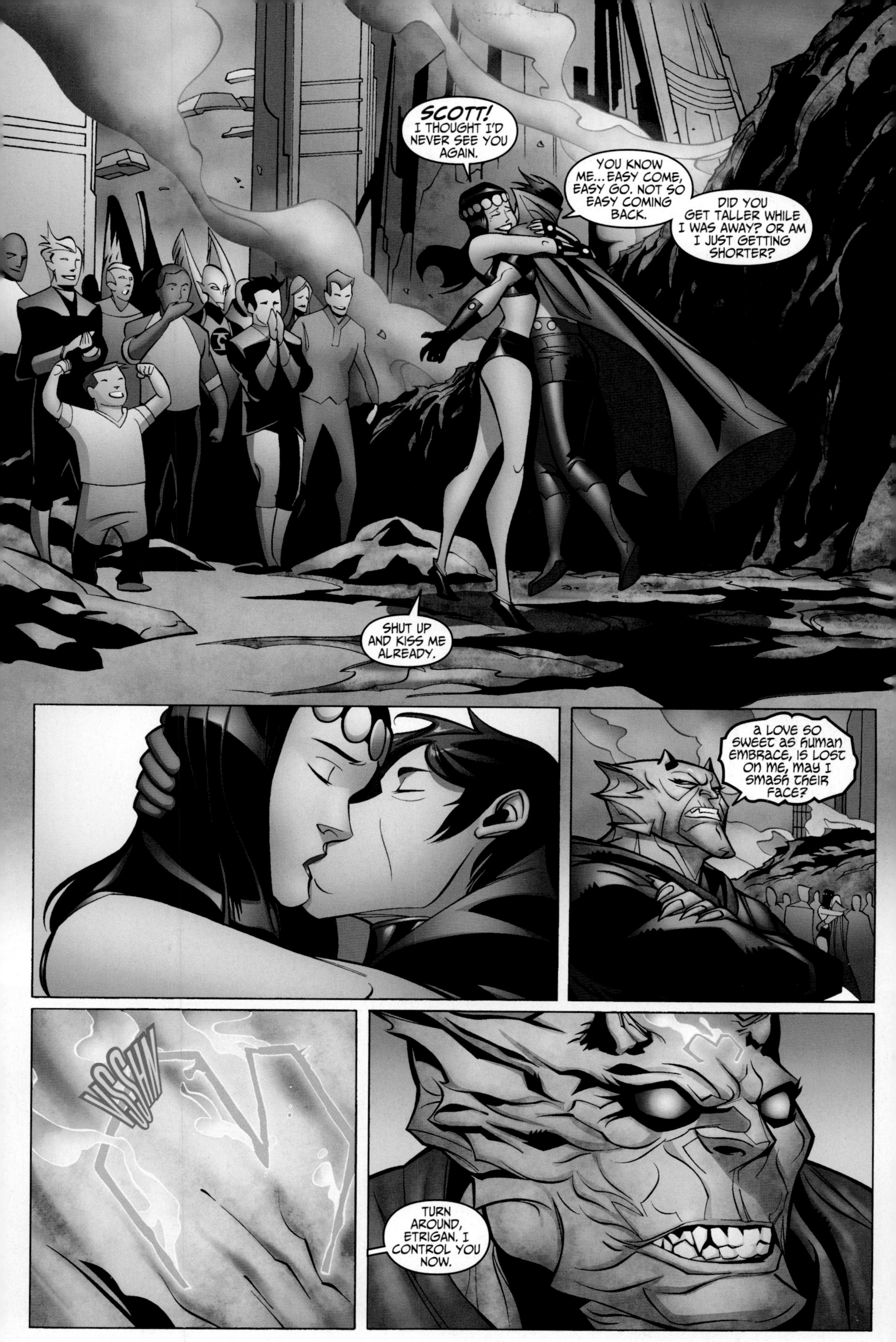
SCOTT! I THOUGHT I'D NEVER SEE YOU AGAIN.
YOU KNOW ME... EASY COME, EASY GO. NOT SO EASY COMING BACK.
DID YOU GET TALLER WHILE I WAS AWAY? OR AM I JUST GETTING SHORTER?
SHUT UP AND KISS ME ALREADY.
A LOVE SO SWEET AS HUMAN EMBRACE, IS LOST ON ME, MAY I SMASH THEIR FACE?
VSSHH
TURN AROUND, ETRIGAN. I CONTROL YOU NOW.

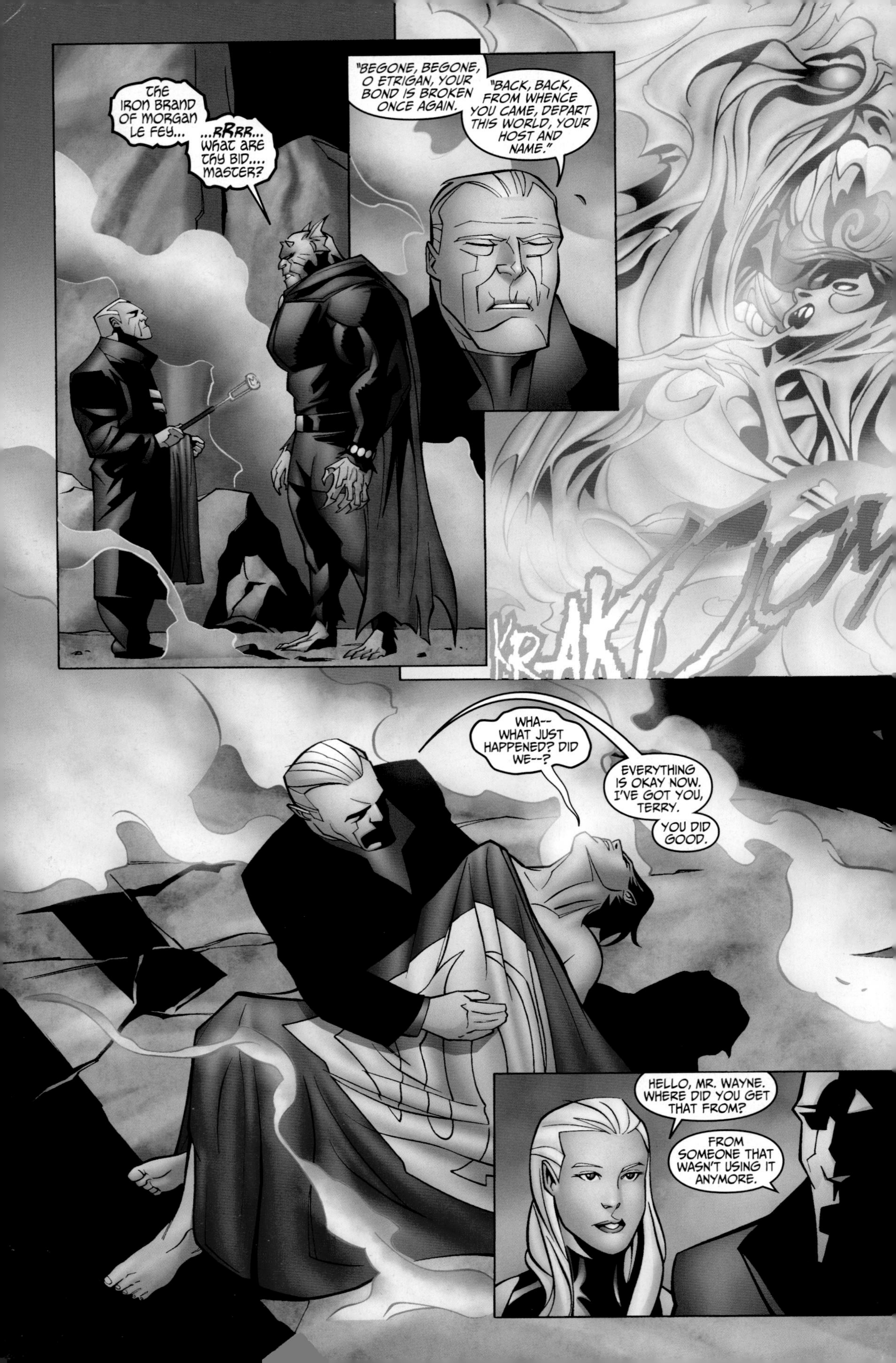

THE IRON BRAND OF MORGAN LE FEY...
...RRRR... WHAT ARE THY BID.... MASTER?
"BEGONE, BEGONE, O ETRIGAN, YOUR BOND IS BROKEN ONCE AGAIN.
"BACK, BACK, FROM WHENCE YOU CAME, DEPART THIS WORLD, YOUR HOST AND NAME."
KRAKADOOM
WHA-- WHAT JUST HAPPENED? DID WE--?
EVERYTHING IS OKAY NOW. I'VE GOT YOU, TERRY.
YOU DID GOOD.
HELLO, MR. WAYNE. WHERE DID YOU GET THAT FROM?
FROM SOMEONE THAT WASN'T USING IT ANYMORE.

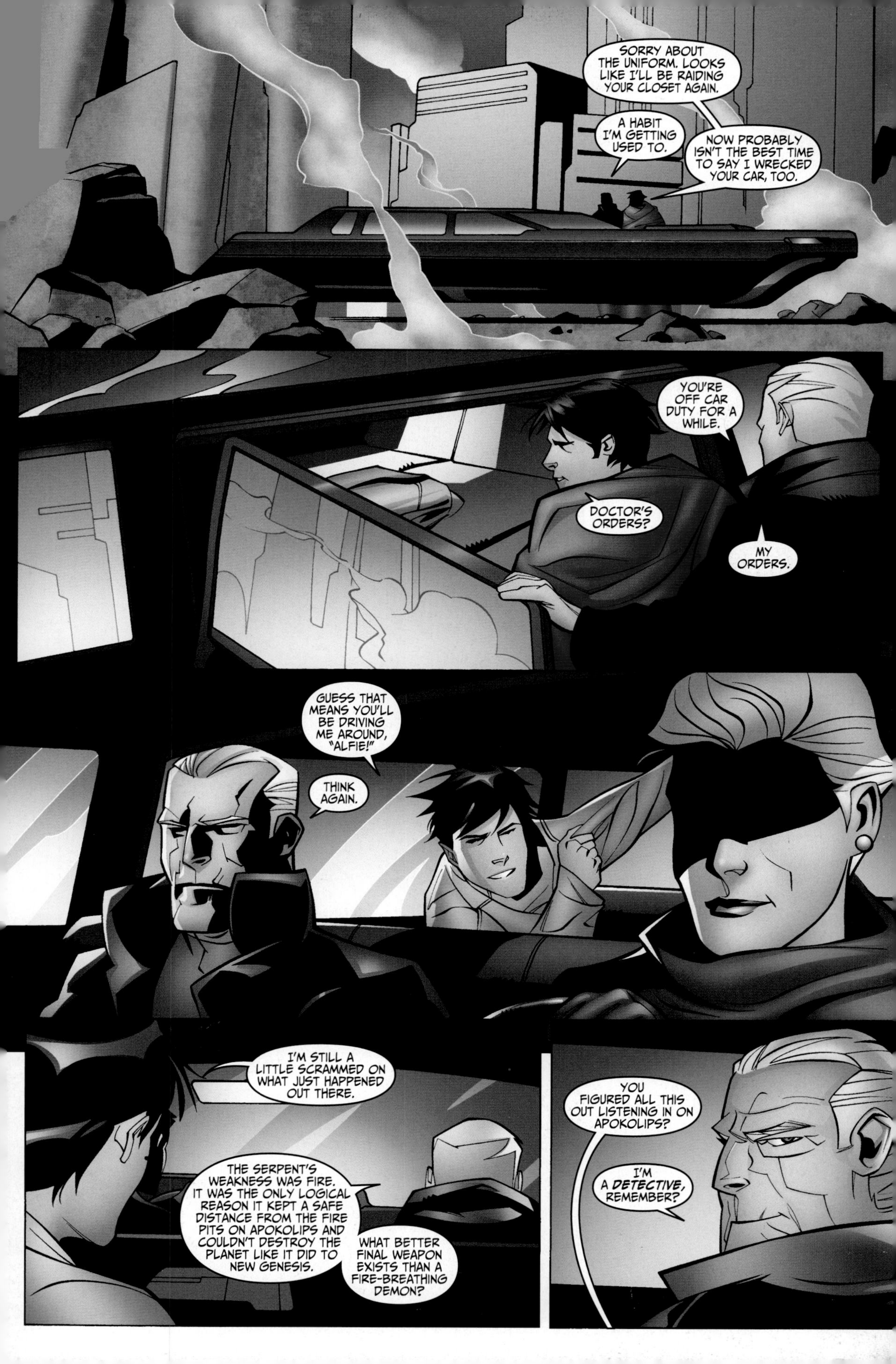
SORRY ABOUT THE UNIFORM. LOOKS LIKE I'LL BE RAIDING YOUR CLOSET AGAIN.
A HABIT I'M GETTING USED TO.
NOW PROBABLY ISN'T THE BEST TIME TO SAY I WRECKED YOUR CAR, TOO.
YOU'RE OFF CAR DUTY FOR A WHILE.
DOCTOR'S ORDERS?
MY ORDERS.
GUESS THAT MEANS YOU'LL BE DRIVING ME AROUND, "ALFIE!"
THINK AGAIN.
I'M STILL A LITTLE SCRAMMED ON WHAT JUST HAPPENED OUT THERE.
THE SERPENT'S WEAKNESS WAS FIRE. IT WAS THE ONLY LOGICAL REASON IT KEPT A SAFE DISTANCE FROM THE FIRE PITS ON APOKOLIPS AND COULDN'T DESTROY THE PLANET LIKE IT DID TO NEW GENESIS.
WHAT BETTER FINAL WEAPON EXISTS THAN A FIRE-BREATHING DEMON?
YOU FIGURED ALL THIS OUT LISTENING IN ON APOKOLIPS?
I'M A *DETECTIVE*, REMEMBER?

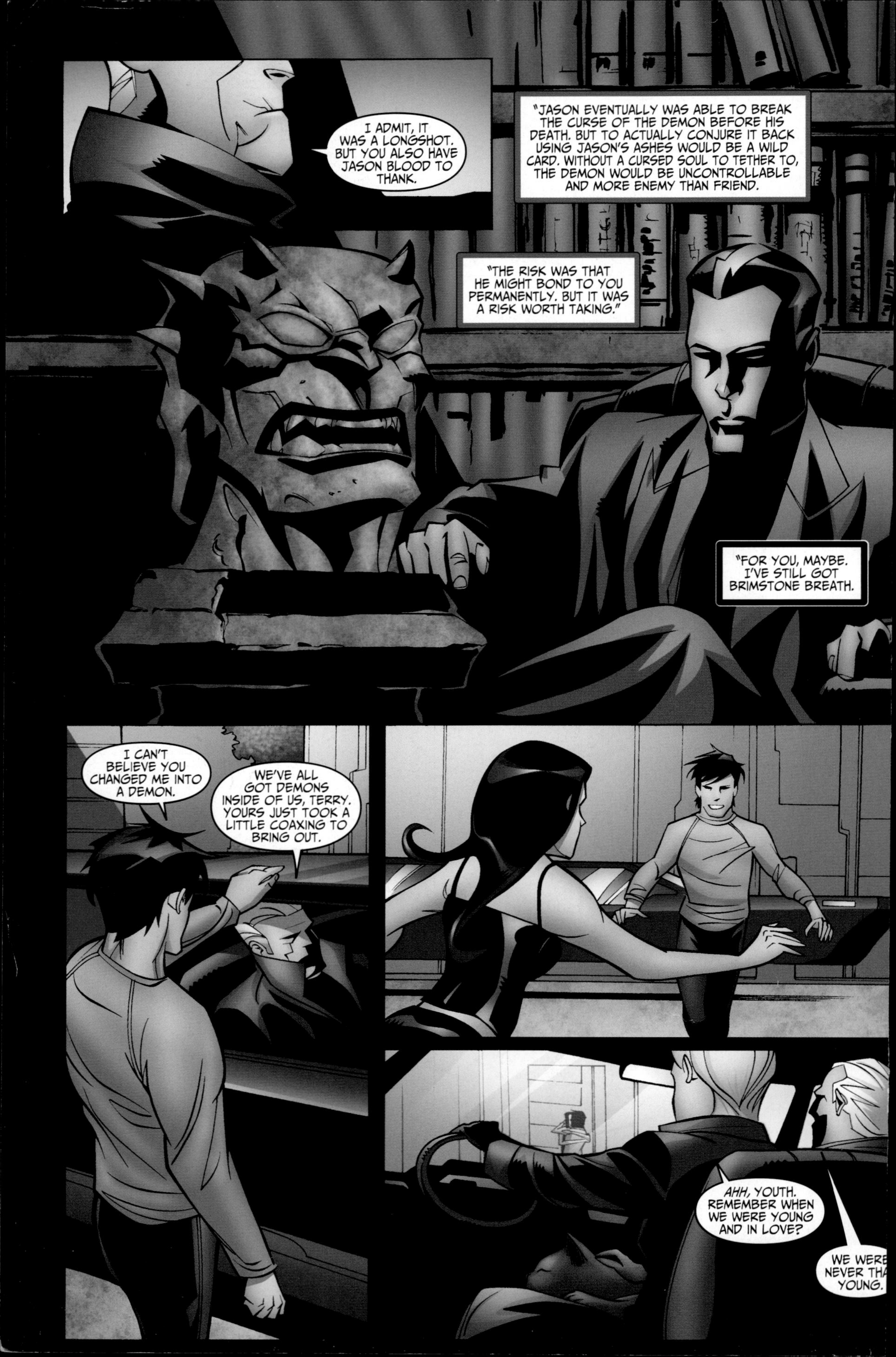
I ADMIT, IT WAS A LONGSHOT. BUT YOU ALSO HAVE JASON BLOOD TO THANK.
"JASON EVENTUALLY WAS ABLE TO BREAK THE CURSE OF THE DEMON BEFORE HIS DEATH. BUT TO ACTUALLY CONJURE IT BACK USING JASON'S ASHES WOULD BE A WILD CARD. WITHOUT A CURSED SOUL TO TETHER TO, THE DEMON WOULD BE UNCONTROLLABLE AND MORE ENEMY THAN FRIEND.
"THE RISK WAS THAT HE MIGHT BOND TO YOU PERMANENTLY. BUT IT WAS A RISK WORTH TAKING."
"FOR YOU, MAYBE. I'VE STILL GOT BRIMSTONE BREATH.
I CAN'T BELIEVE YOU CHANGED ME INTO A DEMON.
WE'VE ALL GOT DEMONS INSIDE OF US, TERRY. YOURS JUST TOOK A LITTLE COAXING TO BRING OUT.
AHH, YOUTH. REMEMBER WHEN WE WERE YOUNG AND IN LOVE?
WE WERE NEVER THA YOUNG.

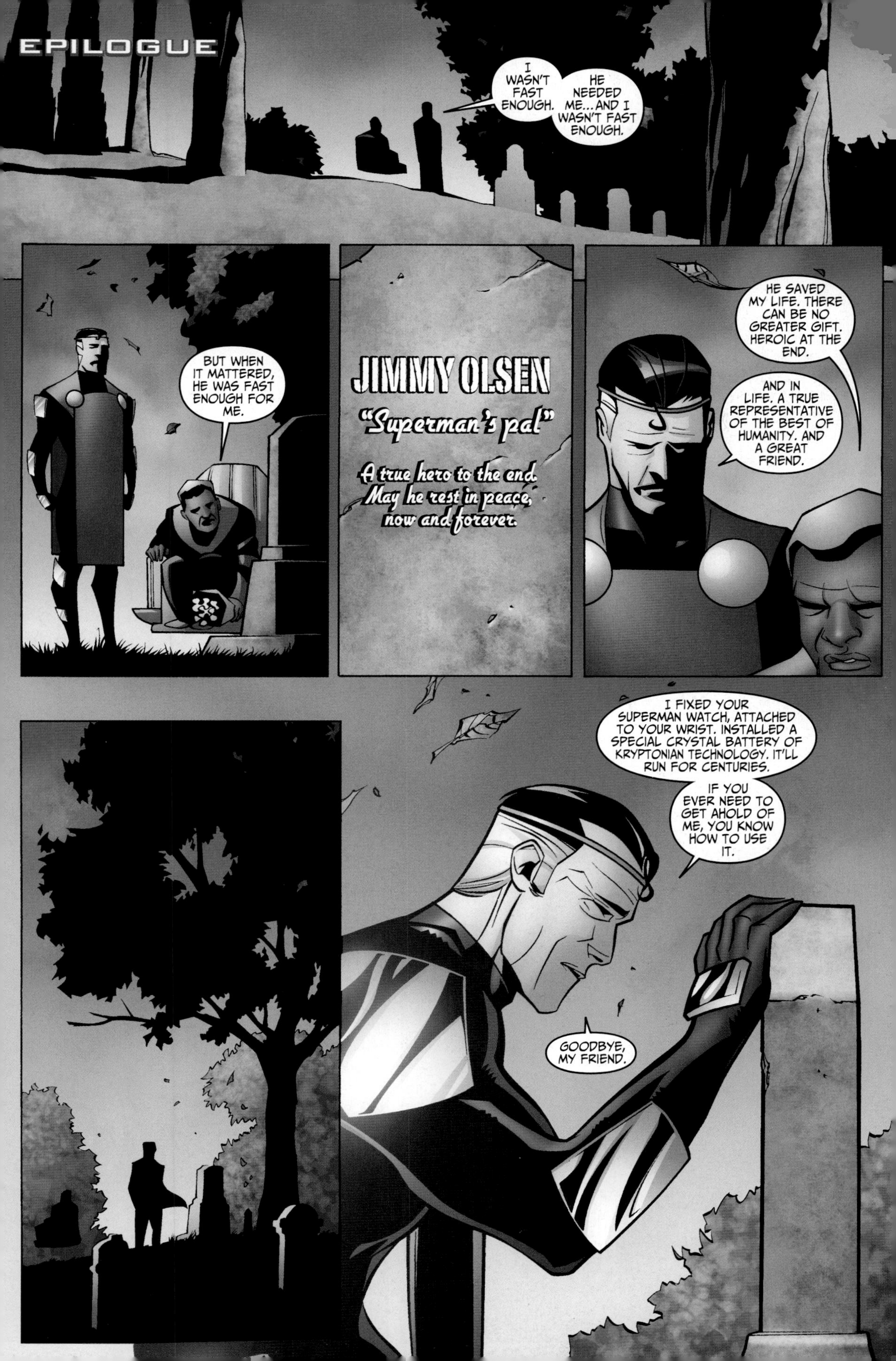
EPILOGUE
I WASN'T FAST ENOUGH.
HE NEEDED ME...AND I WASN'T FAST ENOUGH.
BUT WHEN IT MATTERED, HE WAS FAST ENOUGH FOR ME.
JIMMY OLSEN
"Superman's pal"
A true hero to the end. May he rest in peace, now and forever.
HE SAVED MY LIFE. THERE CAN BE NO GREATER GIFT. HEROIC AT THE END.
AND IN LIFE. A TRUE REPRESENTATIVE OF THE BEST OF HUMANITY. AND A GREAT FRIEND.
I FIXED YOUR SUPERMAN WATCH, ATTACHED TO YOUR WRIST. INSTALLED A SPECIAL CRYSTAL BATTERY OF KRYPTONIAN TECHNOLOGY. IT'LL RUN FOR CENTURIES.
IF YOU EVER NEED TO GET AHOLD OF ME, YOU KNOW HOW TO USE IT.
GOODBYE, MY FRIEND.

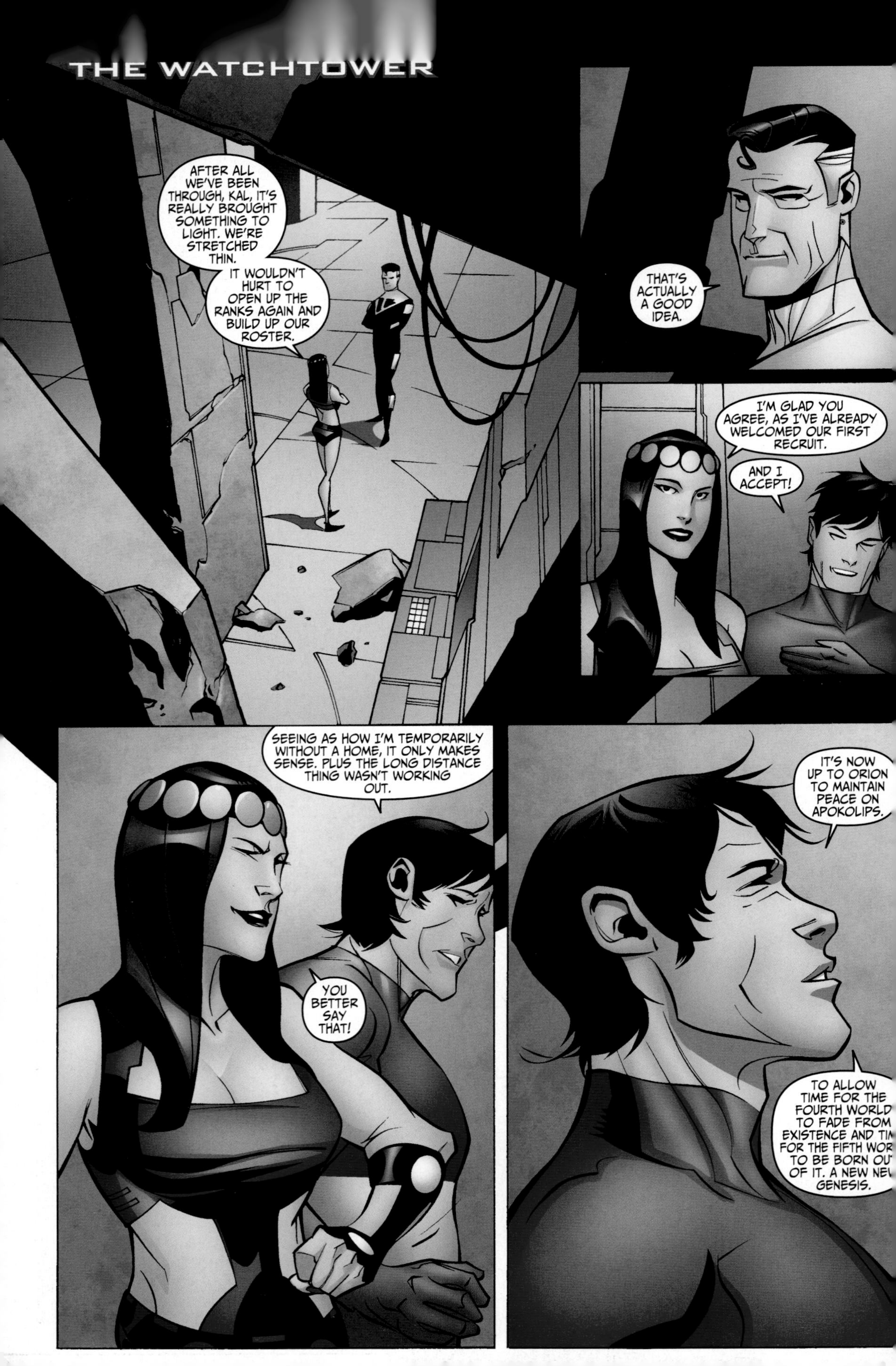

THE WATCHTOWER
AFTER ALL WE'VE BEEN THROUGH, KAL, IT'S REALLY BROUGHT SOMETHING TO LIGHT. WE'RE STRETCHED THIN.
IT WOULDN'T HURT TO OPEN UP THE RANKS AGAIN AND BUILD UP OUR ROSTER.
THAT'S ACTUALLY A GOOD IDEA.
I'M GLAD YOU AGREE, AS I'VE ALREADY WELCOMED OUR FIRST RECRUIT.
AND I ACCEPT!
SEEING AS HOW I'M TEMPORARILY WITHOUT A HOME, IT ONLY MAKES SENSE. PLUS THE LONG DISTANCE THING WASN'T WORKING OUT.
YOU BETTER SAY THAT!
IT'S NOW UP TO ORION TO MAINTAIN PEACE ON APOKOLIPS.
TO ALLOW TIME FOR THE FOURTH WORLD TO FADE FROM EXISTENCE AND TIM
FOR THE FIFTH WOR
TO BE BORN OU
OF IT. A NEW NEV
GENESIS.

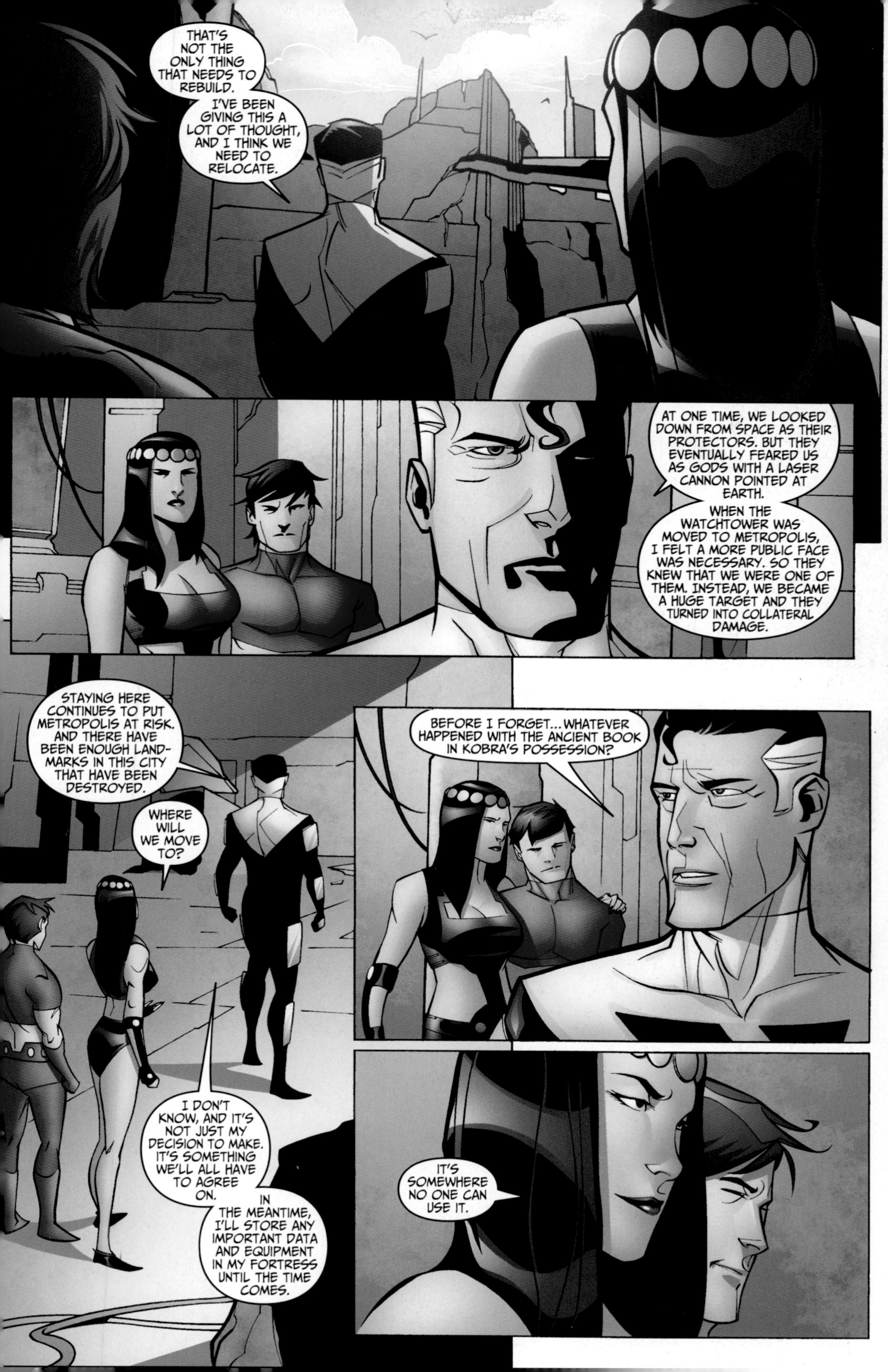
THAT'S NOT THE ONLY THING THAT NEEDS TO REBUILD.
I'VE BEEN GIVING THIS A LOT OF THOUGHT, AND I THINK WE NEED TO RELOCATE.
AT ONE TIME, WE LOOKED DOWN FROM SPACE AS THEIR PROTECTORS. BUT THEY EVENTUALLY FEARED US AS GODS WITH A LASER CANNON POINTED AT EARTH.
WHEN THE WATCHTOWER WAS MOVED TO METROPOLIS, I FELT A MORE PUBLIC FACE WAS NECESSARY. SO THEY KNEW THAT WE WERE ONE OF THEM. INSTEAD, WE BECAME A HUGE TARGET AND THEY TURNED INTO COLLATERAL DAMAGE.
STAYING HERE CONTINUES TO PUT METROPOLIS AT RISK. AND THERE HAVE BEEN ENOUGH LAND-MARKS IN THIS CITY THAT HAVE BEEN DESTROYED.
WHERE WILL WE MOVE TO?
I DON'T KNOW, AND IT'S NOT JUST MY DECISION TO MAKE. IT'S SOMETHING WE'LL ALL HAVE TO AGREE ON.
IN THE MEANTIME, I'LL STORE ANY IMPORTANT DATA AND EQUIPMENT IN MY FORTRESS UNTIL THE TIME COMES.
BEFORE I FORGET... WHATEVER HAPPENED WITH THE ANCIENT BOOK IN KOBRA'S POSSESSION?
IT'S SOMEWHERE NO ONE CAN USE IT.

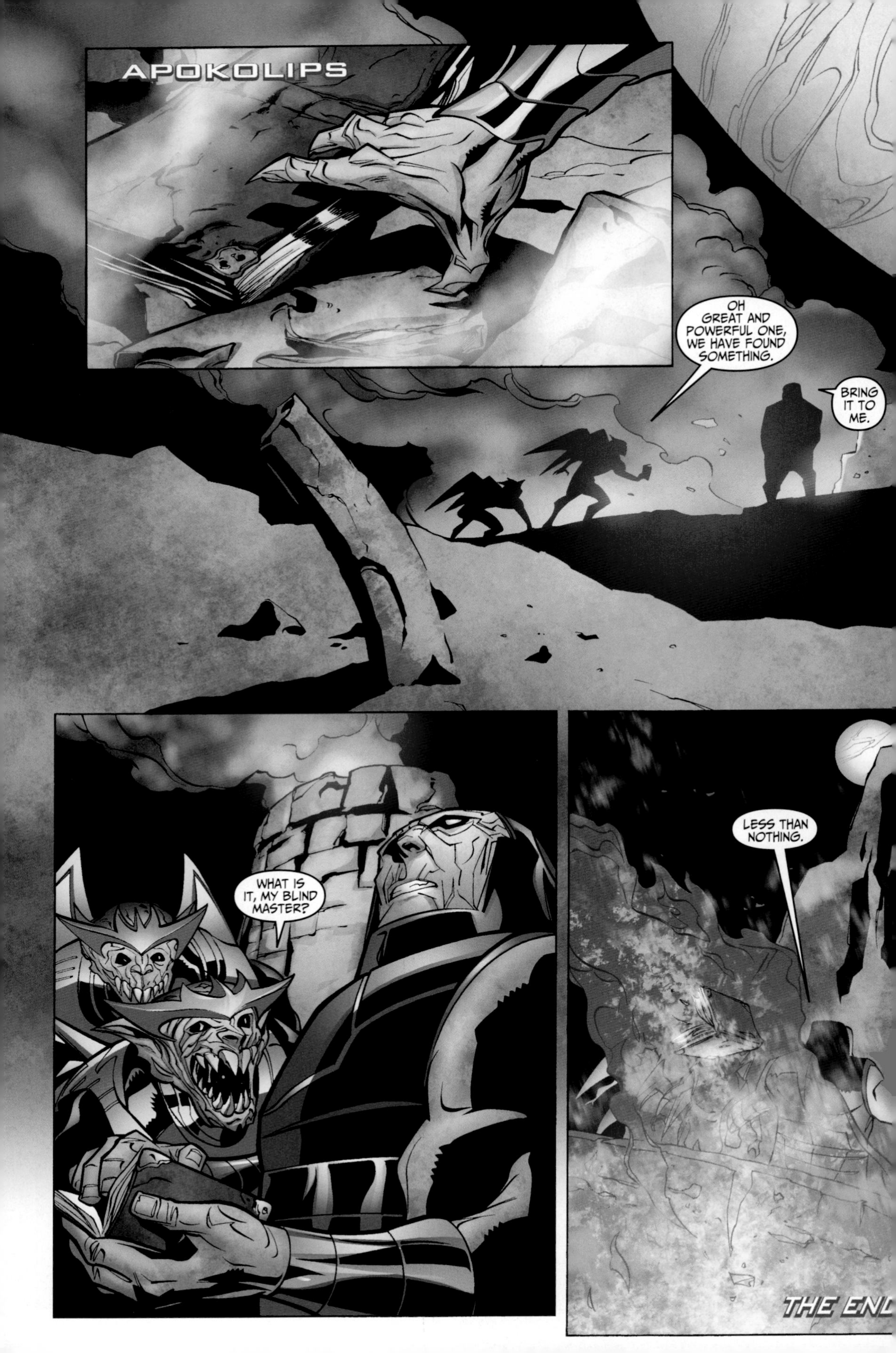
APOKOLIPS
OH GREAT AND POWERFUL ONE, WE HAVE FOUND SOMETHING.
BRING IT TO ME.
WHAT IS IT, MY BLIND MASTER?
LESS THAN NOTHING.
THE END

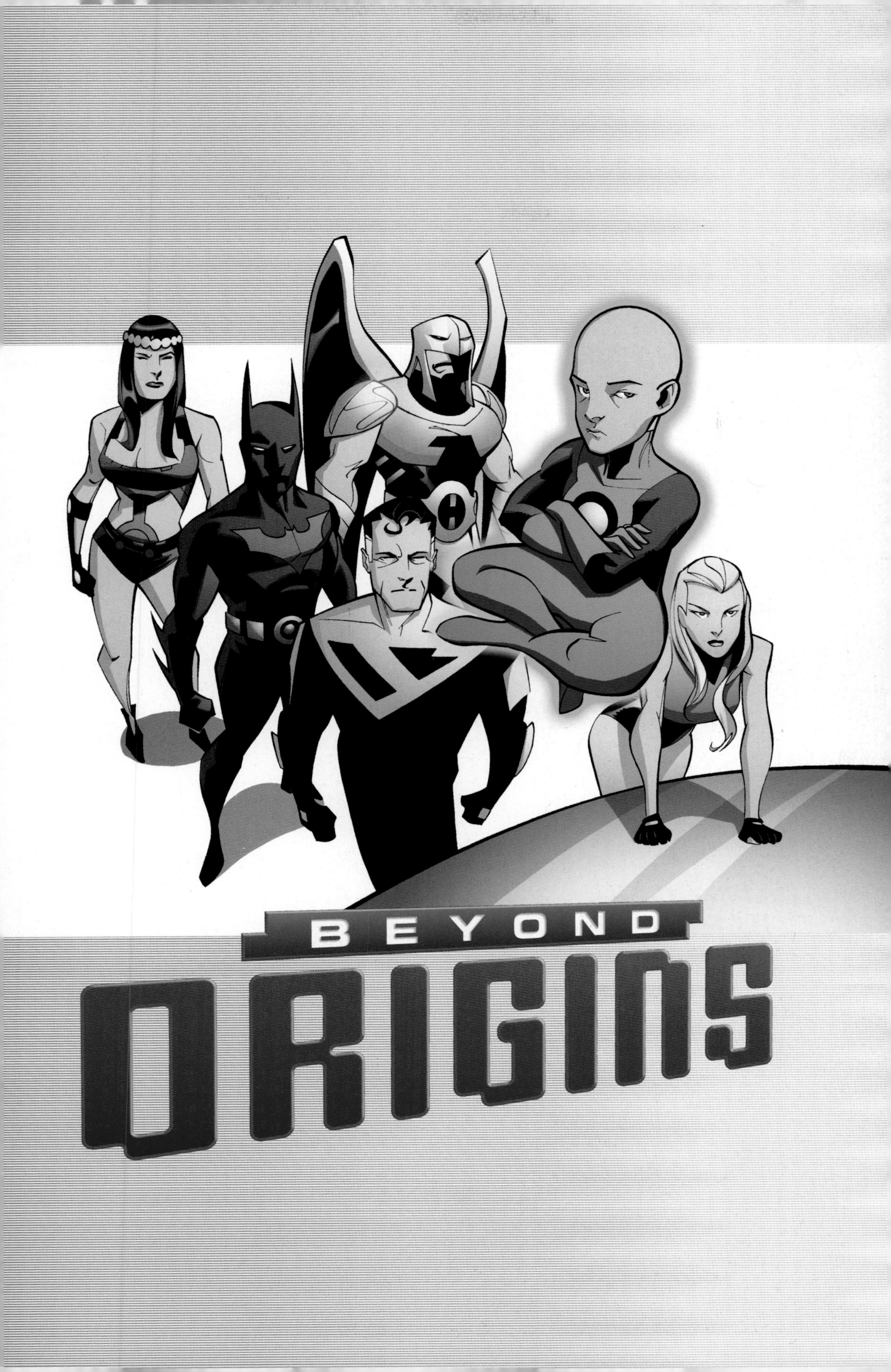

BEYOND ORIGINS

CHAPTER ONE:
WARHAWK
ART BY **ERIC NGUYEN**

CHAPTER TWO:
AQUAGIRL
ART BY **JAMES BROUWER**

CHAPTER THREE:
BARDA
ART BY **BEN CALDWELL**

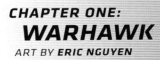

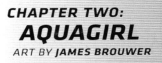

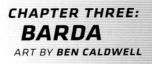

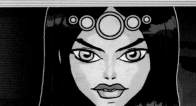

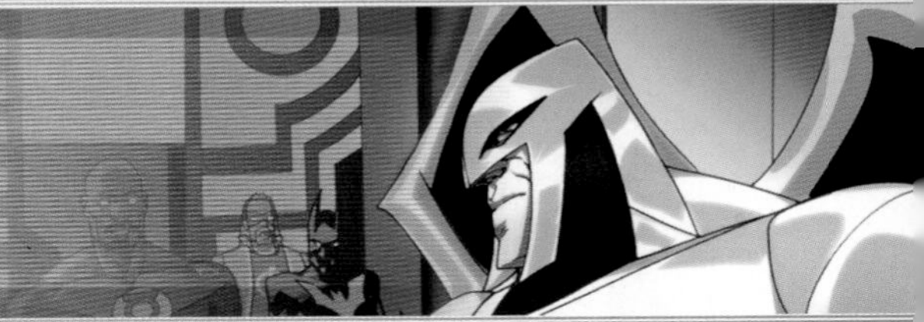

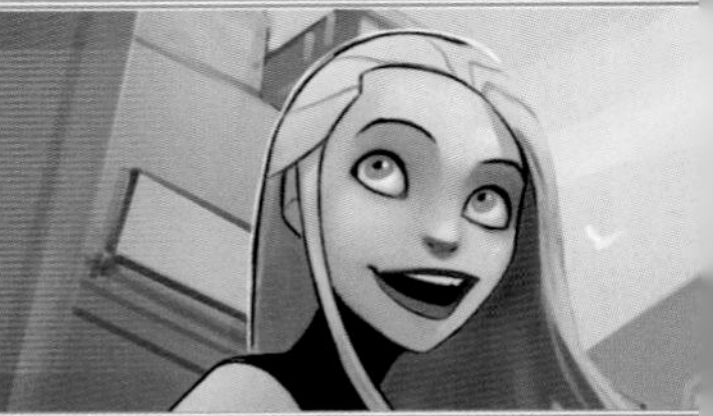

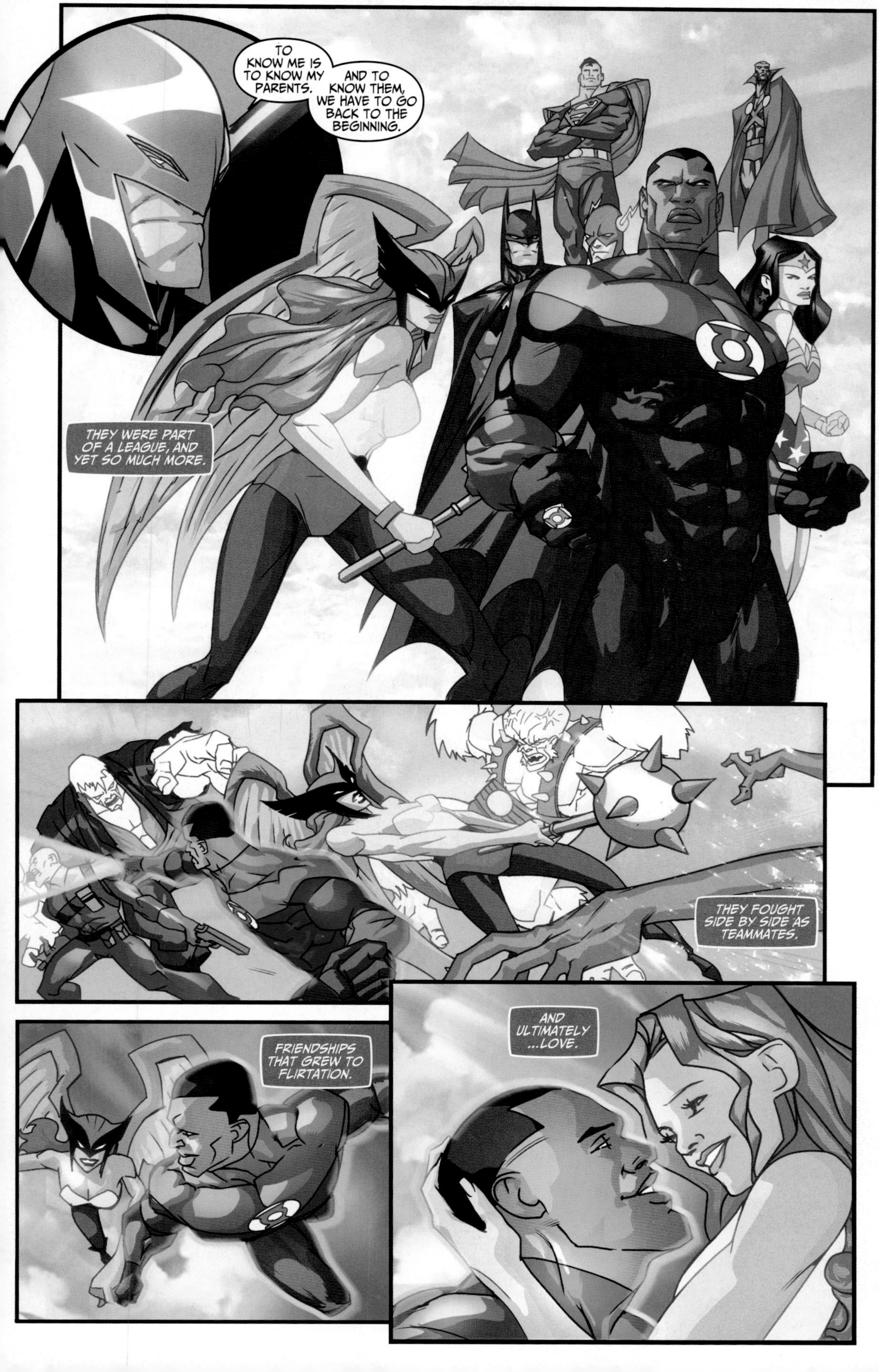
TO KNOW ME IS TO KNOW MY PARENTS.
AND TO KNOW THEM, WE HAVE TO GO BACK TO THE BEGINNING.
THEY WERE PART OF A LEAGUE, AND YET SO MUCH MORE.
THEY FOUGHT SIDE BY SIDE AS TEAMMATES.
FRIENDSHIPS THAT GREW TO FLIRTATION.
AND ULTIMATELY ...LOVE.

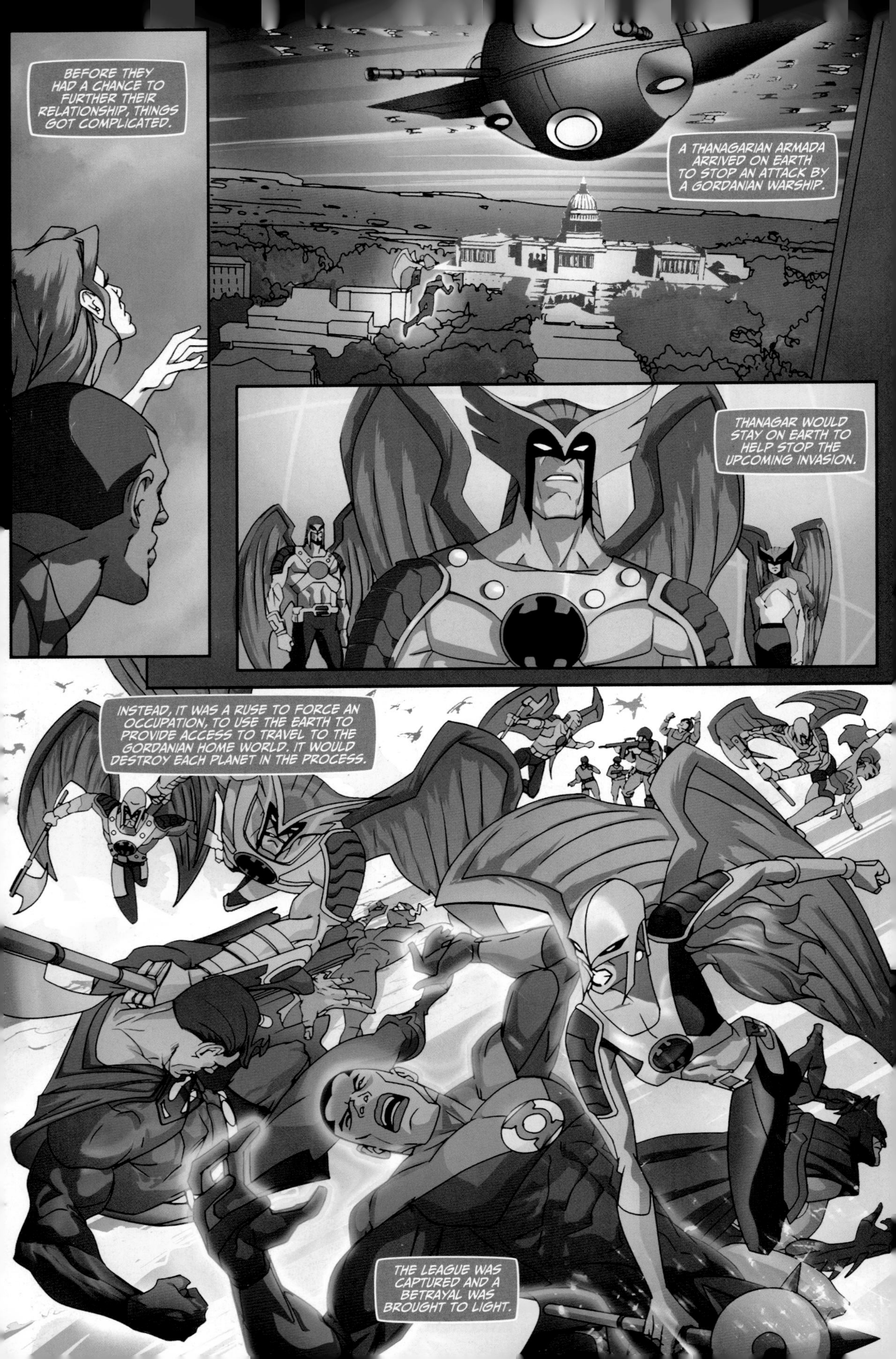
BEFORE THEY HAD A CHANCE TO FURTHER THEIR RELATIONSHIP, THINGS GOT COMPLICATED.
A THANAGARIAN ARMADA ARRIVED ON EARTH TO STOP AN ATTACK BY A GORDANIAN WARSHIP.
THANAGAR WOULD STAY ON EARTH TO HELP STOP THE UPCOMING INVASION.
INSTEAD, IT WAS A RUSE TO FORCE AN OCCUPATION, TO USE THE EARTH TO PROVIDE ACCESS TO TRAVEL TO THE GORDANIAN HOME WORLD. IT WOULD DESTROY EACH PLANET IN THE PROCESS.
THE LEAGUE WAS CAPTURED AND A BETRAYAL WAS BROUGHT TO LIGHT.

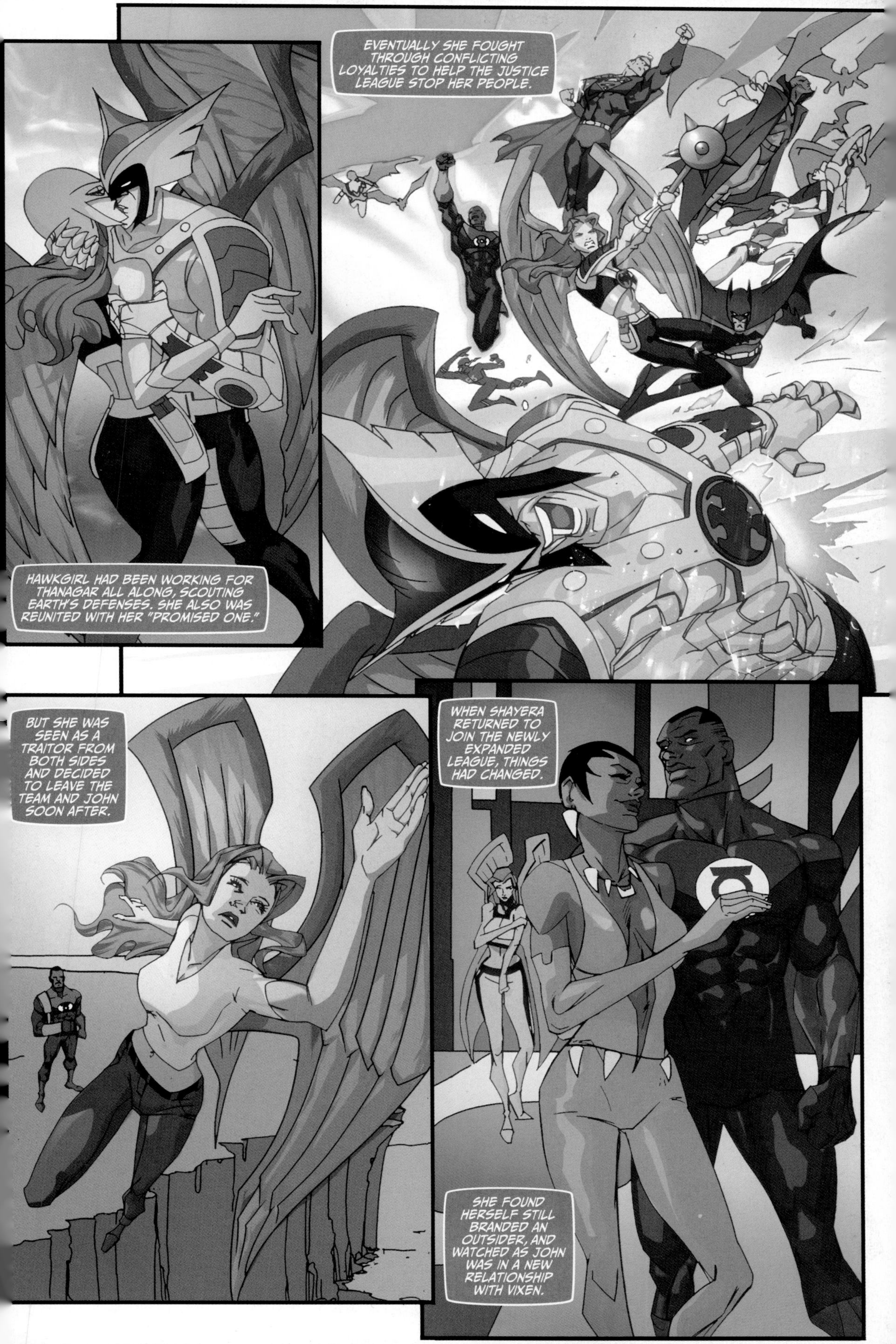
HAWKGIRL HAD BEEN WORKING FOR THANAGAR ALL ALONG, SCOUTING EARTH'S DEFENSES. SHE ALSO WAS REUNITED WITH HER "PROMISED ONE."
EVENTUALLY SHE FOUGHT THROUGH CONFLICTING LOYALTIES TO HELP THE JUSTICE LEAGUE STOP HER PEOPLE.
BUT SHE WAS SEEN AS A TRAITOR FROM BOTH SIDES AND DECIDED TO LEAVE THE TEAM AND JOHN SOON AFTER.
WHEN SHAYERA RETURNED TO JOIN THE NEWLY EXPANDED LEAGUE, THINGS HAD CHANGED.
SHE FOUND HERSELF STILL BRANDED AN OUTSIDER, AND WATCHED AS JOHN WAS IN A NEW RELATIONSHIP WITH VIXEN.

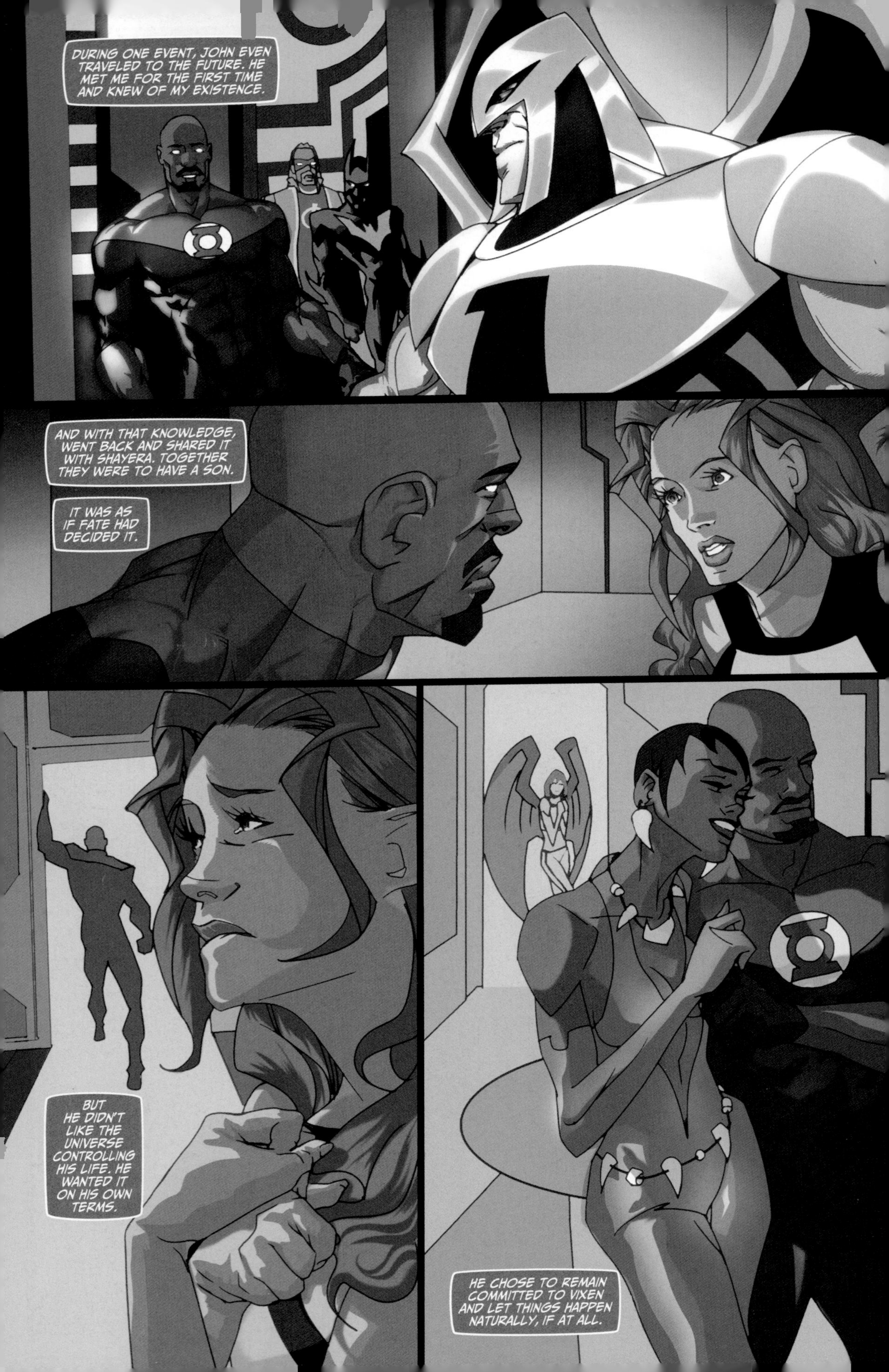
DURING ONE EVENT, JOHN EVEN TRAVELED TO THE FUTURE. HE MET ME FOR THE FIRST TIME AND KNEW OF MY EXISTENCE.
AND WITH THAT KNOWLEDGE, WENT BACK AND SHARED IT WITH SHAYERA. TOGETHER THEY WERE TO HAVE A SON.
IT WAS AS IF FATE HAD DECIDED IT.
BUT HE DIDN'T LIKE THE UNIVERSE CONTROLLING HIS LIFE. HE WANTED IT ON HIS OWN TERMS.
HE CHOSE TO REMAIN COMMITTED TO VIXEN AND LET THINGS HAPPEN NATURALLY, IF AT ALL.

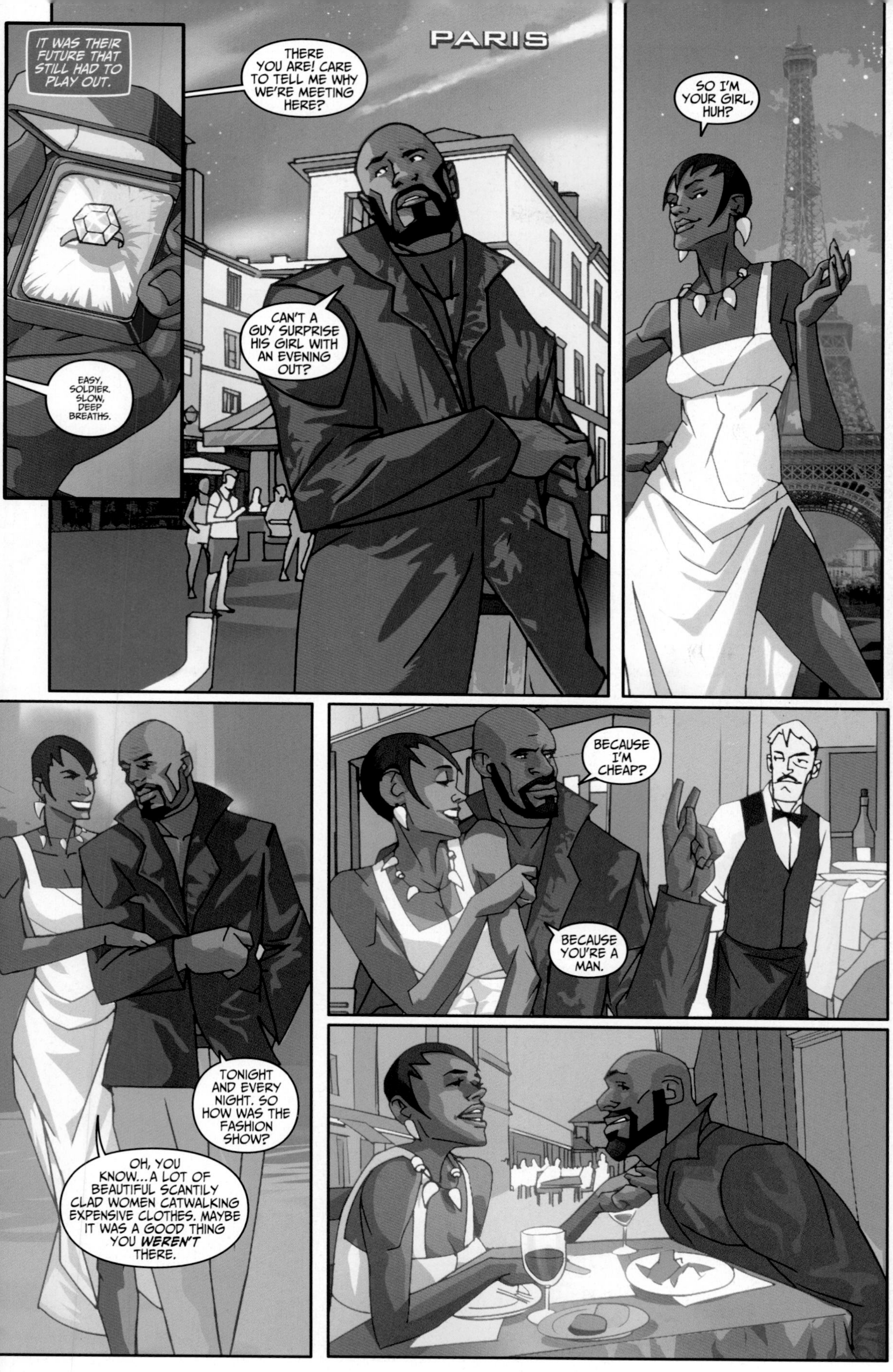
PARIS
IT WAS THEIR FUTURE THAT STILL HAD TO PLAY OUT.
EASY, SOLDIER. SLOW, DEEP BREATHS.
THERE YOU ARE! CARE TO TELL ME WHY WE'RE MEETING HERE?
CAN'T A GUY SURPRISE HIS GIRL WITH AN EVENING OUT?
SO I'M YOUR GIRL, HUH?
TONIGHT AND EVERY NIGHT. SO HOW WAS THE FASHION SHOW?
OH, YOU KNOW...A LOT OF BEAUTIFUL SCANTILY CLAD WOMEN CATWALKING EXPENSIVE CLOTHES. MAYBE IT WAS A GOOD THING YOU ***WEREN'T*** THERE.
BECAUSE I'M CHEAP?
BECAUSE YOU'RE A MAN.

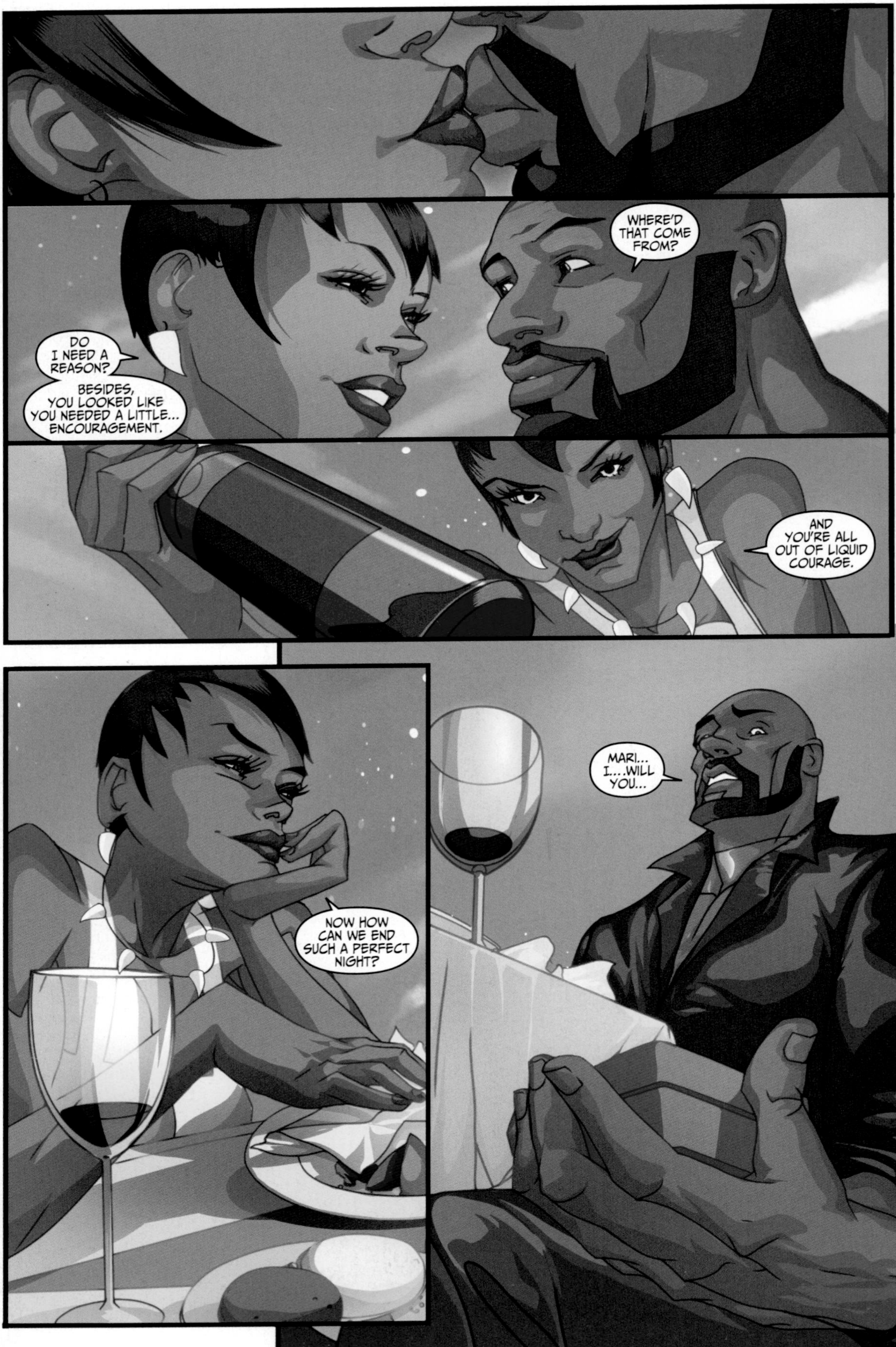
WHERE'D THAT COME FROM?
DO I NEED A REASON?
BESIDES, YOU LOOKED LIKE YOU NEEDED A LITTLE... ENCOURAGEMENT.
AND YOU'RE ALL OUT OF LIQUID COURAGE.
NOW HOW CAN WE END SUCH A PERFECT NIGHT?
MARI... I...WILL YOU...

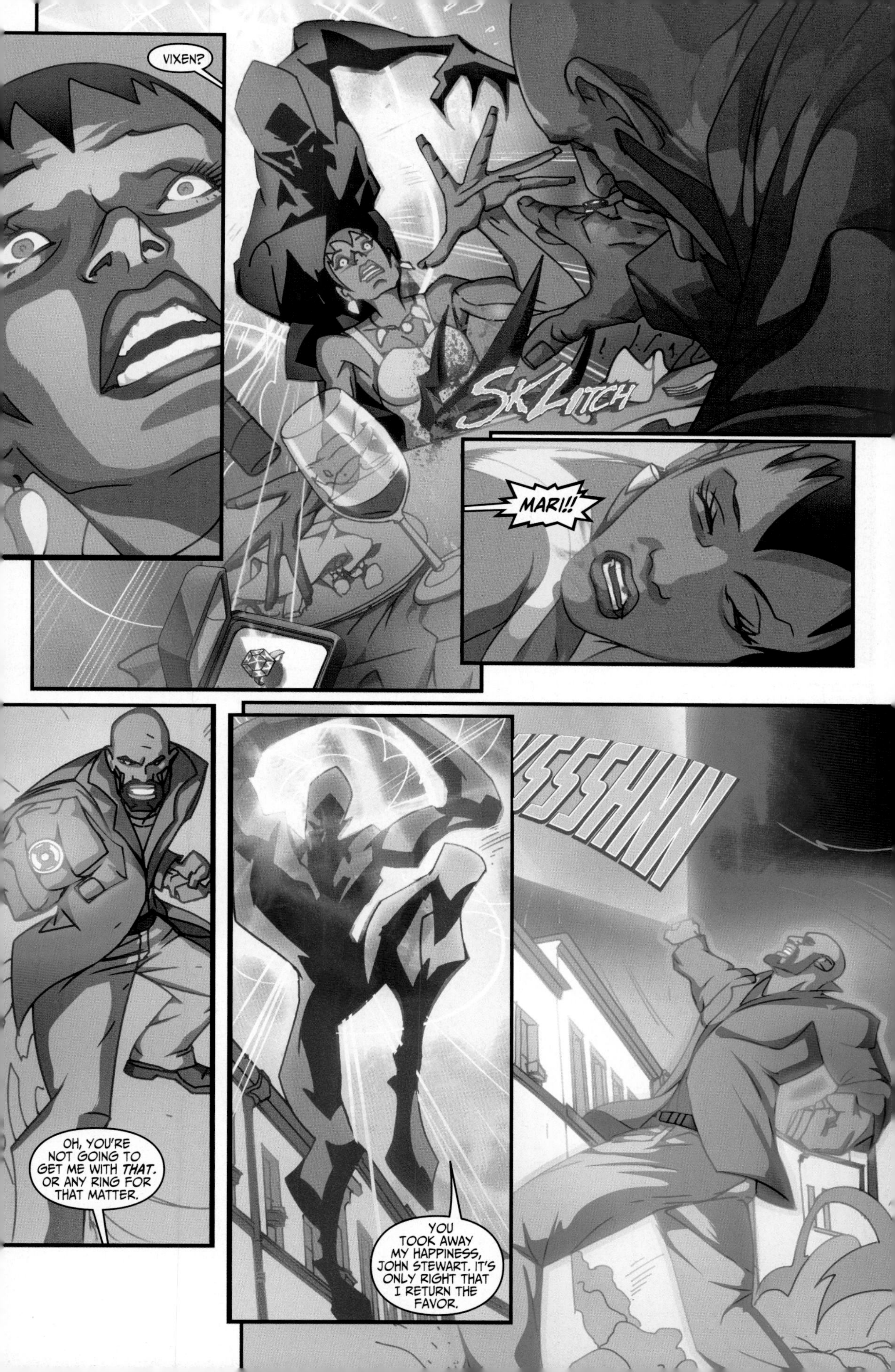
VIXEN?
SKLITCH
MARI!!
OH, YOU'RE NOT GOING TO GET ME WITH *THAT*. OR ANY RING FOR THAT MATTER.
YOU TOOK AWAY MY HAPPINESS, JOHN STEWART. IT'S ONLY RIGHT THAT I RETURN THE FAVOR.

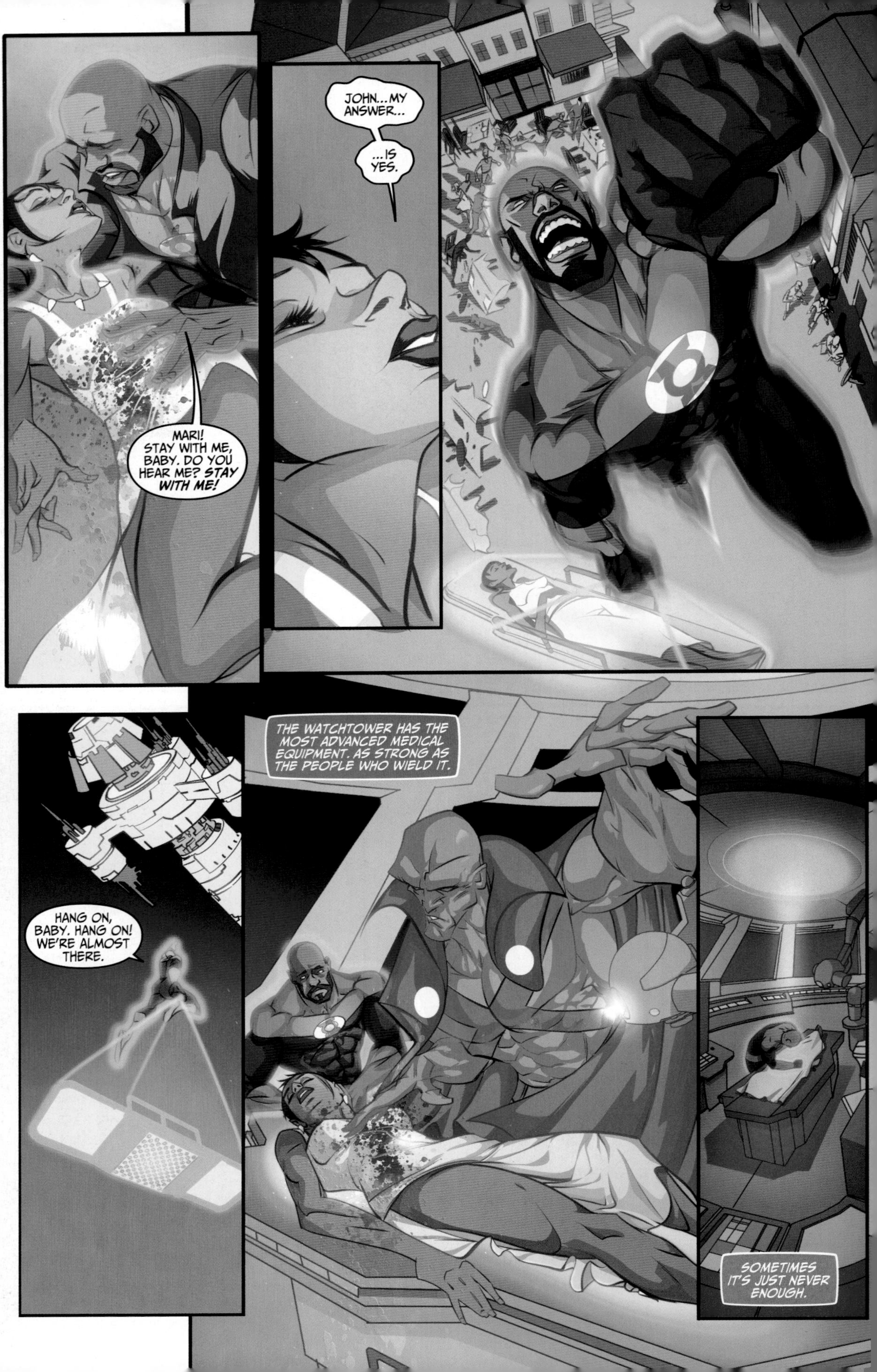
MARI! STAY WITH ME, BABY. DO YOU HEAR ME? STAY WITH ME!
JOHN... MY ANSWER...
...IS YES.
HANG ON, BABY. HANG ON! WE'RE ALMOST THERE.
THE WATCHTOWER HAS THE MOST ADVANCED MEDICAL EQUIPMENT. AS STRONG AS THE PEOPLE WHO WIELD IT.
SOMETIMES IT'S JUST NEVER ENOUGH.

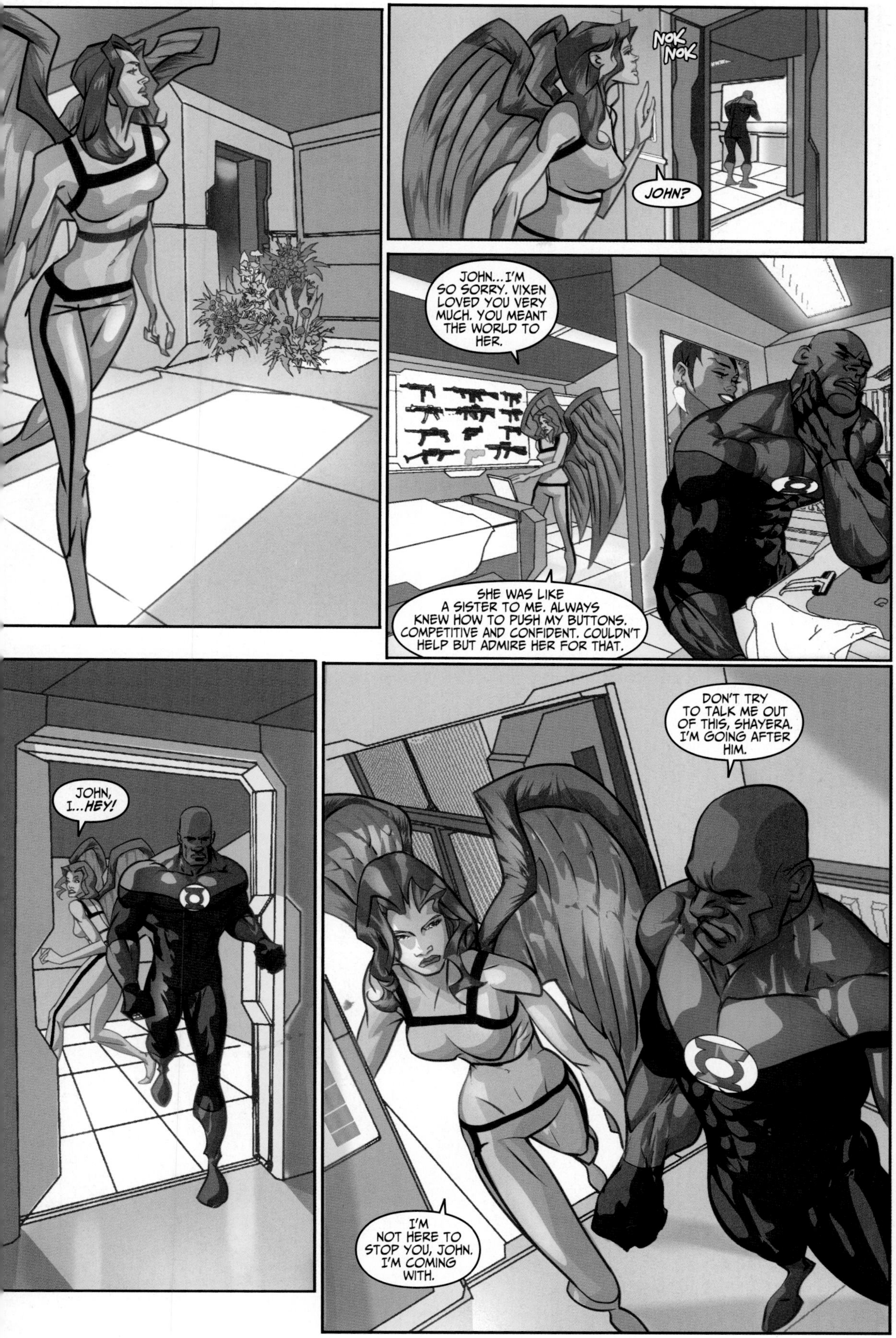
NOK NOK
JOHN?
JOHN...I'M SO SORRY. VIXEN LOVED YOU VERY MUCH. YOU MEANT THE WORLD TO HER.
SHE WAS LIKE A SISTER TO ME. ALWAYS KNEW HOW TO PUSH MY BUTTONS. COMPETITIVE AND CONFIDENT. COULDN'T HELP BUT ADMIRE HER FOR THAT.
JOHN, I...HEY!
DON'T TRY TO TALK ME OUT OF THIS, SHAYERA. I'M GOING AFTER HIM.
I'M NOT HERE TO STOP YOU, JOHN. I'M COMING WITH.

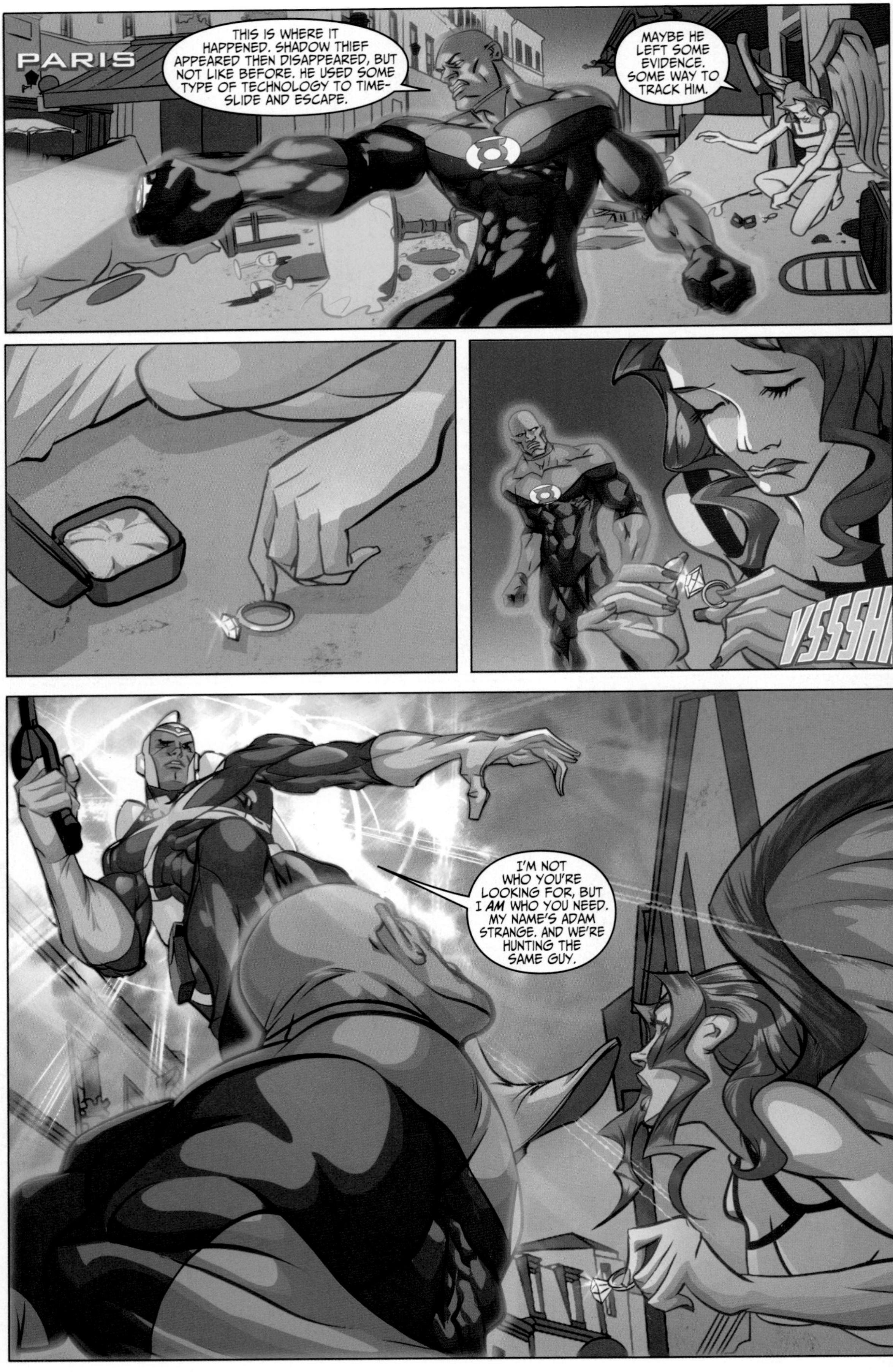
PARIS
THIS IS WHERE IT HAPPENED. SHADOW THIEF APPEARED THEN DISAPPEARED, BUT NOT LIKE BEFORE. HE USED SOME TYPE OF TECHNOLOGY TO TIME-SLIDE AND ESCAPE.
MAYBE HE LEFT SOME EVIDENCE. SOME WAY TO TRACK HIM.
VSSSHH
I'M NOT WHO YOU'RE LOOKING FOR, BUT I *AM* WHO YOU NEED. MY NAME'S ADAM STRANGE. AND WE'RE HUNTING THE SAME GUY.

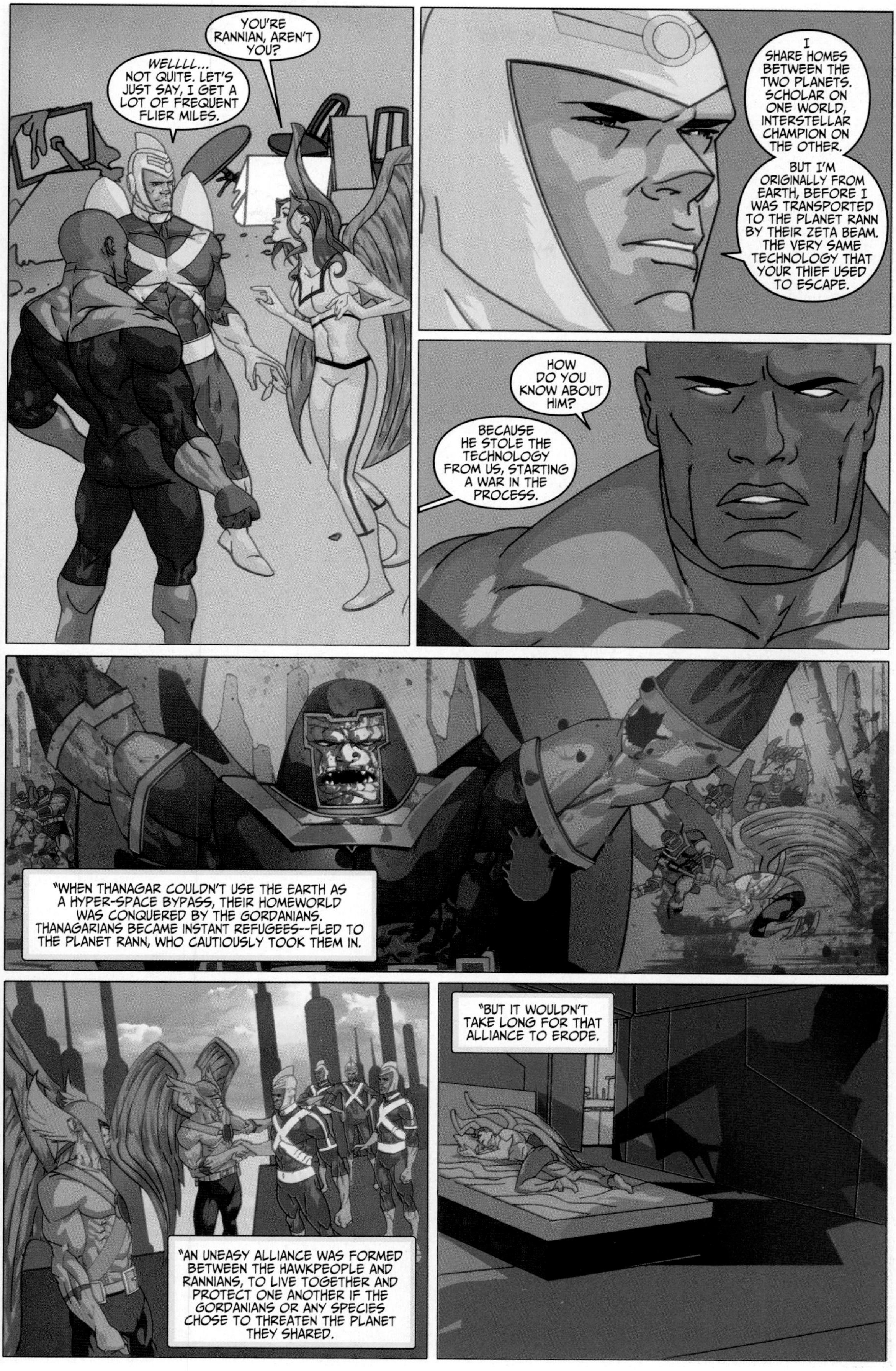
YOU'RE RANNIAN, AREN'T YOU?
WELLLL... NOT QUITE. LET'S JUST SAY, I GET A LOT OF FREQUENT FLIER MILES.
I SHARE HOMES BETWEEN THE TWO PLANETS. SCHOLAR ON ONE WORLD, INTERSTELLAR CHAMPION ON THE OTHER.
BUT I'M ORIGINALLY FROM EARTH, BEFORE I WAS TRANSPORTED TO THE PLANET RANN BY THEIR ZETA BEAM. THE VERY SAME TECHNOLOGY THAT YOUR THIEF USED TO ESCAPE.
HOW DO YOU KNOW ABOUT HIM?
BECAUSE HE STOLE THE TECHNOLOGY FROM US, STARTING A WAR IN THE PROCESS.
"WHEN THANAGAR COULDN'T USE THE EARTH AS A HYPER-SPACE BYPASS, THEIR HOMEWORLD WAS CONQUERED BY THE GORDANIANS. THANAGARIANS BECAME INSTANT REFUGEES--FLED TO THE PLANET RANN, WHO CAUTIOUSLY TOOK THEM IN.
"AN UNEASY ALLIANCE WAS FORMED BETWEEN THE HAWKPEOPLE AND RANNIANS, TO LIVE TOGETHER AND PROTECT ONE ANOTHER IF THE GORDANIANS OR ANY SPECIES CHOSE TO THREATEN THE PLANET THEY SHARED.
"BUT IT WOULDN'T TAKE LONG FOR THAT ALLIANCE TO ERODE.

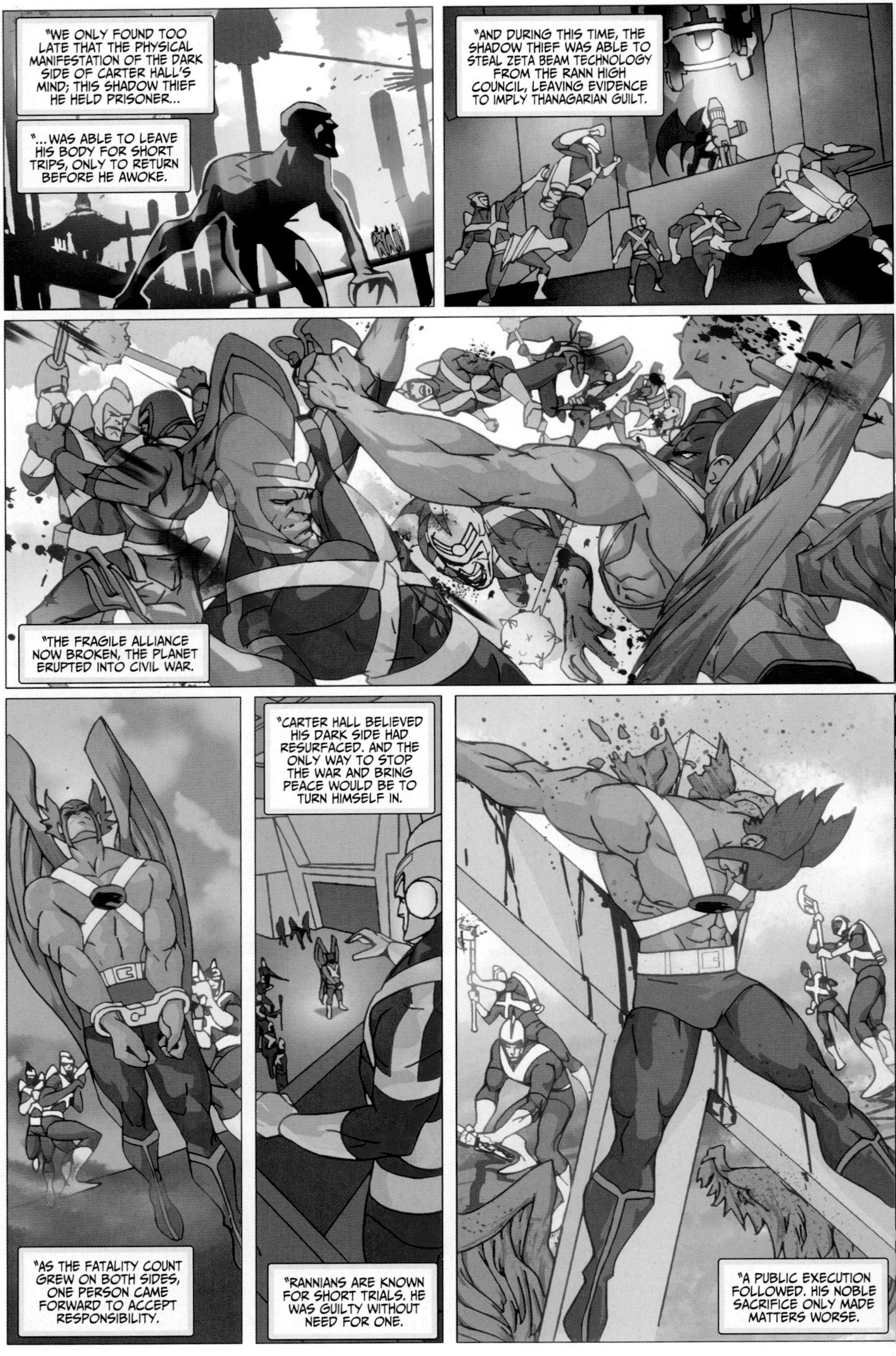
"WE ONLY FOUND TOO LATE THAT THE PHYSICAL MANIFESTATION OF THE DARK SIDE OF CARTER HALL'S MIND; THIS SHADOW THIEF HE HELD PRISONER...
"...WAS ABLE TO LEAVE HIS BODY FOR SHORT TRIPS, ONLY TO RETURN BEFORE HE AWOKE.
"AND DURING THIS TIME, THE SHADOW THIEF WAS ABLE TO STEAL ZETA BEAM TECHNOLOGY FROM THE RANN HIGH COUNCIL, LEAVING EVIDENCE TO IMPLY THANAGARIAN GUILT.
"THE FRAGILE ALLIANCE NOW BROKEN, THE PLANET ERUPTED INTO CIVIL WAR.
"AS THE FATALITY COUNT GREW ON BOTH SIDES, ONE PERSON CAME FORWARD TO ACCEPT RESPONSIBILITY.
"CARTER HALL BELIEVED HIS DARK SIDE HAD RESURFACED. AND THE ONLY WAY TO STOP THE WAR AND BRING PEACE WOULD BE TO TURN HIMSELF IN.
"RANNIANS ARE KNOWN FOR SHORT TRIALS. HE WAS GUILTY WITHOUT NEED FOR ONE.
"A PUBLIC EXECUTION FOLLOWED. HIS NOBLE SACRIFICE ONLY MADE MATTERS WORSE.

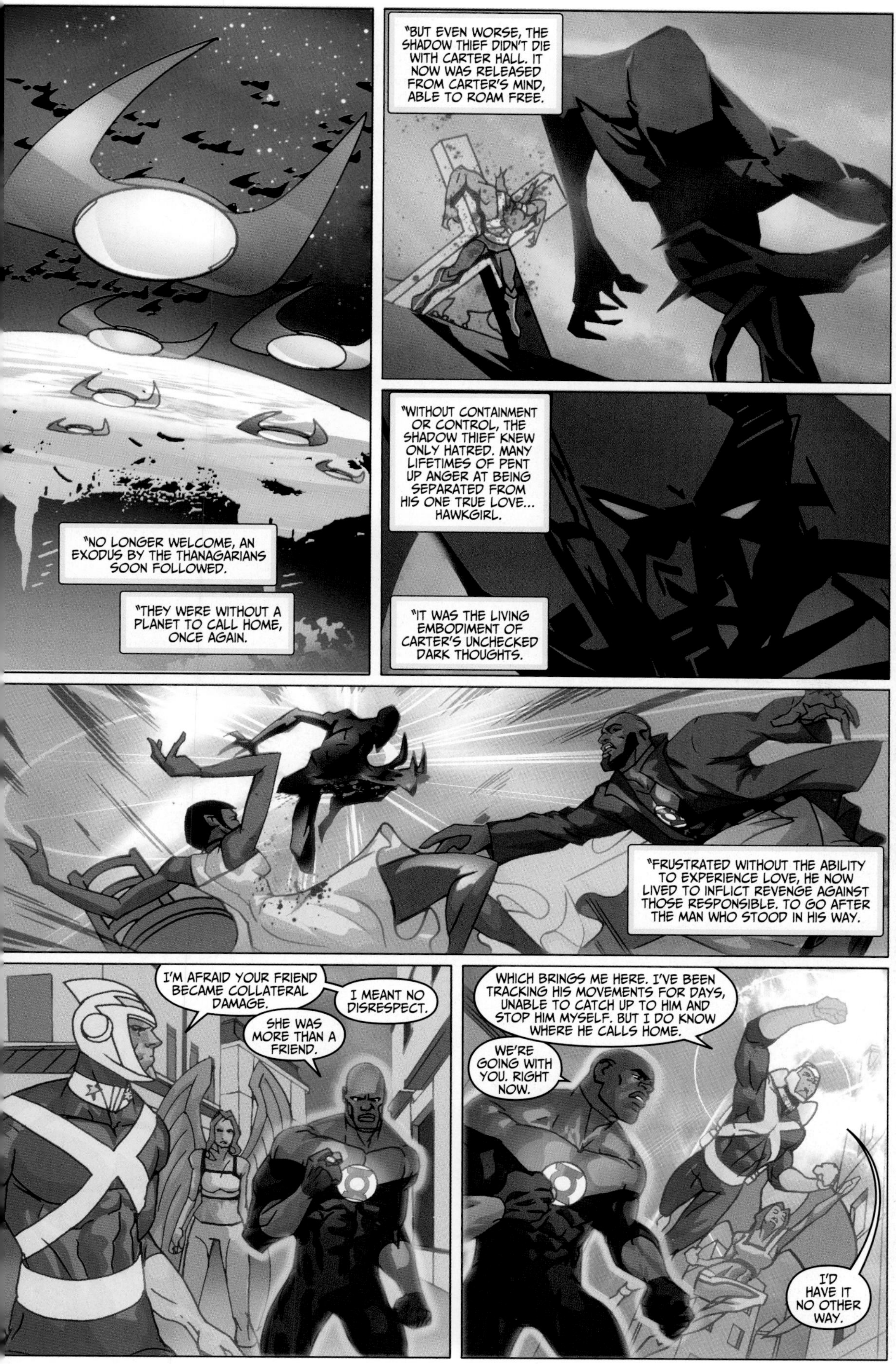
"NO LONGER WELCOME, AN EXODUS BY THE THANAGARIANS SOON FOLLOWED.
"THEY WERE WITHOUT A PLANET TO CALL HOME, ONCE AGAIN.
"BUT EVEN WORSE, THE SHADOW THIEF DIDN'T DIE WITH CARTER HALL. IT NOW WAS RELEASED FROM CARTER'S MIND, ABLE TO ROAM FREE.
"WITHOUT CONTAINMENT OR CONTROL, THE SHADOW THIEF KNEW ONLY HATRED. MANY LIFETIMES OF PENT UP ANGER AT BEING SEPARATED FROM HIS ONE TRUE LOVE... HAWKGIRL.
"IT WAS THE LIVING EMBODIMENT OF CARTER'S UNCHECKED DARK THOUGHTS.
"FRUSTRATED WITHOUT THE ABILITY TO EXPERIENCE LOVE, HE NOW LIVED TO INFLICT REVENGE AGAINST THOSE RESPONSIBLE. TO GO AFTER THE MAN WHO STOOD IN HIS WAY.
I'M AFRAID YOUR FRIEND BECAME COLLATERAL DAMAGE.
I MEANT NO DISRESPECT.
SHE WAS MORE THAN A FRIEND.
WHICH BRINGS ME HERE. I'VE BEEN TRACKING HIS MOVEMENTS FOR DAYS, UNABLE TO CATCH UP TO HIM AND STOP HIM MYSELF. BUT I DO KNOW WHERE HE CALLS HOME.
WE'RE GOING WITH YOU. RIGHT NOW.
I'D HAVE IT NO OTHER WAY.

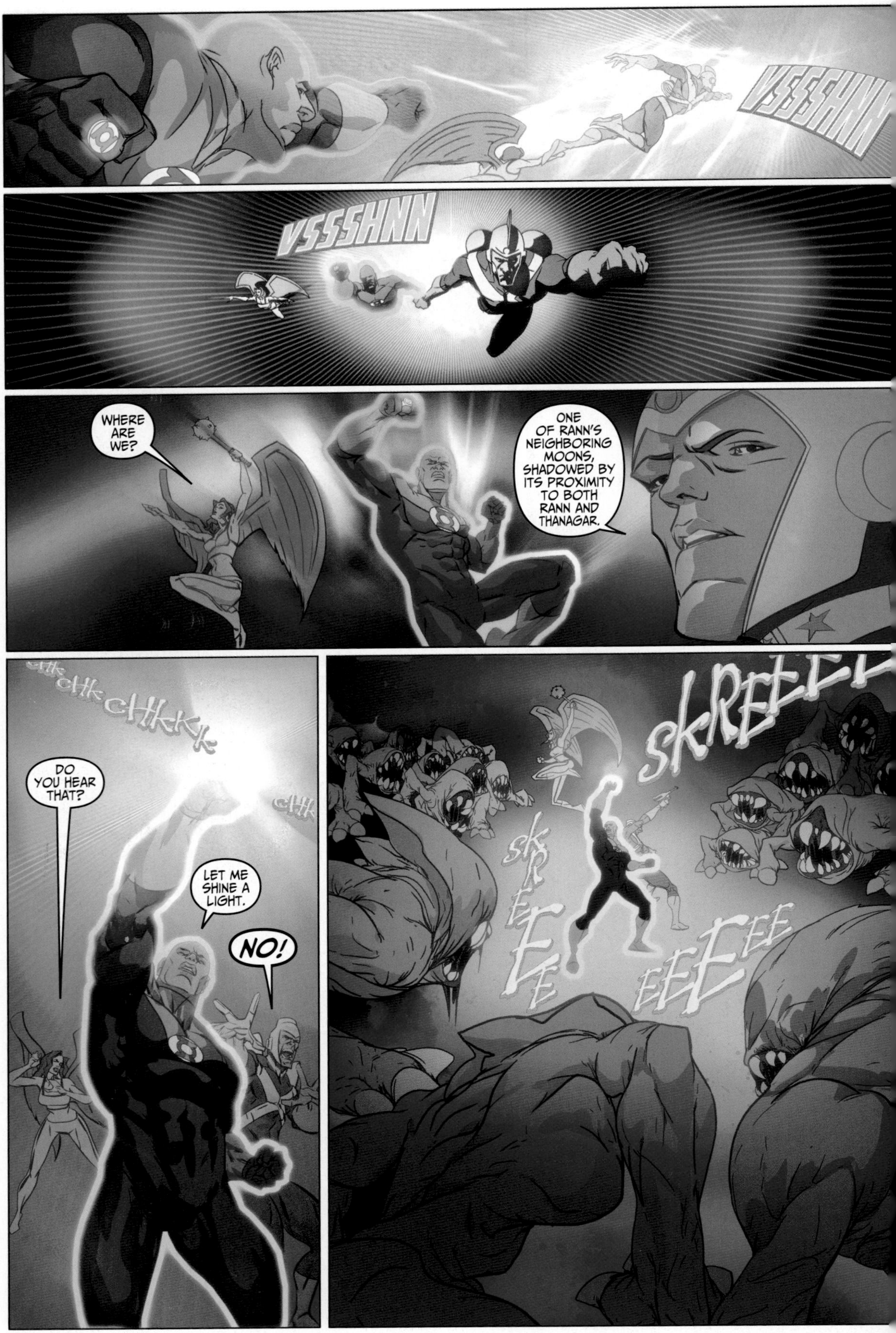
VSSSHNN
VSSSHNN
WHERE ARE WE?
ONE OF RANN'S NEIGHBORING MOONS, SHADOWED BY ITS PROXIMITY TO BOTH RANN AND THANAGAR.
CHK CHK CHKKK
DO YOU HEAR THAT?
LET ME SHINE A LIGHT.
NO!
SKREEEE
SKREEEE
EEEEEE

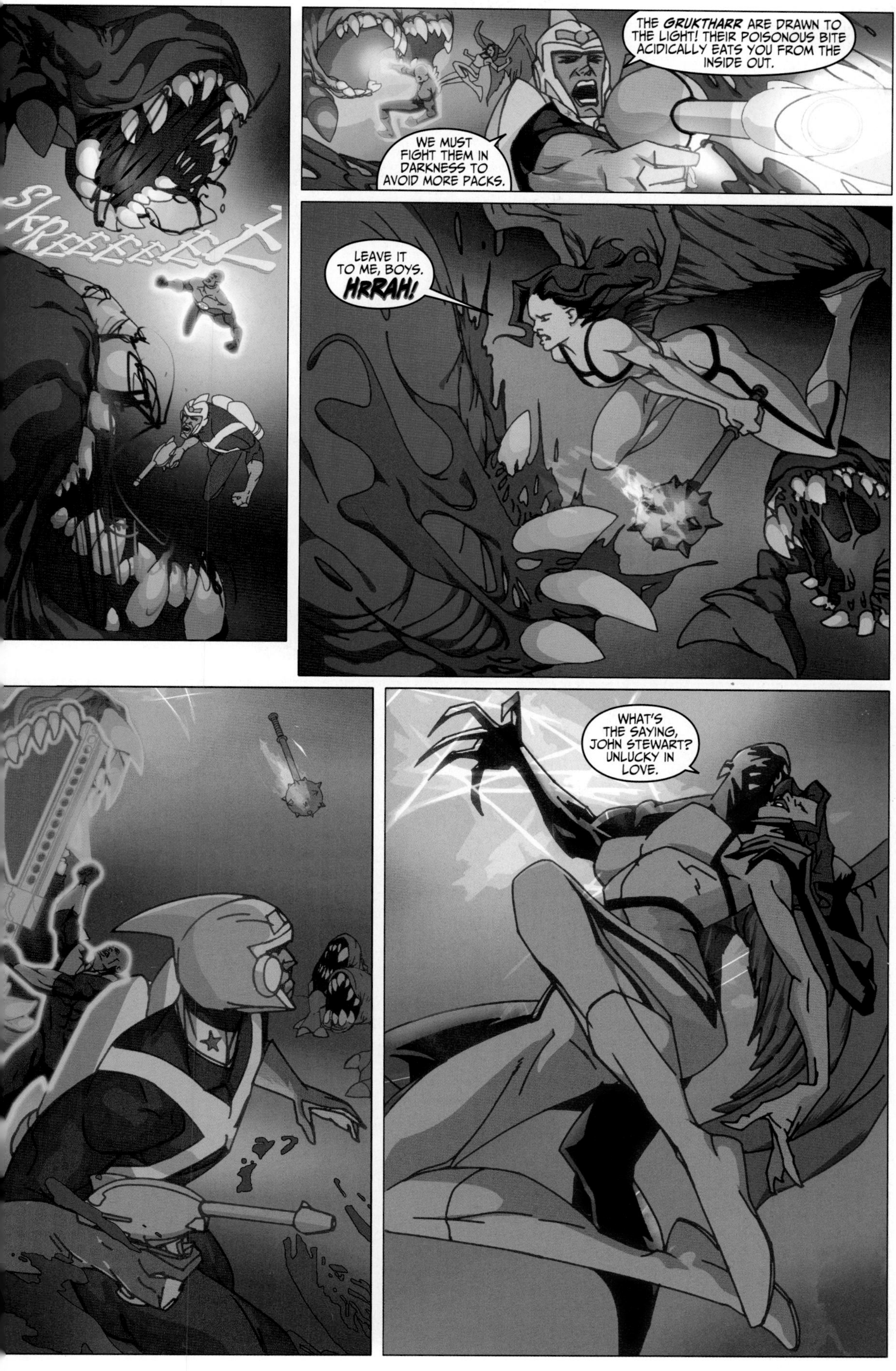
THE **GRUKTHARR** ARE DRAWN TO THE LIGHT! THEIR POISONOUS BITE ACIDICALLY EATS YOU FROM THE INSIDE OUT.
WE MUST FIGHT THEM IN DARKNESS TO AVOID MORE PACKS.
LEAVE IT TO ME, BOYS. **HRRAH!**
WHAT'S THE SAYING, JOHN STEWART? UNLUCKY IN LOVE.

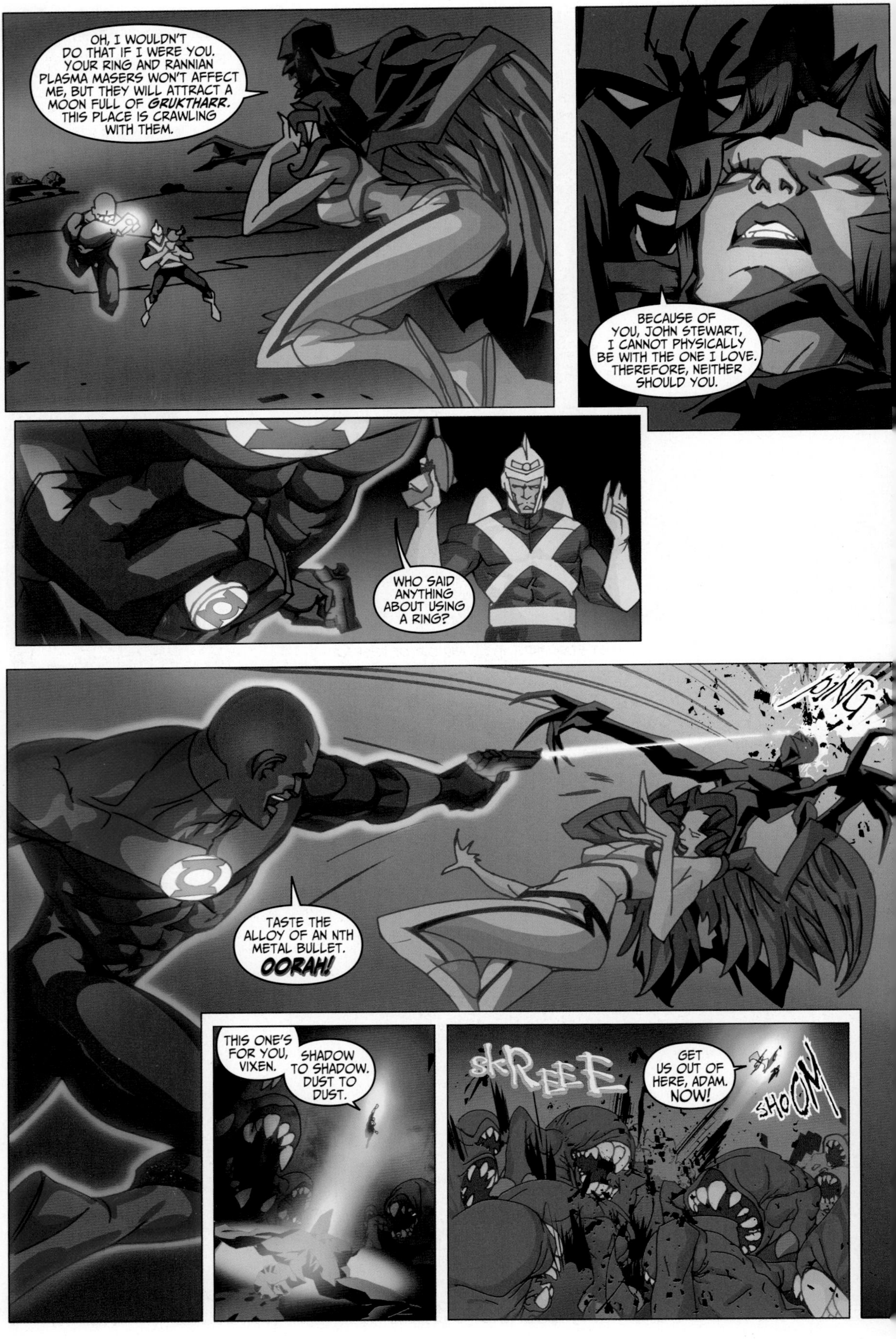
OH, I WOULDN'T DO THAT IF I WERE YOU. YOUR RING AND RANNIAN PLASMA MASERS WON'T AFFECT ME, BUT THEY WILL ATTRACT A MOON FULL OF GRUKTHARR. THIS PLACE IS CRAWLING WITH THEM.
BECAUSE OF YOU, JOHN STEWART, I CANNOT PHYSICALLY BE WITH THE ONE I LOVE. THEREFORE, NEITHER SHOULD YOU.
WHO SAID ANYTHING ABOUT USING A RING?
PING
TASTE THE ALLOY OF AN NTH METAL BULLET. OORAH!
THIS ONE'S FOR YOU, VIXEN.
SHADOW TO SHADOW. DUST TO DUST.
SKREEE
GET US OUT OF HERE, ADAM. NOW!
SHOOM

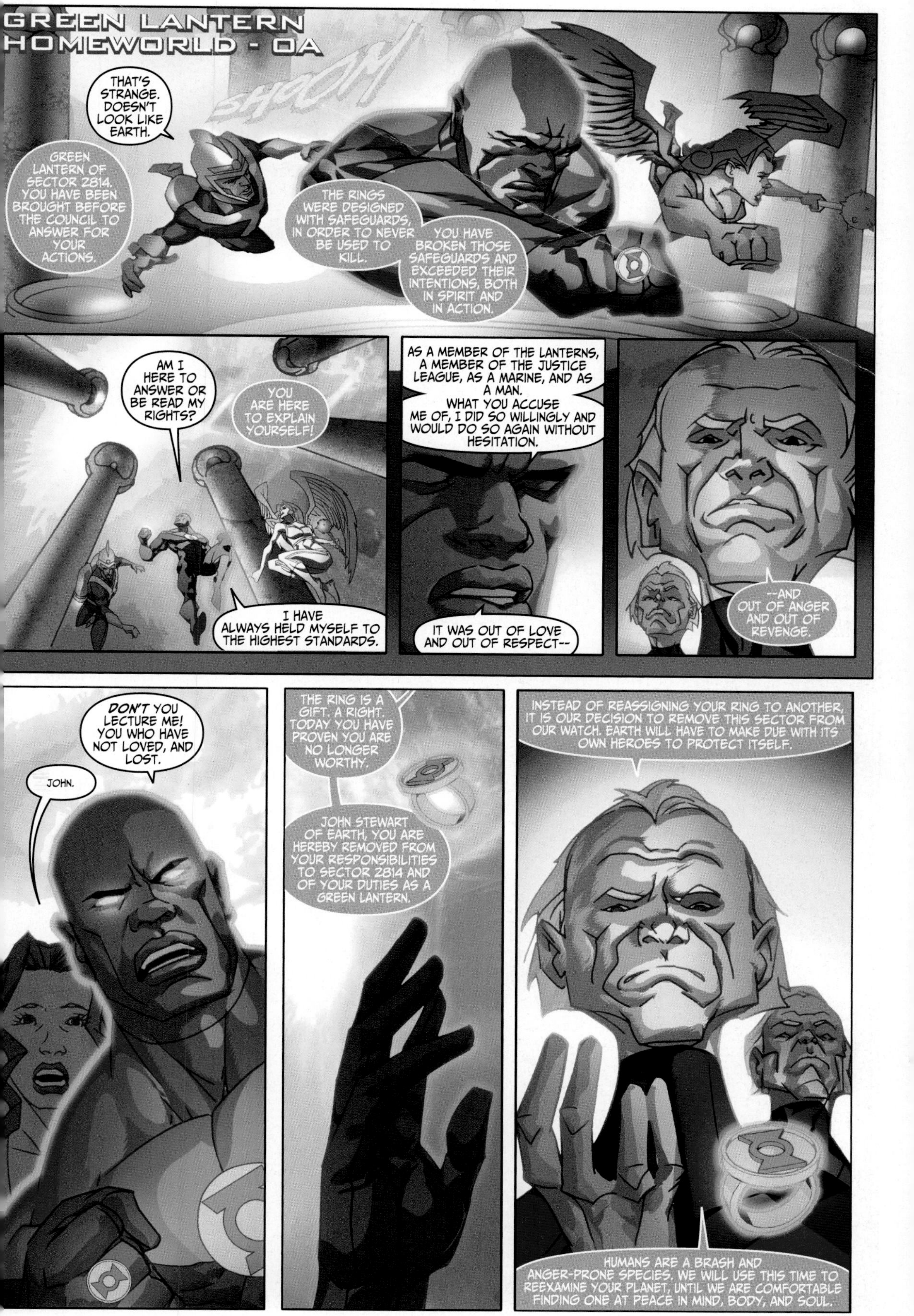
GREEN LANTERN HOMEWORLD - OA
SHOOM
THAT'S STRANGE. DOESN'T LOOK LIKE EARTH.
GREEN LANTERN OF SECTOR 2814. YOU HAVE BEEN BROUGHT BEFORE THE COUNCIL TO ANSWER FOR YOUR ACTIONS.
THE RINGS WERE DESIGNED WITH SAFEGUARDS, IN ORDER TO NEVER BE USED TO KILL.
YOU HAVE BROKEN THOSE SAFEGUARDS AND EXCEEDED THEIR INTENTIONS, BOTH IN SPIRIT AND IN ACTION.
AM I HERE TO ANSWER OR BE READ MY RIGHTS?
YOU ARE HERE TO EXPLAIN YOURSELF!
I HAVE ALWAYS HELD MYSELF TO THE HIGHEST STANDARDS.
AS A MEMBER OF THE LANTERNS, A MEMBER OF THE JUSTICE LEAGUE, AS A MARINE, AND AS A MAN.
WHAT YOU ACCUSE ME OF, I DID SO WILLINGLY AND WOULD DO SO AGAIN WITHOUT HESITATION.
IT WAS OUT OF LOVE AND OUT OF RESPECT--
--AND OUT OF ANGER AND OUT OF REVENGE.
DON'T YOU LECTURE ME! YOU WHO HAVE NOT LOVED, AND LOST.
JOHN.
THE RING IS A GIFT. A RIGHT. TODAY YOU HAVE PROVEN YOU ARE NO LONGER WORTHY.
JOHN STEWART OF EARTH, YOU ARE HEREBY REMOVED FROM YOUR RESPONSIBILITIES TO SECTOR 2814 AND OF YOUR DUTIES AS A GREEN LANTERN.
INSTEAD OF REASSIGNING YOUR RING TO ANOTHER, IT IS OUR DECISION TO REMOVE THIS SECTOR FROM OUR WATCH. EARTH WILL HAVE TO MAKE DUE WITH ITS OWN HEROES TO PROTECT ITSELF.
HUMANS ARE A BRASH AND ANGER-PRONE SPECIES. WE WILL USE THIS TIME TO REEXAMINE YOUR PLANET, UNTIL WE ARE COMFORTABLE FINDING ONE AT PEACE IN MIND, BODY, AND SOUL.

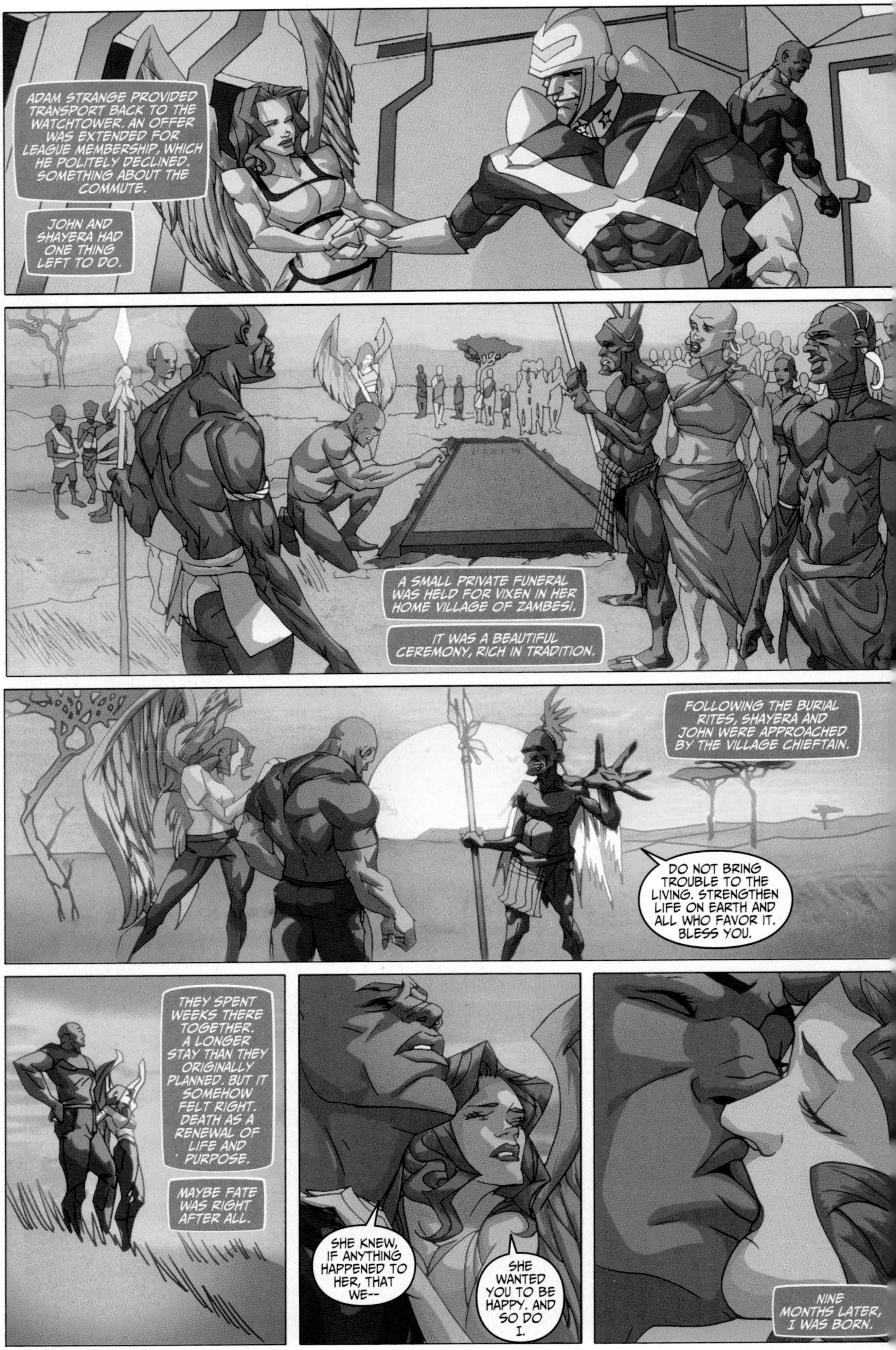
ADAM STRANGE PROVIDED TRANSPORT BACK TO THE WATCHTOWER. AN OFFER WAS EXTENDED FOR LEAGUE MEMBERSHIP, WHICH HE POLITELY DECLINED. SOMETHING ABOUT THE COMMUTE.
JOHN AND SHAYERA HAD ONE THING LEFT TO DO.
VIXEN
A SMALL PRIVATE FUNERAL WAS HELD FOR VIXEN IN HER HOME VILLAGE OF ZAMBESI.
IT WAS A BEAUTIFUL CEREMONY, RICH IN TRADITION.
FOLLOWING THE BURIAL RITES, SHAYERA AND JOHN WERE APPROACHED BY THE VILLAGE CHIEFTAIN.
DO NOT BRING TROUBLE TO THE LIVING. STRENGTHEN LIFE ON EARTH AND ALL WHO FAVOR IT. BLESS YOU.
THEY SPENT WEEKS THERE TOGETHER. A LONGER STAY THAN THEY ORIGINALLY PLANNED. BUT IT SOMEHOW FELT RIGHT. DEATH AS A RENEWAL OF LIFE AND PURPOSE.
MAYBE FATE WAS RIGHT AFTER ALL.
SHE KNEW, IF ANYTHING HAPPENED TO HER, THAT WE--
SHE WANTED YOU TO BE HAPPY. AND SO DO I.
NINE MONTHS LATER, I WAS BORN.

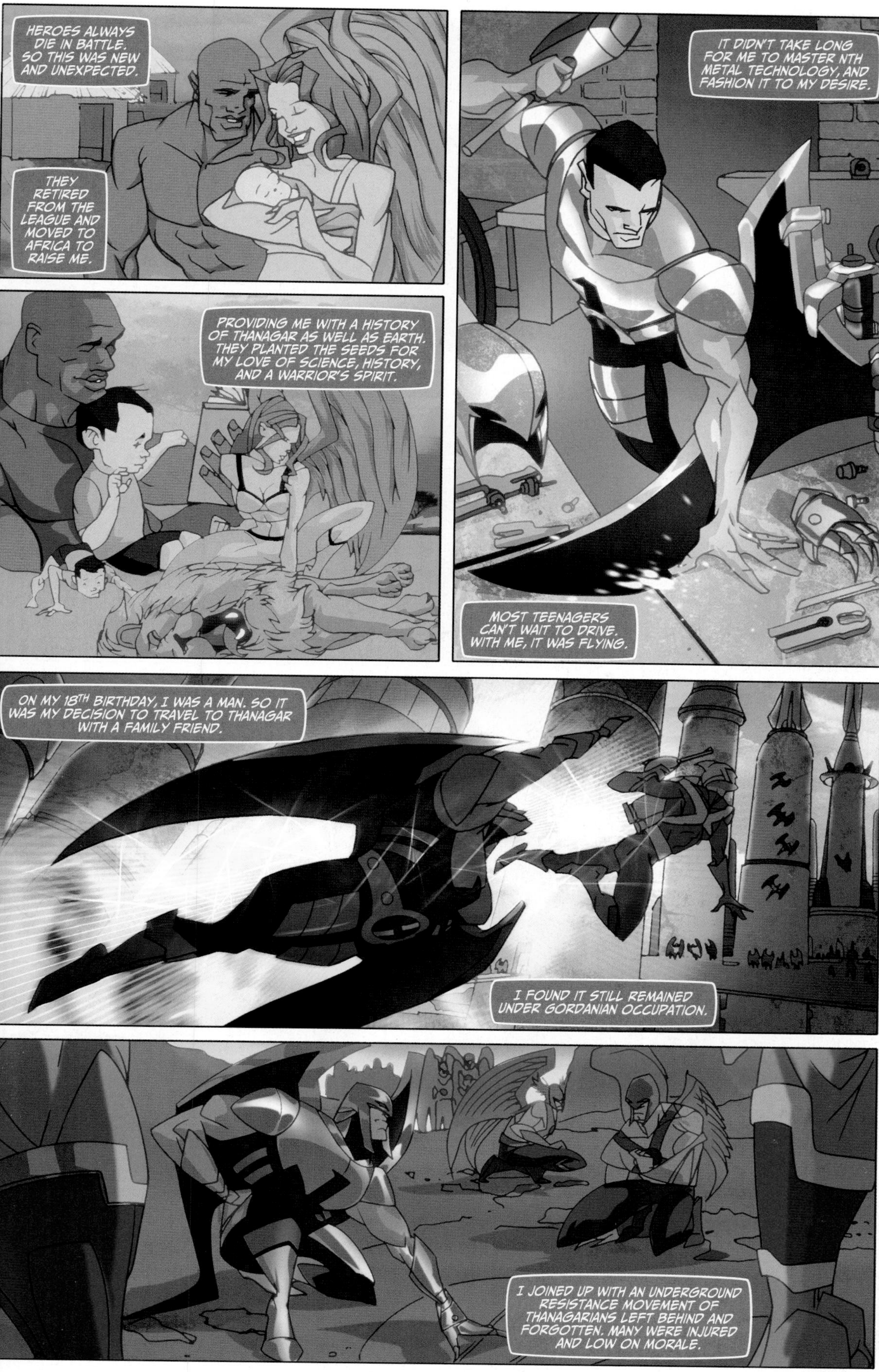
HEROES ALWAYS DIE IN BATTLE. SO THIS WAS NEW AND UNEXPECTED.
THEY RETIRED FROM THE LEAGUE AND MOVED TO AFRICA TO RAISE ME.
IT DIDN'T TAKE LONG FOR ME TO MASTER NTH METAL TECHNOLOGY, AND FASHION IT TO MY DESIRE.
PROVIDING ME WITH A HISTORY OF THANAGAR AS WELL AS EARTH. THEY PLANTED THE SEEDS FOR MY LOVE OF SCIENCE, HISTORY, AND A WARRIOR'S SPIRIT.
MOST TEENAGERS CAN'T WAIT TO DRIVE. WITH ME, IT WAS FLYING.
ON MY 18TH BIRTHDAY, I WAS A MAN. SO IT WAS MY DECISION TO TRAVEL TO THANAGAR WITH A FAMILY FRIEND.
I FOUND IT STILL REMAINED UNDER GORDANIAN OCCUPATION.
I JOINED UP WITH AN UNDERGROUND RESISTANCE MOVEMENT OF THANAGARIANS LEFT BEHIND AND FORGOTTEN. MANY WERE INJURED AND LOW ON MORALE.

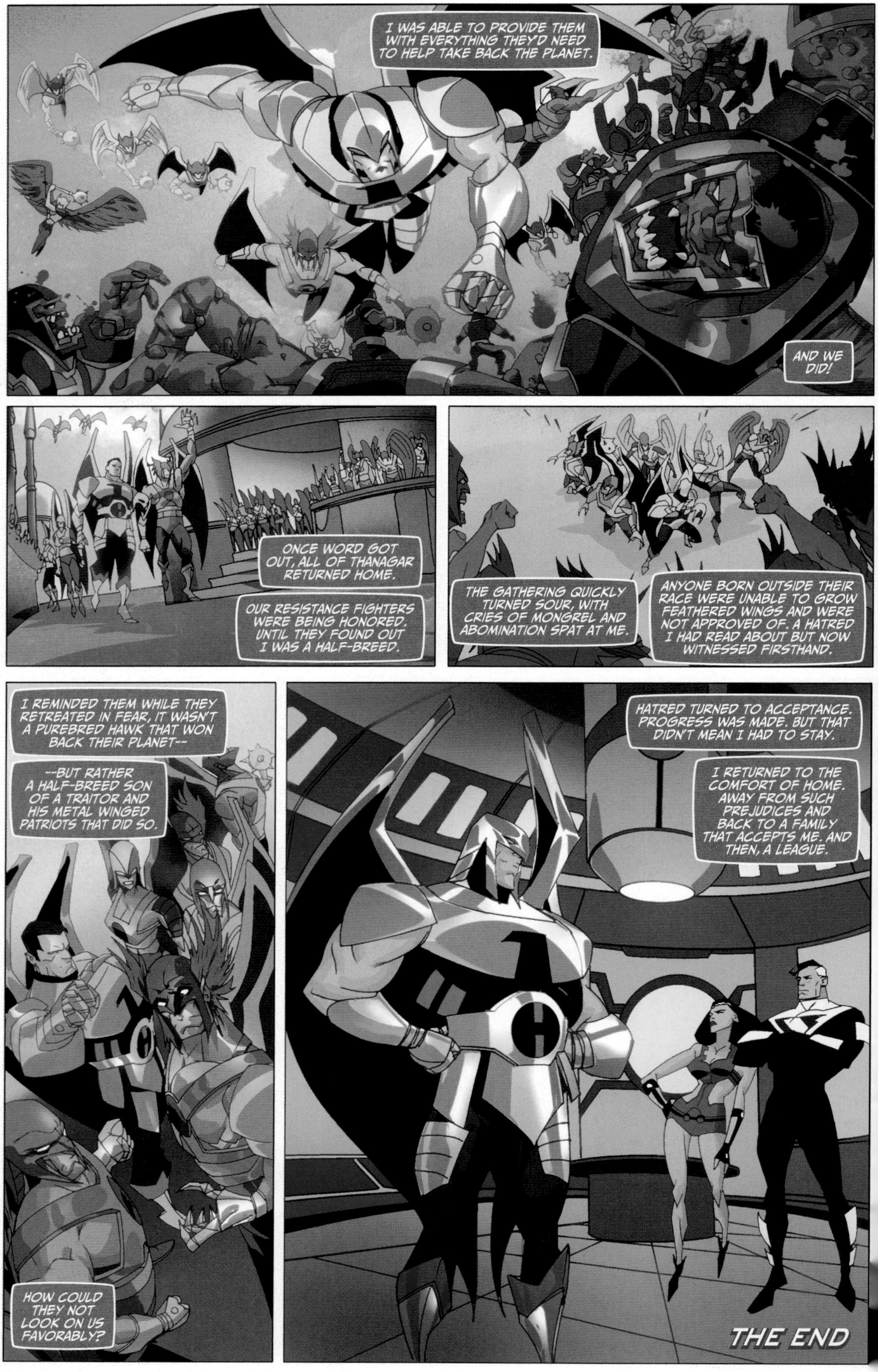
I WAS ABLE TO PROVIDE THEM WITH EVERYTHING THEY'D NEED TO HELP TAKE BACK THE PLANET.
AND WE DID!
ONCE WORD GOT OUT, ALL OF THANAGAR RETURNED HOME.
OUR RESISTANCE FIGHTERS WERE BEING HONORED. UNTIL THEY FOUND OUT I WAS A HALF-BREED.
THE GATHERING QUICKLY TURNED SOUR, WITH CRIES OF MONGREL AND ABOMINATION SPAT AT ME.
ANYONE BORN OUTSIDE THEIR RACE WERE UNABLE TO GROW FEATHERED WINGS AND WERE NOT APPROVED OF. A HATRED I HAD READ ABOUT BUT NOW WITNESSED FIRSTHAND.
I REMINDED THEM WHILE THEY RETREATED IN FEAR, IT WASN'T A PUREBRED HAWK THAT WON BACK THEIR PLANET--
--BUT RATHER A HALF-BREED SON OF A TRAITOR AND HIS METAL WINGED PATRIOTS THAT DID SO.
HOW COULD THEY NOT LOOK ON US FAVORABLY?
HATRED TURNED TO ACCEPTANCE. PROGRESS WAS MADE. BUT THAT DIDN'T MEAN I HAD TO STAY.
I RETURNED TO THE COMFORT OF HOME. AWAY FROM SUCH PREJUDICES AND BACK TO A FAMILY THAT ACCEPTS ME. AND THEN, A LEAGUE.
THE END

MOST PEOPLE VIEW ROYALTY AS A COMMONER WOULD, FROM THE OUTSIDE.

MY VIEW IS A LITTLE MORE INCLUSIVE. I WAS BORN INTO IT. MY HOME. THE BEAUTIFUL KINGDOM OF ATLANTIS.

FIRST CAME MY BROTHER. BORN TO THE KING AND QUEEN, ARTHUR AND MERA.

A GRAND CELEBRATION FOR THE FUTURE HEIR TO THE KINGDOM.

AND HE WAS LOVED.

MY FATHER RARELY TRAVELED TO THE SURFACE WORLD, UNLESS UNDER DURESS OF GREAT DIPLOMATIC IMPORTANCE.

AND SO IT WAS VERY TRAGIC THAT A FAILED ASSASSINATION ATTEMPT PLACED MY FATHER IN A MEDICAL STASIS. THE FUTURE OF HIS KINGDOM IN JEOPARDY.

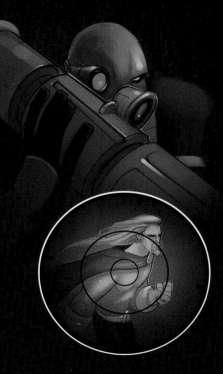

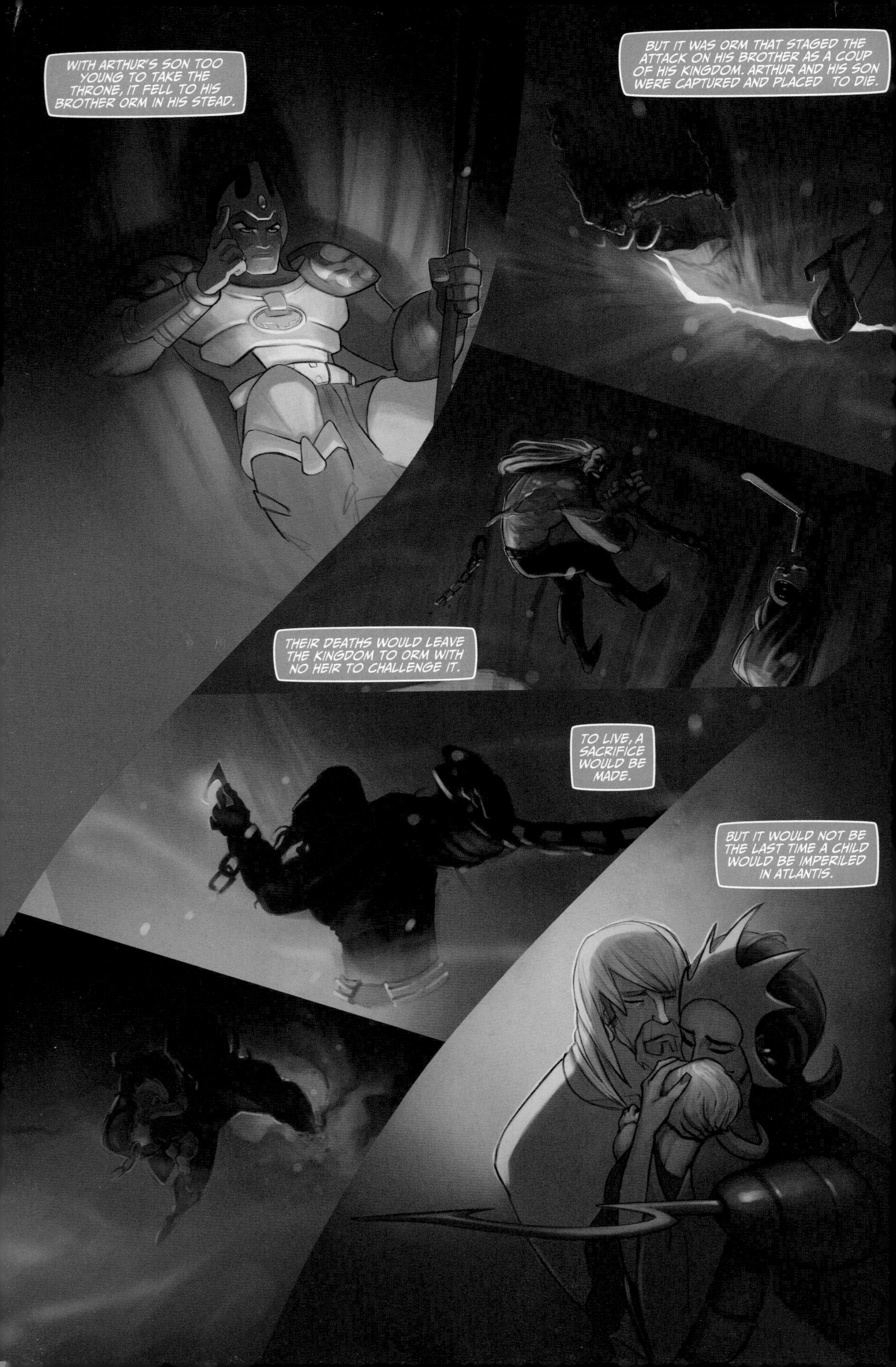
WITH ARTHUR'S SON TOO YOUNG TO TAKE THE THRONE, IT FELL TO HIS BROTHER ORM IN HIS STEAD.
BUT IT WAS ORM THAT STAGED THE ATTACK ON HIS BROTHER AS A COUP OF HIS KINGDOM. ARTHUR AND HIS SON WERE CAPTURED AND PLACED TO DIE.
THEIR DEATHS WOULD LEAVE THE KINGDOM TO ORM WITH NO HEIR TO CHALLENGE IT.
TO LIVE, A SACRIFICE WOULD BE MADE.
BUT IT WOULD NOT BE THE LAST TIME A CHILD WOULD BE IMPERILED IN ATLANTIS.

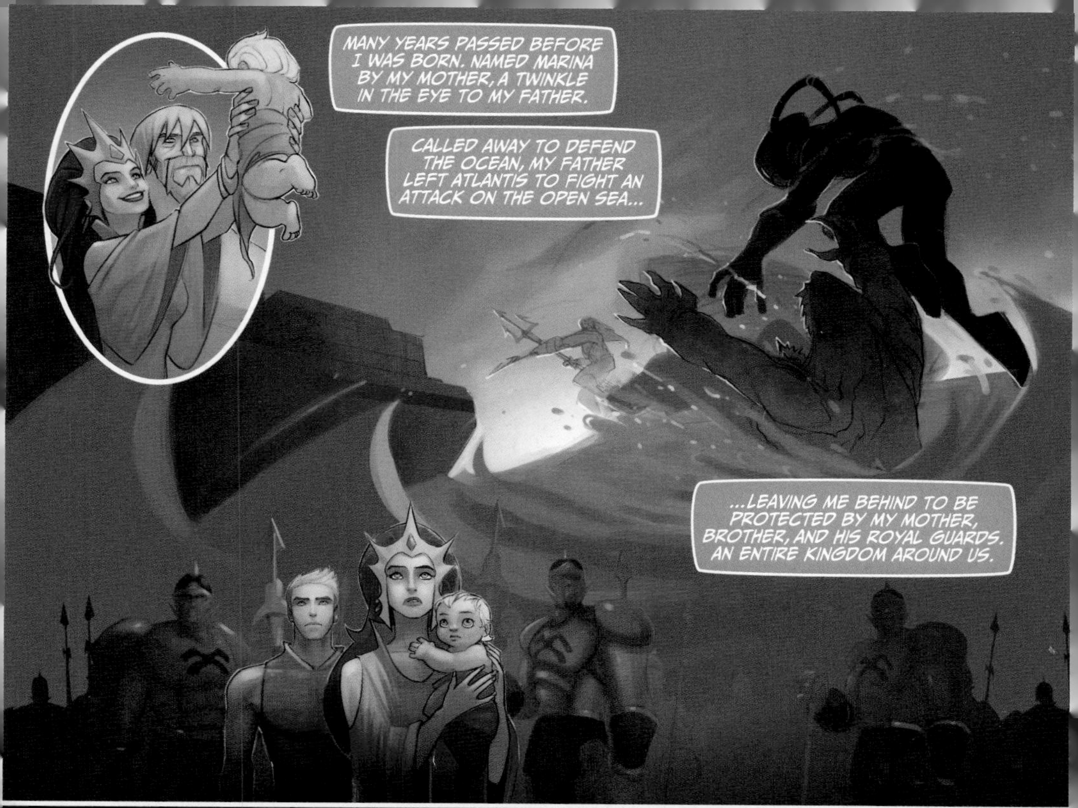
MANY YEARS PASSED BEFORE I WAS BORN. NAMED MARINA BY MY MOTHER, A TWINKLE IN THE EYE TO MY FATHER.
CALLED AWAY TO DEFEND THE OCEAN, MY FATHER LEFT ATLANTIS TO FIGHT AN ATTACK ON THE OPEN SEA...
...LEAVING ME BEHIND TO BE PROTECTED BY MY MOTHER, BROTHER, AND HIS ROYAL GUARDS. AN ENTIRE KINGDOM AROUND US.

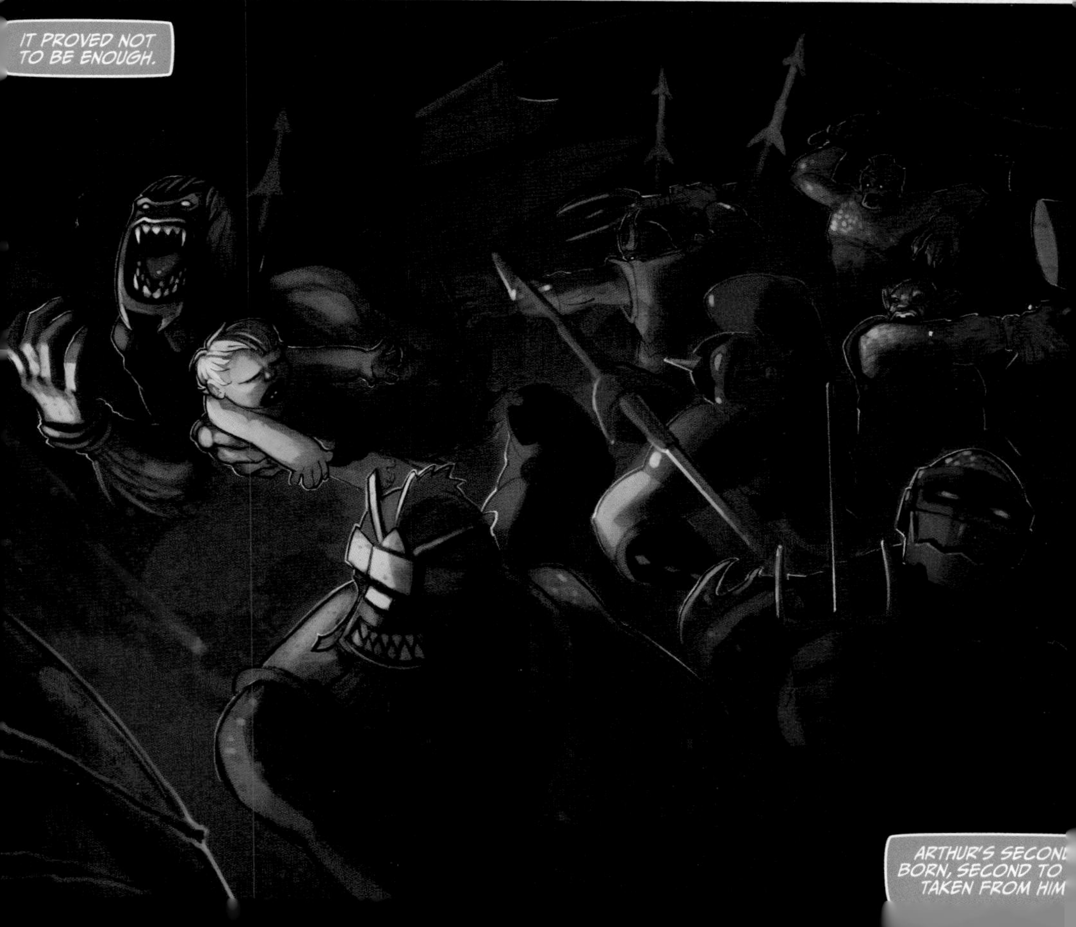
IT PROVED NOT TO BE ENOUGH.
ARTHUR'S SECON
BORN, SECOND TO
TAKEN FROM HIM

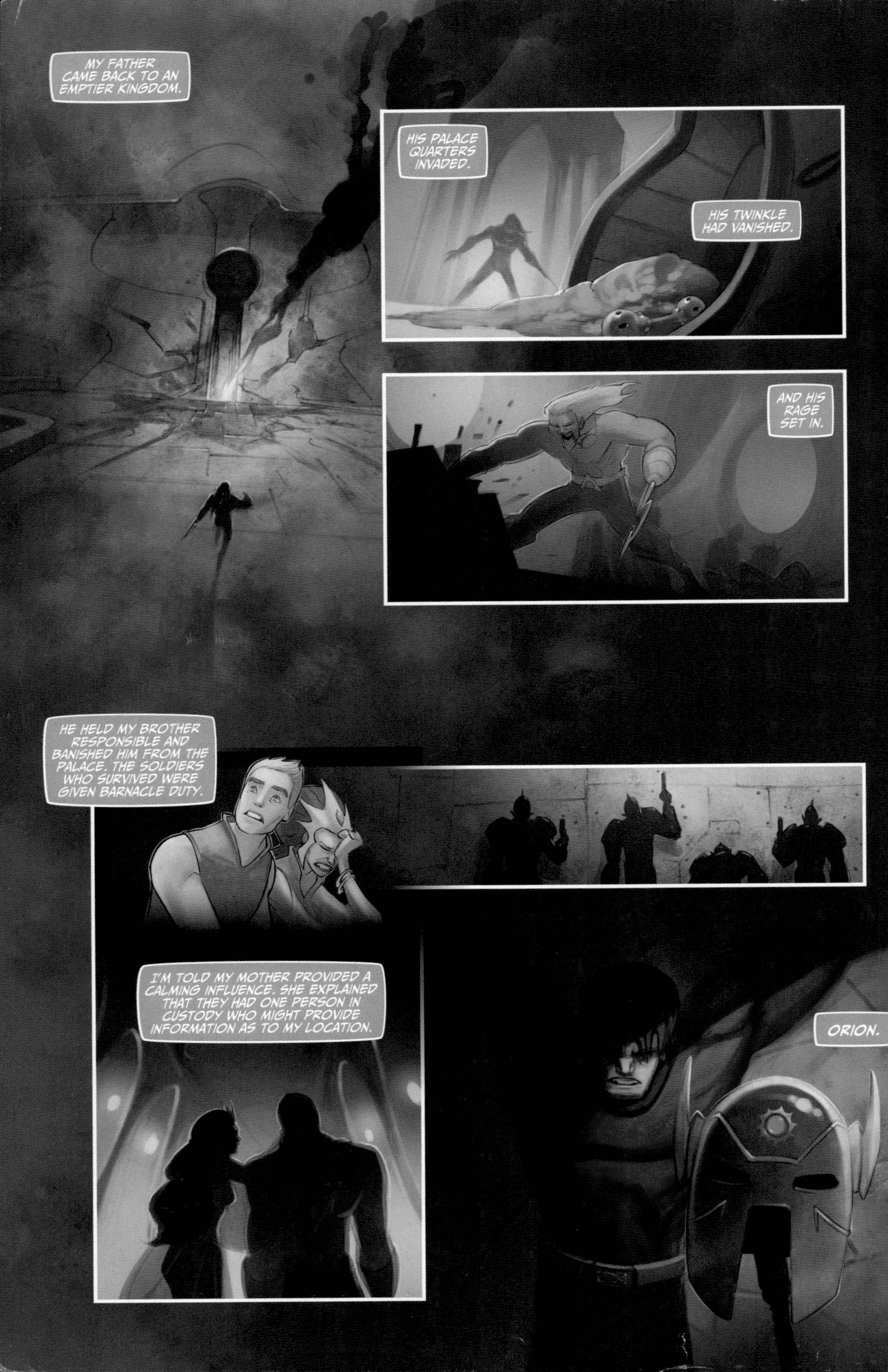
MY FATHER CAME BACK TO AN EMPTIER KINGDOM.
HIS PALACE QUARTERS INVADED.
HIS TWINKLE HAD VANISHED.
AND HIS RAGE SET IN.
HE HELD MY BROTHER RESPONSIBLE AND BANISHED HIM FROM THE PALACE. THE SOLDIERS WHO SURVIVED WERE GIVEN BARNACLE DUTY.
I'M TOLD MY MOTHER PROVIDED A CALMING INFLUENCE. SHE EXPLAINED THAT THEY HAD ONE PERSON IN CUSTODY WHO MIGHT PROVIDE INFORMATION AS TO MY LOCATION.
ORION.

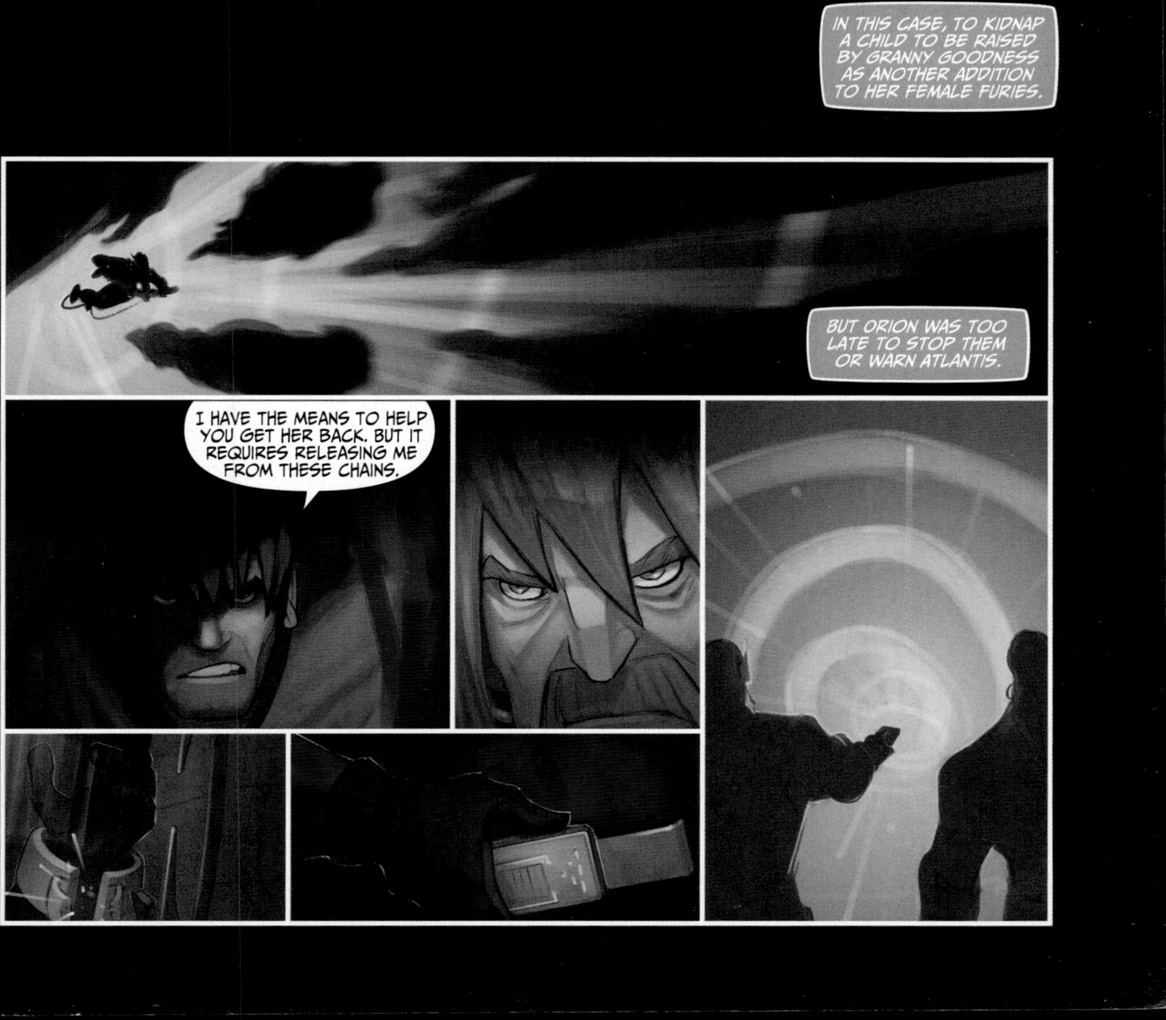
IN THIS CASE, TO KIDNAP A CHILD TO BE RAISED BY GRANNY GOODNESS AS ANOTHER ADDITION TO HER FEMALE FURIES.
BUT ORION WAS TOO LATE TO STOP THEM OR WARN ATLANTIS.
I HAVE THE MEANS TO HELP YOU GET HER BACK. BUT IT REQUIRES RELEASING ME FROM THESE CHAINS.

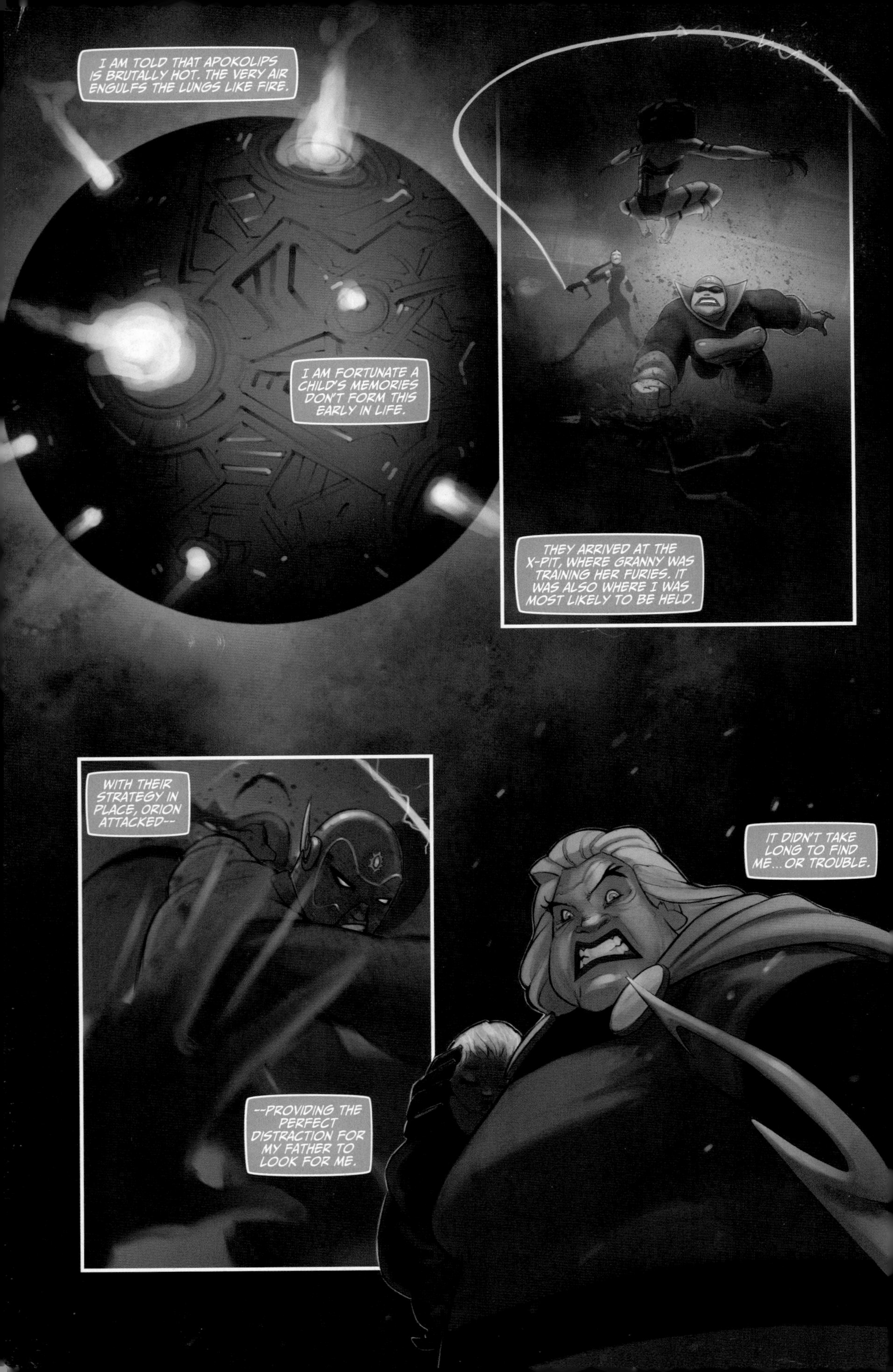
I AM TOLD THAT APOKOLIPS IS BRUTALLY HOT. THE VERY AIR ENGULFS THE LUNGS LIKE FIRE.
I AM FORTUNATE A CHILD'S MEMORIES DON'T FORM THIS EARLY IN LIFE.
THEY ARRIVED AT THE X-PIT, WHERE GRANNY WAS TRAINING HER FURIES. IT WAS ALSO WHERE I WAS MOST LIKELY TO BE HELD.
WITH THEIR STRATEGY IN PLACE, ORION ATTACKED--
--PROVIDING THE PERFECT DISTRACTION FOR MY FATHER TO LOOK FOR ME.
IT DIDN'T TAKE LONG TO FIND ME...OR TROUBLE.

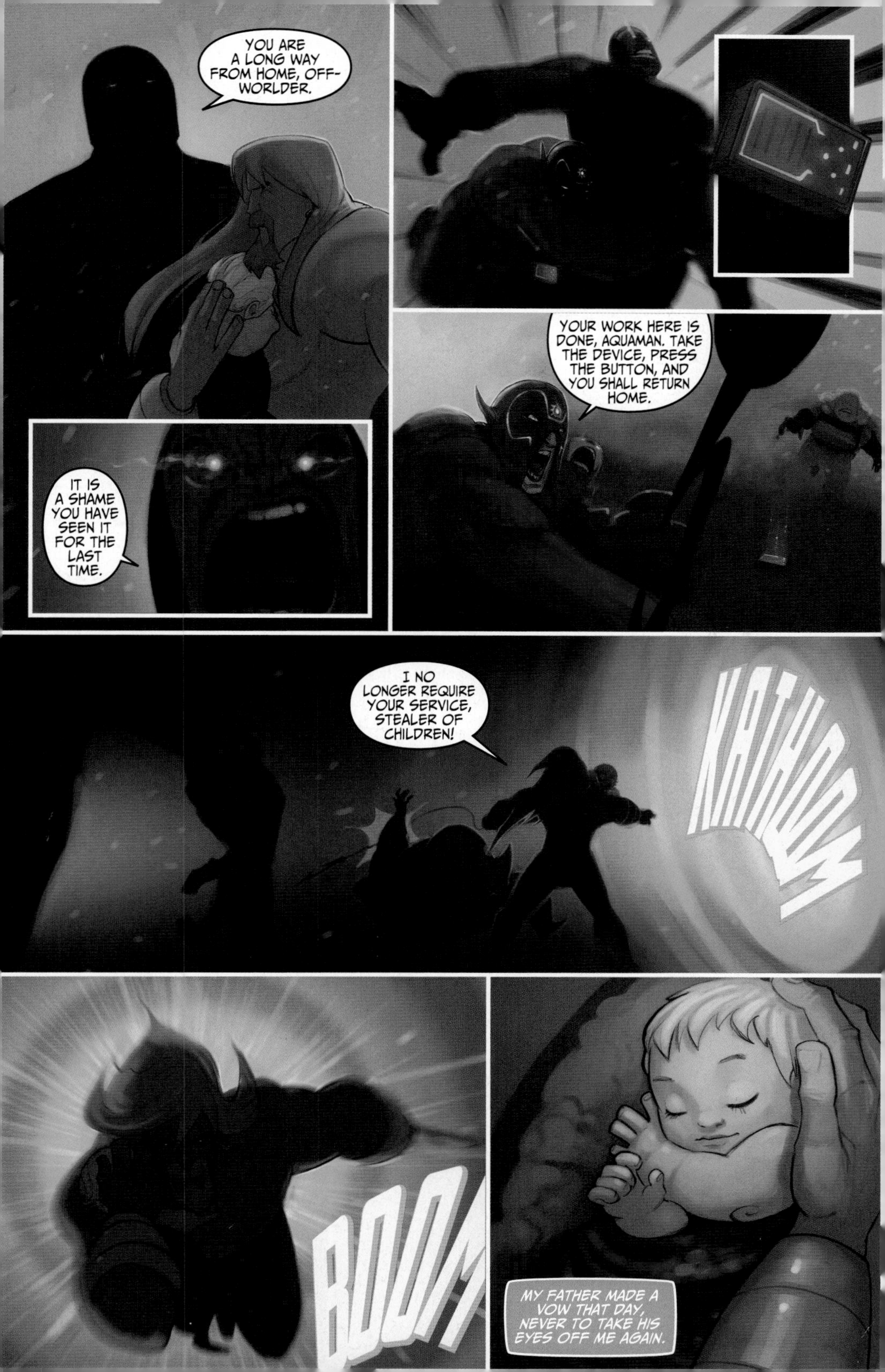
YOU ARE A LONG WAY FROM HOME, OFF-WORLDER.
IT IS A SHAME YOU HAVE SEEN IT FOR THE LAST TIME.
YOUR WORK HERE IS DONE, AQUAMAN. TAKE THE DEVICE, PRESS THE BUTTON, AND YOU SHALL RETURN HOME.
I NO LONGER REQUIRE YOUR SERVICE, STEALER OF CHILDREN!
KATHOOM
BOOM
MY FATHER MADE A VOW THAT DAY, NEVER TO TAKE HIS EYES OFF ME AGAIN.

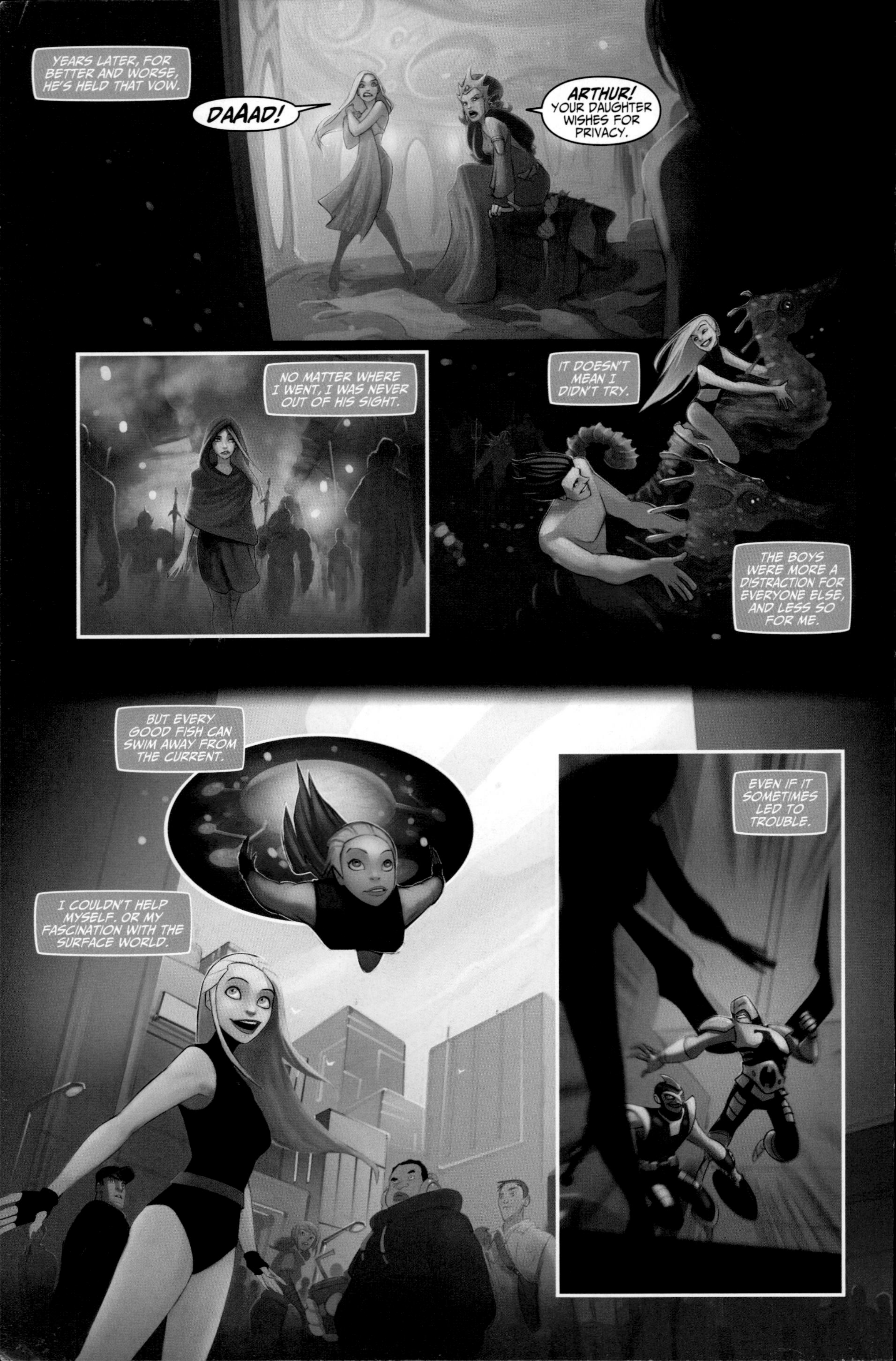
YEARS LATER, FOR BETTER AND WORSE, HE'S HELD THAT VOW.
DAAAD!
ARTHUR! YOUR DAUGHTER WISHES FOR PRIVACY.
NO MATTER WHERE I WENT, I WAS NEVER OUT OF HIS SIGHT.
IT DOESN'T MEAN I DIDN'T TRY.
THE BOYS WERE MORE A DISTRACTION FOR EVERYONE ELSE, AND LESS SO FOR ME.
BUT EVERY GOOD FISH CAN SWIM AWAY FROM THE CURRENT.
I COULDN'T HELP MYSELF. OR MY FASCINATION WITH THE SURFACE WORLD.
EVEN IF IT SOMETIMES LED TO TROUBLE.

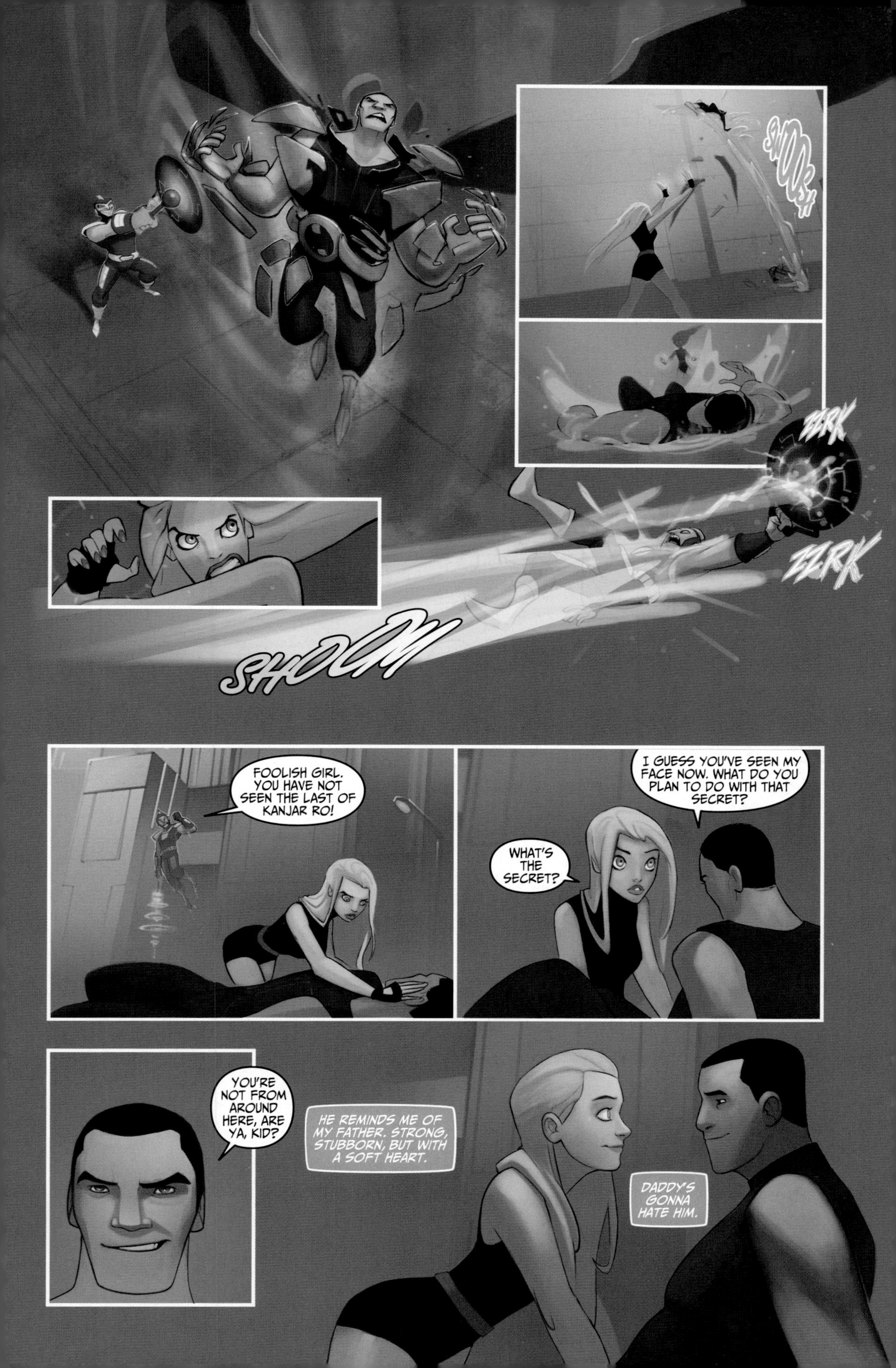
SHOOSH
ZZRK
ZZRK
SHOOM
FOOLISH GIRL. YOU HAVE NOT SEEN THE LAST OF KANJAR RO!
I GUESS YOU'VE SEEN MY FACE NOW. WHAT DO YOU PLAN TO DO WITH THAT SECRET?
WHAT'S THE SECRET?
YOU'RE NOT FROM AROUND HERE, ARE YA, KID?
HE REMINDS ME OF MY FATHER. STRONG, STUBBORN, BUT WITH A SOFT HEART.
DADDY'S GONNA HATE HIM.

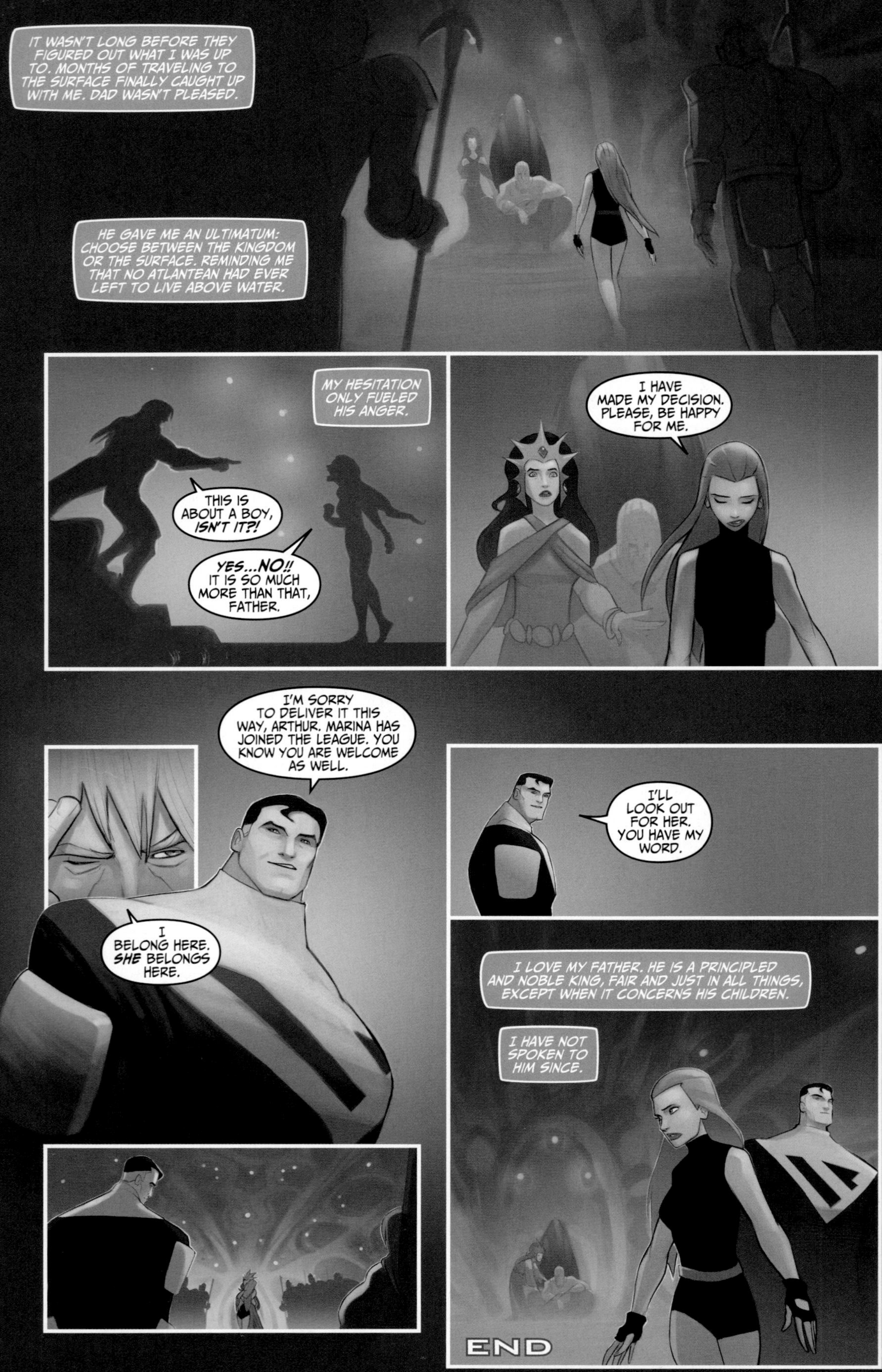
IT WASN'T LONG BEFORE THEY FIGURED OUT WHAT I WAS UP TO. MONTHS OF TRAVELING TO THE SURFACE FINALLY CAUGHT UP WITH ME. DAD WASN'T PLEASED.
HE GAVE ME AN ULTIMATUM: CHOOSE BETWEEN THE KINGDOM OR THE SURFACE. REMINDING ME THAT NO ATLANTEAN HAD EVER LEFT TO LIVE ABOVE WATER.
MY HESITATION ONLY FUELED HIS ANGER.
THIS IS ABOUT A BOY, ISN'T IT?!
YES...NO!! IT IS SO MUCH MORE THAN THAT, FATHER.
I HAVE MADE MY DECISION. PLEASE, BE HAPPY FOR ME.
I'M SORRY TO DELIVER IT THIS WAY, ARTHUR. MARINA HAS JOINED THE LEAGUE. YOU KNOW YOU ARE WELCOME AS WELL.
I BELONG HERE. SHE BELONGS HERE.
I'LL LOOK OUT FOR HER. YOU HAVE MY WORD.
I LOVE MY FATHER. HE IS A PRINCIPLED AND NOBLE KING, FAIR AND JUST IN ALL THINGS, EXCEPT WHEN IT CONCERNS HIS CHILDREN.
I HAVE NOT SPOKEN TO HIM SINCE.
END

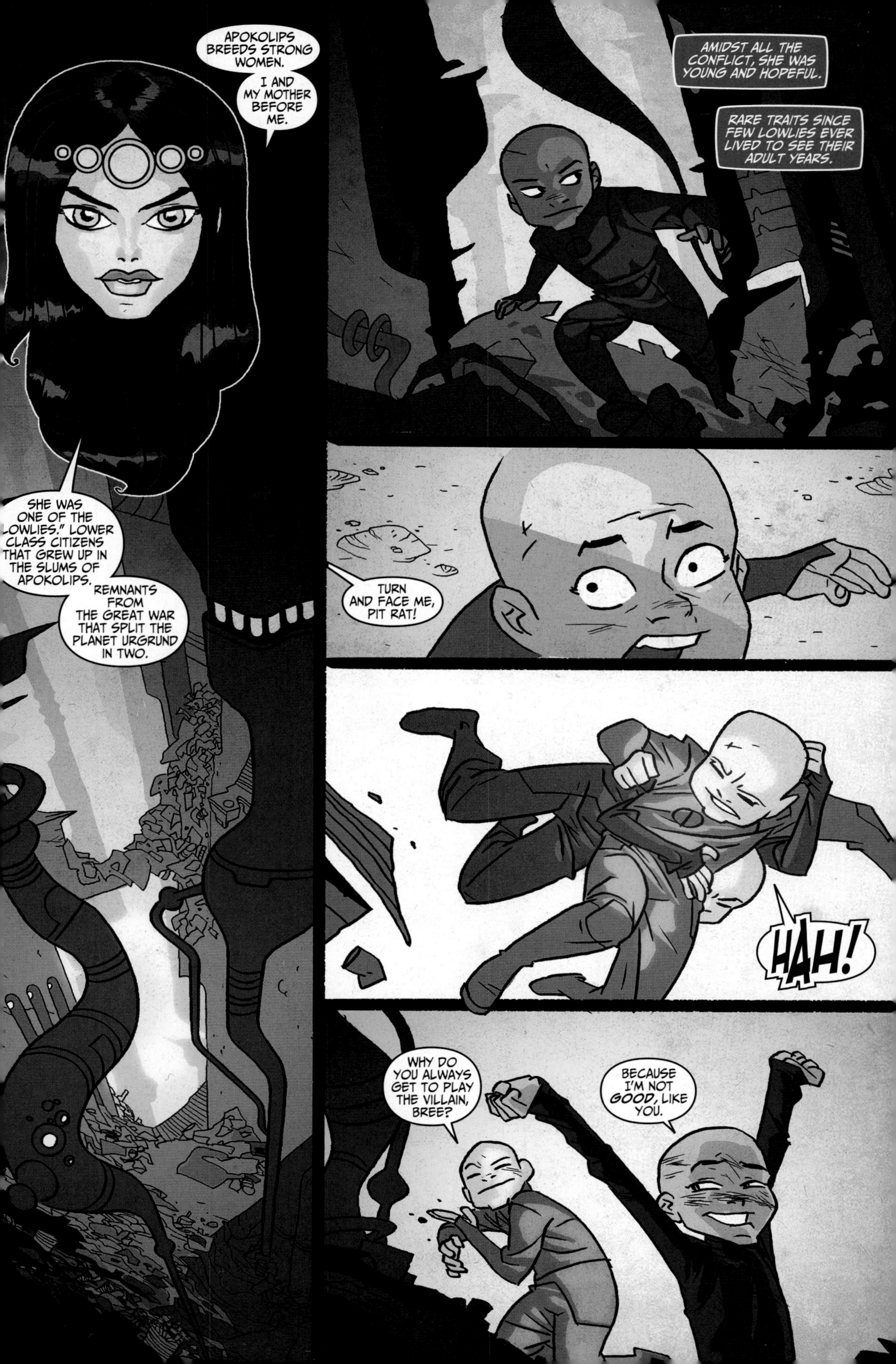
APOKOLIPS BREEDS STRONG WOMEN.
I AND MY MOTHER BEFORE ME.
SHE WAS ONE OF THE "LOWLIES." LOWER CLASS CITIZENS THAT GREW UP IN THE SLUMS OF APOKOLIPS.
REMNANTS FROM THE GREAT WAR THAT SPLIT THE PLANET URGRUND IN TWO.
AMIDST ALL THE CONFLICT, SHE WAS YOUNG AND HOPEFUL.
RARE TRAITS SINCE FEW LOWLIES EVER LIVED TO SEE THEIR ADULT YEARS.
TURN AND FACE ME, PIT RAT!
HAH!
WHY DO YOU ALWAYS GET TO PLAY THE VILLAIN, BREE?
BECAUSE I'M NOT GOOD, LIKE YOU.

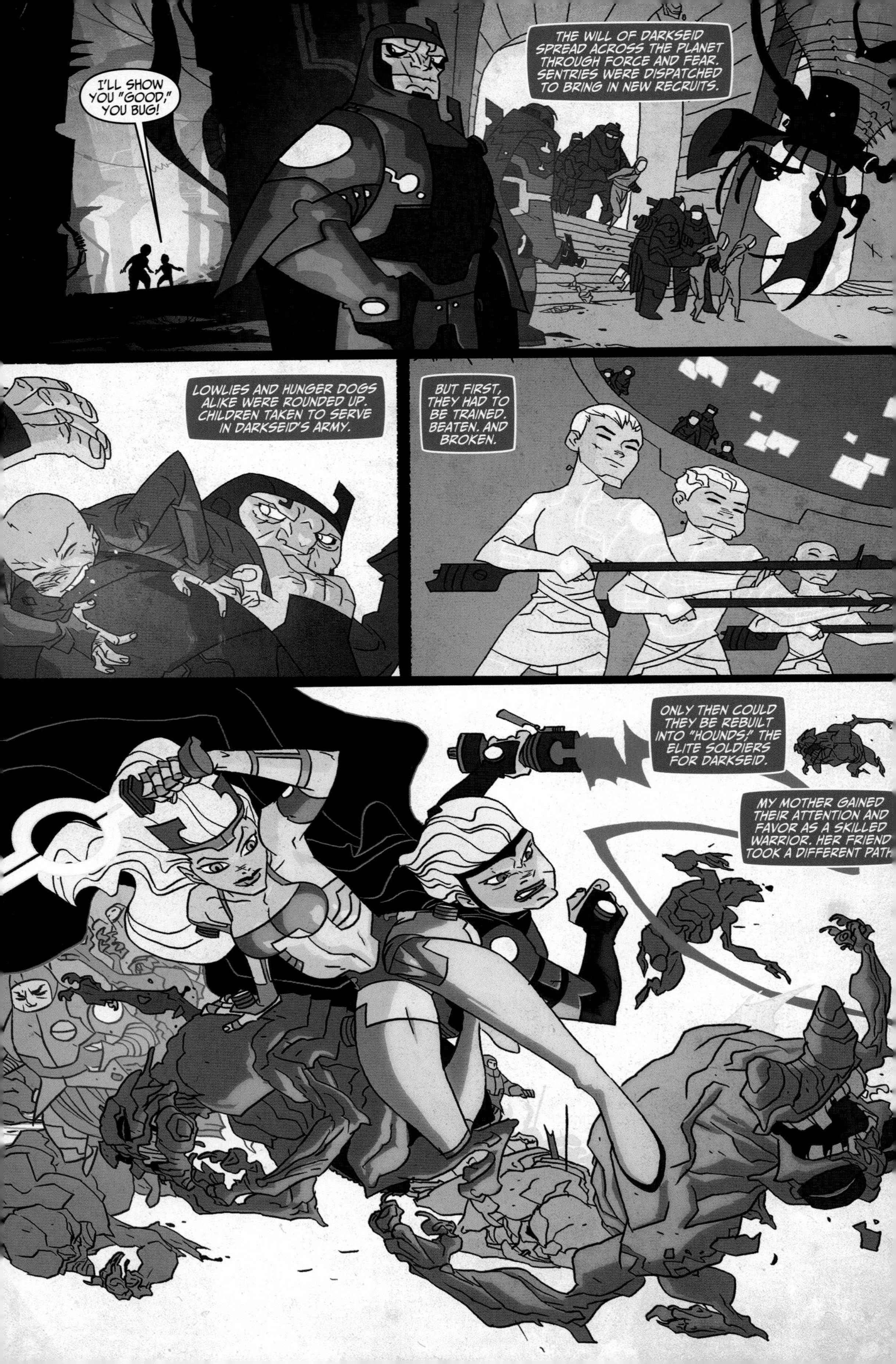
I'LL SHOW YOU "GOOD," YOU BUG!
THE WILL OF DARKSEID SPREAD ACROSS THE PLANET THROUGH FORCE AND FEAR. SENTRIES WERE DISPATCHED TO BRING IN NEW RECRUITS.
LOWLIES AND HUNGER DOGS ALIKE WERE ROUNDED UP. CHILDREN TAKEN TO SERVE IN DARKSEID'S ARMY.
BUT FIRST, THEY HAD TO BE TRAINED. BEATEN. AND BROKEN.
ONLY THEN COULD THEY BE REBUILT INTO "HOUNDS," THE ELITE SOLDIERS FOR DARKSEID.
MY MOTHER GAINED THEIR ATTENTION AND FAVOR AS A SKILLED WARRIOR. HER FRIEND TOOK A DIFFERENT PATH

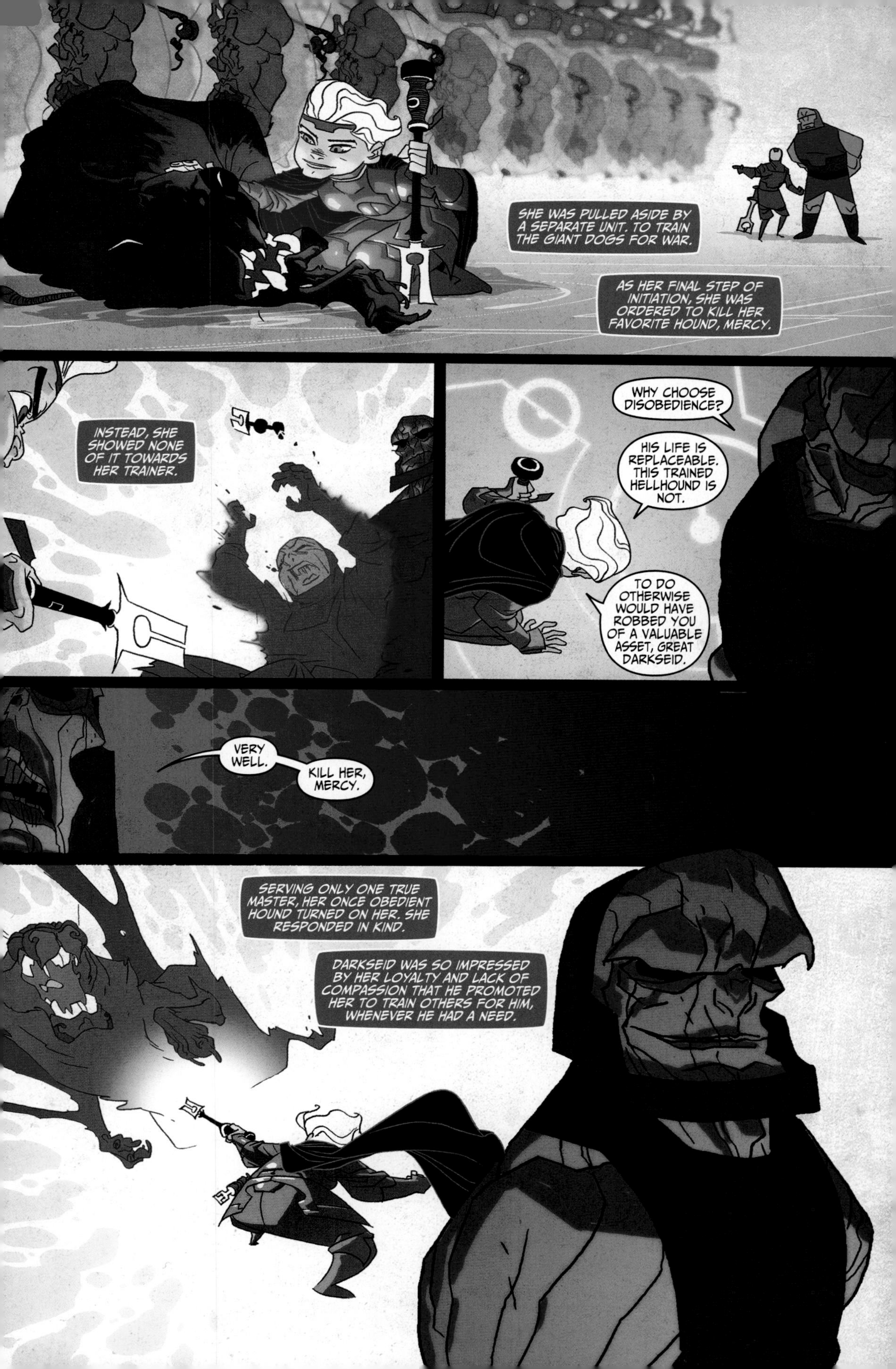
SHE WAS PULLED ASIDE BY A SEPARATE UNIT. TO TRAIN THE GIANT DOGS FOR WAR.
AS HER FINAL STEP OF INITIATION, SHE WAS ORDERED TO KILL HER FAVORITE HOUND, MERCY.
INSTEAD, SHE SHOWED NONE OF IT TOWARDS HER TRAINER.
WHY CHOOSE DISOBEDIENCE?
HIS LIFE IS REPLACEABLE. THIS TRAINED HELLHOUND IS NOT.
TO DO OTHERWISE WOULD HAVE ROBBED YOU OF A VALUABLE ASSET, GREAT DARKSEID.
VERY WELL.
KILL HER, MERCY.
SERVING ONLY ONE TRUE MASTER, HER ONCE OBEDIENT HOUND TURNED ON HER. SHE RESPONDED IN KIND.
DARKSEID WAS SO IMPRESSED BY HER LOYALTY AND LACK OF COMPASSION THAT HE PROMOTED HER TO TRAIN OTHERS FOR HIM, WHENEVER HE HAD A NEED.

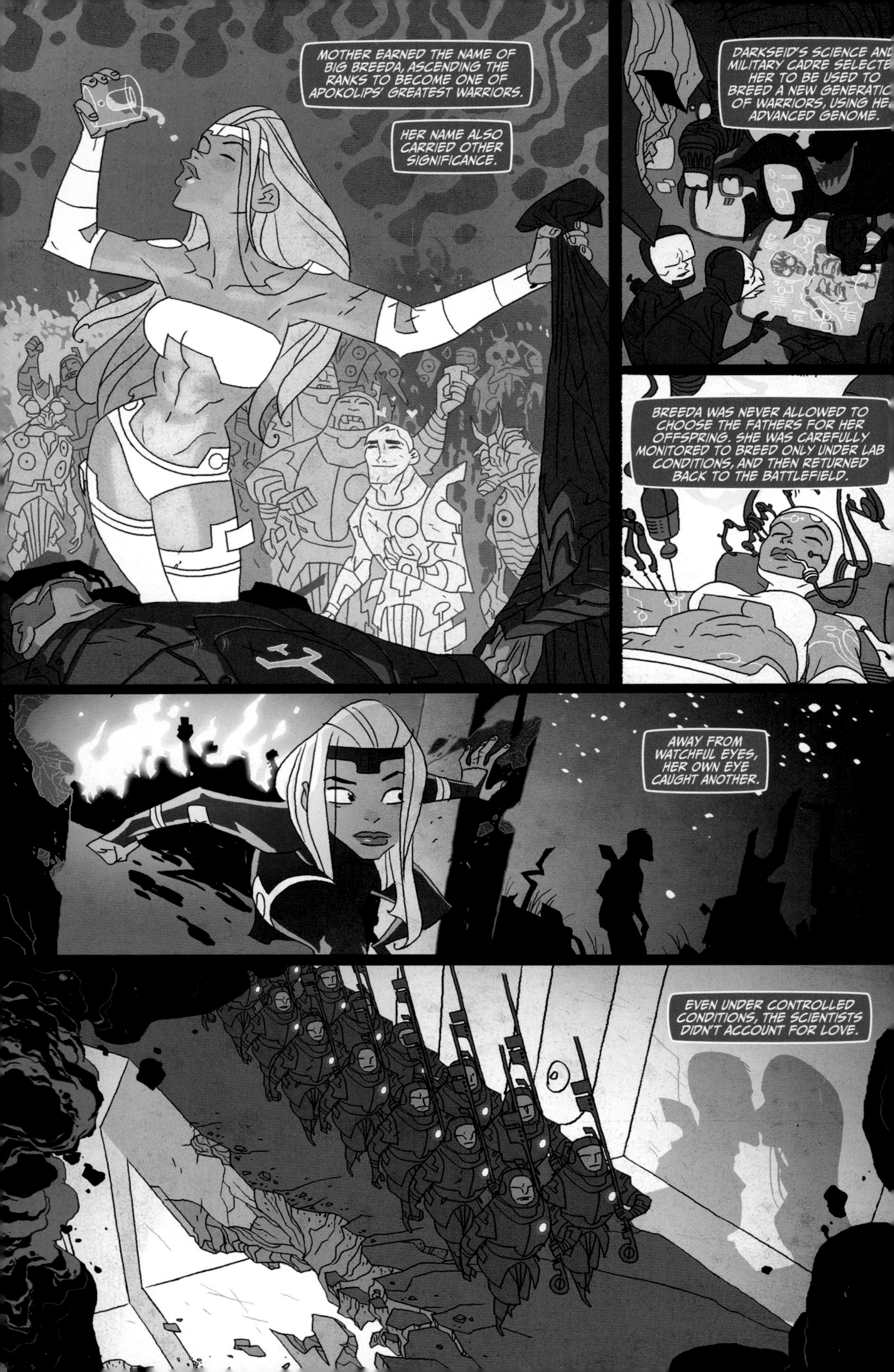
MOTHER EARNED THE NAME OF BIG BREEDA, ASCENDING THE RANKS TO BECOME ONE OF APOKOLIPS' GREATEST WARRIORS.
HER NAME ALSO CARRIED OTHER SIGNIFICANCE.
DARKSEID'S SCIENCE AND MILITARY CADRE SELECTE HER TO BE USED TO BREED A NEW GENERATI OF WARRIORS, USING HE ADVANCED GENOME.
BREEDA WAS NEVER ALLOWED TO CHOOSE THE FATHERS FOR HER OFFSPRING. SHE WAS CAREFULLY MONITORED TO BREED ONLY UNDER LAB CONDITIONS, AND THEN RETURNED BACK TO THE BATTLEFIELD.
AWAY FROM WATCHFUL EYES, HER OWN EYE CAUGHT ANOTHER.
EVEN UNDER CONTROLLED CONDITIONS, THE SCIENTISTS DIDN'T ACCOUNT FOR LOVE.

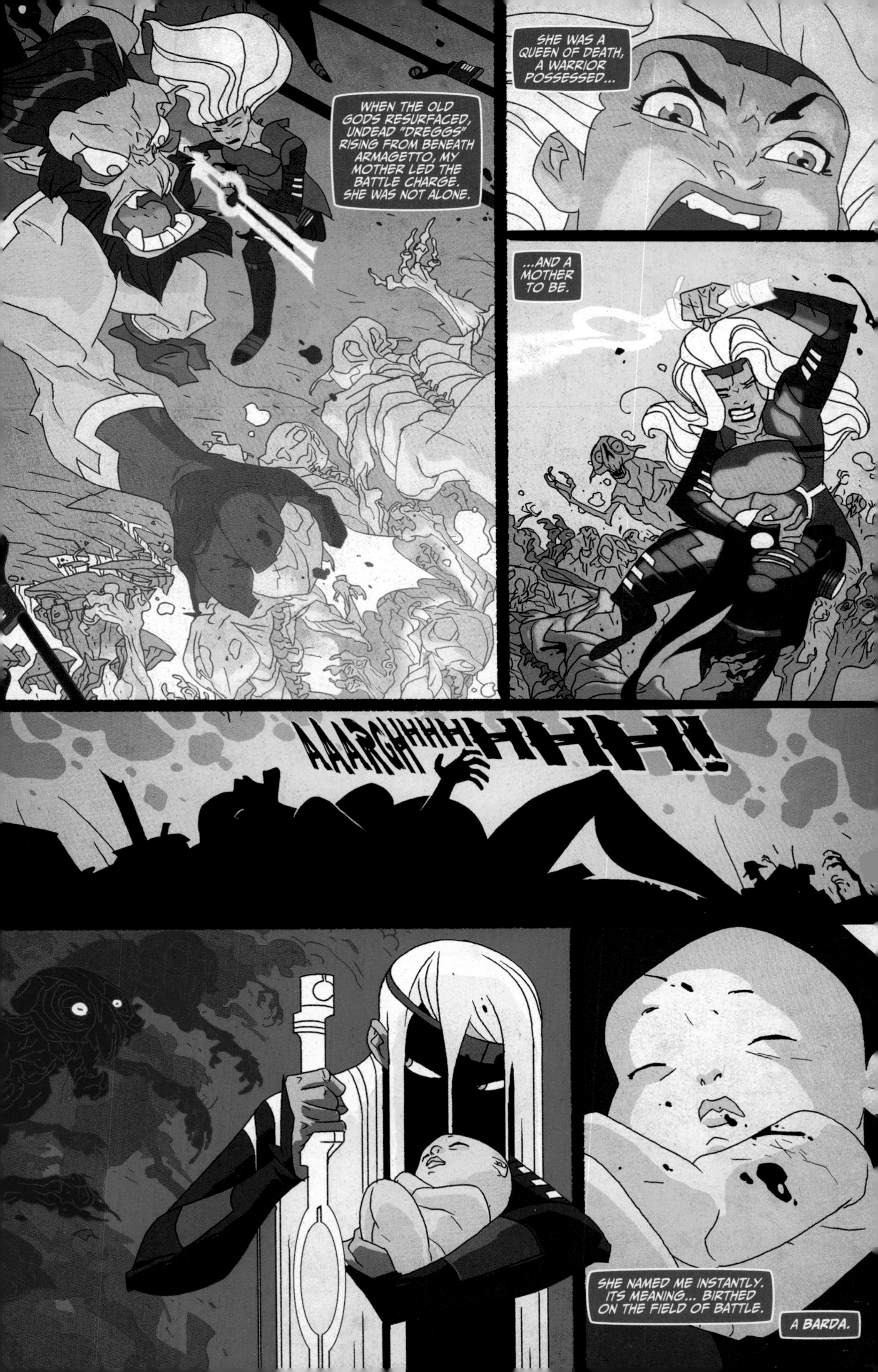

WHEN THE OLD GODS RESURFACED, UNDEAD "DREGGS" RISING FROM BENEATH ARMAGETTO, MY MOTHER LED THE BATTLE CHARGE. SHE WAS NOT ALONE.
SHE WAS A QUEEN OF DEATH, A WARRIOR POSSESSED...
...AND A MOTHER TO BE.
AAARGHHHHHHHH!
SHE NAMED ME INSTANTLY. ITS MEANING... BIRTHED ON THE FIELD OF BATTLE.
A BARDA.

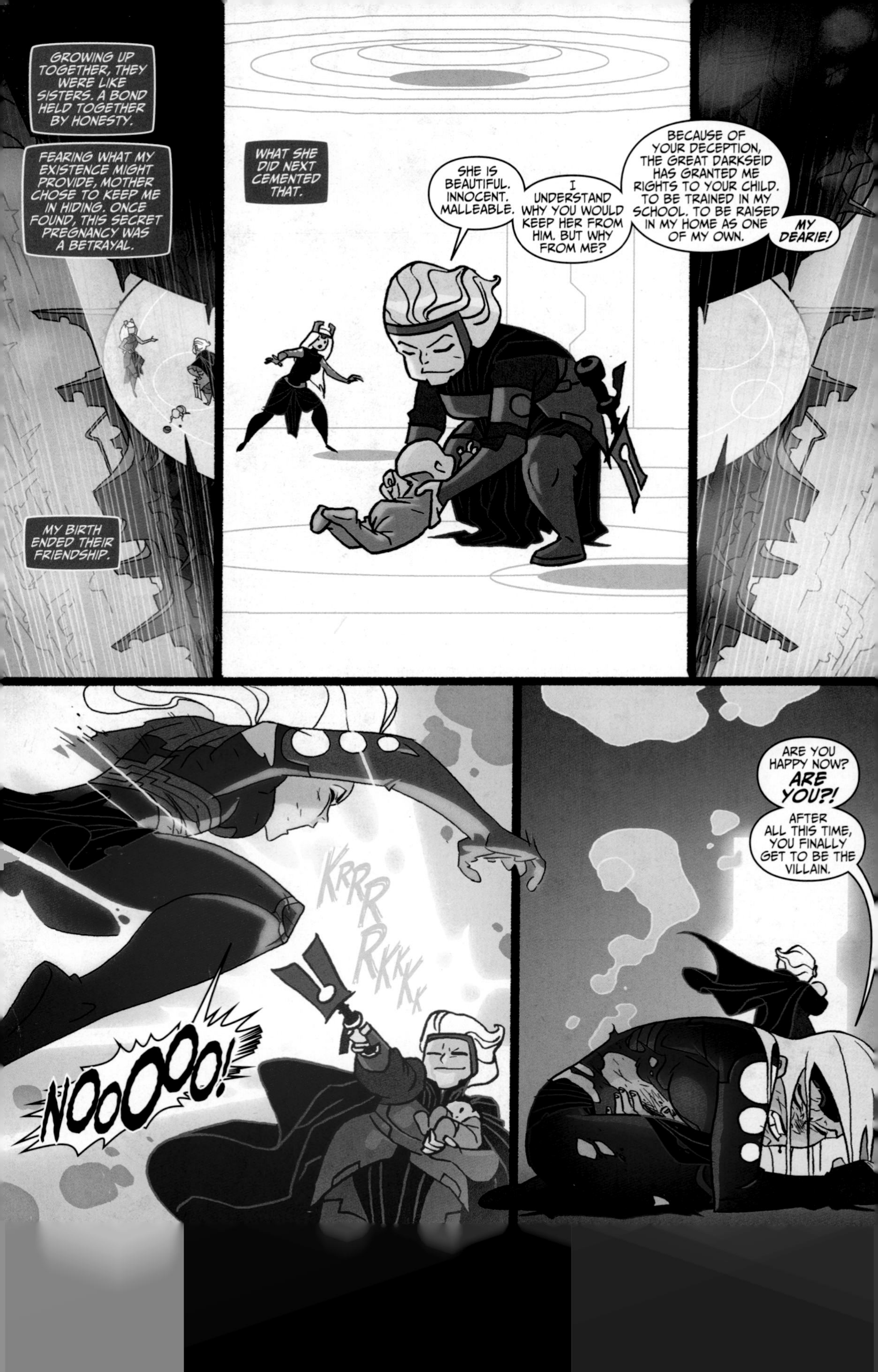
GROWING UP TOGETHER, THEY WERE LIKE SISTERS. A BOND HELD TOGETHER BY HONESTY.
FEARING WHAT MY EXISTENCE MIGHT PROVIDE, MOTHER CHOSE TO KEEP ME IN HIDING. ONCE FOUND, THIS SECRET PREGNANCY WAS A BETRAYAL.
MY BIRTH ENDED THEIR FRIENDSHIP.
WHAT SHE DID NEXT CEMENTED THAT.
SHE IS BEAUTIFUL. INNOCENT. MALLEABLE.
I UNDERSTAND WHY YOU WOULD KEEP HER FROM HIM. BUT WHY FROM ME?
BECAUSE OF YOUR DECEPTION, THE GREAT DARKSEID HAS GRANTED ME RIGHTS TO YOUR CHILD. TO BE TRAINED IN MY SCHOOL. TO BE RAISED IN MY HOME AS ONE OF MY OWN.
MY DEARIE!
KRRRRRKKKK
NOOOOO!
ARE YOU HAPPY NOW? ARE YOU?!
AFTER ALL THIS TIME, YOU FINALLY GET TO BE THE VILLAIN.

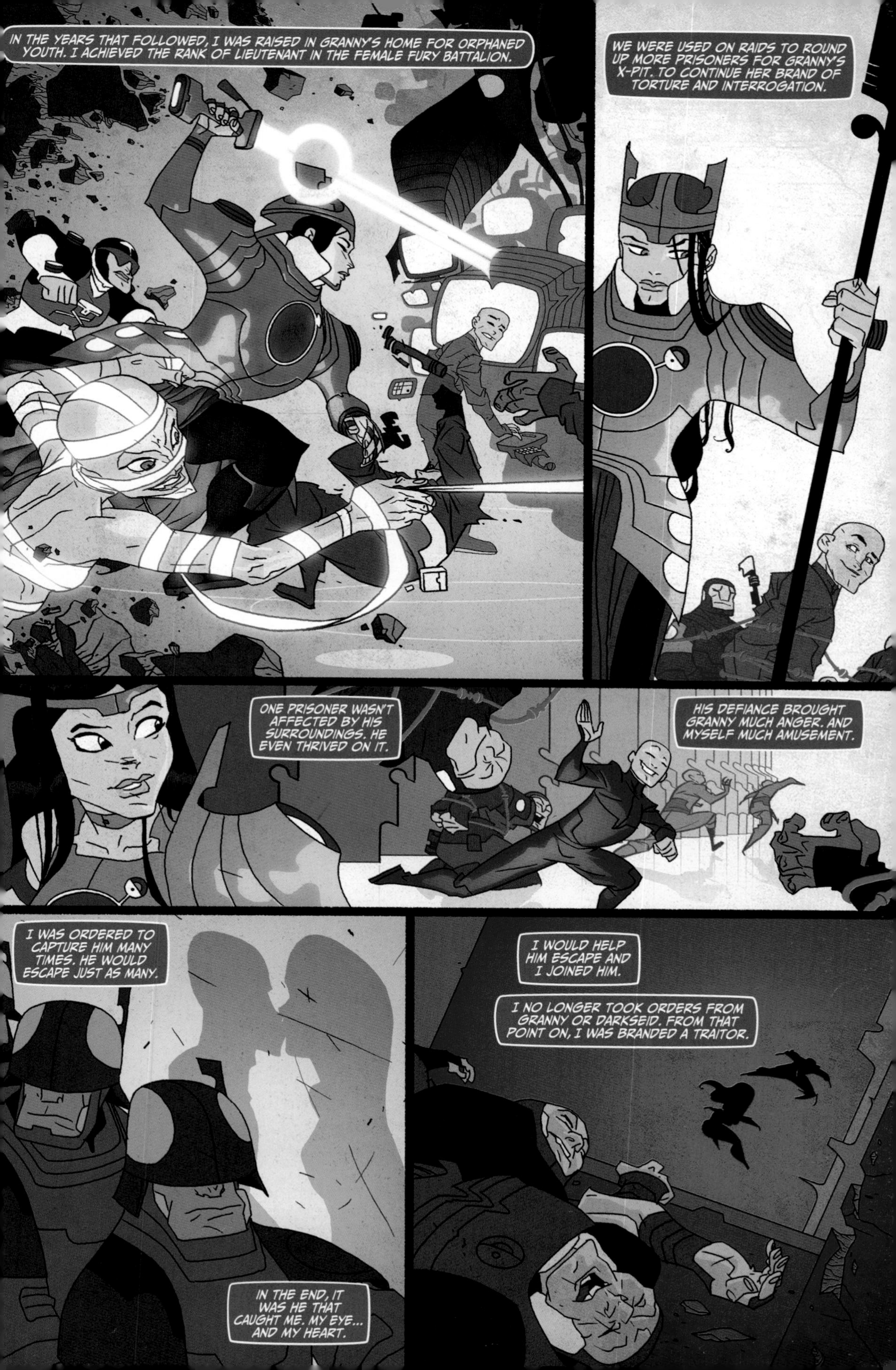

IN THE YEARS THAT FOLLOWED, I WAS RAISED IN GRANNY'S HOME FOR ORPHANED YOUTH. I ACHIEVED THE RANK OF LIEUTENANT IN THE FEMALE FURY BATTALION.
WE WERE USED ON RAIDS TO ROUND UP MORE PRISONERS FOR GRANNY'S X-PIT. TO CONTINUE HER BRAND OF TORTURE AND INTERROGATION.
ONE PRISONER WASN'T AFFECTED BY HIS SURROUNDINGS. HE EVEN THRIVED ON IT.
HIS DEFIANCE BROUGHT GRANNY MUCH ANGER. AND MYSELF MUCH AMUSEMENT.
I WAS ORDERED TO CAPTURE HIM MANY TIMES. HE WOULD ESCAPE JUST AS MANY.
IN THE END, IT WAS HE THAT CAUGHT ME. MY EYE... AND MY HEART.
I WOULD HELP HIM ESCAPE AND I JOINED HIM.
I NO LONGER TOOK ORDERS FROM GRANNY OR DARKSEID. FROM THAT POINT ON, I WAS BRANDED A TRAITOR.

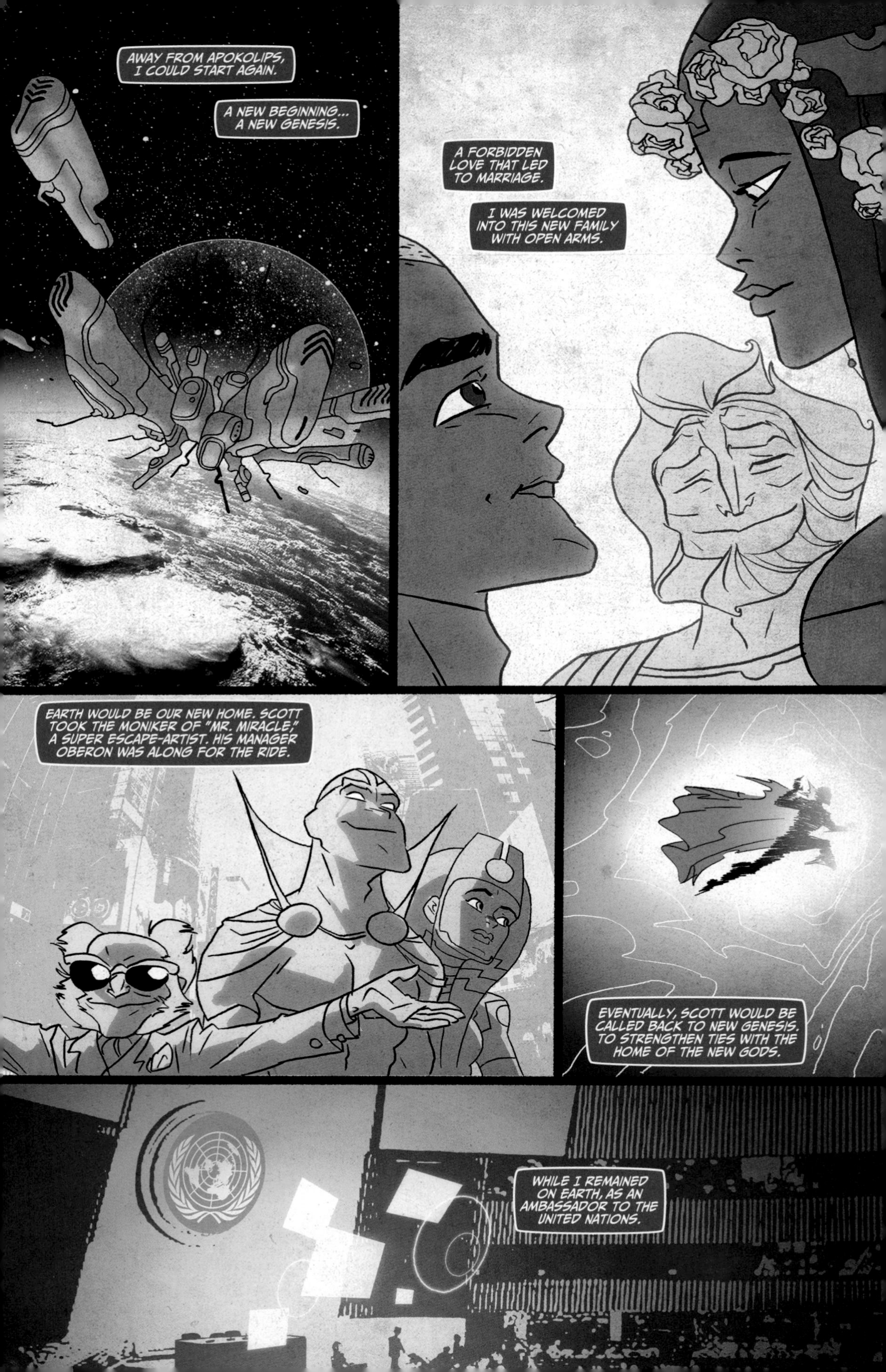
AWAY FROM APOKOLIPS, I COULD START AGAIN.
A NEW BEGINNING... A NEW GENESIS.
A FORBIDDEN LOVE THAT LED TO MARRIAGE.
I WAS WELCOMED INTO THIS NEW FAMILY WITH OPEN ARMS.
EARTH WOULD BE OUR NEW HOME. SCOTT TOOK THE MONIKER OF "MR. MIRACLE," A SUPER ESCAPE-ARTIST. HIS MANAGER OBERON WAS ALONG FOR THE RIDE.
EVENTUALLY, SCOTT WOULD BE CALLED BACK TO NEW GENESIS. TO STRENGTHEN TIES WITH THE HOME OF THE NEW GODS.
WHILE I REMAINED ON EARTH, AS AN AMBASSADOR TO THE UNITED NATIONS.

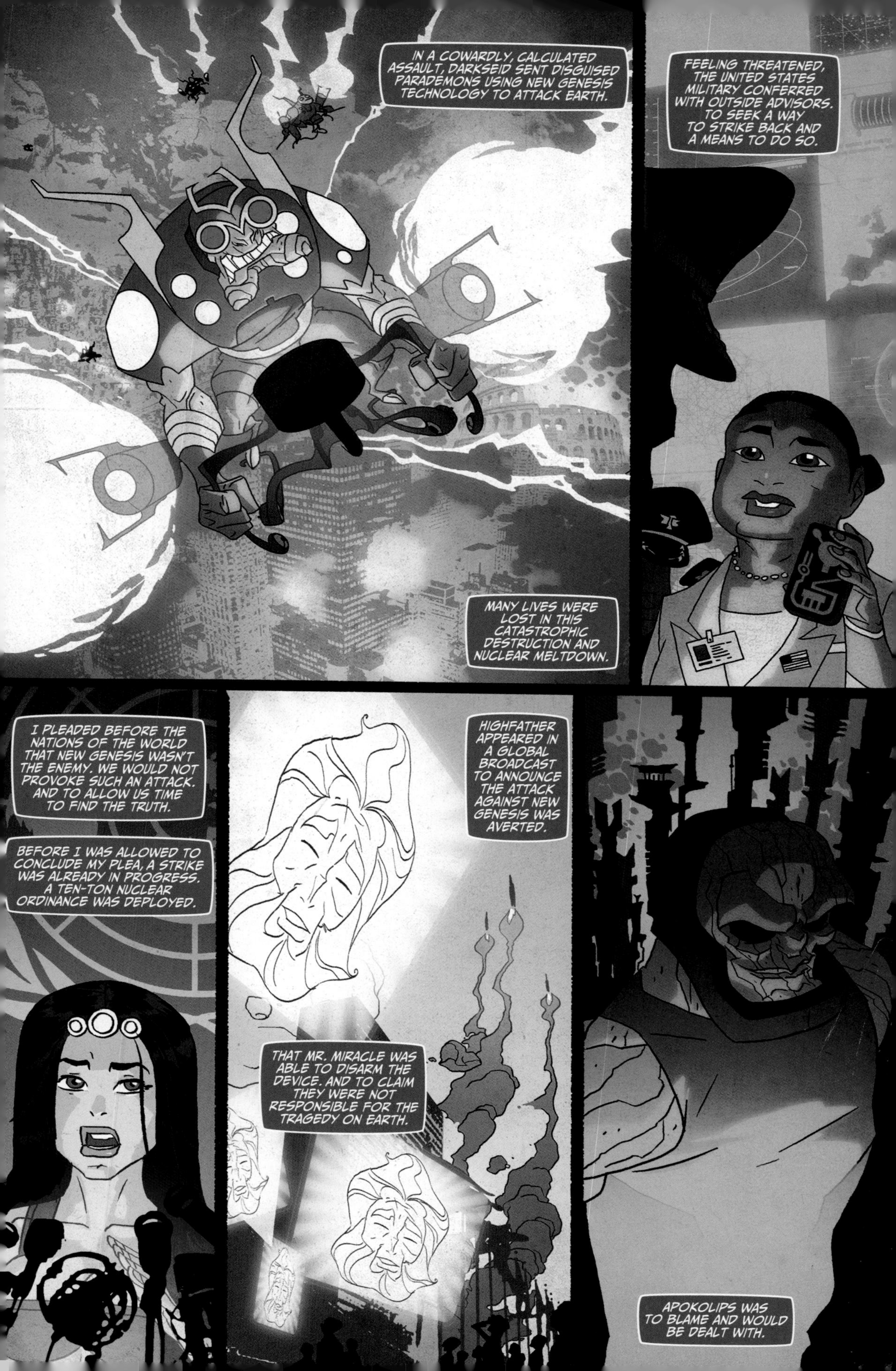
IN A COWARDLY, CALCULATED ASSAULT, DARKSEID SENT DISGUISED PARADEMONS USING NEW GENESIS TECHNOLOGY TO ATTACK EARTH.
MANY LIVES WERE LOST IN THIS CATASTROPHIC DESTRUCTION AND NUCLEAR MELTDOWN.
FEELING THREATENED, THE UNITED STATES MILITARY CONFERRED WITH OUTSIDE ADVISORS. TO SEEK A WAY TO STRIKE BACK AND A MEANS TO DO SO.
I PLEADED BEFORE THE NATIONS OF THE WORLD THAT NEW GENESIS WASN'T THE ENEMY. WE WOULD NOT PROVOKE SUCH AN ATTACK. AND TO ALLOW US TIME TO FIND THE TRUTH.
BEFORE I WAS ALLOWED TO CONCLUDE MY PLEA, A STRIKE WAS ALREADY IN PROGRESS. A TEN-TON NUCLEAR ORDINANCE WAS DEPLOYED.
HIGHFATHER APPEARED IN A GLOBAL BROADCAST TO ANNOUNCE THE ATTACK AGAINST NEW GENESIS WAS AVERTED.
THAT MR. MIRACLE WAS ABLE TO DISARM THE DEVICE. AND TO CLAIM THEY WERE NOT RESPONSIBLE FOR THE TRAGEDY ON EARTH.
APOKOLIPS WAS TO BLAME AND WOULD BE DEALT WITH.

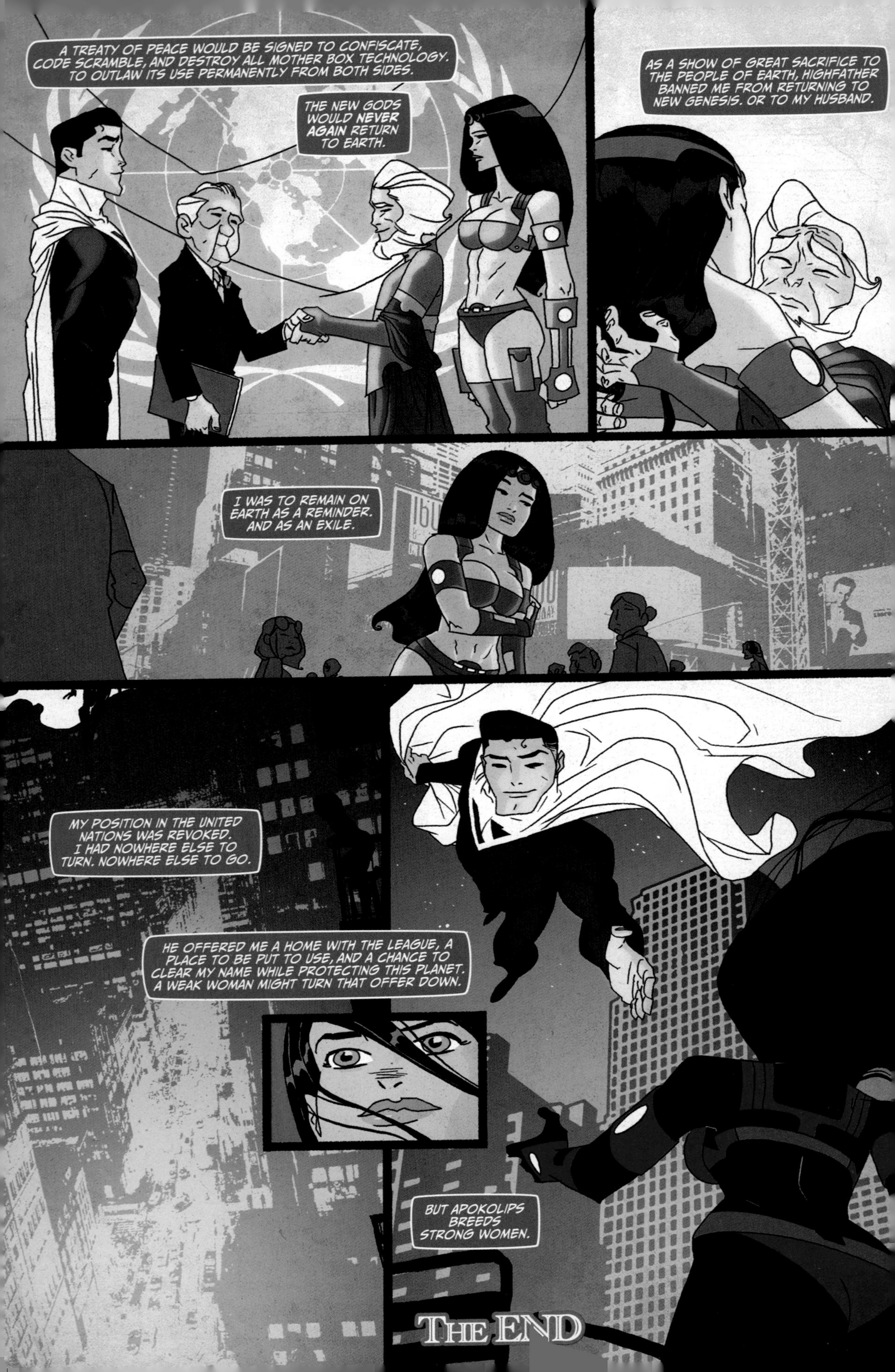
A TREATY OF PEACE WOULD BE SIGNED TO CONFISCATE, CODE SCRAMBLE, AND DESTROY ALL MOTHER BOX TECHNOLOGY. TO OUTLAW ITS USE PERMANENTLY FROM BOTH SIDES.
THE NEW GODS WOULD NEVER AGAIN RETURN TO EARTH.
AS A SHOW OF GREAT SACRIFICE TO THE PEOPLE OF EARTH, HIGHFATHER BANNED ME FROM RETURNING TO NEW GENESIS. OR TO MY HUSBAND.
I WAS TO REMAIN ON EARTH AS A REMINDER. AND AS AN EXILE.
MY POSITION IN THE UNITED NATIONS WAS REVOKED. I HAD NOWHERE ELSE TO TURN. NOWHERE ELSE TO GO.
HE OFFERED ME A HOME WITH THE LEAGUE, A PLACE TO BE PUT TO USE, AND A CHANCE TO CLEAR MY NAME WHILE PROTECTING THIS PLANET. A WEAK WOMAN MIGHT TURN THAT OFFER DOWN.
BUT APOKOLIPS BREEDS STRONG WOMEN.
THE END

JUSTICE LEAGUE BEYOND
Digital cover • Chapters #1–3

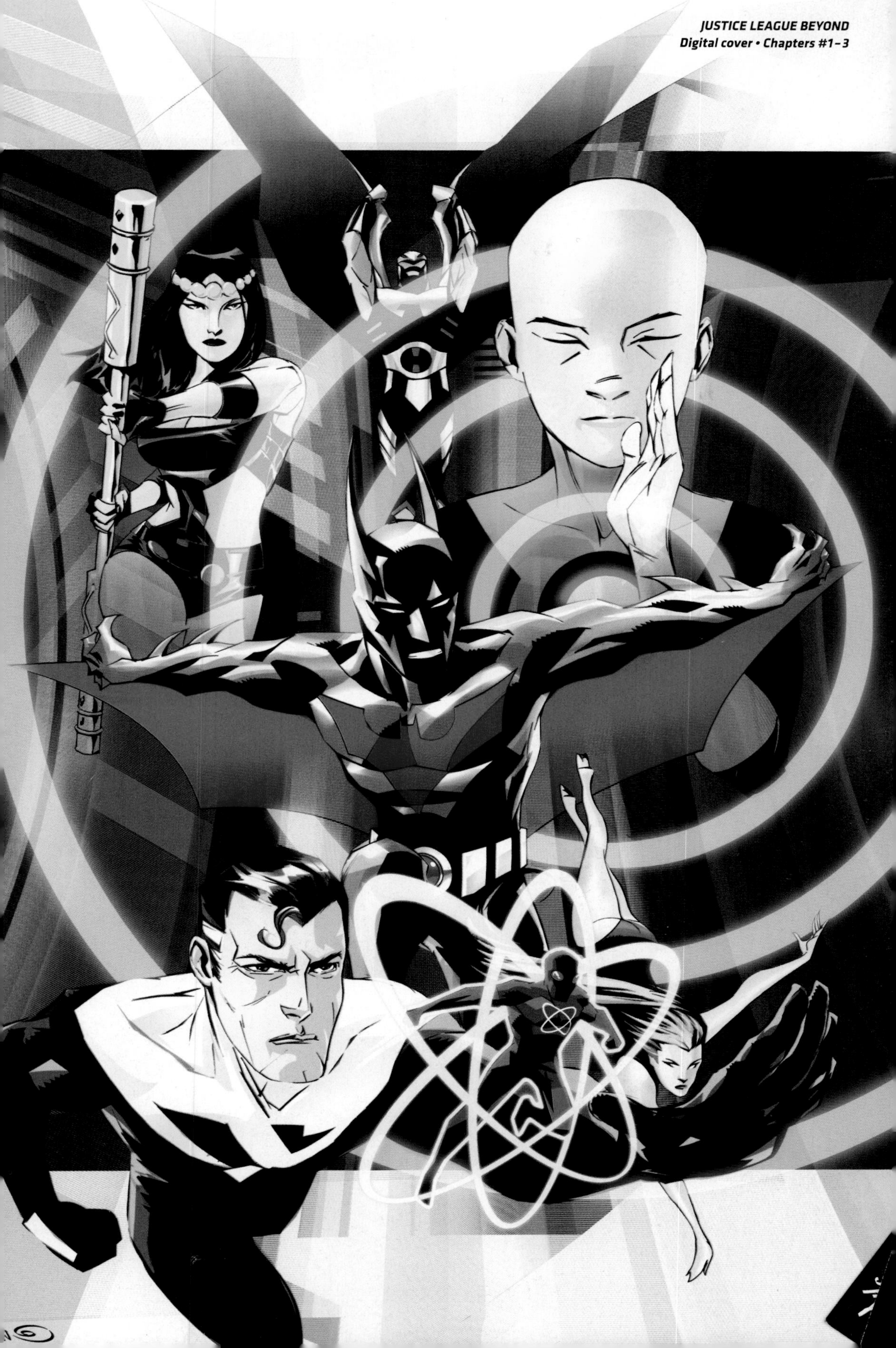

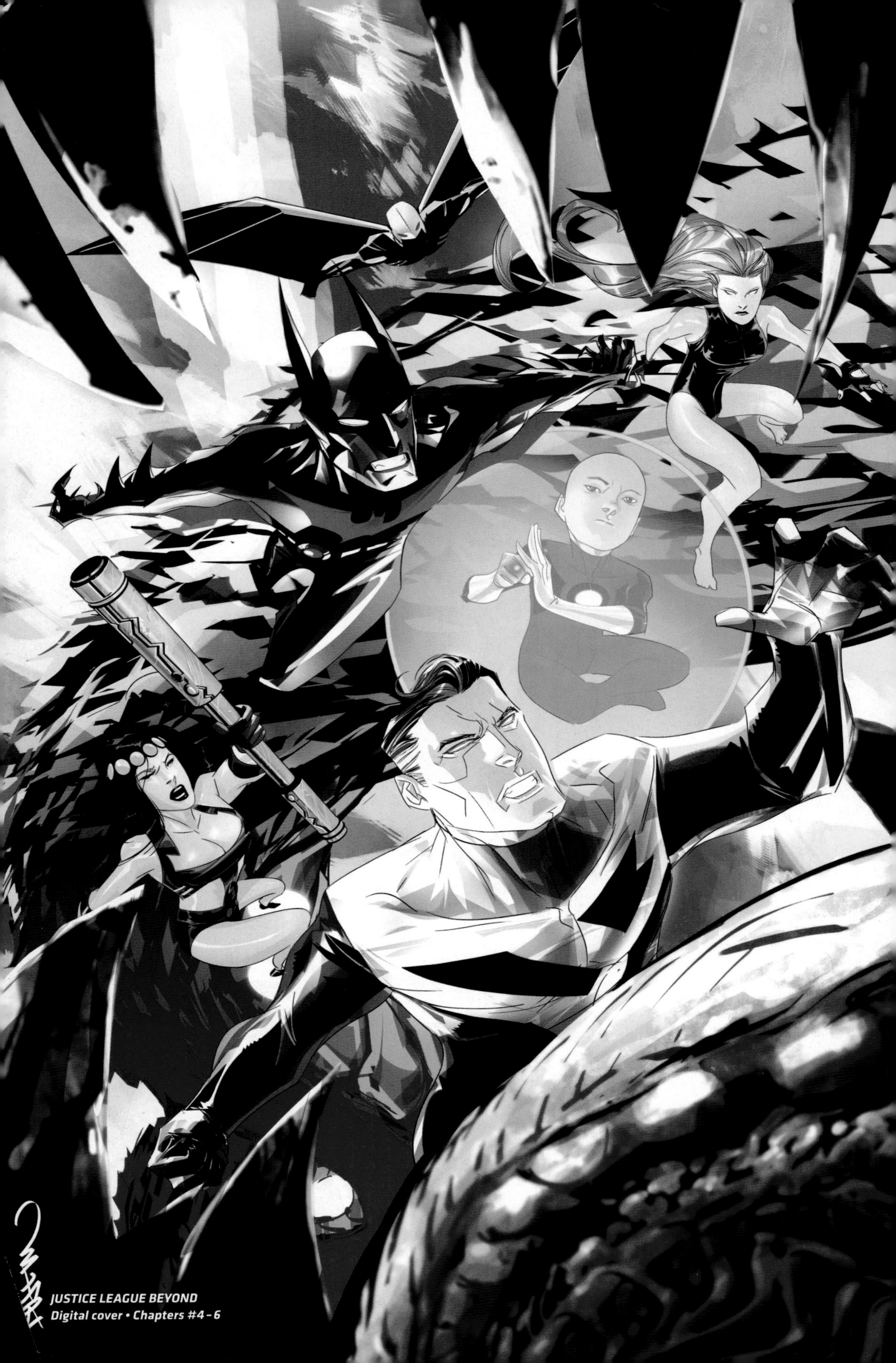

JUSTICE LEAGUE BEYOND
Digital cover • Chapters #4–6

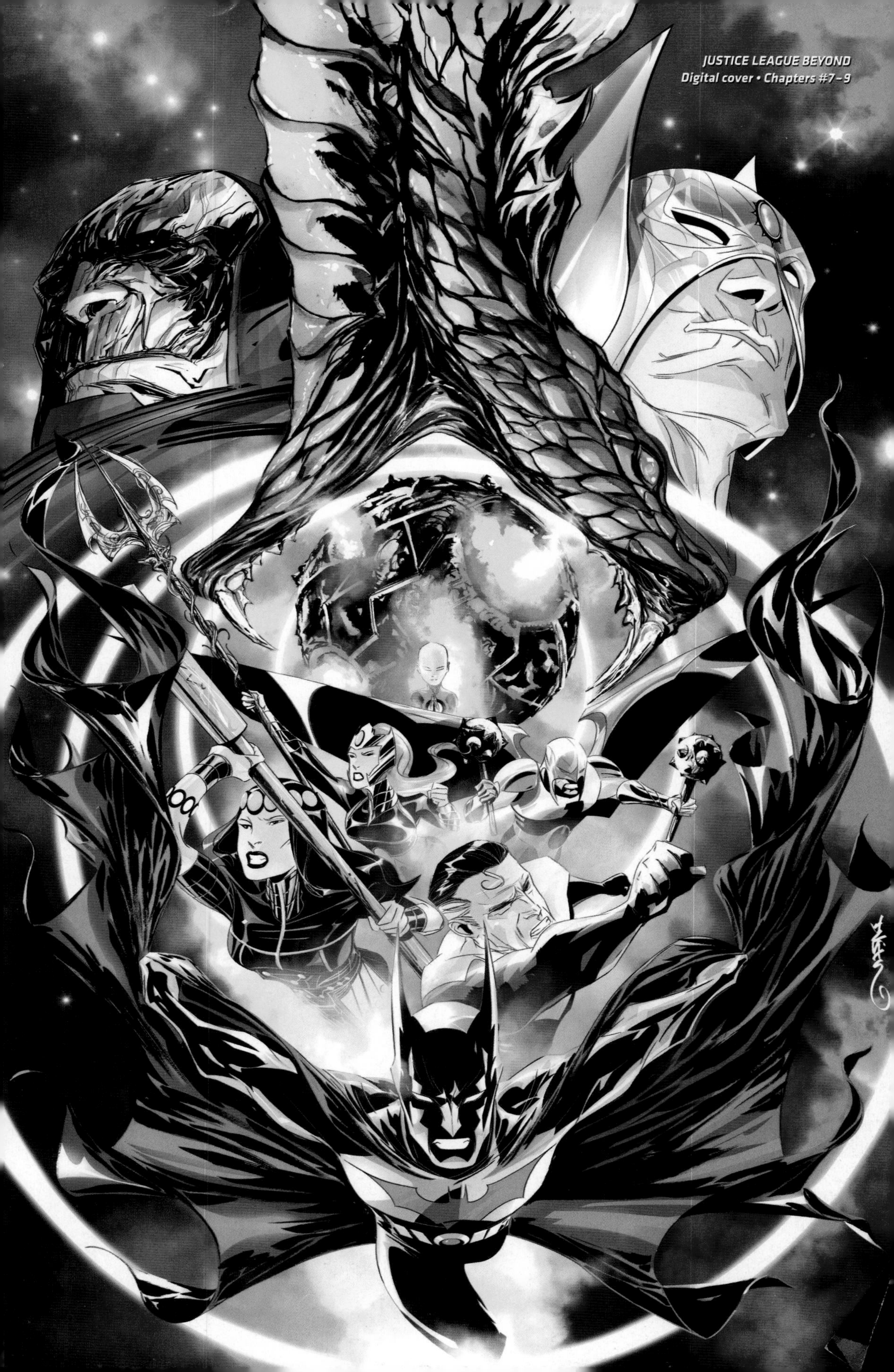

JUSTICE LEAGUE BEYOND
Digital cover • Chapters #7–9

JUSTICE LEAGUE BEYOND
Digital cover • Chapters #10 – 12

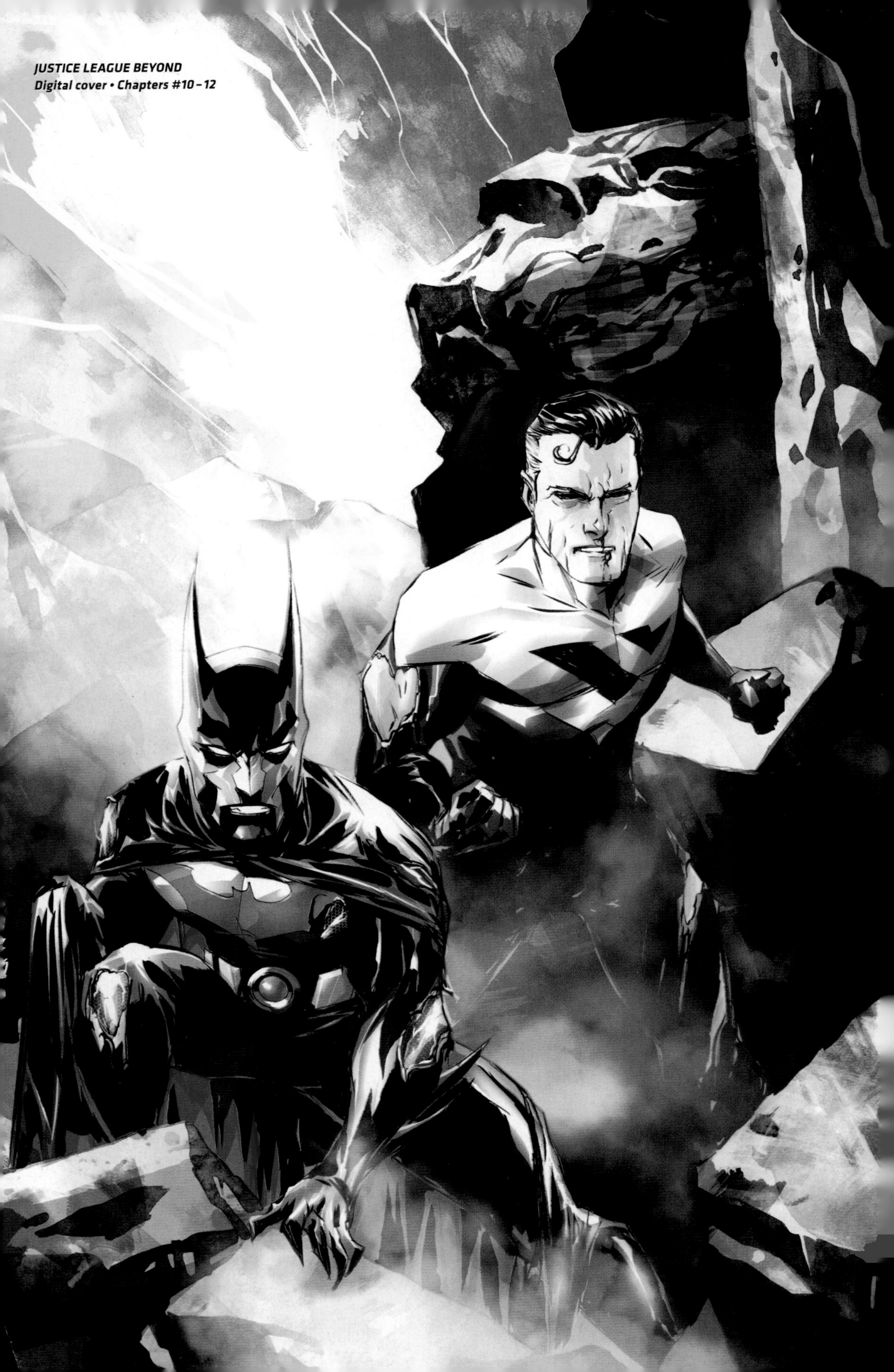

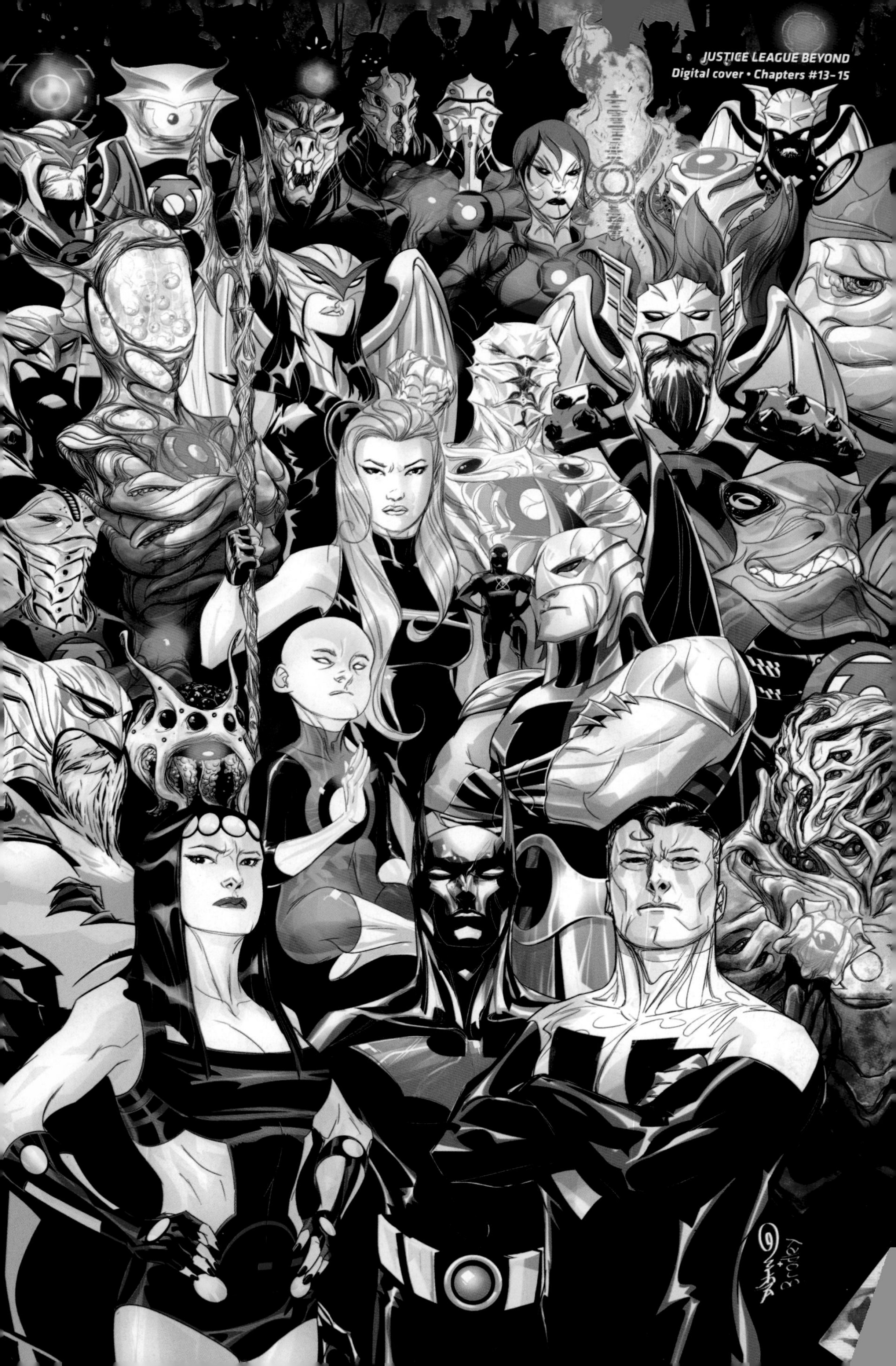
JUSTICE LEAGUE BEYOND
Digital cover • Chapters #13–15

JUSTICE LEAGUE BEYOND
Digital cover • Chapter #16

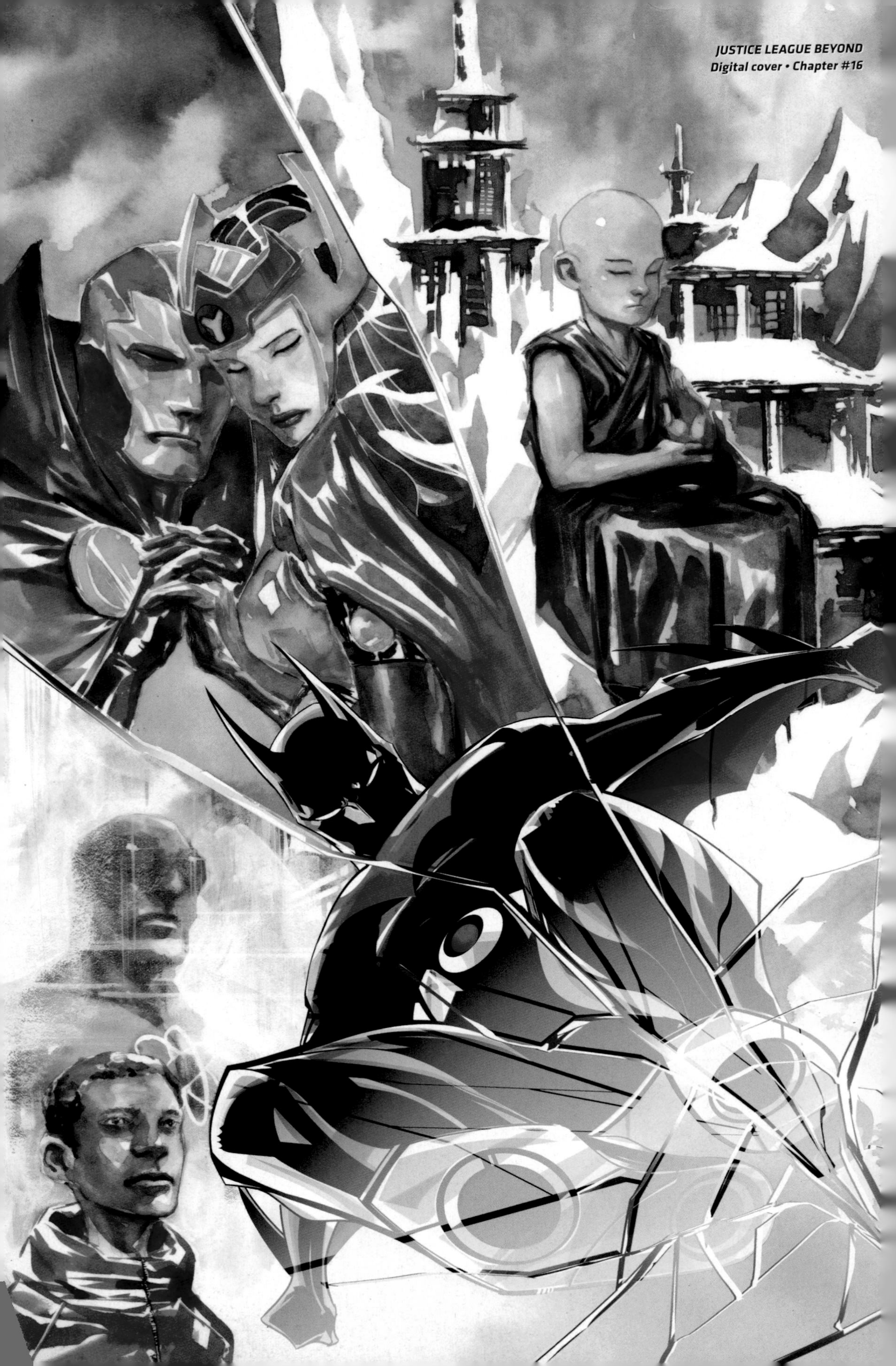

JUSTICE LEAGUE BEYOND cover sketch gallery by Dustin Nguyen

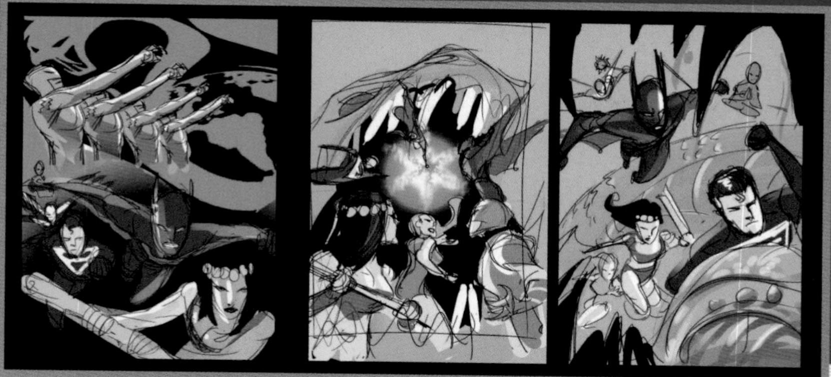

JUSTICE LEAGUE BEYOND **Digital cover • Chapters #4-6**

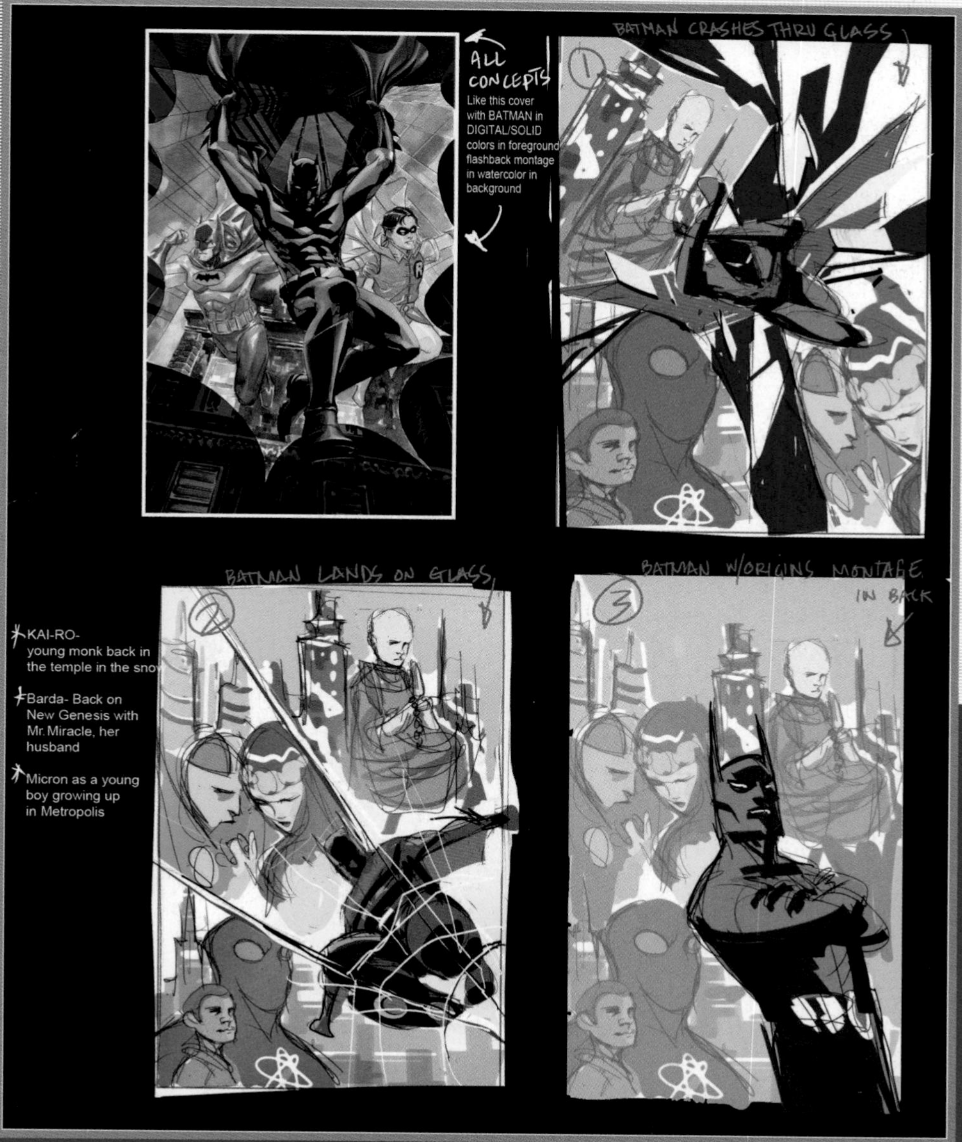
ALL CONCEPTS
Like this cover with BATMAN in DIGITAL/SOLID colors in foreground flashback montage in watercolor in background
BATMAN CRASHES THRU GLASS
1
BATMAN LANDS ON GLASS
2
BATMAN W/ORIGINS MONTAGE IN BACK
3
*KAI-RO- young monk back in the temple in the snow
*Barda- Back on New Genesis with Mr. Miracle, her husband
*Micron as a young boy growing up in Metropolis

JUSTICE LEAGUE BEYOND **Digital cover • Chapters #15-17**

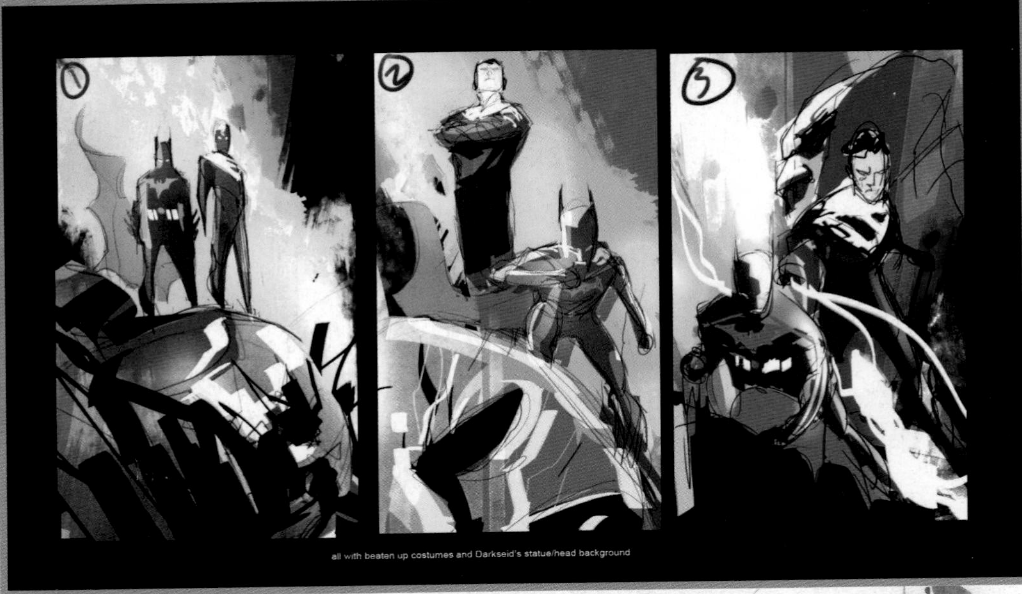
all with beaten up costumes and Darkseid's statue/head background

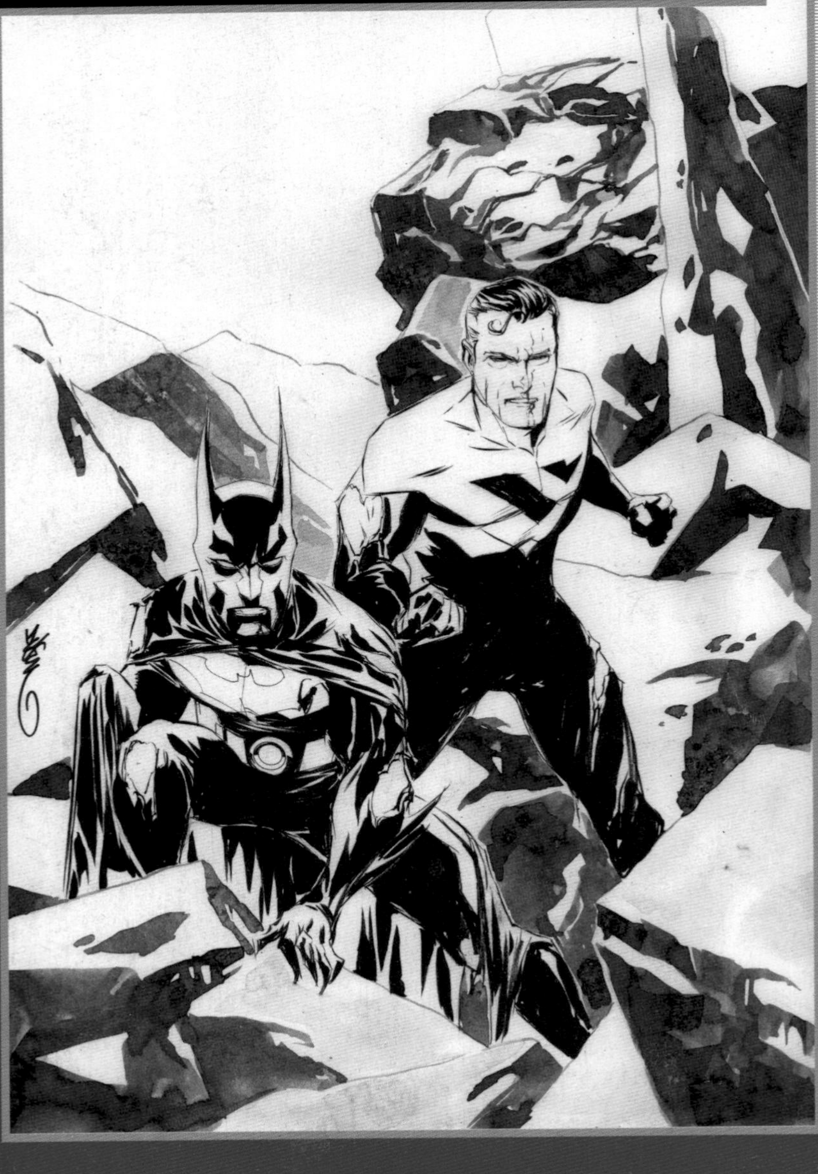

JUSTICE LEAGUE BEYOND
Digital cover • Chapters #10-12

Apokolips in the background here
BATMAN IN HIS NEW OUTFIT burning Metropolis in BG behind him
ORION on his flying thing
snake wrapped around Apokolips
DARKSEID
ORION
HIGHFATHER

JL team bursting thru BOOM TUBE on both
burning Apokolips
NOTE BATMAN has NEW TEMPORARY costume with cape

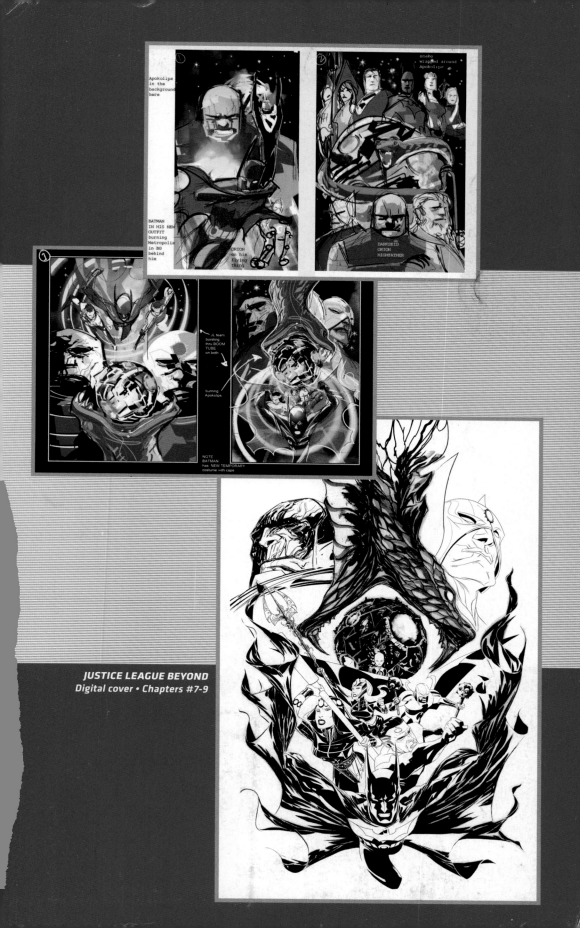

JUSTICE LEAGUE BEYOND
Digital cover • Chapters #7-9

*Artist Dustin Nguyen asked his eight-year old son to help design concepts for Green Lanterns of the future for **JUSTICE LEAGUE BEYOND** cover #5.*

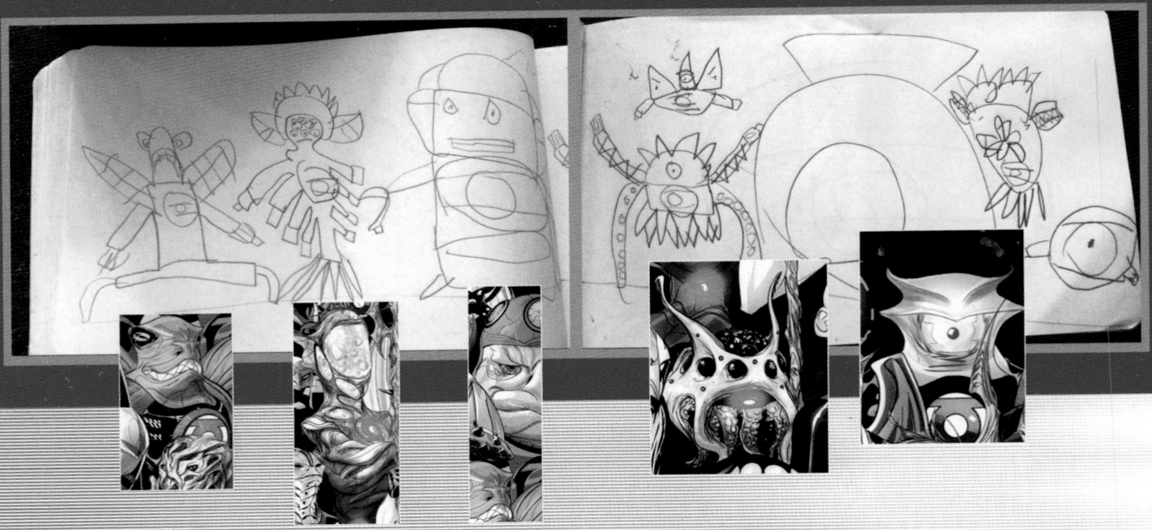

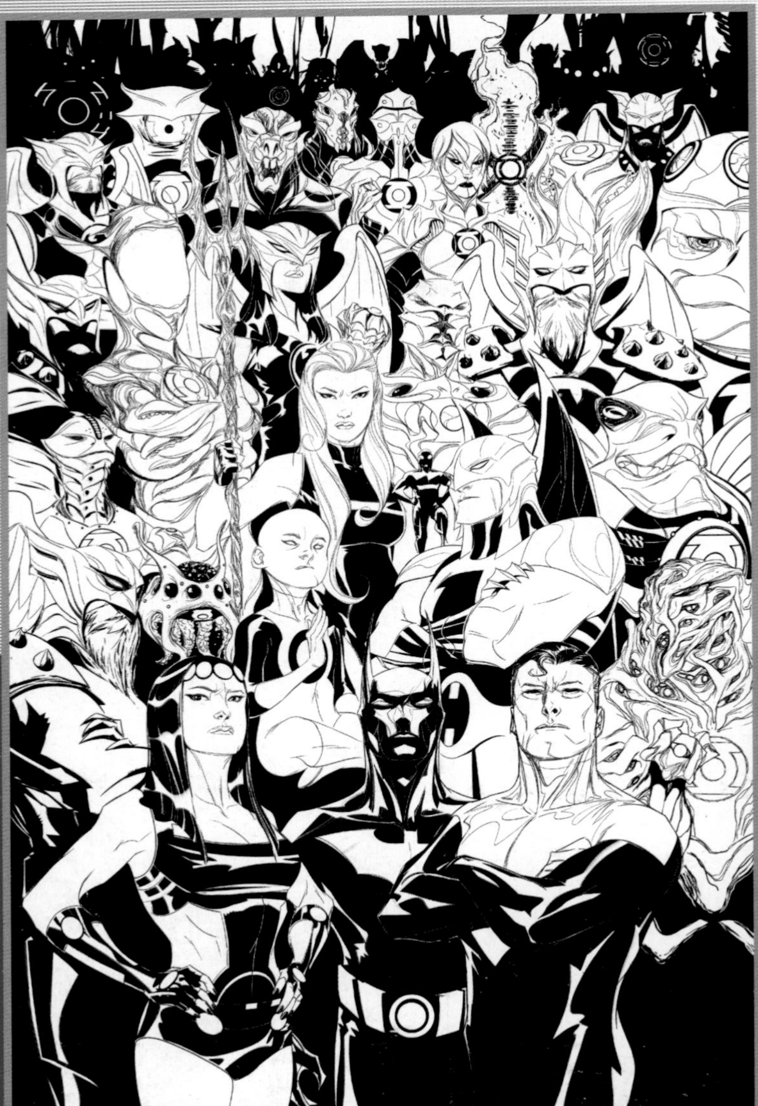